Bob Dylan
FAQ

Bob Dylan FAQ

All That's Left to Know About the Song and Dance Man

Bruce Pollock

Backbeat Books

An Imprint of Hal Leonard LLC

Published in 2017 by Backbeat Books
An Imprint of Hal Leonard LLC
7777 West Bluemound Road
Milwaukee, WI 53213

Trade Book Division Editorial Offices
33 Plymouth St., Montclair, NJ 07042

All images are from the author's collection unless otherwise noted.

The FAQ series was conceived by Robert Rodriguez and developed with Stuart Shea. Printed in the United States of America

Book design by Snow Creative

Library of Congress Cataloging-in-Publication Data

Names: Pollock, Bruce.
Title: Bob Dylan FAQ : all that's left to know about the song and dance man / Bruce Pollock.
Description: Montclair, NJ : Backbeat Books, 2017. | Includes bibliographical references and index.
Identifiers: LCCN 2016046568 | ISBN 9781617136078
Subjects: LCSH: Dylan, Bob, 1941—Miscellanea.
Classification: LCC ML420.D98 P656 2017 | DDC 782.42164092 [B] —dc23
LC record available at https://lccn.loc.gov/2016046568

www.backbeatbooks.com

To my family for their love and support
and to Bob Dylan for being Bob Dylan

Contents

Introduction

L ike many men of my generation, I grew up not only wanting to be Bob Dylan, but thinking I already *was* Bob Dylan. The Bob Dylan of my block in Brooklyn, and then, once I moved to Greenwich Village, the Bob Dylan of my apartment building on West 10th Street and 6th Avenue. Like Dylan, I too went under a poetic songwriting *nom de plume* (although I never officially changed my name), Larry Byron, in collaboration with my roommate, Richard Keats. Every Tuesday night at the Gaslight, from 1965 through '68, we watched all the other Bob Dylans of their neighborhoods, or their blocks, or their imaginations, strut their stuff for the approval of the big, bearded, curmudgeonly Dave Van Ronk, ringleader of the weekly hoots, determined to one day get up there as Byron and Keats, much as one night Simon and Garfunkel got up there, in suits and ties, announced as Columbia recording artists, and got booed out of the room. Although we never did take that leap (or learn how to sing in tune), at least we knew enough to dress accordingly, in rumpled jeans, work shirts, and boots (Dylan's famous cap was already passé).

It was at the Gaslight that I had my "Bob Dylan moment" in 1965, just as Bob Dylan had had his "Buddy Holly moment" in Duluth in 1959, a few days before Buddy died, seeing him in concert from the front row, close enough to look into his eyes and gaze at the future, his future as a world famous rock star. I saw Dylan on a Tuesday night at a half-empty Gaslight in 1965 when he interrupted a set by Gordon Lightfoot, taking the stage to sing "Mr. Tambourine Man" and several other songs to a suddenly packed house. This was Dylan in the ascendant, post–Newport '65 Dylan. I'd missed him at Newport, spending the night on Second Beach instead because all the cool kids were the ones who didn't have tickets. But I'd seen him at Town Hall and Carnegie Hall, Forest Hills, and Philharmonic Hall—all of those times from the cheap seats, without binoculars. This time I was sitting six feet from the stage, close enough to gaze into his sunglasses and see my future.

It turned out my future was not to be the next Bob Dylan.

Frantically reassessing things, I determined that my future was to be the next J. D. Salinger.

Byron and Keats soon broke up in favor of my endless, expanding novel.

Eventually I gave up on becoming the next J. D. Salinger and settled on becoming the next Studs Terkel. Interviewing Paul Simon in 1976 at his apartment on Central Park West for a *Saturday Review* cover story, I brought up that disastrous night at the Gaslight.

"We were being represented by the William Morris Agency," Simon recalled, with agony in his voice, "and they were looking for a way to sell us, with typical disregard for the content. They wanted us to be the Smothers Brothers. I arrived at the Gaslight that night with a terrible sense of foreboding, because I used to go there to watch the other acts—in normal attire—and now here I was, knowing I shouldn't be wearing this jacket and tie. I told our agent we were making a big mistake, and he said, 'It doesn't matter what the audience thinks, there are television people here.'"

I never got that close to Bob Dylan again, in person or in performance. But his old pal Dave Van Ronk, who presided over those Tuesday night hoots, had been following Dylan very carefully ever since his arrival in 1961. "He was nothing like what he subsequently became," Van Ronk told me in a 1981 interview. "He seemed very extroverted on the stage, and he did all kinds of little Charlie Chaplin turns. His sense of timing was incredibly good, and he was hilariously funny. He was nervous; he was obviously quaking in his boots, but he used it. He had a kind of herky-jerky patter: a one-liner, long pause, another one-liner, a mutter, a mumble, a slam at the guitar. It was very effective."

He even seemed to recall the night I was there, when Dylan filled the Gaslight with one strum of his guitar. "Every guest set the man did, by the time he'd do the second song, the word was out on the street that Dylan was onstage, and his coterie would start pouring in."

More than any other musician of the time, Dylan's development as an artist and a person was of a piece with his generation, continuously intriguing and influential. A few years ahead of the first wave of the baby boom, he was in a perfect position to lead the way with his dramatic changes, the antisocial antihero hiding behind his guitar, using it to speak for him when the usual conversational platitudes with shiksa goddesses and Jewish princesses failed. His 1960 Dinkytown experience in Minneapolis, with its politics and poetry and pot, mirrored the coming-of-age experience of hordes of middle-class kids in many other college towns in the '60s who dropped out of school and adopted folk airs and repertoires, myself among them. By the end of the decade we all looked like him, too, growing our hair out to resemble "a walking mountain range" and lusting after girls like the one pictured walking with him down Jones Street in the snow on the cover of *Freewheelin'*. Segueing out of Woody Guthrie, he became the last of the Beats, Kerouac's *On the Road* set to music, Ginsberg's "Howl" topping the record charts, outdoing the Beatles with "Like a Rolling Stone." It seemed there were no limits to his verbiage, his mania, his desire.

But Dylan was human after all. By this time he'd left Greenwich Village, moved to Woodstock, gotten married, had a kid. Soon he was recovering from the same kind of motorcycle accident that had killed his friend Richard Fariña only a few months before. As the '60s neared their end, I was not alone in dreaming of one day making a pilgrimage to Woodstock, to show up at his door with my expanding novel, the way he'd shown up at Woody Guthrie's door in Queens with his guitar. Unlike many of my contemporaries, I managed to quell the urge. Instead, on the very weekend of the Woodstock mud bath in August of '69 (when Dylan would have been in England, anyway), I traveled to a town near Providence, Rhode Island, to read my 600-page work in progress to a friend and her husband, before abandoning it to become the next Richard Goldstein (one of the original rock journalists, who gave my first paper an encouraging review in the class I took with him when I returned to college).

With a writing prize and a degree from CCNY in my pocket, I reentered the now-flourishing field of rock journalism in the early '70s, just in time to interview Bruce Springsteen at Black Rock on the heels of his debut album, for which he was being hailed as "the next Bob Dylan."

Dylan wasn't done with the name yet, although his Rolling Thunder comeback tour of 1975 didn't save him from an otherwise rocky seventies. When he wrote what was widely thought of (except by Dylan) as his "divorce albums," *Blood on the Tracks*, *Desire*, and *Planet Waves*, a lot of his baby-boomer constituency could identify, much as they had with his earlier anthems of freedom. As he pointed out, at the time he wasn't divorced, just on the precipice. But when he hit the road in '74 and '75, he was in the grip of a newfound desire, once again mirroring a generation caught between punk and disco, rebellion and rejuvenation; hitting the age at which none of us could be trusted anymore (thirty), and attempting to turn back the clock, if not stop time entirely. But as the decade neared its end, the pendulum that had briefly swung back to the left, knocking Richard M. Nixon off his perch and ending the war in Vietnam and the draft, lurched toward the right again, bringing to power the former governor of California, Ronald "If It Takes a Bloodbath" Reagan. Many an aging rock star about that time began to lose faith in the mission—Dylan included. With his marriage gone, the drugs no longer working, the albums no longer landmarks, the songs not coming through the unconscious pipeline like they used to, he turned to Jesus, as if for divine and career counseling.

The songs started coming again, but his fans rebelled, as his fans had been known to do in the past. As usual, Dylan prevailed, gaining new fans before discarding them a few years later. Always a work in progress, he weathered storms of critical abuse throughout the eighties and early nineties while continuing to perform in any emotional or political climate, marrying and divorcing again, shedding bands at the drop of a missed chord, all the while regularly turning out the occasional masterpiece, even if he was sometimes unaware of it. With a bootleg market keeping track of every false move he made in the studio and every redeeming performance he gave on the road, true fans were able to chart his progress, while the rest of humanity just presumed he'd finally reached the end of the road.

But then the songwriting god in his twilight years confounded all expectations again, finding a creative fountain of youth a few years shy of the millennium. And if the healing waters did nothing in particular to heal his singing voice, his poetic voice was stronger than ever, still speaking clearly to the thought dreams of a generation heading toward the highlands, in language as new as tomorrow and as old as the hills. Though he rarely (purposely) revealed himself in these songs of the endgame, and even more rarely revealed himself in interviews, the occasional glimpse behind the many masks revealed a man whose life had been saved, not by Jesus, not by any one woman, but by the songs he'd written and the songs he'd cherished and devoured for so many years.

Never was this more clear than on the night of February 6, 2015, when Bob Dylan received the National Academy of Recording Arts and Sciences MusiCares "Person of the Year" award in Los Angeles, to go along with his Kennedy Center Honors (1997), Pulitzer Prize Special Citation (2008), National Medal of Arts (2009), Presidential Medal of Freedom (2012), and, most controversially, Nobel Prize for Literature (2016). As surprising as his latter-day incarnation as a satellite radio deejay helming *Theme Time Radio Hour* as a cross between Alan Lomax, Wolfman Jack, and Jean Shepherd, the seventy-three-year-old troubadour's speech lasted over half an hour, probably exceeding the combined total of every one of his in-concert song introductions for his entire career (except for his extended preaching during the "born-again" era).

The unpredictable Dylan's previous podium experiences ranged from the outrageous (claiming he could identify with Lee Harvey Oswald in accepting the Tom Paine Prize in 1963) to the merely inscrutable (invoking the name of his father and Our Father in the same disturbing sentence when picking up his Grammy Lifetime Achievement award in 1993). But on this night he was remarkably forthright as he thanked everyone from likely suspects the Byrds; Joan Baez; and Peter, Paul and Mary, to his first record producer, John Hammond, and his first music publisher, Lou Levy. "Levy told me I was either before my time or after it," he said.

As he often did on his radio show, when the subject was other songs and artists, Dylan proceeded to deconstruct his own catalog—something he has only rarely done in interviews, and certainly never in front of the heavyweights of the music industry. To answer the accusations always following him of copping, co-opting, copying, or outright stealing the songs of his peers and predecessors, he pointed to specific songs that inspired some of his own classics: "Key to the Highway" = "Highway 61 Revisited"; "Five Feet High and Rising" = "It's Alright, Ma (I'm Only Bleeding)"; "Pretty Boy Floyd" = "The Times They Are a-Changin'."

"All these songs are connected," he continued. "I learned lyrics and how to write them from listening to folk songs. I sang them everywhere, clubs, parties, bars, coffeehouses, fields, festivals. I met other singers along the way who did the same thing and we just learned songs from each other. They were the only kinds of songs that made sense. I didn't think I was doing anything different. I thought I was just extending the line."

That line stretches way back. But for the purposes of this book, it begins in Duluth, Minnesota, in 1941.

He Fought with His Twin

Becoming Bob Dylan

The First Sign

As far as being born and raised, about the only thing Bob Dylan and Bobby Zimmerman could originally agree on was the time and place: St. Mary's hospital, Duluth, Minnesota, May 24, 1941, at 9:05 p.m. Astrologers would have you believe his fate was sealed from birth. "Geminis are perfectly represented by the Twins," says Astrology.com. "The fact is, you're not sure which Twin will show up half the time. Geminis may not know who's showing up either, which can prompt others to consider them fickle and restless."

In a *TV Guide* interview from 1976, Dylan agreed with this assessment. "My being a Gemini explains a lot," he said. "It forces me to extremes. I'm never really balanced in the middle. I go from one side to the other without staying in either place very long."

In a *Playboy* interview in 1978, however, he backed away from that statement. "Well, maybe there are certain characteristics of people who are born under certain signs. But I'm not sure how relevant it is."

Old friends, girlfriends, his family, as well as Dylan's entire audience for most of his career, would come to know this pattern well.

Almost from the beginning, Bob Dylan fought for control over Bobby Zimmerman. Bobby Zimmerman was a quiet kid from a middle-class Jewish household in Minnesota who went to a Jewish summer camp and whose grandmother lived with the family. As he wrote in the program notes for his April 12, 1963, concert at Town Hall, in a piece entitled "My Life in a Stolen Moment," Bob Dylan came across like a character straight out of a John Steinbeck novel or Woody Guthrie song, riding freight trains at night and witnessing Indian festivals in Gallup, New Mexico, in the morning, getting beaten up, busted, or jailed during the day. "I ran away [from home] when I was 10, 12, 13, 15, 15½, 17, and 18," he wrote. "I been caught and brought back all but once."

The idea of Bob Dylan, if not the name, probably came to him around 1954, when puberty and rock 'n' roll struck at the same time. Like many a striving Jewish family, the Zimmermans had a piano in their living room. This was where Bobby Zimmerman found the most solace, when his younger brother David wasn't hogging it, filling his after-school hours with the newly minted sounds of Little Richard, Elvis Presley, and Buddy Holly, much to the family's dismay. Later, he bought a cheap acoustic guitar. From there, he transitioned to an equally cheap Silvertone, before moving on to a solid-body electric and starting to play out.

Heard It on the Radio

In Hibbing, as in most American cities and towns at the time, rock 'n' roll was the province of the outsiders, especially the ones who found it first,

Where Bob Dylan was partly raised: 2425 Seventh Avenue, South Hibbing, Minnesota.

Jonathunder/Wikimedia Commons/Public domain

crackling through the static of the radio dial late at night from what felt like a world away, even if it was only a small station in a nowhere town right down the road. Zimmerman and his best friend John Bucklen were big fans of the radio show *No Name Jive*, hosted by the street-talking deejay Gatemouth Page and beamed into their bedrooms out of Shreveport, Louisiana, and they routinely spent their allowances ordering the singles he hawked on the program. A local show hosted by Ron Marinelli began to attract their attention when the deejay handed the last half-hour to a black-sounding man named Jim Dandy, who operated out of a tiny station in the nearby town of Virginia (population 12,000).

Zimmerman and Bucklen were so enamored of the man and the music he played that they paid a call to Marinelli one day, much like the intrepid seekers in the movie *American Graffiti*, descending unannounced at the studio to collar the voice of rock 'n' roll, Wolfman Jack. Finding out from Marinelli that Jim Dandy was in actuality James Reese, a black man in a white part of the country, only deepened the mystery, enhanced the thrill. In possession of his phone number, the boys made a call and were invited over. For months after that, they were regular visitors to the Reese

Downtown Hibbing.   *Sulven Angela Skeie/Wikimedia Commons/Public domain*

household, sitting at the deejay's feet, these hungry and thirsty sixteen-year-olds, at the base of his mountainous record collection, absorbing his wisdom, soaking it up as if it were the Gospel.

The Shadow Blasters, the Golden Chords, the Satintones, and the Night the Principal Pulled the Plug

Collaring some neighborhood kids he'd known for most of his life—Chuck Nava (drums), Bill Marinac (bass), and Larry Fabbro (electric guitar)—Bobby Zimmerman formed the Shadow Blasters. In 1957, they auditioned for a Chamber of Commerce–sponsored talent show honoring the high school's homecoming queen to the tune of Little Richard's "Jenny Jenny." They were either laughed or booed off the stage and didn't make the cut. A year later, he would be back facing the school elders at the Jacket Jamboree with a more properly trained band, the Golden Chords, featuring the acrobatic lead guitarist Monte Edwardson and the threatening-looking Leroy Hoikkala on the gold-plated drums—perhaps the closest Bobby would get to finding real rock musicians in a country music– and polka-loving town one hundred miles south of the Canadian border. Hoikkala dressed like a Hollywood hood, with greased-back hair and biker boots. Edwardson collaborated with him on one of his earliest songs, "Big Black Train."

Zimmerman, the self-appointed leader of the band, hadn't changed his performing style much in the intervening year, and the shocked principal, Mr. Pederson, pulled the plug on the noise soon after his efforts at "Rock and Roll Is Here to Stay" wound up breaking the pedal on the school piano, the crowd of clean teens laughing in shock or embarrassment like the kids in the scene from *Back to the Future* when Michael J. Fox goes all Eddie Van Halen on a Chuck Berry tune. When even the lack of amplification couldn't stop young Mr. Zimmerman from launching into another song, Pederson dropped the curtain.

"It was something different," John Bucklen proclaims in Bob Spitz's biography. "Very slowly after that the kids really got into it."

As if warming up for the abuse he'd take seven years later, when he brought the noise of "Maggie's Farm" and "Like a Rolling Stone" to the previously staid Newport Folk Festival, from his earliest days Dylan seemed unconcerned with if not oblivious to the reaction of the audience. Or maybe, since he performed without his glasses, he couldn't see (or hear) what was going on five feet in front of him; he was in a world of his own, this quiet and unassuming kid in class finding his inner rebel with a cause onstage, becoming an outlaw without having to commit armed robbery or pick a pocket.

The Golden Chords wound up acquiring something of a local following of kids who gathered whenever they practiced at Colliers Barbeque on Sundays. Shortly after the fiasco at the Jacket Jamboree, they took second place at the Chamber of Commerce Winter Frolic. They played the National Guard Armory, too, before capping their career with an appearance on the Chmielewski Brothers' ever-popular Minneapolis TV show *The Polka Hour*, where they introduced the show's traditional audience to the work of Little Richard.

Following that performance, Zimmerman and the Golden Chords parted ways, citing artistic differences, the remaining Golden Chords morphing into the Rockets and becoming the premier rock 'n' roll covers band in town. At the St. Louis County Fair later in '58, the Rockets stole the show, while Zimmerman's new band, the Satintones, consisting of himself and some cousins from Duluth, settled for a blue ribbon.

At the 1959 edition of the Jacket Jamboree, the undaunted Zimmerman had recruited a new band and a strikingly new approach. With John Bucklen making his public performing debut beside him on guitar, and the reliable Bill Marinac on string bass, their leader was flanked by a trio of glamorous female backup singers, Fran Matosich, Kathy Dasovic, and Mary DeFonso, all former contenders for Queen of the Keewatin Centennial. Their tame renditions of "As Time Goes By" and "Swing, Dad, Swing" were probably as disheartening and confusing to those in the crowd, who expected (perhaps feared) Bobby Zimmerman's usual histrionics, as similarly dramatic shifts in his repertoire, image, singing style, and overall demeanor would be to distraught diehards in future eras.

Bob Dylan Triumphs

As Bobby Zimmerman's high-school graduation approached, whether he would go to college in September or instead hitch a ride on the first flatbed freight rumbling out of town, he probably knew in his heart that the day was soon approaching when he would have to leave the comfortable trappings of his boyhood behind forever. Whether he was consciously aware of it or not, this meant leaving something else behind forever.

His last name.

Unlike his fellow Zimmerman, Broadway singer Ethel Merman, Bob wanted no part of his father's surname. He liked the sound of Dillon,

A football card issued by Bowman in 1952.
Wikimedia Commons/Public domain

undoubtedly aware of Dillon Road, right off Route 169, if not Bobby Dillon, the one-eyed defensive back who played for the Green Bay Packers. His girlfriend, Echo Helstrom, was familiar with the long, winding road, too, living on Maple Hill, about a minute away. But Bob wanted to spell it "Dylan," like the poet Dylan Thomas, whom he may or may not have read as early as 1958.

It wouldn't have surprised Echo if Bob had become enamored of the Welsh poet, who died in 1952. In fact, some biographies claim it was a copy of Thomas's poems Dylan was carrying when he came to call on her on the fateful day he arrived to tell her of his *nom de plume*.

Echo was always impressed with her boyfriend's budding literary taste, like the time he came to her house carrying a copy of *Cannery Row* and raving about its author, John Steinbeck, whose subsequent work, *East of Eden*, had recently been made into a movie starring Dylan's instant idol, James Dean. Dylan devoured all of Steinbeck after that, and was moved especially by the plight of the Okies in *The Grapes of Wrath*. He got an "A" on a paper he wrote about the book in Mr. Rolfsen's English class.

When he went off to college, Bob would claim that "Dillion" was his mother's maiden name. It was actually Stone, originally Solemovitz, but he was still into this fabrication as late as 1965, when he told a reporter for the *Chicago Daily News*, "I took [Dylan] because I have an uncle named Dillion." In 1978, he cleared up the matter in a *Playboy* interview. "No, I haven't read that much of Dylan Thomas. It wasn't that I was inspired by reading some of his poetry and going 'Aha.' If I thought he was that great I would have sung his poems and could just as easily have changed my name to Thomas." In 1986, he thought it was high time his biographer, Robert Shelton, put a lid on this matter for good. "Straighten out in your book that I did not take my name from Dylan Thomas."

Evidently unsatisfied, he went into a lengthy explanation in his own 2004 memoir, *Chronicles*, claiming his first choice had been Robert Allen or Robert Allyn. "Then sometime later, unexpectedly, I'd seen some poems by Dylan Thomas. But Robert Dylan didn't sound or look good and Bobby Dylan sounded so skittish to me."

Tell that to the Green Bay Packers.

2

Woody and Bob

Five Artists That Formed Bob Dylan and One Album That Transformed Him

Jimmie Rodgers

Though Bob Dylan had a fondness for sampling from the record collections of his friends, his favorite album was one he owned, *Hank Snow Salutes Jimmie Rodgers*. Snow, a traditional country singer from Nova Scotia who ran away from home at the age of twelve to join the Merchant Marines, pays tribute, in songs like "Jimmy the Kid," "Southern Cannonball," and "Mississippi River Blues," to Rodgers, country music's founding father, who ran away from home at the age of twelve or thirteen to join a medicine show. (Here you begin to get the source and the motive behind Dylan's early fabrications.)

Known as "the singing brakeman," Rodgers was adept at merging country music with rhythm 'n' blues to produce a true reflection of America's roots. When the country was deeply segregated and the audiences for music equally segregated, Rodgers utilized black musicians on his records, a famed example of which is Louis Armstrong's appearance, playing lead trumpet, alongside his wife, Lil Hardin Armstrong, on piano, on "Blue Yodel Number 9 (Standing on the Corner)" in 1930, a song acknowledged as one of the building blocks of rock 'n' roll. Discovered by Ralph Peer of Victor Records, Rodgers, at the time of his death from tuberculosis in 1933, at the age of thirty-five, accounted for 10 percent of the label's total sales, thanks to hits like "Blue Yodel Number 1 (T for Texas)" and "In the Jailhouse Now."

Leadbelly

A rather odd high-school graduation gift from an uncle helped shift Bob Dylan's focus from the rock 'n' roll of Little Richard and Buddy Holly (to

Jimmie Rodgers, the Father of Country Music.
Wikimedia Commons/Public domain

say nothing of Bobby Vee) to the folk music and blues of Hudie Ledbetter (a.k.a. Leadbelly). Adopted as a *cause célèbre* by the progressive folk music elites of the 1930s, Leadbelly was discovered in prison by noted folklorists John Lomax and his young son, Alan. Responsible for introducing to the wider public such future folk standards as "Goodnight Irene," "Rock Island Line," "Midnight Special," and "Cotton Fields," Leadbelly frequently toured with Dylan's idol, Woody Guthrie, whenever he wasn't incarcerated for assault, murder, or attempted murder.

While serving as a driver for Alan Lomax, Leadbelly appeared with the distinguished academic at a series of college lectures on the subject of Negro folk songs, including one at Harvard. In 1950, a year after Leadbelly's death, "Goodnight Irene," as recorded by the Weavers, hit the top of the pop charts, selling two million copies, inaugurating a brief period of

Blues singer Hudie Ledbetter (Leadbelly) was a
favorite of the folk intelligentsia.
Wikimedia Commons/Public domain

heightened interest in folk music among the wider populace. This lasted
until 1952, when some members of the Weavers, including Pete Seeger, were
blacklisted for Communist affiliations. Their 1955 reunion had a profound
effect on the folk boom of the late '50s and early '60s, featuring the Kingston
Trio and the Brothers Four, as well as contributing to Bob Dylan's nascent
political education.

Robert Johnson

Born Robert Dodds and initially going by the name of Robert Spencer, this
vastly influential Delta blues singer became Robert Johnson (adopting the
name of his natural father) soon after leaving school in 1929, at the age
of eighteen. After his first two wives died in childbirth, some, including
Johnson, saw this as a sign that he'd made a pact with the Devil when he
decided to play the blues. One of his early mentors, Son House, attributed
Johnson's almost overnight mastery of the guitar to the same pact. In fact,
the Devil was probably a black man named Ike Zimmerman (no relation to
Bobby's father, Abe), who took young Johnson under his wing.

If it was a deal with the Devil he'd made, Johnson was by far the loser of the bargain. Although he played all across the country, he recorded only twenty-nine songs during his career, over the course of two sessions. At the first session, with Don Law in 1936, Johnson put down the future classics "Come on in My Kitchen," "I Believe I'll Dust My Broom," "Crossroads Blues," and "Terraplane Blues." Of all his songs, only "Terraplane Blues" was a minor regional hit. His acclaim would come posthumously, when *King of the Delta Blues* was released by Columbia Records in 1961. This was the record John Hammond gave to the scruffy Bob Dylan when he signed him to his first record contract. In his autobiography, *Chronicles*, Dylan states, "If I hadn't heard the Robert Johnson record when I did, there probably would have been hundreds of lines of mine that I wouldn't have felt free enough to write. I immediately differentiated between him and anyone else I had ever heard."

Not only well versed in the blues, Johnson could play almost any style of music, from pop to swing, endearing him to a whole generation of guitarists, from Keith Richards to Eric Clapton to Jimi Hendrix. One particular aspect of the Robert Johnson legend that may have especially appealed to Bob Dylan was the profligate nature of his love life, where a lover in one town would be unaware of his romantic partners elsewhere. At one point, he went under at least eight last names.

Ramblin' Jack Elliott

Almost as important an influence on young Bob Dylan as Woody Guthrie, Jack Elliott was similar in many ways to Bob. Both were extremely devoted to Guthrie; both had a predilection for obscuring their Jewish roots behind poetic surnames. A graduate of Brooklyn's Midwood High School, and ten years Dylan's senior, Jack Elliott was born Elliott Adnopoz. At the age of fifteen he ran away from his appointed destiny as a surgeon to join the rodeo. He only stayed a few months before his parents found him, but his life's work had been revealed to him. By 1953, he was an early regular down in Greenwich Village, helping to establish the folk scene that would welcome Dylan in 1961.

By that time he had recorded three important folk albums for the Topic label in the UK. These albums, representing Elliott at his most Guthrie-esque, feature tunes that would become the backbone of Dylan's Dinkytown and early Greenwich Village repertoire, including "San Francisco Bay Blues," "Dink's Song," and "New York Town," as well as Guthrie classics like "Pretty Boy Floyd," "So Long, It's Been Good to Know You," and "1913 Massacre."

Rambling Jack Elliott was jokingly called "the father of Bob Dylan."

Diana Davies, courtesy of the Ralph Rinzler Folklife Archives and Collections, Smithsonian Institution

These were also among the albums Dylan lifted from a friend's collection one night in an unsavory incident that has since become legendary, representing Dylan's unquenchable desire to acquire by any means necessary whatever he needed to advance his musical education.

Even as he was becoming established in the Village, many in the audience, taking note of his performing style, his patter, his general demeanor, as well as his repertoire, would refer to Dylan as "Jack's son," a moniker that usually tickled rather than offended the much mellower Elliott, who made use of it himself, introducing the Dylan songs in his own repertoire with the words, "Here's a song from my son."

Woody Guthrie

As much as any record or artist, it was a book that probably changed Bob Dylan's outlook on his life and his music the most. The book was Woody Guthrie's memoir, *Bound for Glory*, which, among the many other attributes that immediately endeared it to Dylan, opens up on a scene of hoboes jumping a train in Duluth. Where Bobby Zimmerman was born and partly raised. No wonder Dylan, who for a while would all but become the Minneapolis version of Guthrie, would mistake some of the events portrayed in the book as episodes from his own life, going so far as to present them as such in his early press releases, either as a joke on the press or a joke on himself.

"Bob talked about going east to meet Woody all the time," a college girlfriend, Ellen Baker, told Toby Thompson in *Positively Main Street*. "We'd be at a party someplace and Bob would have been drinking and somebody would say, 'Woody's outside, Bob. Woody wants to meet you.' Bob's head would jerk up and sometimes he'd stumble outside screaming, 'I'm coming Woody, I'm coming.'"

By the fall of 1960, he was performing all around town as Bob Dylan, breaking open the Woody Guthrie songbook at local coffeehouses the Ten O'Clock Scholar, the Bastille, and the Purple Onion, whenever and wherever an open mic beckoned, but mostly at people's parties, where he used his guitar like a swizzle stick, to stir the juices of friends and strangers alike. In the manner of a wizened hobo, or Woody Guthrie himself, he'd often don an old brown hat to regale the throng.

According to Howard Sounes, in *Down the Highway*, it was University of Minneapolis student Harry Weber who loaned Dylan his spare copy of *Bound for Glory*. "You'd go to a party and Bob would get a chair and move right into the center of the room and start singing," said Weber, "and if you didn't want to listen you got the hell out of the room."

After dreaming of joining Little Richard's band, Dylan moved seamlessly into cloning Woody Guthrie.   World Telegram *Al Aumuller/ Wikimedia Commons/ Public domain*

"For a while people probably went to parties to hear Dylan play," another student, Harvey Abrams, told Robert Shelton in *No Direction Home*. "After a while, nobody wanted to go to a party because Dylan would inevitably come and play."

As a newcomer invading the established turf of his elders, Dylan offended as many of them as he pleased with this kind of behavior. Among those who straddled the fence were a pair of regulars on the Dinkytown scene, guitarist Spider John Koerner and harmonica player Tony Glover (who would later achieve a measure of fame with blues guitarist Dave Ray as the folk/blues trio Koerner, Ray, and Glover). To Glover, he admitted his fixation with Guthrie was an act at first, but only for a few days. "After that, he said, 'It was me,'" Glover recalled to Shelton.

To some people, Woody Guthrie's persona was also an act at first—until he grew into it. Far from being born into poverty, Guthrie came from a well-to-do Oklahoma family. His father was a businessman turned politician.

Although he dropped out of high school before graduation, Guthrie was an avid reader and skilled writer from an early age, writing columns for a Communist newspaper in an affected hillbilly dialect, similar to the dialect Bob Dylan would affect when he came to New York City. When Guthrie arrived in New York, he was thought of as a cowboy, much like Ramblin' Jack Elliott. He made his first recordings for Alan Lomax, roomed with Pete Seeger, and performed on the radio with Leadbelly, whose apartment on 10th Street was a hub for the folk scene. Speaking of the wisdom he acquired from Guthrie, Elliott recalled to Randy Sue Coburn in *Esquire* magazine a nugget Bob Dylan would also absorb: "He said, If you want to learn something, just steal it—that's the way I learned from Leadbelly."

The Anthology of American Folk Music

The hunchbacked filmmaker Harry Smith, an all-purpose bohemian record-hoarder, turned his personal collection of hard-to-find country, blues, zydeco, and gospel 78s into one of the most important musical documents of the twentieth century, *The Anthology of American Folk Music.* The eighty-six-track collection would be an essential tour guide for Bob Dylan in his journey from Minnesota to New York, and from Bob Dylan to immortality. *The Anthology* features old-timey stalwarts like the Carter Family, Clarence Ashley, Gus Cannon's Jug Stompers, and Uncle Dave Macon, as well as Dock Boggs and Buell Kazee, who appear side by side with future blues revivalists Mississippi John Hurt, Furry Lewis, and Blind Lemon Jefferson. The fact that it was technically an illegal release, since neither Smith nor Folkways Records owner Moses Asch ever got the permissions required to properly license these tracks from the labels that owned them, like Columbia, RCA, Mercury, and Paramount, somehow made the four-disc set even more authentic to those lucky few who could get their hands on it. It was an outlaw record cherished by an outlaw community of purists to whom the conceits and restraints of the bourgeoisie were no longer relevant in their quest for meaning in a crazy world.

Dylan's Minneapolis contemporary Jon Pankake snagged an assignment to write an essay included in the liner notes for the much-anticipated 1997 CD boxed-set reissue of the legendary sides. In these notes, he reveals it was his first hearing and subsequent immersion in the music and the lyrics and the world of Harry Smith at his friend Paul Nelson's apartment in Minneapolis over a six-hour period of time in 1959 that led this particular Jon and Paul to create their own Beatles moment in founding the highly influential *Little Sandy Review* (1959–1965), a publication dedicated to holding the line against the cruel incursion of "commercial" folk music into the pure waters represented by the music of the collection. "We found the music emotionally shattering yet culturally incomprehensible," he writes. "These lost, archaic, savage sounds seemed to carry some peculiarly American meaning for us, albeit in a syntax we couldn't yet decipher."

Pankake notes that Dylan himself had returned to the *Anthology* for inspiration as late as 1993's *World Gone Wrong*, which "contains a performance of 'Stackalee' derived from the *Anthology* version by Frank Hutchison." The Dylan album preceding it, *Good as I Been to You*, also dips into the same well.

Greil Marcus, whose essay "The Old, Weird America," adapted from his book *Invisible Republic: Bob Dylan's Basement Tapes* (eventually retitled *The Old, Weird America*) takes up the bulk of the reissued *Anthology*'s liner notes, goes even further, suggesting Dylan's mid-'60s Woodstock hiatus was nothing less than an homage to Smith and the mysterious tangled roots of American music the *Anthology* represents. "In the *Basement Tapes* an uncompleted world was haphazardly constructed out of Smith's *Anthology* and the like, out of the responses Bob Dylan and Mike Seeger and so many others brought to that music." In his book he is even more specific. "Smith's *Anthology* is a backdrop to the *Basement Tapes*. More deeply, it is a version of them."

At many a different crossroads in his life and his career, Dylan was drawn to the world and the music of the *Anthology* for inspiration and rejuvenation as if it were the Bible (maybe his second biggest influence). Before he left home for college, when his rock 'n' roll career was in shambles and the blues of Jimmie Rodgers and Leadbelly called out to him; in Dinkytown, competing for the bodies, hearts, minds, and souls of the men and women he met and competed with, under the guise and the protection of a Woody Guthrie hat; in the cold New York City winter, before and after the recording of his first album, a record populated with the country blues he was sleeping with on people's floors and humming to himself as he scribbled in neighborhood drug stores, bars, and coffeehouses, memorizing, adapting, and rearranging or downright stealing them. Later, when the demands of fame were crushing him, from the outside and the inside, in 1967, and he just wanted to find a room with a wooden stove where he could hang his hat and sit with his friends—Richard Manuel, Rick Danko, Robbie Robertson, Garth Hudson, and Levon Helm—and work on songs he knew the public would never hear. And then, at the top of the '90s, when it seemed his endless road had hit a dead end, and the traditional sounds he had known and loved were on the brink of extinction, or perhaps already extinct, like Bob

Harry Smith's *Anthology of American Folk Music* collection was revered as "The Bible" by folk purists; Dylan disagreed.

Dylan himself, he once again made a visit to the land of Harry Smith, like someone kneeling at a gravesite, giving testimony to the fact this magical music once existed and would never entirely leave this world as long as he could help it.

Dylan, of course, denied this, especially Marcus's writerly thesis. "Well, he makes too much of that," he told Mikal Gilmore, in a *Rolling Stone* interview from 2001. "He intellectualizes it too much. Performers did know of that record but they weren't in retrospect the monumental iconic recordings that he makes them out to be. It wasn't like someone discovered this pot of gold somewhere."

The records were one thing, but Dylan's greatest joy in those bygone days of the early '60s was seeing performers like Clarence Ashley, Doc Boggs, the Memphis Jug Band, and Furry Lewis "live and in person."

Now only Dylan remains.

3

Once Upon a Time

Eight Benchmark Songs

"Blowin' in the Wind"

Soon after writing about a slain black youth named Emmett Till in February 1961, Bob Dylan moved on to a singular gem about fallout shelters called "Let Me Die in My Footsteps," before stumbling across the ditty that was to change his life even more than meeting Woody Guthrie, or the appearance and prompt disappearance of his first album in March 1962. Obsessed by the wind since using the image in December '61, in the song "I Was Young When I Left Home," Dylan put it to better use in April '62 during a writing session one afternoon across the street from the Gaslight. He was so impressed by the two verses he wrote for "Blowin' in the Wind," based on the melody of a Negro spiritual "No More Auction Block for Me," which one of his favorite folk singers, Odetta, had released on her 1960 album *Live at Carnegie Hall*, that he immediately raced toward Washington Square Park, his hair blowing in the wind, to show it to his friend and mentor at Folk City, Gil Turner, who was performing there that night. Equally impressed, Turner immediately included it in his set, singing it with a copy of the chords and lyrics on his knee. He brought down the house, with the proud author drinking in the praises along with his mug of beer at the bar.

Still, with his first headline appearance at Folk City scheduled for the next week, there was work to do: another verse to add to the song, which he failed to complete in time for the gig but managed to deliver for the May issue of *Broadside*, although still not in its finished form, as he would reverse the final two verses when it appeared on his second album. By this time, Albert Grossman's moneymaking trio Peter, Paul and Mary would have heard it and decided to record it; Dylan would have a new publishing deal with the legendary Witmark Music (home of Victor Herbert), having bought

Dylan's "Blowin' in the Wind" was derived from Odetta's performance of "No More Auction Block for Me."
Diana Davies, courtesy of the Ralph Rinzler Folklife Archives and Collections, Smithsonian Institution

his way out of his original publishing deal with Leeds Music (home of Sammy Cahn); and Grossman would be his manager (having bought out Roy Silver). By the middle of 1963, when the single of Peter, Paul and Mary's version of the song sold 300,000 copies in its first week of release, the world would be a very different place.

"Don't Think Twice, It's All Right"

In the face of fame's onslaught following the writing of "Blowin' in the Wind," in April of '62, Bob Dylan's live-in girlfriend Suze Rotolo withdrew into her own world. "I remember thinking, 'I am not giving myself over to him 100 percent,'" she told Bob Spitz. "I cannot become dependent on him. If I do, I'm no person at all."

In an effort to become more independent, Rotolo would spend the last six months of 1962 studying art in Italy. In her absence, the grieving songwriter, who had gone down on his knees trying to prevent her from leaving, proposing marriage several times, would create some of his most devastatingly personal and poignant songs, including "Tomorrow Is a Long Time," the stark emotionality of which he eventually tried to disown, and "Don't Think Twice, It's All Right," the melody and arrangement of which he patently lifted from his friend and traveling companion Paul Clayton. But the feelings were all his own: abandonment, betrayal, and unrequited love, interrupted every so often by some of the other terrible things going on in the world outside his universe of pain and suffering.

A year later, at the Newport Folk Festival in July of 1963, where Bob Dylan walked around backstage cracking a bullwhip given to him by Joan Baez's flaky friend Geno Foreman (son of Clark Foreman, the noted civil rights advocate), Suze Rotolo probably would have liked to have a crack at that bullwhip herself, so she could wind it around the neck of her wandering boyfriend—especially when that wandering boyfriend's rumored new lover, Joan Baez, had the temerity to introduce her version of "Don't Think Twice, It's All Right," with a caustic aside ("This is a song about a relationship that went on too long") that had her running for the exits in tears.

"A Hard Rain's a-Gonna Fall"

In late October 1962, the face-off over missile bases in Cuba between John F. Kennedy and Russian leader Nikita Khrushchev brought about a fearful week in the life of America that had every citizen dreading World War III, especially down in the trenches of MacDougal Street, where Dylan and the rest of the folk community huddled together to weather the storm on the night of the 27th, just before the crisis broke on Sunday the 28th.

"That night we had a really drunken, depressed evening of music," Dave Van Ronk told me, "everybody saying, 'This is it. Adios.' Later, we went down to Chinatown and did up an incredible feast. Then there was this wild party at my apartment. We went through all the mood swings right there. Nobody who went through that experience came out of it the same as they were when they went in."

Lonesome and depressed over Suze's extended stay in Italy, and now scared out of his wits, Dylan could only write about it in a letter to the girl who'd left him behind. "Sitting in the Figaro all nite waiting for the world to end," he wrote. "I honest to God thought it was all over. If the world did end that nite, all I wanted was to be with you—and it was impossible cause you're so far away."

In the meantime, if any songs were to be extracted from the rubble of nuclear annihilation, he had already written the lyrics of his life up to then, typing them out at sixteen words a minute on comedian Wavy Gravy's Smith-Corona in his apartment above the Gaslight, about a month earlier. It was a manifesto up there with Ginsberg's "Howl," putting everything he knew and felt and observed into a five-verse, seven-minute extravaganza of apocalyptic rage and despair called "A Hard Rain's a-Gonna Fall." As he told the radio host Studs Terkel in April of 1963, "When I wrote that song I didn't know how many other songs I would be able to write."

While the specific Cuban crisis to which this song has always been viewed as a direct response was still a month away, Dylan debuted "Hard Rain" at a multi-artist Carnegie Hall hootenanny, under the auspices of *Sing Out!* magazine, programed and headlined by Pete Seeger (and witnessed in the audience by Dylan's University of Minnesota pals Dave and Gretel Whittaker), at which Seeger advised all the performers to limit their sets to three songs and ten minutes. In an eerie precursor to his epic battles against Seeger's strictures three years later, Dylan performed the seven-minute song anyway, along with four others: "Sally Gal," "Highway 51," "Talking John Birch Paranoid Blues," and "Ballad of Hollis Brown." Unlike the purists at Newport, the Carnegie Hall crowd was thunderously on his side. "He walked out on the stage and this roar went up," Gretel Whittaker recalled to Bob Spitz in awe, "this absolute roar."

"With God on Our Side"

In December 1961, Bob Dylan journeyed to England for the first time and stayed for several weeks to perform in a BBC TV production called *The Madhouse on Castle Street.* During the early rehearsals he found his role winnowed down from costar to Greek chorus, due to his inability to learn his lines or to refrain from smoking weed with the friends he ran into, namely Eric Von Schmidt and Richard Fariña. Hardly disappointed by his failure to follow James Dean and Elvis Presley into the acting trade, Dylan sang four songs in the production, including "Blowin' in the Wind."

By far more important were his forays with Von Schmidt and Fariña into the English folk scene via the legendary Earl's Court cellar coffeehouse the Troubadour, where he soaked up and incorporated into his repertoire easily a year's worth of inspirational influences over the course of a couple of hard-listening nights. Though many of these songs may not have been an unknown quantity to the ten o'clock scholar who absorbed music the way Dracula absorbed blood, hearing them so far from home seemed to activate an immediate transport system directly from the stage of the Troubadour into his guitar.

Thus, Bob Davenport's rendition of Jean Ritchie's "Nottamun Town" was turned into "Masters of War." Martin Carthy's arrangements of "Lord Franklin" and "Scarborough Fair" became "Bob Dylan's Dream" and "Girl from the North Country," respectively. Louis Killen's version of "The Leaving of Liverpool" was transformed into "Farewell." Nigel Denver's interpretation of Dominic Behan's "The Patriot Game," itself derived from the 1950 Jo Stafford tune "The Nightingale," found on her Capitol album *American Folk Songs* (which in turn was derived from "The Merry Month of May"), became "With God on Our Side." Subsequent protests from Jean Ritchie, the Clancy Brothers, and even the brooding Irish poet Dominic Behan himself failed to penetrate Dylan's fortress of indifference.

"With God on Our Side" turned out to be the song with which Dylan apparently began his official courtship of Joan Baez, who would eventually replace Suze Rotolo as his muse and political conscience—and, more importantly, the voice behind at least twenty-seven of his songs.

Traveling down to Cambridge a week or so after his Town Hall concert in April 1963, to play a gig at Cafe Yana, he decided to moonlight the following evening at Club 47's Sunday hoot, among an all-star cast that included Jim Kweskin and members of his Jug Band, as well as Ramblin' Jack Elliott and Eric Von Schmidt. Later, at a party above a dry goods store on Harvard Square, his first words upon being reintroduced to Joan Baez were something on the order of, "Where's Mimi?"—carrying on a running joke that his true interest was in Joan's younger sister, a ruse begun the night he first met Joan at Folk City two years before, shrewdly and correctly intuiting the quickest path to the magisterial folk Madonna's heart. (Then again, it's possible he really was more interested in the younger sister.)

His next words were equally reminiscent of that first meeting.

"Wanna hear a song?"

While her reaction to "Song to Woody" that night at Folk City was relatively muted, after hearing "With God on Our Side," Baez was "bowled over. I never thought anything so powerful could come out of that little toad," she writes in her memoir. "When I heard that song, it changed the way I thought of Bob. I even thought he looked a little better." Before she left that night, she and Dylan made plans to meet the following month in California, where he was appearing just down the road from her house, at the Monterey Folk Festival, to promote "Blowin' in the Wind."

As promised, Dylan and Baez did get together during that time, but, as was the case with one of his college girlfriends, Ellen Baker, nothing more sexual than playing folk songs together occurred. "We didn't need to make love," Baez writes. "The music seemed like enough."

When next he spent some quality time with Baez, a year later, the relationship moved to a deeper level as he brought more than one change of clothes, along with his Olivetti typewriter. "He was so shy and fragile, I wanted to mother him," Baez adds.

Baez also wanted to show Dylan off by introducing him to her cultured neighbors, the writer Alan Marcus and his wife. Much as he'd been among the great minds of Dinkytown during his college year at the University of Minnesota, Dylan was somewhat intimidated by the intellectual Marcus, who'd obviously never heard of him. "We sat back and waited for a conversation to flourish," Marcus recalled, in Howard Sounes's biography of Dylan. "It didn't flourish. He just sat there staring at us." Undeterred, Baez, doing her best Suze Rotolo impression, next arranged a visit with the notorious bohemian novelist Henry Miller, who was much more interested in Joan.

"The Times They Are a-Changin'"

In the summer of 1963, Dylan returned to Minneapolis, mainly to jam with his friends and to continue his debate with Paul Nelson and Tony Glover over the relative value of the new protest songs he was writing, like "Masters of War" and "Only a Pawn in Their Game." With the argument hardly resolved, he was swayed by a request from Joan Baez to join her at the huge civil rights march on Washington in August, where Martin Luther King Jr. would deliver his famous "I Have a Dream" speech. It was here, in front of 100,000 people, that they performed "With God on Our Side," "When the Ship Comes In," and "Only a Pawn in Their Game." Moved by the event, the speech, and Baez—most likely in that order—and in open defiance of Paul Nelson and Tony Glover, Dylan wrote "The Times They Are a-Changin'" right after the march.

Though he was certainly ambivalent about protest music, there's no denying that Dylan had become quite adept at it. Not only did he have Suze Rotolo in one ear and Joan Baez in the other, telling him about the power and necessity of such material, but he'd also found a community of peers over whom to preside, at the regular meetings of the new fanzine *Broadside*, put out by Pete Seeger and Sis Cunningham from her apartment in the west nineties. A launching pad for the best topical songs of the day, the periodical also named Dylan one of its contributing editors.

With the world suddenly attuned to his every wink and grimace and discarded matchbook cover, Dylan ramped up his writing efforts, scribbling away in Village bars and coffeehouses from midnight to dawn. Now the reigning king of the protest songwriters, in a veritable league of his own, he had crusades to launch, windmills to upend. But no sooner had he completed his protest album to end all protest albums, *The Times They Are a-Changin'*, than Dylan would disavow many of the songs on the album including the title song as merely giving the people what they wanted. He

Shortly after the assassination of President John F. Kennedy, Dylan played "The Times They Are a-Changin'" at St. Lawrence University, knowing that "something had gone haywire in the country." *St. Lawrence College Yearbook/ Wikimedia Commons/Public domain*

claimed they were part and parcel of his New York City experience, borne on the air of Greenwich Village in the early '60s—songs he was compelled to write before Tom Paxton or Phil Ochs or Eric Andersen wrote them first. "I'd never have written any of them," he told Jann Wenner in *Rolling Stone*, "if I hadn't been sitting around listening to performers in the New York cafes and the talk in all the dingy parlors."

He nevertheless continued performing them until he could hide his disdain no longer. He confessed as much to Baez in March of '65. Like most of her cronies in the folk field, still engaged in fighting the good fight to end war and unite the races, Joan was not enamored of Dylan's more personal, anti-protest material, considering it nihilistic, although she may have kept her harshest criticisms to herself for the sake of their relationship. Knowing it was a sore point for her, Dylan couldn't resist pushing her buttons, once even telling her he wrote "Masters of War" because he thought it would sell. On the last night of the tour he told her to take care of his audience. "I can't be responsible for those kids' lives," he said.

"I think he was just afraid," Baez told the writer David Hajdu, in his book *Positively 4th Street*, "but it was real. He meant it."

"The Times They Are a-Changin'," the song as well as the album, would symbolize Dylan's ambition but not his fear. Clearly speaking for his generation's desire to break free of restrictions, traditions, laws, rules, and their parents, he tied this universal truth into an all-encompassing vision of a young nation on the brink of radical change and unprecedented freedom. It was supposed to be the last song he recorded for the new album, and the song he chose to put in the leadoff spot, not only on the album but also at his Carnegie Hall concert two days later.

Less than a month after the concert, the Kennedy assassination changed everything—for a generation, no less than for Bob Dylan. Watching the news reports of the assassination, the funeral cortege, and then the point-blank murder of Lee Harvey Oswald by nightclub operator Jack Ruby unfold on TV, Dylan was apparently as blown away as anyone—certainly as blown away as any topical songwriter in Greenwich Village. But while Phil Ochs would write several songs about JFK, most notably "That Was the President" and "The Cruxifiction," Dylan's only response was a six-line poem he scribbled the next morning, with lines describing church bells tolling, that would turn into "Chimes of Freedom," a key song for his next album, on which he began to turn away from the past.

The next night, biographer Anthony Scaduto recounts, Dylan had a college concert upstate (several websites list this concert as taking place a few days later, on November 26, at St. Lawrence University in Canton, New York, just outside of Potsdam). "To my amazement the hall was filled," Scaduto quotes Dylan as saying. "The song I was opening with was 'The Times They Are a-Changin'.' That song was just too much for the day after the assassination, but I had to sing it. My whole concert takes off from there. Something had just gone haywire in the country and they were applauding that song and I couldn't understand why they were clapping or why I wrote that song."

As Dylan further reflected, the whole notion of writing protest songs now suddenly seemed not only bogus but also dangerous. "If somebody really had something to say to help somebody out, just bluntly say the truth, well obviously they're going to be done away with. They're gonna be killed."

Although by the time of this interview (1970) truth-tellers like Martin Luther King and Bobby Kennedy had also been murdered, Dylan's comment speaks directly to the fears rising up inside him that the role of truth-teller to a generation—a generation that could contain any number of nameless psychos like Lee Harvey Oswald and Jack Ruby—was no fit profession for a diminutive poet.

Dylan, of course, would brush this aside. "The whole thing about my reaction to the assassination is overplayed," he said. "If I was more sensitive to it than anyone else, I would have written a song about it." Instead, the assassination convinced Dylan that there was no longer a point in pointing fingers, except at himself.

Crystalizing his confusion, Dylan continued to lead off his concerts through 1964 with "The Times They Are a-Changin'," a song that would become a defining anthem of the decade, along with his other protest lyrics, cementing a role and an image he no longer wanted or needed and was plainly living in mortal fear of.

Adding more than a little absurdity to this role was his appearance at the Americana Hotel in New York City in December 1963, to accept the Tom Paine award for contributions to social justice from the Emergency Civil Liberties Committee (ECLC). Invited to say a few words to the audience of aging left-wing contributors to the cause, and impaired by nerves and drink, Dylan succumbed to an always ill-advised attempt at public speaking. In short, he'd have been much better served singing a few songs from his forthcoming album than trying to explain himself in his own words. Of the many lines he crossed in his alternately satiric and tasteless remarks, claiming he could see some of himself in Lee Harvey Oswald was the most egregious.

Later, informed that his impromptu harangue had probably cost the committee upward of $10,000 in lost contributions from offended attendees, he wrote an apologetic letter to the ECLC and offered to give a benefit concert (but never did).

"Mr. Tambourine Man"

Taking to the road in February 1964 with some pals in an old Ford station wagon to explore the mythic West en route to a concert in Berkeley later in the month must have seemed like just the kind of escape route a beleaguered artist determined to shed one skin for another needed. The trip consisted of several symbolic stops, including delivering clothes to coalminers in Hazard, Kentucky, and delivering his ego to the doorstep of Carl Sandburg in Hendersonville, North Carolina (where the aged poet and folk-song aficionado had much the same mystified reaction as had Alan Marcus and Henry Miller). A brief, embarrassing visit was curtailed when Sandburg excused himself to take a nap, prompting Dylan's fellow passenger, the journalist Paul Karman, to hiss, "How do you write the stuff you do when you don't even understand what it means?"

Dylan ignored Karman to begin work on "Chimes of Freedom" as the car headed toward New Orleans, where "Mr. Tambourine Man" would be born, and Denver, where he'd introduce "Chimes of Freedom" at the Denver Folklore Center. Along the way, the car radio played "I Want to Hold Your Hand," introducing Bob Dylan and the rest of America to the Beatles.

A soaring break with his tradition of traditional melodies tied to political or romantic protest lyrics, "Mr. Tambourine Man" was Dylan's first genuine merger of the personal and the poetic, referred to by Robert Shelton in his review of Dylan's concert at New York's Philharmonic Hall in October 1964 as "an introspective symbolist piece that moved in and out of this listener's comprehension but still conveyed a strong mood." Obviously, this was a clue, to the Dylanologically inclined, that Shelton was more of a drinker than a devotee of psychedelics. Had he been a raging acidhead, he'd have surely comprehended the song in all of its hallucinatory entirety, a swirling French surrealistic trip to the Mardi Gras, dedicated to mystic sideman Bruce Langhorne's legendary Turkish tambourine. However, in 1964, the use of LSD was still a rarefied activity, even among the hip intelligentsia Dylan was addressing in many of his new songs.

Dylan, of course, has always denied that the use of drugs had anything to do with opening up his own doors of perception regarding the songwriter's trade. But he is a notoriously unreliable narrator, especially of his own work. What's definitely true is that his audience's perception of his work from '65 through '67 was increasingly informed (some might say addled) by the use of any number of legal and illegal substances.

"Subterranean Homesick Blues"

The use of mind-expanding drugs may have had more to do with Dylan's first major rock 'n' roll song, "Subterranean Homesick Blues," than any of his others (with a bit of credit to the Beatles, and a tip of the cap to Chuck Berry). While on that post-beatnik journey west in the car with his friends in 1964, when the Beatles hit the radio waves of America, Dylan apparently heard the lyrics in the bridge to "I Want to Hold Your Hand" as "I get high" instead of "I can't hide." Upon this misunderstanding the foundations of '60s rock were built.

A few months later, on August 28, with the songs of the Beatles in the midst of their unprecedented domination of the American charts, Al Aronowitz, a journalist who had interviewed both principals, set up an encounter between Dylan and the Beatles at the Delmonico Hotel in New York City. This event has since achieved legendary status not only as a kind of mythical meeting of the Gods of the Rock Sixties, but also as the occasion when Dylan, thinking the lads were already experienced tokers, wound up introducing the Beatles to pot for the first time, thus propelling the former mop tops into a new level of creativity. This bit of rock lore was partially debunked in later years, as Harrison and Lennon came forward to admit they were hardly virgins in matters of the medieval weed. But perhaps, as dedicated drinkers who utilized speed to get them through seven sets a night in Germany, they'd just *never inhaled*. At any rate, after passing around a joint or two, McCartney, for one, found himself looking down at the room from the ceiling. From that rarefied remove, it's very probable yesterday looked far away indeed.

Similarly stoked by the Beatles' success, Dylan leaned into Chuck Berry's all-purpose song of personal protest, "Too Much Monkey Business," as he prepared the *Bringing It All Back Home* album that fall and winter. Utilizing some of the writing techniques he'd absorbed from reading Jack Kerouac and Allen Ginsberg, and was already tapping into in the formation of his novel in progress, *Tarantula*, Dylan railed against the establishment, the counterculture, the government, the educational system, and the natural order of things to bring forth one of his most cogent diatribes to date—in a two-and-a-half-minute song you could dance to, recorded on January 14, 1965, and released on March 8.

The initial release of "Subterranean Homesick Blues"—while failing to dent the consciousness, expanded or otherwise, of the top half of the singles-buying market—caused reverberations almost as seismic as the sessions that produced it. This was true for Dylan's diehard fans, but it was equally true for the fellow musicians tuned in to his evolving sonic palette. John Lennon, for one, is reported to have been so stunned by its drive and manic verbiage that he wondered how he could possibly compete with it.

Many other artists and groups dove into the fray headfirst. Following "Subterranean Homesick Blues" to the radio in May was the Byrds' version of "Mr. Tambourine Man." The Rolling Stones released "Satisfaction" in

June. Cher debuted as a solo artist on July 3 with Dylan's "All I Really Want to Do." A week later, Sonny and Cher put out the Dylan-esque "I Got You Babe." A week after that, Dylan switched his affections from the Beatles to their friendly competitors, deciding after all this time and all these many disguises that he really wanted to be "Like a Rolling Stone." On August 7, the Beatles finally responded with "Help!" before going into the studio to record *Rubber Soul*, which would contain the Dylan-esque "Norwegian Wood," penned mainly by Lennon. On that same August 7 date, the Turtles released their cover of Dylan's "It Ain't Me Babe." Two weeks later, Barry McGuire released the Dylan-esque "Eve of Destruction," written by Dylan-obsessed P. F. Sloan, and Greenwich Village's own the Lovin' Spoonful, featuring the songwriting talents of sometime Dylan sideman John B. Sebastian, released the gloriously celebratory "Do You Believe in Magic."

Dylan followed up "Like a Rolling Stone" with another angry missive to his detractors, the non-album single "Positively 4th Street," an actual and metaphorical address that could have applied just as well to his Dinkytown critics as to the naysayers of Greenwich Village and Newport, Rhode Island. By the time it succeeded "Like a Rolling Stone" in the Top 10 late in '65, the merger of Dylan's brand of caustic folk-rock with the Beatles brand of rock 'n' roll magic had created the dominant sound of the decade.

"Like a Rolling Stone"

Bob Dylan did sixty-three concerts in 1965, up from a previous personal high of twenty-eight in 1964, during many of which he was subjected to constant booing from his previously devoted audience. From September 24, 1965, through May 27, 1966, he and his backing band, the Hawks, gave seventy-seven concerts in two hundred and ten days in forty-seven North America cities, plus twelve in the UK, six in Australia, and one each in Paris, Dublin, Belfast, Copenhagen, and Stockholm. At the same time, he wrote all the songs for and recorded two of the most influential albums of the rock 'n' roll era, *Bringing It All Back Home* (released in March) and *Highway 61 Revisited* (released in August), which include some of the most searing, iconic, and complicated songs in his entire catalog. This is not including the thirty-page diary entry he turned into "Like a Rolling Stone" in March or the post–Newport '65 rant "Positively 4th Street."

He started writing "Like a Rolling Stone" in England, where he officially broke up with Joan Baez, the breakup occurring only when Joan happened upon Dylan's new love, Sara, at Dylan's London hotel room. But he'd been throwing her hints for quite a while, even writing her two kiss-off songs, "Love Is Just a Four-Letter Word" and "Farewell Angelina," both of which, instead of taking to heart, she took to the recording studio and covered.

Whether she sensed the coming breakup or not, Baez had high hopes that Dylan would do for her in England what she'd done for him in the United States: open up a previously untapped audience. Dylan was reluctant to take her on his May tour of the UK and claimed to Robert Shelton that he told her in no uncertain terms that he wouldn't be inviting her to participate in any of his concerts, but Baez couldn't hear him. Instead, her pain and humiliation was there for all the world to see in the documentary of that tour filmed by D. A. Pennebaker, *Dont Look Back*, Dylan's nasty answer to the Beatles filmic debut, the rollicking *A Hard Day's Night*.

Directing his rage inward—perhaps thinking of Baez, or maybe Gretel Hoffman, the earlier crush he'd had before Dave Whittaker swept her away from him, or maybe his more recent rejection by Marianne Faithfull, reigning rock goddess girlfriend of Mick Jagger, the leader of the Rolling Stones—Dylan spewed his venom in a long screed again written in the hyped-up manner of a beat(en) Jack Kerouac, filled with more imagery of the type he had discovered in free-writing his "novel," *Tarantula*. As opposed to that hopelessly aimless manuscript, here he eventually found the focus he needed to extract a four-verse, thirty-six-line, three-hundred-and-thirteen-word song (excluding choruses); and, even more miraculously, he proceeded to capture its essence in the studio through several excruciating takes before he nailed it (on take seven). Clocking in at 6:00—an unheard-of length for a rock 'n' roll single—it was nevertheless one of his proudest achievements.

"Here was a sound I myself could dig," he told Nat Hentoff.

Along for the ride during the sessions for the *Highway 61* album and later at Newport, was Michael Bloomfield, spontaneously appointed by Dylan as his musical director. "All these studio cats are standing around," Bloomfield told Jim Delahunt in *Hit Parader*, thinking of people like guitarist Charlie McCoy, bass players Harvey Brooks and Russ Savakus, drummers Bobby Gregg and Sam Lay, and keyboard players Paul Griffin and Frank Owens. "I come in like a dumb punk with my guitar over my back, no case, and I'm telling people, this is the arrangement, do this on the bridge. . . . Dylan remained completely isolated from that. He just sang his tunes and they fitted the music around him."

4

He Was Young When He Left Home

Dylan in Dinkytown

ambridge, Massachusetts, and Berkeley, California, were the reigning college towns of the 1960s—reputations they would burnish throughout that smoldering decade. But there were also Ann Arbor (University of Michigan), Austin (University of Texas), and Madison (University of Wisconsin). Honorary college towns included the Old Town neighborhood of Chicago, which was home to the Old Town School of Folk Music, where Jim McGuinn, future founder of the Byrds, first learned the twelve-string guitar in the style of Bob Gibson. San Francisco played host to the Beat generation in North Beach, followed by the hippie generation in Haight-Ashbury. Greenwich Village was in many ways the ultimate college town, containing NYU and the New School and every acoustic folkie within walking distance of a subway station, plus Sundays in Washington Square, Monday nights at Folk City, and Tuesday nights at the Gaslight. The University of Minnesota, which Dylan nominally attended, called its radical neighborhood Dinkytown.

What all these neighborhoods had in common was at least one if not several haunts like Dylan's favorite hangout, the Ten O'Clock Scholar, where the collegiate elite would gather in a smoky haze for heady talk and the music of revolution. Gradually, as the new decade of JFK commenced and the events of the world began to get absurd and dangerous, these smoky haunts would be filled by many more college dropouts than students, an unkempt, unruly, unforgiving, and extremely opinionated lot. Their opinion back in 1959, shared by the soon-to-be Bob Dylan, was that rock 'n' roll was entirely beside the point, and folk music, as consumed by the college audience and performed by spiffy groups like the Highwaymen, the Brothers Four, the Limeliters, and the Kingston Trio, was entirely inauthentic. That being the most cuttingly snide assessment any self-respecting purist need muster.

Besides, Bobby Zimmerman had already washed out as a rocker, after auditioning for Buddy Holly clone Bobby Vee's backup band the summer before he left for college. For two dances in Gwinner, North Dakota, he was a Shadow, manning the keyboard wearing a matching plaid shirt. "All I remember is an old crusty piano that hadn't been tuned . . . ever," Vee told Kathleen Mackay in *Bob Dylan: Intimate Insights from Friends and Fellow Musicians*. "The next night was more of the same. He was good spirited about the fact that none of us had the money to secure a piano for him and there were no hard feelings on the part of anyone as he made his exit for the University of Minnesota."

This was the kind of credit that meant nothing to the musical snobs at the Ten O'Clock Scholar, so the future folk musician undoubtedly kept it to himself, like most of the other personal details of his inauthentic, pre-Dylan existence, which, for a while, would safely protect his debt to the early rock 'n' roll of Elvis Presley (although anyone wishing to inspect his high-school yearbook would find his desire to one day be employed by Little Richard glaringly obvious). He'd also keep Hank Williams and Hank Snow in his back pocket, but his appreciation for Leadbelly was deemed authentic enough to admit in mixed company.

The Girls of Dinkytown

Almost as hungry for love as he was for fame and recognition, Bob Dylan did still possess one significant deal-breaker when it came to getting involved with a woman, even if that involvement extended no further than that woman's couch. That requirement was a massive record collection, or at least easy access to historic sides. Back in high school, Echo Helstrom's mother had some great country albums featuring his two favorite Hanks, as well as Johnny and Jack, and the Louvin Brothers. Echo's father had a couple of neat guitars. Although his summer-camp crush, Judy Rubin, didn't seem to be much of a music geek, when she enrolled at the University of Minnesota, she attended all of his shows, shouting out requests. But when the singer mistook her fandom for something more and asked her to marry him, she quickly backed away, getting herself pinned to a future stockbroker instead.

Brimming with nostalgic feelings, Dylan then invited Echo to live with him when she moved to Minneapolis and visited Dinkytown (she turned him down), even while he was actively seeing Bonnie Beecher, a Ten O'

Clock Scholar regular, for whom he wrote "Song to Bonnie," based on a traditional Woody Guthrie melody. The two had become instant friends when she dropped the name of Sleepy John Estes into their first conversation and agreed to lend her new soulmate some records. A theater major at the U of M, it is Bonnie whom most scholars of Dylanology consider to be not only the true "Girl from the North Country" but also "the actress girl" Dylan wrote about in his poem "Life in a Stolen Moment," "who kneed me in the guts."

Of course, Dylan was also dating her friend Lorna at the time, as well as Ellen Baker, a Jewish girl whose father ran the Minneapolis Folklore Society, thus giving her a literal as well as figurative leg up on the competition. Ellen's mother, like Echo's mother, took care of Dylan's basic needs, mending his torn dungarees and providing home-cooked meals and the occasional bed whenever he didn't feel like commuting back to the Sammy house on Fraternity Row, where he was regarded as an oddball and a loner but admired for his inspired use of the house piano.

"My mother would either go tell him to brush his teeth or take a shower or not come to dinner," Ellen Baker told Toby Thompson in *Positively Main Street*. "She was the only person I ever knew who could talk to him like that and not make him mad. I suppose Bob dined and slept at our house for a period of four months."

In Ellen Baker's father, Dylan found a worthy successor to the Virginia deejay Jim Dandy, as far as the sheer size and significance of his record collection. Jim Dandy's route was through rhythm 'n' blues to the blues; Mike Baker's collection plunged through the blues to the heart of Harry Smith territory. Among his artifacts were manuscripts and magazines and old 78s. Bob and Ellen sang Cisco Houston and Woody Guthrie songs together in the living room. It was their way of making out. "He was extremely inarticulate unless he had a guitar in his hands," she added.

Bonnie Beecher was by far Dylan's biggest fan. She would drive him to auditions and sneak him food from her sorority house, or from the hamburger joint where she worked part-time. As opposed to Judy Rubin, who was content to sit in the audience, and Ellen Baker, who never progressed past the harmonizing stage with him, Bonnie Beecher had the foresight to add a third party to their relationship: a tape recorder. Soon after Beecher was asked to leave her sorority house, partly because of her continuing relationship with Dylan and his incessant harmonica playing as he serenaded her at the house, he started visiting her and her tape recorder on a regular basis at her new apartment, which, in the coming years, Dinkytown scene-makers would come to know as the Beecher Hotel.

One of his earliest songwriting efforts captured on these home tapes was called "Bonnie Why'd You Cut My Hair," an autobiographical lament inspired by an upcoming trip to Hibbing to visit his parents. Less specific and topical, "Song to Bonnie" morphed into "Song to Woody" after Bob and Bonnie broke up. (By then, Dylan had met the actual Woody Guthrie on a Sunday afternoon early in 1961.)

The Boys of Dinkytown

Another song captured on Bonnie Beecher's tape recorder was called "Talkin' Hugh Brown," written about one of Dylan's first roommates after his days as a Sammy came to an early end. Brown was part of a larger group of campus-based freethinkers and radicals that also included folk singer Dave Morton; Harvey Abrams, who later became a social worker; and all-around proto-hipster Dave Whittaker, who had traveled with Kerouac and dined with Ginsberg, and at whose house people would gather for high-spirited discussions about life and literature. As he did with the record collections of his girlfriends, Dylan would soak up the essential information without comment. Perhaps they were beyond him at the time, the literary and political references tossed about during these competitive conversations like Molotov cocktails, but he'd never let on.

"He was like an empty vessel waiting to be filled," Whittaker told Dylan biographer Bob Spitz.

Once he'd digested them, Dylan would present these concepts to the world as the thought-dreams of an instinctive poet, while his intellectual betters continued to muse in their easy chairs. (Dave Whittaker, meanwhile, went on to live the life he talked about in those days, in many ways sacrificing his health and family to do so. As late as 2011, the man known as Diamond Dave, "radical raconteur, rabble rouser, revolutionary rebel," was still operating according to the hippie ethic, living in a communal setting in Haight-Ashbury, about to host a program on Pirate Cat Radio and preparing to teach a class at the Free University of San Francisco.)

In addition to being Dylan's mentor, spiritual guru, and source for morning glory seeds, Whittaker soon became his main rival for the affections of Gretel Hoffman, a Bennington dropout returning to her Minnesota roots; a rich, sophisticated, long-haired girl deigning to mingle with the jugglers and the clowns on the Dinkytown folk scene. The rivalry was short-lived, however. Although Dylan and Hoffman were inseparable for a time, it was an entirely intellectual relationship, conducted over steaming cups of coffee and acoustic guitars. In his mind, Dylan may have thought there was chemistry brewing, but he was never very good at chemistry or biology. Chemistry and biology was what Gretel Hoffman and Dave Whittaker had from the instant they set eyes on each other in March of 1960, leading them to elope two months later, and leading Dylan to one of the great lost lyrics of his career, when he spotted Gretel on the street soon after the event, and instead of rushing to hug and congratulate her, shouted, "Call me when you get a divorce."

In this inbred society of festering purists, the purest of the pure were the editors of the startup literary/political journal out of Minneapolis, the *Little Sandy Review*, Jon Pankake and Paul Nelson. Of necessity, they encountered the early Bob Dylan almost everywhere they went. "Dylan seemed to learn so incredibly fast," Nelson told Howard Sounes, speaking as a music critic. "If you didn't see him for two weeks, he had made three weeks of progress."

Pankake was less enthusiastic. "I was not particularly interested in Bob Dylan as a musician or a person," he stressed to Sounes.

Pankake's place in Bob Dylan's history was cemented the night he discovered that his young friend had made off with a number of his record albums, including several by Jack Elliott, as well as his treasured copy of Harry Smith's *Anthology*. When cornered by Pankake, Nelson, and Tony Glover the next day, Dylan broke down, and eventually the records were returned. But Pankake never really forgave him. "I think he believed he needed them more than I did," he told Robert Shelton. "But it expressed a certain amount of contempt for me personally."

Even after he found his fame and fortune in New York City, Dylan would periodically return to Dinkytown, sometimes to record songs at his girlfriend's apartment. More often, he'd collar Jon and Paul at the offices of the *Review*, where they engaged in spirited debates about the value of "protest music." Jon and Paul were unrelenting in their disdain for this type of pandering to the mood of the moment, claiming it was hardly authentic. Dylan went to great lengths to defend himself, although he would soon come to this conclusion himself. Both Pankake and Nelson had been profoundly disturbed by Bob's second album, *Freewheelin'*, after falling hard for the first.

"That such a creative energy and driving force as Dylan would ever be satisfied with some of the material issued here is a great mystery," they wrote in their review. After several hundred more scathing words to the same effect, they did in the end throw the boy a bone. "A failure," they wrote, "but a most interesting one. Don't give up on Dylan yet."

Live at the Beecher Hotel: The Dinkytown Album

The earliest appearance of Bob Dylan on record seems to be a pair of 1961 Minnesota performances, one from May and the other from December, bookending the recording of his first Columbia album, in November (which wouldn't be released until March of 1962). Put out as one disc in 1994 under the title *The Minnesota Party Tape*, the sets were recorded at Bonnie Beecher's apartment, the first supervised by Bonnie, the second, much better one by Tony Glover.

Both tapes feature a repertoire similar to that of Dylan's debut album and his many in-house Dinkytown concert performances. Among the twenty-plus songs on the first tape, standouts include Woody Guthrie's "Pastures of Plenty" and "This Land Is Your Land," the A. P. Carter classic "Will the Circle Be Unbroken," Jesse Fuller's "San Francisco Bay Blues," "James Alley Blues" by Richard "Rabbit" Brown (from the Harry Smith collection), the Muddy Waters tune "Two Trains Running," the Gary Davis tune "Death Don't Have No Mercy," traditional favorites "Man of Constant Sorrow" and "Pretty Polly," and the immortal "Bonnie Why'd You Cut My Hair."

Seven months later, with a professional recording under his belt, Dylan duplicated only two songs from the earlier set: Guthrie's "Ramblin' Round" and "Man of Constant Sorrow," which also appears on his debut album, as do Blind Lemon Jefferson's "See That My Grave Is Kept Clean" and Eric Von Schmidt's "Baby Let Me Follow You Down." Traditional tunes like "Dink's Song," "Poor Lazarus," "Stealin'," and "Wade in the Water" round out the package. Notable also are some songs that would remain in his repertoire throughout much of the early '60s: "Sally Gal," "Hard Times in New York," and "I Was Young When I Left Home."

5

Hard Times in the City

Bob Dylan's Surrogate Families

Meeting Woody Guthrie

After burning his bridges in the Twin Cities with both his Woody Guthrie act and his Bob Dylan act, Dylan knew it was time to put his lack of money where his mouth was and go to New York City, where the national folk scene was, and where, more importantly, Woody Guthrie was. He did this, according to his biographers, by sticking out his thumb and hitchhiking, because no self-respecting authentic hipster would be caught dead asking his father for money to purchase a ticket on Hibbing's own Greyhound bus line as if it were just another Ford convertible or new motorcycle he wanted. Better to hop a freight like one of Steinbeck's hobos. But Dylan, no doubt averse to the actual dangers of riding a boxcar, chose instead to hitch, since in those days hitchhiking was still an acceptable mode of travel for an innocent-looking dude with an acoustic guitar on his back, even in the midst of a snowstorm.

Although he accomplished his mission in one piece, his journey was as fortuitous as it was circuitous. Pausing briefly in Chicago, he received such a poor reception when he tried to entertain at a house party that he seemed to be rethinking his whole plan by doubling back to Madison. In Madison, however, an angel appeared, in the form of Pete Seeger, who was giving a concert the very night Dylan was there. Much like the concert Bobby Zimmerman attended in Duluth by Buddy Holly and the Crickets, given a few nights before Holly died in a plane crash, Seeger seemed to be speaking directly to Dylan through his guitar, telling him it was his destiny to continue east to meet Woody Guthrie and to become one of us. This had a galvanizing, mystical effect on the young seeker; this and the fact that he ran into a couple of guys looking for a third to help them drive all the way to New York.

Without so much as a contact or a cousin to call on, Dylan showed up in this vast, cruel town in January of 1961 as a complete unknown, having to rely on the same lost little boy charisma he used to charm Echo Helstrom's mom and Ellen Baker's mom to gain for himself a number of new surrogate families, now that he'd decided his original Zimmerman family back in Hibbing would have to be erased for the time being, at least as far as the general public was concerned, as if he were living in a personal witness-protection program.

According to legend, no sooner was young Dylan dropped off in Greenwich Village than he secured himself a gig playing harmonica behind Fred Neil at the Cafe Wha?. Not long after that, following his internal agenda, his next stop was at the Queens address he had for Guthrie, arriving unannounced, snow on his boots, dust on his hat, where he was regarded with suspicion like a Jehovah's witness or a Fuller brush man by the housekeeper. Informed that Woody was in the hospital in New Jersey, Dylan refused to go away. He probably had no plan B. Plan B was always his guitar, and eventually he was able to seduce young Arlo with it, thereby at least accomplishing a thirty-minute jam session with a Guthrie, if not the particular Guthrie he had in mind.

Dylan himself gives a slightly different rendering of this fabled meeting with the son of Woody in his memoir, *Chronicles*. Significantly, he has it taking place on Coney Island, after he'd already established himself as a frequent houseguest in several Greenwich Village pads, from which home base he'd already visited Guthrie a few times in the hospital and been told by his deteriorating hero that he had a bunch of unpublished lyrics stashed away that the songwriter was welcome to put melodies to. The existence of these lyrics is evidenced by the appearance in 1998 and 2000 of two volumes of previously unheard songs, *Mermaid Avenue* and *Mermaid Avenue Vol. II*, with melodies by folk icons not named Dylan (Billy Bragg and Jeff Tweedy). However, Marjorie Guthrie was already living in Howard Beach, Queens, by 1961, so the original story sounds more authentic. Which is not to say that Woody, in his near-demented state, never made Dylan the offer.

More likely, young Arlo, obviously feeling something for his mission, directed Dylan to the New Jersey home of Robert Gleason, an East Orange electrician, and his wife, Sidsel, who lived near the Greystone Park hospital where Woody had been since 1956. The Gleasons had been hosting Guthrie for Sunday get-togethers since 1959, at which the cream of the folk

At his first stop in New York town, Dylan was greeted by Woody Guthrie's son Arlo.
Diana Davies, courtesy of the Ralph Rinzler Folklife Archives and Collections, Smithsonian Institution

aristocracy would come to pay homage to a dying legend who could barely reciprocate, including Pete Seeger, Guthrie's manager Harold Leventhal, and the noted folklorist Alan Lomax, along with some of the new generation of acolytes like the native American folk singer Peter LaFarge and New Lost City Ramblers founder John Cohen. Most weekends, Marjorie Guthrie, Woody's ex-wife, was there with her kids, including young Arlo, then thirteen or fourteen.

This is probably where Dylan had his first audience with Guthrie, on January 29, 1961, after gaining Marjorie's approval (no doubt aided by Arlo whispering in her left ear). And while Woody himself may have been hard-pressed to subsequently pick Dylan out of a lineup (even a lineup of folk singers), he did seem to recall one particular youngster he enjoyed hearing do his songs on a weekly basis, that being Bob Dylan. These visits allowed Dylan the immense pleasure of fulfilling an ancient fantasy that he could then rub in the noses of all the Dinkytown naysayers.

Dylan became a regular visitor to Guthrie's bedside, as well as an instant regular at the Gleason's house; by some accounts he never left the party at all, preferring to drop his sleeping bag in a corner of the living room, near Bob Gleason's tape machine, where he could listen all night to Woody's actual record collection of vintage country music. In the early months of 1961, he even had a standing gig at East Orange's top (only?) coffeehouse, the Cave, where the audience was much more interested in playing chess than listening to folk music. In the talking blues he adapted from a traditional tune to become a tale of working at the Cave in East Orange, he claimed to have been paid in chess pieces instead of cash.

Dylan's Surrogate Families

Aside from the Gleasons, several more surrogate families soon emerged for Bob Dylan in the East Village and thereabouts. Mell Bailey, a physician, and his dress-designer wife, Lillian, a black couple who had a small apartment on Avenue B and East Third Street, were the next to take him in. "They let me come over and sleep there when they had nothing but a room," Dylan told Robert Shelton. Their record collection was immense, spanning all the genres that had any meaning for him: blues, gospel, R&B, folk music. They also had a Wollensack tape recorder and a soft spot for wandering minstrels.

The Baileys were regulars at Folk City, on the outskirts of the Village, a few blocks from Washington Square, along with Mac and Eve MacKenzie. The MacKenzies were introduced to Dylan at a Cisco Houston concert by

Godfather to a generation of folkies, Dave Van Ronk often put up Bob Dylan (and put up with him) at his apartment.   *Diana Davies, courtesy of the Ralph Rinzler Folklife Archives and Collections, Smithsonian Institution*

Marjorie Guthrie, who had by this time apparently fallen for his waifish charm. "My mother found the Jewish part of him endearing," Nora Guthrie told Howard Sounes. Soon he was a regular sleepover visitor at the MacKenzies' apartment on East 28th Street, near Bellevue, too, trading a spot on their living room couch for access to some of his early original manuscripts, many of them inspired by and some of them directly copied from the Harry Smith songbook. (These manuscripts were eventually auctioned at Sotheby's by the MacKenzies' son, Peter.)

While Dylan gives a lot of uncorroborated space in his memoir to Ray and Chloe Gooch as another surrogate family, it's probably safer to say that when he wasn't bunking with the MacKenzies or the Baileys or traveling out to Jersey to stay with the Gleasons or visiting Woody Guthrie at the hospital, he could be found on the living-room couch or kitchen floor of Dave and Terri Van Ronk's apartment on 15th Street near 7th Avenue, and then later on Waverly Place. Terri was briefly Dylan's manager, helping him get gigs in New York City, Cambridge, and Saratoga Springs. She also peddled his demo tape to Folkways and Vanguard, both of which declined.

6

Positively Bleecker and MacDougal Street

Three Defining Greenwich Village Gigs, One Chance Meeting

A mecca for the unwashed bohemian dreamer since the nineteenth century, Greenwich Village had been home to generations of poets, painters, writers, and radicals well before Bob Dylan pulled into town. Immediately preceding his arrival, the Beat writers and poets held forth, led by Allen Ginsberg, Jack Kerouac, and William S. Burroughs. Dylan's own not-namesake, Dylan Thomas, drank himself to death at the famed White Horse Tavern on the corner of Hudson and West 11th Street. Washington Square Park sported the fabled fountain where every Sunday bluegrass balladeers from the outer boroughs, having put a token in the subway and hauled their banjos downtown, would perform Appalachian airs. The place was filled with enough innocent-looking but impossibly knowledgeable long-haired girls to make a Dinkytown neophyte (to say nothing of a Brooklyn neophyte) go weak in the knees.

Further south, the corner of Bleecker and West 3rd Street became famous as the hub of the nascent 1960s folk scene, eventually becoming all but impassable, except by human traffic. There were basket houses littering the block where all manner of the talented and the talentless could be found. The Night Owl was the home base of the Lovin' Spoonful, Tim Hardin, and Fred Neil. Aside from the stately Village Gate, a venue known for its jazz lineup, the most influential clubs in the area were the Bitter End, where "commercial" folk acts like Peter, Paul and Mary played, and Folk City and the Gaslight, where the more "authentic" acts were discovered. By mid-decade, the Cafe au Go Go had opened up, attracting high-powered groups like the Butterfield Blues Band, the Blues Project, and Jimi Hendrix, then still operating under the name of Jimmy James. Upstairs from the Au

Spending Sundays at the fountain in Washington Square was a sacred folk tradition.
Diana Davies, courtesy of the Ralph Rinzler Folklife Archives
and Collections, Smithsonian Institution

Go Go was the Garrick Theater, where Frank Zappa spent the summer of '67 playing every night with the Mothers of Invention. Down the block, the Fugs displayed their wicked wares at the Players Theater.

Between sets, the various musicians convened to swill beer, talk politics, scribble poetry, play chess, or indulge in neighborhood gossip at the Kettle of Fish, upstairs from the Gaslight, or the Cafe Figaro, a little further down the block. Established in 1950, the Kettle of Fish eventually left MacDougal Street when the flow of traffic started to ebb, relocating to Christopher Street. The Figaro closed in 1969, replaced by a Blimpie sandwich bar. It later opened up again as a remodeled Figaro, but by then the era was over. "The demise of the Figaro marked the end of a genuine 'golden age' era for Greenwich Village—a time when the Village was a genuine font of cultural ferment and a focal point of American popular culture," offered commentator Benjamin Hemric on the *New York Times*' City Room blog.

Ironically, in the early years of the sixties, when Dylan began to make his first serious inroads into the commercial folk scene, it was not with his voice or his songs but with his harmonica playing, when he began appearing behind the lanky baritone Fred Neil at the Cafe Wha? to blow a few notes.

Gathered nightly over espresso and grenadine, the denizens of Greenwich Village met for musical, political, and spiritual nourishment at the many coffee houses on MacDougal Street.
Diana Davies, courtesy of the Ralph Rinzler Folklife Archives and Collections, Smithsonian Institution

In the studio, he gained credits and credibility backing such blues icons as Victoria Spivey and Big Joe Williams, as well as Harry Belafonte. At Folk City, along with Mark Spoelstra on guitar, he frequently accompanied Brother John Sellers. But it was in his attempt to establish himself as a solo folk singer that he focused the bulk of his attention, quickly garnering an adoring crowd at the Gaslight and Folk City, and even more quickly moving toward his ultimate goal of a recording contract.

Folk City: April 11, 1961

On the night of April 11, 1961, Dylan played the first important New York City gig of his career, starting a two-week engagement opening for the legendary blues singer John Lee Hooker. The gig had come about partly through a gathering of angels—the Van Ronks, the Baileys, and the MacKenzies—who began lobbying club owner Mike Porco to offer the boy a paid slot soon after meeting him. It was at this point that Porco became another father figure in Dylan's continuing quest, actually chaperoning the not-quite-twenty-year-old supposed orphan down to the intimidating offices of the Musicians' Union for his union card, paying the fee for his initiation, and signing the appropriate papers as his guardian. Porco gave Dylan some of his children's old clothes, which a friend named Camilla Adams altered. "I knew she was very fond of Bobby, like a mother," Porco told Shelton, echoing a familiar theme. Sid Gleason reportedly gave Dylan one of Woody Guthrie's old suits to wear on opening night.

Only the night before, Dylan had made an auspicious contact at the very same Folk City that would serve him well in the not-so-distant future. A group of folk singers was convening that night to celebrate a victory over the mayor and the police. As reflected in the front-page headline of the *Daily News* dated April 9, 1961, "10,000 Beatniks Riot in Washington Square," the unlikely combatants in this protest were probably a couple dozen bearded folk singers and their long-haired ladies—and vice versa. Led by Izzy Young, beloved proprietor of the nearby Folklore Center, and chanting "The Star Spangled Banner," they thwarted the proposed idea of requiring amateur musicians to obtain a license to perform, potentially eliminating the "Sundays in the Square" experience.

Celebrating at the regular Monday hoot the next night, the performers included Folk City regulars like Gil Turner and Dave Van Ronk (who had missed the previous day's festivities due to a gig in Oklahoma City), and Dylan's new Village friend and performing partner, Mark Spoelstra, as well as an outsider from Cambridge, the extremely popular barefoot soprano Joan Baez.

Baez heard Dylan sing a couple of Woody Guthrie songs that night and was fairly unimpressed. "He made me smile," she allows in her memoirs. When Baez took the stage, Dylan immediately told John Stein, Joan's friend and driver (of a 1952 Cadillac hearse), that he had a song for her. At about 2:00 a.m. outside Folk City, he flirted with Joan's sister, Mimi, before singing "Song to Woody," kneeling in front of Joan, her guitar balanced on his knee. Even though Joan wound up asking Maynard Solomon at her label, Vanguard Records, to request the song, Dylan withdrew the offer soon after making it, preferring to hold it for himself.

The Folk City series of gigs proved to be disappointing. Dylan's failure to immediately land a record deal—or even a review—sent him into a downward spiral, resulting in a trip back home to Minneapolis in May. He was probably hoping to reconnect with Bonnie Beecher, who had seen him

Dylan met Joan Baez, one of his first important business and romantic connections, at Folk City.
*Diana Davies, courtesy of the Ralph Rinzler Folklife Archives
and Collections, Smithsonian Institution*

in the Village when she visited New York with her theater group in March. Similar to his hegira on the night of his high-school junior prom, when he took Echo Helstrom to visit the black deejay Jim Dandy, Dylan made sure to escort Bonnie to Woody's hospital bedside to prove this wasn't just another one of his usual fabrications. "One of the things he wanted me to do was to tell all our friends he really did know Woody Guthrie," Beecher told Howard Sounes.

In May, Dylan got the chance to gloat in front of his Minneapolis friends in person, at Bonnie's "hotel," while concertizing in the living room with such staples of his repertoire as "Man of Constant Sorrow," "San Francisco Bay Blues," "This Land Is Your Land," "Death Don't Have No Mercy," and "Pastures of Plenty." Any dreams of reconnecting with Bonnie on a more emotional and physical level were dashed, however, when she told him she had a new boyfriend. "I think that had something to do with why he left so soon for New York again," she speculated.

As further evidence that he'd yet to cut the cord on the Bobby Zimmerman part of his life, even in December, with a record contract under his belt (as Bob Dylan), he paid another visit to Minneapolis, where he slept at Dave and Gretel Whittaker's apartment, taped another set of songs at Bonnie Beecher's house, and asked Echo Helstrom to move to New York City to live with him at his West 4th Street apartment—forgetting for the moment that his just-turned-eighteen-year-old girlfriend, Suze Rotolo, was already living there with him . . .

The Gaslight, September 1961

At the Gaslight, Dylan befriended the entertainment director, wacky comedian Hugh Romney, who would eventually change his name to Wavy Gravy and (in a cosmic coincidence recalling the union of Gretel Hoffman and Dave Whittaker) wind up marrying Bonnie Beecher, who then changed her name to Jahanara Romney.

Hugh Romney delivered Dylan a significant gig sharing the bill for a week with Dave Van Ronk, during which he signed a five-year management agreement with Roy Silver, who would also manage the comedian Bill Cosby. At one point during the week, Dylan got to meet the formidable manager and owner of Chicago's Gate of Horn, Albert Grossman, who had helped Joan Baez get her first recording contract at Vanguard Records. The gruff and intimidating Grossman was at the Gaslight to see Van Ronk and to offer him a slot in a group he was putting together featuring Mary Travers and Peter Yarrow. When Van Ronk turned him down, Grossman next offered the gig to Noel Stookey, the Gaslight's nutty new emcee, who at that time was better known as "the toilet man" for his impression of a flushing toilet. Stookey changed his name to Paul, and thus was born Peter, Paul and Mary. As a consolation prize, Van Ronk inherited Stookey's position as the host of the Tuesday night hoots.

Carolyn Hester Rehearsal: West 10th Street, September 1961

Having failed in a couple of attempts to crash the stage at Club 47 in Joan Baez's home turf of Cambridge, Massachusetts, Dylan turned his attention to the next best contact he could muster, Carolyn Hester. He'd known her casually from Folk City, where she was the first act to play there under Mike Porco's new regime in 1960, after Porco wrested control of the club from Izzy Young, his partner at the time. Parlaying this acquaintance into a career move, Dylan was determined to have Hester invite him up to sing a couple of songs during her set at Club 47 in August. Unfortunately, that slot

Joan Baez's younger sister, Mimi, married the dashing songwriter and novelist Richard Fariña; they recorded together as Dick and Mimi Fariña.

Diana Davies, courtesy of the Ralph Rinzler Folklife Archives
and Collections, Smithsonian Institution

was filled by her new husband, Richard Fariña, whom she'd married a year before after a whirlwind two-week courtship.

Dylan did manage to sneak backstage, where he was befriended by Eric Von Schmidt, whom he'd met the last time he was rebuffed at the club, a few weeks before. Von Schmidt then introduced Dylan to a couple of numbers that he would soon add to his permanent repertoire, "He Was a Friend of Mine" and "Baby Let Me Follow You Down." On this particular night, Von Schmidt took Dylan under his wing because he looked so lost.

The next day, Dylan accompanied Von Schmidt, Hester, and Fariña to Revere Beach, where he looked not only lost but also as pale as a ghost. While Von Schmidt and Fariña carried the bulk of the socializing, Dylan sank back into the shadows (if there were shadows), reverting to much the same stance he took during those electric, eclectic conversations held by Dave Whittaker and friends in Dinkytown.

Whatever effort and emotional—to say nothing of physical—discomfort it may have involved, that trip to the beach would prove beneficial. In September, when Carolyn Hester was in New York, getting ready to record her first album for the great American producer John Hammond (who had discovered Billie Holiday, Benny Goodman, and Aretha Franklin, and turned down Joan Baez) at Columbia Records, she tapped Dylan to accompany her on harmonica. During a rehearsal held in the Village, Hammond stopped by unexpectedly to look in on Columbia's competition for Baez, never realizing it would turn out to be the scraggly fellow sitting next to him on the couch.

Folk City, Part II: September 27, 1961

In late September, Bob Dylan was once again cast as an opening act at Folk City, this time for the Greenbriar Boys. He was prepared with lots of fresh material, starting off his set with the recently penned "Sally Gal," a Guthrie-inspired ode to the traveling life, before moving on to the mournful "Dink's Song," his own hilarious "Talking New York," and the ever-popular "House of the Rising Sun," his arrangement of which was remarkably similar to that of his friend and mentor, Dave Van Ronk, who taught it to him. When Dylan went ahead and put this version of "House" on his first record, a few weeks before Van Ronk had been planning to put it on *his* first record, an unspoken line was crossed, much like the line Dylan crossed when he walked off with all those records that belonged to Jon Pankake, just because he thought he needed them more than his friend. It would take years and much intervening by the women in their lives before any semblance of their previous friendship was restored.

In the audience for one of Dylan's sets, Robert Shelton of the *New York Times* was bowled over (some say he was paid off by Albert Grossman) by the young song stylist and stealer. "Mr. Dylan's highly personalized approach toward folk songs is still evolving," Shelon wrote in his review. "But if not for every taste, his music making has the mark of originality and inspiration."

When the review came out, Dylan bought up every copy in the Village, to distribute when he appeared uptown for his recording session with Carolyn Hester—to Carolyn, her husband Richard, and most especially John Hammond. They'd already seen it. Carolyn and Richard were truly delighted, hoping Dylan's new notoriety would spread to Carolyn's record.

It didn't. Hammond had been doing some research on the strange-looking folk singer he'd first met a few days before, perhaps by consulting his son, John Jr., the blues singer, another Greenwich Village regular, who ran in the same circles as Dylan. He got Dylan off to the side, suggesting he come up and see him sometime—an offer that Dylan may or may not have immediately construed as a record deal on the spot. The record deal was nevertheless soon forthcoming.

7

The Great American Folk Scare

The Village Scene Goes National

W e were very conscious that something important was going on," Dave Van Ronk told me in my book *When the Music Mattered*, of the historically fertile era in Greenwich Village between 1964 and 1967. "I remember one time Phil Ochs came back from a recording session. I asked him how it went. 'How did it go?' he said. 'We have just changed the entire course of Western music. That's how it went.'"

"That period in the Village was incredibly exciting, super-euphoric," Phil Ochs reflected in my book *In Their Own Words*. "There was total creativity on the part of a great number of individuals that laid the bedrock for the next ten years."

Propelled by Bob Dylan's leap into the songwriting ether with "Mr. Tambourine Man" and "Like a Rolling Stone," it seemed like every halfway-talented collegiate poet dropped out of school during those years to pick up a guitar and head to Folk City, the Night Owl, or the Gaslight, where they plucked out their insights and miseries in front of a welcoming audience of their peers. Here are some of those peers whose names have largely faded from the view of contemporary pop culture, but whose contributions to the cause of great music were and remain immense.

Dave Van Ronk

"We had five or six real fat years," Van Ronk told me. "Some people bought houses in the country, some people built recording studios, some people acquired expensive drug habits. And while New York was kind of late on the scene, as compared with Boston or Los Angeles, the typical New York attitude was, 'If anything is worth doing, it's worth overdoing.' There weren't three or five rooms to work in, there were fifteen or twenty."

Van Ronk's main hangout became the Gaslight, which opened in 1959 as the Gaslight Poetry Cafe, where the headliner was Roy Berkeley, and the featured attraction was Beat poetry. The big, bearded Van Ronk had been loitering in the neighborhood since 1954, playing tenor banjo at the informal sessions on Spring Street among regulars like Roger Abrams and Paul Clayton, John Cohen, Freddy Gurlaich, Luke Faust, and John Herald. By 1960, he was playing six nights a week at the Gaslight, an outsized presence stitching together precise guitar accompaniments to tunes like "Winin' Boy," "Green Rocky Road," "Cocaine Blues," "Wanderin'," "One Meatball," and "Song of the Wandering Aengus," all delivered in his wizened, grizzled voice—a cross between Tom Waits and a steam engine.

Meanwhile, as the decade progressed and the crowds increased, the Tuesday hoots he hosted at the Gaslight became, like the Monday hoots Gil Turner hosted at Folk City, a ritual and a rite of passage for all neophytes hoping to make an impression, as well as a chance to hear the man do three sets, ending at four in the morning. Way after the scene had moldered to a climax, Van Ronk remained at his apartment on Waverly Place, giving guitar lessons and playing festivals in Europe when the need arose. An astute observer of the scene on the upswing and in decline, he never let sentiment get in the way of a good punch line. "I've always been a doom crier," he told me. "For years I'd been predicting grass growing on MacDougal Street, so I think it gave me some satisfaction when it happened. I probably felt like a Seventh Day Adventist on the day the world really ended."

Gil Turner

Gil Turner was the all-important gatekeeper of Folk City's Monday-night hoots when the mysterious tramp called Bob Dylan introduced himself as a precocious blues singer and would-be son of Jack Elliott in 1961. Even more crucially, Turner was there the night Bob Dylan breathlessly raced in, waving the lyrics and chord chart to his newly written "Blowin' in the Wind." Perusing it downstairs in the boiler room, Turner, who also served as an editor of *Broadside*, immediately recognized a classic when he saw one, performing the partially finished song that night in front of a cheering audience. Not content to stop there, Turner was the first to record the song, doing so with his group, the New World Singers, featuring Happy Traum and Bob Cohen, who'd remain lifelong friends with the author. Quickly, he brought Dylan into the *Broadside* fold in time for the first issue, publishing the soon-to-be-controversial "Talkin' John Birch Paranoid Blues." Two issues later, "Blowin' in the Wind" was the cover story. Turner was a prolific songwriter himself; his best-known effort, "Carry It On," became a civil rights–era anthem, covered by Judy Collins and Joan Baez.

Fred Neil

When Bob Dylan arrived in Greenwich Village in 1961, it was the equally mysterious Fred Neil who gave him his first professional job in town at the Cafe Wha?, as a backup harmonica player. At the end of the sixties, Dylan repaid the favor by taking so long to deliver "Lay Lady Lay" for the soundtrack of *Midnight Cowboy* that the vaunted opening slot went to Neil's much more appropriate "Everybody's Talkin'," as sung by Harry Nilsson, which went on to top the charts and win that year's "Best Song" Oscar.

"Everybody's Talkin'" would be as revealing a title as Neil would write to describe his uneasy relationship with the Great Folk Scare in Greenwich Village in the mid-sixties. On the one hand, his first solo album was entitled *Bleecker & MacDougal*, immortalizing the entire era, as well as the address of the Night Owl Cafe, where he most often played (even though, in fact, the Night Owl was located a couple of blocks north, on the corner of MacDougal and West 3rd Street). On the other hand, he was always a reluctant performer, rumored to be an old Brill Building hand, who had played guitar on Bobby Darin's demo of "Dream Lover" and behind Paul Anka on "Diana," and wrote "Candy Man" for Roy Orbison. He hinted at the mystery in "The Other Side to This Life," which was covered by the Jefferson Airplane, among others. Part of that other side was his devotion to dolphins, extolled in his greatest song, "The Dolphins." It was the success of "Everybody's Talkin'," one presumes, that gave him enough money to retire from this life to Florida, to devote himself to working on the Dolphin Research Project, which he cofounded in 1970 to help stop the capture and destruction of dolphins worldwide.

"Freddy had a classic case of ambivalence," his friend John Sebastian told me. "He hung out with a lot of jazz musicians, to whom making it was synonymous with selling out. He had done a lot of time in Nashville and in the early rock 'n' roll amphetamine and road scene. He was only sort of passing as a folk singer."

Mark Spoelstra

Scrounging for work in any capacity he could, except perhaps as a dish-washer, Bob Dylan's first successful performing gigs were as part of a duo, with the recent West Coast arrival Mark Spoelstra. An adept fingerpicker, well versed in old-timey music and the blues, Spoelstra probably taught Dylan as much musically as Dylan taught him about the songwriting craft. With Dylan breaking down the barriers erected by the elders of the old school, in which folk singers (other than Woody Guthrie) weren't allowed to pen their own material, Spoelstra joined his singing partner as a *Broadside* contributor, where his pacifist consciousness, born of his Quaker upbring-ing, came to the fore in quality protest material like "White Winged Dove." Early Dylan mentor Harry Belafonte recorded Spoelstra's "My Love Is a Dewdrop," and later Janis Joplin covered "Magic of Love."

Spoelstra's convictions were put to the test in 1963, as the war in Vietnam started heating up, when he returned to Fresno, California, to perform alternative service as a conscientious objector. Later on, prefiguring Dylan, he became a Christian and eventually a minister, releasing two gospel albums.

Phil Ochs

Unlike Bob Dylan, Phil Ochs never had any qualms about writing protest songs. A University of Ohio dropout, he saw himself as a singing journalist, while Dylan saw journalists as the enemy. Ochs wrote songs about Freedom Riders, Billy Sol Estes, American imperialism, and the American Medical Association, and performed them in the dank cellars of Cleveland in the days when "The Twist" was dominating the radio waves of America, the Beatles were still scuffling in the bars of Hamburg, and the profession-ally polished and politically neutral Kingston Trio was the definition of folk music.

"Everybody said go to New York and I figured, well, New York is the tiger's den, I can't go up against those pros," Ochs said, when I interviewed him for *In Their Own Words*. But go to New York and meet Dylan he did. He immediately flipped out, not only because of Dylan's talent but also because Dylan was writing folk songs in the face of the implicit ban on such presump-tuous creativity passed down by the elders of the scene. Ochs attributed the breakthrough of the new generation to the songwriter's workshop at the 1963 Newport Folk Festival, "where it suddenly moved from the background into the foreground in just one weekend."

Influenced by Dylan, Phil Ochs used his songs as stinging editorials.
Diana Davies, courtesy of the Ralph Rinzler Folklife Archives
and Collections, Smithsonian Institution

Ochs became completely immersed in writing through the mid-'60s, with his manic editorials excoriating targets on the left and right, from "Draft Dodger Rag" and "Love Me I'm a Liberal" to "I Ain't Marchin' Anymore" and "The Ringing of Revolution." He would remain a loyal friend to Dylan for the rest of his life, which ended with suicide in 1975, although Dylan did not always reciprocate, once going so far as to term Ochs a "journalist" before tossing him from his car.

"I never had anything against Dylan when he stopped writing political songs," Ochs continued. "In that controversy I was always completely on his side. The thing that's important about a writer is whether or not he's writing good stuff. It's not important if he's writing politics, left wing, right wing, or anything. Is it good, is it great, does it work? When Dylan made the switch I said he's writing as good or better. And when he made his *Highway 61* album, I said, this is it, his apex; it's fantastic. But after his hiatus, when he came back and made his recent albums, at that point I couldn't go along with Dylan, because he'd reached his heights, and I couldn't accept what I considered lightweight stuff."

Tom Paxton

In his typically understated fashion, Tom Paxton was as much of a pioneering songwriting rebel as Bob Dylan and Phil Ochs. Arriving on the scene as a visiting clerk typist from Fort Dix, New Jersey, the short-haired, Oklahoma-born Paxton was thought by many backstage and in the audience at the Gaslight as a moonlighting cop. Until he started playing his sly and hilarious topical songs, like "What Did You Learn in School Today" and "Daily News." One of his earliest efforts, the droll children's song "The Marvelous Toy," was picked up on by John Denver and made into a seasonal classic. "Ramblin' Boy" and "Can't Help but Wonder Where I'm Bound" perfectly described the wistfulness and confusion of a generation set loose on new roads with no direction home.

"Dylan is usually cited as the founder of the new song movement," Dave told Elijah Wald in his book *The Mayor of MacDougal Street*, "but the person who started the whole thing was Tom Paxton. He set himself a training regimen of deliberately writing one song every day. Dylan had not yet showed up when this was happening, and by the time Bobby came on the scene, with at most two or three songs he had written, Tom was already singing at least 50 percent his own material."

For one night in 1962 alone, Paxton's historic importance would be enshrined forever, far beyond his many covers and sixty-one album releases. Happening upon the young Dylan laboring on a long poem at the typewriter in Wavy Gravy's apartment above the Gaslight, Paxton looked it over.

"I asked, is this a song?" Clinton Heylin reported Paxton as asking, in his book on the songs of Bob Dylan, *Revolution in the Air.* "He said, no it's a poem. I said, all this work and you're not going to add a melody?" Probably within the next half hour, Dylan found the perfect public-domain melody to contain "A Hard Rain's a-Gonna Fall."

Eric Andersen

With movie-star good looks and ballads of frank sexuality, Eric Andersen seemed perfectly poised to sail on Bob Dylan's superstar coattails in the mid-sixties into the rarefied realms of pop stardom. Alas, he took the ill-advised decision to redo his impressive second album, *'Bout Changes and Things* (which contains his two classics, "Thirsty Boots" and "Violets of Dawn") with electric instruments, à la Simon and Garfunkel, to disastrous results. And then the Beatles' manager, Brian Epstein, died, just prior to signing Andersen as a client. And then, after recovering from these two career setbacks to produce his most successful album to date, *Blue River,* for Columbia Records, the master tapes to his follow-up, *Stages,* were inexplicably lost by the label.

Although his legacy was secured with the civil rights standard "Thirsty Boots," the seductive "Violets of Dawn," which he claims inspired the novelist and poet Leonard Cohen to begin writing songs, and the novelistic ode to the Village "Tin Can Alley," a lot more was left on the table. "I can't look at the sixties with much lucidity," he once told me. "To me it was a negative time, with everybody vying for attention and getting caught up in their own ego trips."

Leaving the Village, he wound up settling in Woodstock from 1975 to 1983, which was most likely just as competitive a scene. No wonder he eventually took off for the Netherlands, where he was able to work on his personal songs unimpeded by thoughts of fame and fortune. As late as 2003, he was still writing lengthy epics, with his album *Beat Avenue* featuring a twenty-six-minute title track devoted to his memories of San Francisco on the day of JFK's assassination.

Tim Hardin

Discovered by producer Erik Jacobsen, who would move on to the Lovin' Spoonful, Tim Hardin emigrated from Boston to the Village, where he was part of the crowd centered around the Night Owl, which included John Sebastian, Buzzy Linhart, and fellow bluesman Fred Neil. His classic "Eulogy to Lenny Bruce," covered by Nico, is a poignant reminder of the talent he squandered in a life that ended when he was just short of forty years old. His erratic performing style and reluctance to tour hid a sensitive soul who could tear into the blues with the best of them and then turn Byron-esque with the delicate "If I Were a Carpenter," made into a hit by Bobby Darin, and the wistful "Reason to Believe," made into a hit by Rod Stewart. Unfortunately, these songwriting successes did not prevent him from succumbing to a long-standing heroin addiction.

John Hammond Jr.

Like Bob Dylan, the musicians who gained the greatest success in the last half of the sixties were the ones who merged folk-rock with rhythm 'n' blues. For the most part, John Hammond Jr., son of the great producer who signed Dylan to Columbia in 1961, resisted this trend, preferring to remain authentically indebted to forbears like Robert Johnson, Reverend Gary Davis, and Mississippi John Hurt. He most notably strayed from this path in 1965, with the album *So Many Roads*, for which he employed the talents of future Dylan sidemen Robbie Robertson, Garth Hudson, and Levon Helm (a.k.a. three fifths of the Band) and a guitar slinger from Chicago named Michael Bloomfield (on keyboards). Predating Bloomfield's next project, the Paul Butterfield Blues Band, by several months, Hammond's choice of material was equal to his choice of sidemen, featuring tracks by Willie Dixon, Bo Diddley, Muddy Waters, Robert Johnson, and Jimmy Reed. One of the visitors during those sessions was Bob Dylan, recruiting instrumentalists for his upcoming *Bringing It All Back Home*.

In 1966, Hammond put together a band featuring an out-of-work guitarist from Seattle named Jimi Hendrix (or perhaps Jimmy James at the time). They played the Cafe au Go Go across the street from the Bitter End, where Jimi was discovered by Chas Chandler of the Animals and brought to England to record. Hammond next ran into Hendrix in '67, just after he'd quit a gig opening for the Monkees. Jimi asked if he could sit in during

Hammond's upcoming sets at the Gaslight, where they were joined the next night by Eric Clapton, who was in the States touring with Cream.

"He was off that week, so he came down to check me out," Hammond told Bill Forman of the *Colorado Springs Independent*. "And there was him and Jimi, and they both wanted to sit in. And so for a week, they sat in with my little group at the Gaslight Café."

John Sebastian

Born and raised in Greenwich Village, John Sebastian was part of the Even Dozen Jug Band, whose one and only album came out on Elektra in 1964. Already known by the denizens of Washington Square for his harmonica playing, his classical harmonica–playing father, and his friendship with the Texas bluesman Lightnin' Hopkins, who briefly became his roommate when John attended the Blair Academy in Massachusetts, Sebastian was home on a visit when he got a call from a Village friend, guitarist Stefan Grossman. "He said, 'Hi, you're in our group and rehearsals start today.' I said, 'Yeah? That's very convenient.'" Sebastian told me in *In Their Own Words*.

Included in the group was an old-time banjo player named Peter Siegel, an accordion player named David Grisman, a guitarist named Steve Katz, and a blues singer named Maria D'Amato, who would become Maria Muldaur when she joined the Jim Kweskin Jug Band and married blues singer Geoff Muldaur. The Even Dozen's eventual album was produced for Elektra by Paul Rothschild, who wound up throwing a lot of backup harmonica work to Sebastian (with his friend Felix Pappalardi on guitarrón). "Soon I was making fifty-three dollars for a three-hour session. I remember writing to my father about it. 'Gee, this is great, this is what I want to do. I'm a studio musician.' And he wrote me back a great letter that I remember to this day. He said, 'You be careful. You'll be selling it note by note, and you'll lose your soul.'"

Lost in Bob Dylan's transition to electricity in the summer of 1965 was the fact that Sebastian and his new group, the Lovin' Spoonful, had already been playing electric rock for audiences in the Village for over a year, as the house band at the Night Owl on the corner of MacDougal and West 3rd Street. "To avoid any false modesty, the Spoonful was what was happening on that street," Sebastian said. "Everything else was very exciting, of course, and if you were into traditional music, Mississippi John Hurt was what was happening. But for the younger people who didn't know anything about that, it was rock 'n' roll. The Spoonful were heartily frowned upon by all the traditional blues and folk music people, inasmuch as any place we'd play we'd be louder than anything else they'd ever heard, and people would be terrified. But we were sure we were the cutting edge."

For fans of the rock 'n' roll single in its modern incarnation as good-time jug-band music with a touch of folk-rock, this was by far the right assessment. Filled with the sheer shimmering optimism of "Do You Believe in Magic," "You Didn't Have to Be So Nice," "Did You Ever Have to Make Up Your Mind," "Daydream," and "Summer in the City," the work of the Spoonful was all but the dream of the alternate culture personified in a loopy T-shirt and ten-year-old jeans. By the end of the decade, Sebastian had built up enough goodwill to be invited to be one of the hosts at the era-defining event in Woodstock.

Richie Havens

Another icon remembered mostly now for his bravura performance at Woodstock, Richie Havens was much better known earlier in the decade for the power of his voice. As I wrote in the liner notes to his best-of collection, *Resume*: "It's a voice you remember, possessing in its cavernous reaches the smoky essence of an age." It was an age when the singers, the songwriters, and the audience were often one and the same, all of us prowling the three Squares of Greenwich Village—Sheridan, Washington, and Tompkins—for the same slum goddesses dressed in the image of Dylan's girl, Suzy Rotolo, slouching down a snowy Jones Street on the cover of the *Freewheelin'* album.

As an interpreter of Bob Dylan's finest songs, from "Boots of Spanish Leather" to "Just Like a Woman," Richie Havens was equally known for beating out tunes like "Drown in My Own Tears," "Follow," "The Clan," and "San Francisco Bay Blues" in his unique, self-taught, battering ram of a guitar style, which would usually result in approximately six broken strings a set.

"I was fortunate enough to come to the Village at a time when music was into the communication business rather than the music business," he told me, in his famous spacey drawl. "And I was fortunate enough to go onstage and sing when anybody could jump up out of the audience and sing. You know, the stage is a very peculiar place, because a lot of people think it belongs to them when they get on it. Wrong. It belongs to the audience only, 'cause if they don't pay, it's dark. I never felt it was an equal exchange in any kind of way. I don't think you can get paid in equal exchange for going onstage, 'cause there's no way of equating that exchange."

One of Dylan's oldest friends and best interpreters, Richie Havens was a basket-house regular until he was "discovered" at Woodstock.

Diana Davies, courtesy of the Ralph Rinzler Folklife Archives and Collections, Smithsonian Institution

The Blues Project

Formed by Dylan's Dinkytown compatriot, blues guitarist Danny Kalb, the Blues Project took much more advantage of the heady fusion of folk, rock, the blues, and psychedelia than most New York City bands. Some people called them the East Coast version of the Grateful Dead, which started out as Mother Macree's Uptown Jug Champions. Recruiting guitarist Steve Katz from the Even Dozen Jug Band and session guitarist Al Kooper—who was creating a new career for himself as an organ player after passing for one on Bob Dylan's recent "Like a Rolling Stone"—Kalb and company took the Village by storm. Showcasing their chops as well as their taste in contemporary musical styles, they filled their debut album, *Live at the Cafe au Go Go*, with such choice gems as Eric Andersen's "Violets of Dawn," Donovan's "Catch the Wind," Chuck Berry's "I Want to Be Your Driver," "Spoonful" by Willie Dixon, "Who Do You Love" by Bo Diddley, and "Goin' Down to Louisiana" by Muddy Waters.

Plagued by personnel changes and a lack of sales, the group soon fell apart, with Katz and Kooper leaving to form the original Blood, Sweat, and Tears, whose lineup included Randy Brecker on trumpet, Dick Halligan on trombone, Fred Lipsius on alto sax, and Bobby Colomby on percussion. Their masterful first album, *Child Is Father to the Man*, contains the Kooper classics "I Love You More Than You'll Ever Know" and "I Can't Quit Her," along with songs by Tim Buckley, Harry Nilsson, and Randy Newman.

By the second album, Kooper had left the group.

Dick and Mimi Fariña

While Bob Dylan's erratic courtship of Joan Baez was marked by frequent playfully indirect inquiries as to the health and welfare of her younger sister, Mimi, Brooklyn-born songwriter, novelist, and dulcimer player Richard Fariña was a good deal more blatant in his approach, quickly shedding his wife, folk singer Carolyn Hester (whom he married after an eighteen-day courtship), in favor of the seventeen-year-old Mimi, whom he would marry in 1963. A noted drinking buddy at the White Horse Tavern of Tommy Makem and writing buddy at Cornell of classmate Thomas Pynchon (who wrote the intro to his posthumous novel, *Been Down So Long It Looks Like Up to Me*, as well as a celebratory blurb), Fariña's rakish charm enabled him to make friends easily and quickly, soon gaining him the trust of Bob Dylan and Eric Von Schmidt, to say nothing of Mimi's protective older sisters, Joan and Pauline (with whom he wrote one of his best songs, "Pack up Your Sorrows").

On their 1965 debut album, *Celebrations for a Grey Day*, Fariña in turn paid tribute to Makem with "Tommy Makem Fantasy" as well as Pynchon's era-defining novel *V* (on an instrumental cowritten by Bruce Langhorne), along with fallen civil rights workers Schwerner, Chaney, and Goodman ("Michael, Andrews, and James"). Their second album, *Reflections in a Crystal Wind*, also released in '65, brought Richard into Phil Ochsian protest territory, with "House Un-American Blues Activity Dream," "Sell-Out Agitation Waltz," and "Mainline Prosperity Blues." Judy Collins had a minor hit with "Hard Lovin' Loser."

On April 30, 1966, two days after the publication of his novel, Richard Fariña was thrown from a motorcycle and instantly killed on his return from a book signing party in Carmel, California. Three months later, Bob Dylan was thrown from his motorcycle in Woodstock, but escaped with minor injuries.

The Fugs

When the anarchic conglomeration of professional poets and part-time instrumentalists known as the Fugs took over the Players Theater on MacDougal Street for an extended run in 1967, their scatological gems may have seemed like a breath of fresh, dirty air compared to the arch and earnest proclamations of the entrenched folkies on the block. It was also a distinct incursion of an era and a sensibility waiting to happen, as well as an example of the different lifestyle changes and choices indulged in once you crossed Fifth Avenue from the West Village to the East. By then, the West was laden with souvenir shops and tourist traps, just another Disney version of the French Quarter. The East Village was far more dangerous, a virtual grazing ground for dropouts, druggies, runaways, longhairs, and would-be rock-and-rollers. The Fugs arose from the filth to make poetry out of the particulars of slum living.

"We used to read at the Metro on Second Avenue," Tuli Kupferberg, an original Fug, recalled in my book *When the Music Mattered*. "After the readings, we'd go to the Dom on St. Marks Place. The jukebox had Beatles and Stones albums on it, and some of the kids would dance. Ed Sanders got the idea it might be good to try to combine some of our poetry with rock music. Suddenly poetry jumped off the page and became a performing art, which is what it should be. My poetry became simpler. It became cruder, more sexual, more emotional. Politically it became less polite; it became more openly bitter and disrespectful. It was a very immediate thing. But we felt that our songs were as great as any being written."

According to Tuli Kupferberg of the Fugs (*far right*), Bob Dylan was the first performer to give poets a rock platform.

Diana Davies, courtesy of the Ralph Rinzler Folklife Archives and Collections, Smithsonian Institution

Inspired by Dylan's forays into the rhythms of wild language, the Fugs put an East Village spin on it with instant odes to personal and sexual freedom like "Super Girl," "Group Grope," "Coca Cola Douche," and "I Saw the Best Minds of My Generation Rot," based not on ancient folk airs but derived more from the inspired amateurism of garage rock and punk.

"I always thought of us as theater," said Tuli. "Ed thought we should be high art. I was afraid we'd get lost in trying to become fine musicians."

The Velvet Underground and Nico

If the Fugs' brand of rock was the theater of the absurd, what the Velvet Underground played was more like the theater of cruelty. As the house band at Andy Warhol's New Cinematheque at the Balloon Farm (soon to become the Electric Circus) on St. Marks Place, Lou Reed applied his rudimentary skills as a singer and melodist in the service of a bleak vision of sexual deviation, drugs, and death, with songs like "Heroin," "Black Angel Death Song," and "I'm Waiting for My Man," opposing both the free love and daffodils ethos of the hippies in San Francisco and the save the world mentality of their neighbors in the West Village. "It was a show by and for freaks," Reed said proudly, when I interviewed him in 1974, "of which there turned out to be many more than anyone had suspected."

The addition of the Nordic fashion model Nico and her brooding ice-queen vocals only added to the mystique. On her first solo album, 1967's *Chelsea Girl*, Nico did her part in discovering another important songwriting voice: that of her current flame, Jackson Browne ("These Days," "Somewhere There's a Feather," "The Fairest of the Seasons"), ex of the Nitty Gritty Dirt Band, who briefly passed through the Village scene as a staff songwriter for EMI Publishing.

Reed's dyspeptic message didn't travel well once it got outside the borders of the Lower East Side. "Bill Graham hated us, said we were the lowest trash ever to hit Frisco," he continued. "Let's say we were a little bit sarcastic about the love thing, which we were right about, because look what happened. We knew that in the first place. They thought acid was going to solve everything. We said, that's not the way it is and you're kidding yourselves."

In the early years of the next decade, a vibrant rock scene would emerge on the Lower East Side, with Lou Reed more of its (anti-)spiritual leader than Bob Dylan.

From the Green Pastures of Harvard University

It was left to Harvard's own Tom Rush, one of the stalwarts of the Cambridge scene that operated out of Club 47 (starring Joan Baez, Eric Von Schmidt, Buffy Sainte-Marie, the Kweskin Jug Band, and Bonnie Raitt), to record the album that would define the era-ending late-sixties years of the Folk Scare, leading into the singer/songwriter era of the seventies. *The Circle Game* contains worthy early efforts by three artists who passed through Bleecker and MacDougal Streets on their way to greater glory—Jackson Browne ("Shadow Dream Song"), James Taylor ("Something in the Way She Moves," "Sunshine Sunshine"), and Joni Mitchell ("Tin Angel," "Urge for Going," and the title song)—as well as a brave farewell to all that by Rush himself ("No Regrets").

Dave Van Ronk described the disruptive effect the ending of the era had on most of its principals. "The economic facts of life changed," he told me. "People who grew up in the sixties, who made what they thought were their final adjustments to the real world, must have found terrific consternation in the fact that the 1960s weren't the real world. All that loose money ain't gonna be around forever. And the check is *not* in the mail."

8

The Could-Be Dream Lover

Dylan Meets His Muse

Bob Dylan met Suze Rotolo a couple of months before his career broke wide open, the breaking open due in no small part to the inspiration she provided, as his girlfriend, his political conscience, and his muse. On the last day of July 1961, at the Riverside Church on the Upper West Side, he was part of an all-day folk concert broadcast over WRVR-FM, where he sang five songs, on some of them accompanied by an old friend from the Dinkytown scene, ace guitarist Danny Kalb, who would later record with the influential Greenwich Village group, the Blues Project. At the end of the concert, Dylan was introduced to a seventeen-year-old girl with long blonde hair who he may have dimly remembered meeting a few months before at Folk City, where she'd been immediately attracted to . . . Dylan's guitar-playing friend from California, Mark Spoelstra.

At this meeting he had Suze all to himself. "He made me think of Harpo Marx, impish and approachable," she writes in her memoir, *A Freewheelin' Time*, "but there was something about him that broadcast an intensity that was not to be taken lightly." For Dylan, the deal was probably sealed once he learned that Suze's sister Carla worked as a personal assistant to folk historian Alan Lomax.

Carla and Suze immediately fell to tackling the no small feat of cleaning up and educating the great unwashed, intuitive, starving artist known to them only as Bob Dylan. Carla introduced him to her estimable record library, in which were found many of the country, blues, and folk music gems discovered and recorded by her boss. At 129 Perry Street, Dylan would while away the afternoons, listening to these formative sides; in the evenings, he made use of Carla's couch. Suze introduced him to poets and playwrights and political concepts way beyond his naive understanding. Carla and her friend Sybil wrote to John Hammond suggesting he produce

Dylan with Suze Rotolo, his true love and songwriting muse.

Joe Alper, courtesy of the Joe Alper Photo Collection, LLC

a "New Faces in Folk"–type record, including Jack Elliott and Dave Van Ronk, where Dylan's voice and style was sure to dazzle and predominate. It's possible Hammond never saw or read the letter, but in any case the record never happened.

Meanwhile, Suze, a red-diaper baby, brought up around radical politics all her life, who was then working part-time as a volunteer at CORE (the Campaign of Racial Equality), began encouraging her new boyfriend to expand his horizons beyond the paltry limits of traditional folk music, to trust his instinctual way with words to illuminate the injustices of the world around him. Eager to please, eager to learn, Dylan increased his output of original-sounding material, the words pouring out of him as he walked down 8th Street. He wrote songs about ramblers and gamblers, cowboys and hookers, giving way to poignant observations about homeless men on the street, topped off by a seventeen-verse ballad about a dope fiend and a couple of stinging satires on city life, one of them based on an article about a boat trip to Bear Mountain handed to him one afternoon by Noel Paul Stookey and returned as "Talking Bear Mountain Massacre Blues" the next day.

At the 1963 March on Washington, Dylan bonded with Joan Baez.

Rowland Scherman of the US Information Agency Press and Publications Service/Wikimedia Commons/Public domain

Carla approved. Suze approved. Going against the usual grain in these matters, Suze's mother emphatically did not. Politically astute, world-weary, and widowed since Suze was fourteen, she was suspicious of Dylan's motives and his stories, convinced he was hiding something, which, of course, he was: his entire past, as tame and inoffensive as it was.

Nevertheless, Dylan's relatively meteoric rise to the stature of recording artist was more than a little hard for Suze to handle. "You can't treat a genius like they're precious China objects," she told Shelton. "They're just human beings." In Dylan's case, a difficult one to live with. "He could always express himself better with what he wrote than with what he said," she added.

Already committed to a once-postponed sojourn to study in Italy the following spring, Suze may indeed have not been all there emotionally to participate in the planning of Bob Dylan's first solo concert, at Carnegie Chapter Hall in November, a week after his gig opening for the Greenbriar Boys ended. Indeed, his repertoire—both for the concert and his upcoming recording sessions at Columbia, in which about half the songs were identical—may have been shaped more by what he was listening to at Carla's apartment than what he and Suze were discussing in their spare moments alone at the apartment on West 4th Street. In any case, the point was moot, as only about fifty people showed up at the concert.

9

He Knew His Song Well

Bob Dylan's First Album

L
ike the pilot of a classic TV series, Bob Dylan's first commercial album, *Bob Dylan*, recorded on the cheap at Columbia studios and produced by John Hammond, contains all the components of what would soon make him famous, as well as all the ingredients that would sustain him over a long and legendary career. Fans (and detractors) from his earliest days in Dinkytown (if not Hibbing) will recognize the old-timey blues, country, folk, and traditional tunes that made up his repertoire on the coffeehouse and party circuit in those days, and the hopped-up, rough-edged Woody Guthrie voice that delivered them, at least a country mile away from the smoother sounds of reigning pop folkies like the Kingston Trio, the Highwaymen, and the Brothers Four, to say nothing of charting pop stars like Frankie Avalon and (his former boss for a day) Bobby Vee. Like one of his idols, Elvis Presley, he found himself intuitively merging his favorite styles of roots music.

"I was singing stuff like 'Ruby Lee' by the Sunny Mountain Boys, and 'Jack O'Diamonds' by Odetta," Dylan told Cameron Crowe, for the liner notes to his *Biograph* set, "and somehow because of my earlier rock 'n' roll background I was unconsciously crossing the two styles. This made me different from your regular folk singers, who were either folk song purists or concert-hall singers, who just happened to be singing folk songs."

Even the uncredited appearance of Dave Van Ronk's arrangement of the traditional "House of the Risin' Sun" (written, according to Dave, about a women's prison) was a pure Dylan move. Preferring to ask for forgiveness rather than permission, he'd already recorded the song before he mentioned it to Van Ronk, who was about to put this version on his own album. When Van Ronk said he'd prefer it if Dylan didn't use the song, Dylan said, "Oops, too late." In the liner notes, in tiny type, Stacey Williams (a pseudonym for Robert Shelton) writes that Dylan learned the song from Van Ronk. "I'd always known 'Risin' Sun,'" Dylan adds, "but I never really knew I knew it until I heard Dave sing it." This reasoning led Dylan to take the "House of the Risin' Sun" arrangement credit for himself.

Many people mistrusted Dylan for this move, among others, for his naked ambition, his cavalier attitude toward sources ("Freight Train Blues," for which he took another arrangement credit, was written by John Lair and made famous by Roy Acuff and Hank Williams), to say nothing of his obviously fabricated background. But they couldn't deny his intensity, his phrasing, the power of his voice—one among many he'd display, one for each of his personalities, all evident on his debut disc. With a foot in the blues (Blind Lemon Jefferson, Blind Willie Johnson, Bukka White), a foot in country music ("Freight Train Blues"), an eye on the Alan Lomax songbook ("Man of Constant Sorrow," "Pretty Peggy-o"), an elbow on the neck of his folk contemporaries ("Baby Let Me Follow You Down" and "You're No Good," credited; "Freight Train Blues" and "House of the Rising Sun," uncredited), a nod to Woody Guthrie ("Talkin' New York," "Song to Woody"), and a finger on the pulse of a generation morbidly fascinated with death in the Cold War era ("Fixin' to Die," "In My Time of Dyin'," "See That My Grave Is Kept Clean"), he immediately had a leg up on his peers.

As with all of his future recorded works, the songs that didn't make the cut are almost as interesting as the ones that did, offering a vital insight into his creative process. Featuring among the outtakes is an undistinguished original called "Man on the Street"; a Woody Guthrie tune, "Ramblin' Blues"; "He Was a Friend of Mine," popularized by Dylan pals Von Schmidt and Van Ronk; and the traditional "House Carpenter," which has been called "the most extraordinary performance of the sessions, as demonically driven as anything Robert Johnson put out in his name" by noted Dylan authority Clinton Heylin. Taken from the handy *Anthology of American Folk Music*, on which it is performed by Clarence Ashley, Dylan's version was finally let out of the vault by Columbia in 1991, on *The Bootleg Series Vol. 1–3: (Rare and Unreleased) 1961–1991*.

Though Dylan claimed arrangement credits for most of the older material, the album contains only two originals, simply because he wasn't writing much quality material in those days, having only recently met his New York City muse. One of the originals, the humorous "Talkin' New York," is based on Woody Guthrie's "Talking Dustbowl Blues"; the other, the evocative "Song to Woody," was also a rewrite of a Woody Guthrie tune, "1913 Massacre," and is, even more fittingly, a rewrite of one of his earliest songs,

"Song to Bonnie," dedicated to his Minneapolis muse and earliest producer, Bonnie Beecher.

Many purists contend that some of her informal recording sessions far surpass Dylan's efforts on his official first album. This would make historical sense, in that Dylan in performance is quite a different animal than Dylan in the confines of the recording studio. "I'd never worked with anyone so undisciplined before," John Hammond recalled in his memoir, *On the Record*.

Dylan even refused to do second takes in those days, claiming he couldn't see himself singing the same song twice in a row. Thus it's not hard to believe the figure of $402, which is what Hammond claimed the record cost to produce, making its initial sales of 2,500–5,000 copies (according to Hammond, it was closer to 10,000) a bit easier to swallow.

10

One More Chance

The Make-Or-Break Second Album

Bob Dylan's second album, *The Freewheelin' Bob Dylan*, took a year to produce. It was recorded over the course of eight sessions, starting just a month after the release of his first, which was already known in the halls of Columbia Records as "Hammond's Folly."

"By the time I cut a second record with him six months had passed and people were running out of patience," Hammond notes in his memoir, forgetting the sessions of April 24–25, which resulted in "Rambling Gambling Willie," "Talking John Birch Paranoid Blues," "Corrina Corrina," "Rocks and Gravel," and "Let Me Die in My Footsteps," all of which were slated to appear on the record, then titled *Bob Dylan's Blues*. Dylan also dropped by Studio A to record "Blowin' in the Wind" on July 6, a couple of months after premiering it at Folk City on April 16, as well as "Bob Dylan's Blues," "Down the Highway," and "Honey Just Allow Me One More Chance."

At any rate, the A&R department at Columbia was less than thrilled by what it had heard thus far. "Dylan impressed a few, not many," Hammond notes, pointing particularly to Dave Kapralik, the new head of A&R at Columbia, who told Hammond he was planning to drop him. "You'll drop him over my dead body," Hammond replied.

The date that Hammond is referring to is probably October 26, a month after Dylan had showcased his epic "A Hard Rain's a-Gonna Fall" as part of a hootenanny concert at Carnegie Hall. At this session, as well as the one in December and a final one the following April, Dylan was provided with a backup band consisting of guitarists Bruce Langhorne and Howie Collins, Leonard Gaskin on bass, Herb Lovelle on drums, and Dick Westwood on piano. One of the songs recorded at that October date was a cover of Elvis Presley's first Sun single, "That's All Right Mama," as well as a version of Dylan's first single, the rockabilly "Mixed-Up Confusion," which was an instant stiff when it was released in December, with "Corrina, Corrina" on the B-side. Two dates in November produced little aside from "Don't Think

Twice, It's All Right" (with a brilliant guitar part that some experts believe is by an uncredited Langhorne), which would go on to become Peter, Paul and Mary's Top 10 follow-up to "Blowin' in the Wind" in September 1963.

In April '63, following a legal dustup over the potentially libelous "Talking John Birch Paranoid Blues," Dylan returned to the studio to cut several replacement tracks. Out with the bathwater went John Hammond, replaced as producer, at Albert Grossman's insistence, by an African American studio hand, Tom Wilson, who'd cut his teeth on John Coltrane and would soon turn Simon and Garfunkel into a folk-rock act with some studio sleight of hand, before moving on from Dylan to Frank Zappa and Lou Reed.

"I didn't particularly like folk music," Wilson told Michael Watts in *Melody Maker*. "But then these words came out. I was flabbergasted. I said to Albert Grossman, who was there in the studio, 'If you put some background to this you might have a white Ray Charles with a message.' But it wasn't until a year later that everyone agreed that we should put a band behind him."

With Wilson at the boards, Dylan revised the *Freewheelin'* album on the fly, dropping "Rocks and Gravel," "Rambling Gambling Willie," and the stellar "Let Me Die in My Footsteps" in favor of "Talking World War III Blues" and three songs he'd written during a brief sojourn to England late in '62.

Under the sway of the vibrant British folk scene and the wing of devout traditionalist Martin Carthy, Dylan continued to perfect his penchant for rewriting ancient melodies with modern angst, using "Scarborough Fair" for "Girl from the North Country" and "Lady Franklin's Lament" for "Bob Dylan's Dream," a pair of nostalgic remembrances of his lost youth and lost loves in Hibbing. During this time he also wrote the caustic "Masters of War," but failed to give credit to Jean Ritchie's "Nottamun Town" for the arrangement of this timeless melody. (John Lennon would use the same arrangement and melody for "Working Class Hero" in 1970.) Ritchie later won a small lawsuit from Dylan's publishing company.

Similarly, "Blowin' in the Wind" occupies the structure and melody of the Negro spiritual "No More Auction Block for Me"; "I Shall Be Free" is based on Leadbelly's "We Shall Be Free"; "Don't Think Twice, It's All Right" uses many of the lyrical and musical phrases found on Dylan's pal Paul Clayton's "Who's Gonna Buy You Ribbons (When I'm Gone)." Unlike Ritchie, or Van Ronk on the previous album, Clayton wasn't heard to complain (and neither were the folks in England, as *Freewheelin'* went to No. 1 on the album charts over there—No. 22 in the US).

By the time Peter, Paul and Mary's version of "Blowin' in the Wind," released a month after *Freewheelin'*, blew the roof off Tin Pan Alley, the sense was that Dylan's success was about to lift all the boats trolling in the folk-music harbors of Greenwich Village. And it did. By the end of '63, Joan Baez ("We Shall Overcome") and Pete Seeger ("Little Boxes," written by Malvina Reynolds) had made their first appearances on the Top 100. In 1964, songs written by Village regulars Tom Paxton ("The Marvelous Toy" by the Chad Mitchell Trio) and Len Chandler ("Beans in My Ears" by the Serendipity Singers) followed Dylan's lead, joined in '65 by Buffy Sainte-Marie ("Universal Soldier" by Donovan), Richard Fariña ("Hard Lovin' Loser" by Judy Collins), Sylvia Fricker of the duo Ian and Sylvia ("You Were on My Mind" by the We Five), and Phil Ochs ("There but for Fortune" by Joan Baez).

Propelled by the instant success of Peter, Paul and Mary's "Blowin' in the Wind" (a hit while Dylan's valuable single of the same song, backed with "Don't Think Twice, It's All Right," sank without a trace), *Freewheelin'* established Dylan as a voice for his generation, wracked with yearning for better times, better leaders, his good girl Suze back in his arms again. The protest songs on the album ("Masters of War," "Blowin' in the Wind," "A Hard Rain's a-Gonna Fall," "Oxford Town") were among the best he'd ever write, balanced by songs of lost or unrequited love ("Down the Highway," "Girl from the North Country," "Honey Just Allow Me One More Chance," "Corrina Corrina," "Don't Think Twice, It's All Right").

On the Cutting-Room Floor

The album's outtakes are just as fascinating, even with "Hero Blues" (a precursor to "It Ain't Me Babe"), the eerie "The Walls of Red Wing," "Let Me Die in My Footsteps," the early concert staple "Sally Gal," "Talking John Birch Society Paranoid Blues" (the song Ed Sullivan wouldn't let him play on TV), and "The Death of Emmet Till" all remaining in mothballs or on bootlegs until Columbia started *The Bootleg Series* in 1991. "Ballad of Hollis Brown," which was also recorded during these sessions, was a true rarity: a song that Dylan was to rerecord and put on his next album.

The last-minute replacing of songs resulted in a collectible item for those few who possessed an album whose track list contained "Rocks and Gravel" and "Let Me Die in My Footsteps" as the second and third tracks on side one, and "Gamblin' Willie's Dead Man's Hand" and "Talkin' John Birch Paranoid Blues" as the second and fifth tracks on side two.

Thanks to Peter, Paul and Mary's covers of "Blowin' in the Wind" and "Don't Think Twice," Dylan became a folk hero. *Diana Davies, courtesy of the Ralph Rinzler Folklife Archives and Collections, Smithsonian Institution*

Even the cover had a story—a cover story—with Dylan's already estranged girlfriend Suze posing for the camera's eye like a good devoted "rock chick," thus establishing the "rock chick" image for the rest of the decade, even while the girl inside the photo had one foot out the door, unwilling to settle for her boyfriend's heart when his soul belonged to Joan Baez. For years she must have cringed when looking at it, or when reading what critic Janet Maslin wrote of its impact: "It was a photograph that inspired countless young men to hunch their shoulders, look distant, and let the girl do the clinging."

Noted musicologist Nat Hentoff (a huge leap forward from Stacey Williams on the first album) sums it all up in the liner notes: "Throughout everything he writes and sings, there is the surge of a young man looking into as many diverse scenes and people as he can find. It is this continuing explosion of a total individual, a young man growing free rather than absurd, that makes Bob Dylan so powerful and so personal and so important a singer." Dylan himself must have been happy enough with this description at the time, since he would subsequently allow Hentoff to profile him in *Playboy* and the *New Yorker*, with superior access to future recording sessions, but in later years he would change his mind about his early success.

"Once in a while I would have to rise up and offer myself for an interview so they wouldn't beat the door down," he writes in his memoir, *Chronicles*. "Later an article would hit the streets with the headline 'Spokesman Denies That He's a Spokesman.' I felt like a piece of meat that someone had thrown to the dogs."

Adventures on the Day Shift

Bob Dylan the Staff Songwriter

The Bootleg Series Vol. 9: The Witmark Demos: 1962–1964

The period between February 2, 1962, and January 1964 shows Bob Dylan to be as dedicated a songwriter, grinding the creative stone, as he'd ever be. While his concert appearances remained sporadic during those two years, and his time in Columbia's Studio A necessarily limited, especially from November 1962 through January 1964, he was a fairly regular presence in the tiny Witmark studio ensconced in the *Look* Building on 51st Street and Madison Avenue in New York City, two (long) blocks from the CBS building, fondly dubbed Black Rock. Here he provided guitar or piano demos of his greatest works, alongside lesser-known gems and little-known throwaways, to be dispensed by the publisher to a growing market for quality folk songs.

The first song he demoed in July of '62, after moving his publishing to the venerable Witmark Music—founded around the turn of the century and sold to Warner Bros. in 1929—from the almost-as-venerable Duchess Music—founded by Lou Levy and pop songwriters Saul Chaplin and Sammy Cahn in 1939—was "Blowin' in the Wind," which gained covers by the Chad Mitchell Trio and Gil Turner before Peter, Paul and Mary turned it into a No. 2 single in 1963, after which Odetta, Sam Cooke, the Kingston Trio, Duke Ellington, and Stan Getz added it to their repertoires. The next Peter, Paul and Mary hit, "Don't Think Twice, It's All Right," became Dylan's most covered song of the period, with versions by Joan Baez, Lawrence Welk, the Brothers Four, and the Village Stompers in 1964, and Johnny Cash, Chad and Jeremy, Cher, the Wonder Who, the Seekers, and Trini Lopez in 1965.

Toiling in a cubicle in the Tin Pan Alley tradition.
Joe Alper, courtesy of the Joe Alper Photo Collection, LLC

"Tomorrow Is a Long Time" was a particular favorite of Ian and Sylvia, Bud and Travis, and Judy Collins. Elvis Presley picked up on it in 1966, his version providing one of the high points of Dylan's career as a songwriter. Once "Mr. Tambourine Man" became a No. 1 song in 1965, courtesy of the Byrds, some of the regulars, like the Brothers Four, Chad and Jeremy, and Judy Collins, recorded it, as did the Four Seasons; Johnny Rivers; and the venerable Dino, Desi, and Billy. Honoring an early pledge to Nico, whose version of the song appears on her *Chelsea Girl* album, Dylan never released a version of the lovely "I'll Keep It with Mine" (except on this collection) or performed it live.

Aside from Gil Turner's New World Singers, one of Dylan's earliest champions was Turner's fellow New World Singer Happy Traum, whose version of "Let Me Die in My Footsteps," under the alternate title of "I Will Not Go Down Under the Ground," was on the same *Broadside Ballads, Vol. 1* as the Singers' "Blowin' in the Wind." Pete Seeger backed up his opinion that "A Hard Rain's a-Gonna Fall" was one of the greatest protest songs ever written by recording it in 1964. But perhaps the greatest early adopter was the singer/actor Hamilton Camp, who put seven Dylan songs on his first album, *Paths of Victory*, in 1964: "Guess I'm Doin' Fine," "North Country Blues," "Walkin' down the Line," "Long Time Gone," "Only a Hobo," "Paths of Victory," and "Tomorrow Is a Long Time."

Some unexpected revelations about the amount of money Dylan's new manager Albert Grossman received from the publisher every time a Dylan song got played or covered caused a falling-out between the two in the mid-'60s, which may have indirectly led to Dylan's casual attitude to writing and recording from '66 through '69. But in fairness to Grossman, many of those early covers were from artists he managed, Peter, Paul and Mary chief among them. And Dylan was notoriously sloppy when it came to reading over legal documents before signing them. Nevertheless, when it came to publishing income, Dylan had relatively little to complain about, soon forming several imprints of his own, among them Dwarf Music and Special Rider Music.

Left in the cold like Dylan's first manager, Al Silver, was his first publisher, Lou Levy, who had signed him in January '62 on the recommendation of John Hammond. Dylan's first lunch with Levy, at the famed Jack Dempsey's restaurant in the heart of Tin Pan Alley, made so profound an impression on the young man that it forms the opening of *Chronicles*. Hammond also devotes some space to the monumental meeting in *John Hammond on the Record*, as well as detailing Dylan's monumental shift in publishers—a music business tale on a par with Babe Ruth being sold by the Boston Red Sox to the New York Yankees for a hundred grand.

"Dylan sang 'Blowin' in the Wind' one night in a Greenwich Village joint before his record was out," Hammond writes. "Peter, Paul and Mary happened to hear it, liked it, and took it to their manager, Albert Grossman, to arrange for recording it in their next album for Warner Brothers records. Their songs were being published by Artie Mogull at Witmark, and when he heard 'Wind' he wanted it. Of course, Dylan told him that Lou Levy had already signed him for all his songs. Mogull said he thought he could take care of that."

Lou Levy's son Leeds, now a music publisher himself, filled in the sordid details. "I once asked my father, how did you know enough to sign Bob Dylan," said Leeds, when I interviewed him in 2012. "His story is that Dylan had been sent over by John Hammond, a guy who everybody respected, so he had that going for him. He had a record deal, although that didn't necessarily impress my father. My father was never impressed with self-contained artists. If they're a true artist, let's see them do a song by Sammy Cahn or by George and Ira Gershwin, he'd say. With Dylan he said he was intrigued with his performance of 'House of the Rising Sun,' and he said on that basis he signed him. But the irony of course is, when my dad was out of the office, his number two couldn't stand the way Dylan looked."

Artie Mogull was working at Witmark, and he gave Dylan $1,000 to buy back his contract from Levy. "So my dad was in Europe, and his second in command said, 'Let me get this straight. I get the hundred bucks back that Lou Levy blew on you, and I make a profit? Great!' Lou had made some demos with him and was trying to find a vehicle, a lyrical theme for Dylan to write to that maybe he could take some of these songs to some other people. Once the deal was cancelled, the only two my father kept were 'Talking New York' and 'Song to Woody,' which were also on that debut album."

Mogull was no stranger to folk music, having worked the catalog of the Kingston Trio, in 1958 the biggest selling act on Capitol Records. Though he was well aware that Grossman's top act, Peter, Paul and Mary, wanted to record "Blowin' in the Wind," he still wanted to hear it for himself. "In walks this little guy, and he's got a guitar with some kind of contraption around his neck so that the harmonica is up to his mouth, and he starts singing for me," Mogull told liner-notes writer Colin Escott in 2010. "And when I heard, 'How many ears must one man have before he can hear people cry?' I flipped. I said, 'That's it. I want you.'"

The last of the Witmark demos is "Mr. Tambourine Man," the song that hit the top of the charts in 1965, in an abbreviated version by the Byrds, ushering in Dylan's most explosive era, the folk-rock era, when electric guitars started to merge with folk melodies and lyrics. Ironically, the era was kicked off late in '64 by the Animals' rousing rendition of "House of the Rising Sun," the song that had caused Dylan so many problems when he lifted Van Ronk's arrangement and claimed it as his own on his first album—causing Lou Levy to offer him a publishing deal. Now the Animals had done a double reverse, lifting Dylan's lift. In interviews, however, Animals lead singer Eric Burdon gave credit to the traditional English folk singer Johnny Handle for the arrangement, while keyboard player Alan Price also claimed credit. Van Ronk got over the whole thing, but Dylan, who jumped out of his seat the first time he heard the Animals' song on his car radio, had to stop playing the song because fans of the Animals accused him of plagiarism.

On the same radio station, Dylan was also hearing and absorbing the songs of the Beatles, who were dominating the American charts in 1964 the way Elvis had in '56. The biggest difference between the two eras was that Lennon and McCartney, like Dylan, wrote (and eventually published) their own songs. "Bob Dylan almost single-handedly eradicated Tin Pan Alley," said Mogull. "Previous to that, if Nat Cole recorded an album of twelve songs, twelve different writers and twelve different publishers were involved."

Dylan himself had no problem with that assessment. "Tin Pan Alley is gone, and I put an end to it," he said.

12

No, No, No

Another Side of Bob Dylan

Bob Dylan has always complained about the title of his fourth album, *Another Side of Bob Dylan*, calling it "corny." Based on the evidence of the track list, the album title could easily have been *Chimes of Freedom*, although that might have given the wrong impression to Dylan's devoted followers that he was still in the forefront of the good political fight.

A little on the negative side, *It Ain't Me Babe* would nonetheless have conveyed his intentions perfectly. A message song to end all message songs, "It Ain't Me Babe" expands the vision first attempted in "Hero Blues," in which Dylan playfully castigates a girlfriend who'd just as soon see him dead so she could memorialize him to her friends. Now the girlfriend had turned into a nationwide army of diehards who saw folk music as the savior of the pop charts and Dylan as the savior of folk music. If they knew Dylan had been enamored of the Beatles as soon as he heard them on the radio, they'd have been mortally wounded as well as morally offended. The Beatles were a bubblegum act, pandering to the lowest of common teenyboppers, while Dylan was at the other extreme, a new breed of entertainer, an Elvis of the mind, a poet in street clothes who hobnobbed with Allen Ginsberg and Carl Sandberg.

While folk purists on 4th Street and in his wider audience claimed *Another Side* was nothing but a money-grab, filled with slight pop songs designed to capture the youth market, Dylan's label failed to share that opinion. It chose instead to release "The Times They Are a-Changin'" as a single, a year after its parent album's release. The song skied to No. 9 in England in 1965, while both the Turtles and Cher hit the Top 20 with covers of songs from *Another Side*, "It Ain't Me Babe" and "All I Really Want to Do," respectively.

Hardly a money-grab, if anything *Another Side* seems to be a prime example of Dylan's erratic approach toward writing and recording. After introducing "Chimes of Freedom," "Mr. Tambourine Man," and "It Ain't Me

Babe" (as well as "Restless Farewell") to an extremely receptive audience at the Royal Festival Hall in England on May 17, Dylan took off for the small Greek town of Vernilya with Nico for a work-and-play vacation to finish writing the songs for the album, seeing it as the perfect antidote to help him recover from his final breakup with Suze Rotolo, played out in extreme detail in "Ballad in Plain D."

As painfully autobiographical as "Restless Farewell," "Ballad in Plain D" was another song Dylan wished he'd never written, or at least written so soon after the inciting incident. Having gotten it out of his system, however, he never performed it in public. Also written that week, with Nico and her small child at his side, were "To Ramona" (which some have seen as a more considered version of "Ballad in Plain D"), "All I Really Want to Do," "Spanish Harlem Incident," "Black Crow Blues," and the classic outtakes "Mama You've Been on My Mind" and "I'll Keep It with Mine."

A Historic Night of Music

On June 9, Dylan took these songs into the recording studio, along with several friends, several bottles of wine, and the writer Nat Hentoff, intending to record the entire album in one night, starting at 7:00 p.m. Aside from misfiring on "Mr. Tambourine Man," which he set aside for his next album, Dylan accomplished his task, completing the brilliant protest-scene kiss-off "My Back Pages" at around one in the morning. Subsequent critics of the album have noted occasional lapses in word choice and arrangement; compared with the dour tone of *The Times They Are a-Changin'*, the results were perhaps a bit too whimsical. It also failed to crack the Top 40 on the American album charts. But Dylan didn't care; he'd fulfilled his obligation and gotten the songs out of his system and into the world, where he could redo them in performance or forget them entirely (or both).

Dylan's refusal to put the wonderful "I'll Keep It with Mine" on the album was an omission that would irk his fans for decades. Apparently he'd promised it to Nico. But Nico was busy fronting the Velvet Underground, whose leader, Lou Reed, preferred not to include any songs by Dylan on the band's debut album. By the time Nico got around to doing a solo album, *Chelsea Girl*, in 1967, Judy Collins had already covered it. That song and "Mama You've Been on My Mind" would have made for a nice change of pace among the more cynical anti-love songs ("It Ain't Me Babe," "All I Really Want to Do"), one-night stands ("I Don't Believe You (She Acts Like

We Never Have Met)," "Spanish Harlem Incident"), and heartbreak dirges ("Black Crow Blues," "To Ramona," "Ballad in Plain D") that made the cut.

As for "message" songs, Dylan's main message from that sunny isle to the folks back home was that he was done with "message" songs, preferring to castigate his former self for self-righteousness and to offer in no uncertain terms a new creative (perhaps drug-inspired) vision ("My Back Pages," "Chimes of Freedom") expansive enough to include the old and the young, the left and the right, as well as the lame, the crippled, and the halt. Even the roundly reviled "Ballad in Plain D" nevertheless represents the songwriter at his most nakedly emotional, recounting details of his final row with Carla and Suze (Suze in the middle, getting pummeled by both sides) in about as straightforward and linear a manner as he'd ever done before or ever would again. As Suze later said, he could always present his feelings so much better in songs than in person.

By the time Dylan walked out of the studio on that June morning, Nat Hentoff trailing behind, pen poised, he was already on to something bigger. When he elaborated at length the next day, Hentoff had apparently neglected to do his required reading, allowing Dylan to reaffirm in '64 the same stories of running away from home to join the carnival that had been so thoroughly debunked in *Newsweek* in '63. Nevertheless, one gem emerged. "The way I like to write is for it to come out the way I walk or talk," he said. "Not that I even walk or talk yet like I'd like to. I don't carry myself yet the way Woody, Big Joe Williams, or Lightnin' Hopkins have carried themselves. I hope to someday, but they're older."

13

The Electric Bard

Bringing It All Back Home, Highway 61 Revisited

Bringing It All Back Home

ere is where the drugs start to kick in. Not only for Bob Dylan, but for all the early adopters in the baby-boom rock culture for whom Dylan's lyrics about this time began to take on an import just shy of the *Bhagavad Gita*, the cherished seven-hundred-verse Hindu poem about liberation that Mahatma Gandhi called his "spiritual diction-ary." As well as raising the consciousness of the Beatles at least as high as marijuana could take them, Dylan also had his first taste of LSD in 1964, as reported by Bob Spitz. While this may or may not be true, he was certainly reading surrealist French poets like Arthur Rimbaud (1854–1891), Charles Baudelaire (1821–1867), Paul Verlaine (1844–1896), and the later Jacques Prévert (1900–1977) by then, having been introduced to them by Suze Rotolo. And he was now trying his hand at the kind of free verse found in his liner notes and soon to show up the book he was writing for Macmillan that would become *Tarantula*.

What's more, he'd been hanging out with Allen Ginsberg since the end of '63. The bearded buddy of Jack Kerouac and the author of the era-defining Beat poem "Howl," Ginsberg had been hip to the salutatory effects of acid since befriending Dr. Timothy Leary around 1962, when he tried to become part of Leary's pioneering Harvard Psilocybin Project. When the French scholar George Izambard exhumed an old letter from Rimbaud to a friend claiming "the poet makes himself a seer by a long, prodigious and rational disordering of the senses. . . . He reaches [for] the unknown and even if, crazed, he ends up by losing the understanding of his visions, at least he has seen them," the sentiments were something Dylan could easily have identified with—before turning them into a song.

But could this alone have been the reasoning behind his decision not to perform the true breakthrough track of *Bringing It All Back Home*, the leadoff ode to Chuck Berry, "Subterranean Homesick Blues," the first chance he got, except in an improvised music video with Ginsberg as his cue-card

Under the poetic and psychedelic tutorage of Beat poet Allen Ginsberg, Dylan tapped the outer limits of his inner world.   *Diana Davies, courtesy of the Ralph Rinzler Folklife Archives and Collections, Smithsonian Institution*

man? Too many words? Too much monkey business? Or was it perhaps a perverse aversion to promoting something so beneath him as a rock 'n' roll single? "That's not me, that's the company," he told an interviewer for the Sheffield University newspaper in England. "The company says, 'It's time to do your next album,' so I go along and record tracks for the next album. What they do with the songs then we leave it up to them." Without much help, the single still broke into the Top 40, while the album crashed the Top 10 in the US and hit No. 1 in Britain.

It would take some twenty-three years before Dylan felt free enough from the demands of commerce to break "Subterranean Homesick Blues" out in public for the first time, opening a show and a tour with it in Concord, California, on June 6, 1988, with G. E. Smith on guitar, Kenny Aaronson on bass, and Chris Parker on drums. He liked it so much that he continued to use it as his opening song for the entire seventy-two dates of the tour, before losing sight of it again sometime during 1989.

Though making use of no fewer than four guitarists (Bruce Langhorne, John Hammond Jr., Al Gorgoni, and Kenny Rankin), three bass players (John Sebastian, Bill Lee, and Joseph Macho Jr.), two piano players (Paul Griffin and Frank Owens), and Bobby Gregg on drums, in addition to Dylan's contributions on acoustic guitar, harmonica, and piano, the quasi-rock 'n' roll instrumentation on the album was less of a shocker and a conversation piece at underground watering holes than were his forays into the theater of the lyrically absurd on "Gates of Eden" and, especially, the quotable "It's Alright, Ma (I'm Only Bleeding)." Songs like these, when performed in concert, demanded a level of concentration from the singer exceeding even that required of the listener. Mix them in with his existing epics, along with the new ones he was producing on an almost weekly basis, and the Rimbaud letter begins to loom even larger in the saga of Dylan's amazing 1965–1966 creative spree, when he most definitely "reached for the unknown and, crazed, ended up [nearly] losing the understanding of his visions."

Highway 61 Revisited

Six short months after completing *Bringing It All Back Home,* Dylan cut the album that was to redefine rock 'n' roll as rock and make him a rock star, *Highway 61 Revisited,* an ode to the blues routes of his youth, culminating with his postcard from the hanging, "Desolation Row," about as poetic

To find some stellar backup players for his new works, Dylan consulted Village pal John Hammond Jr., the son of his original mentor.

Diana Davies, courtesy of the Ralph Rinzler Folklife Archives and Collections, Smithsonian Institution

a portrait of a culture in ferment as a rock song masquerading as a Red Grooms painting could get.

Where two albums earlier he'd pictured himself writing and singing for "every hung up person in the whole wide universe," a mere year and a half later he was now attacking every know-nothing pseudo-intellectual on the planet in "Ballad of a Thin Man." But he shows little mercy for himself, either, charting his own druggy decline in "Just Like Tom Thumb's Blues" as well as the decline of Western civilization in "Desolation Row." Just about the only pure fun he has on the record is his hilarious ode to his childhood, the blues, and the Bible, "Highway 61 Revisited." Of all the important and much-quoted lines from the songs on this album, probably the most revealing is one from this title track, in which God is instructing Abraham to kill one of his sons. In the case of Bob Dylan, who changed his name and disowned his family in the press, the opposite may have been closer to the truth.

By this time, Dylan had been to England, filmed the tour documentary *Dont Look Back*, broken up with Joan Baez (in person and on camera), and written and recorded the most important song on *Highway 61 Revisited*—and

Dylan used the legendary blues highway as the setting for one of his blazing masterworks.
Ken Lund/Wikimedia Commons/Public domain

arguably the most important song in rock history. On the occasion of the release of "Like a Rolling Stone" on July 24, he headed to Newport, as was his regular summertime custom, to showcase the single, as well some of the tunes on the as yet unfinished album.

As has been well documented in many places, that's when all hell broke loose.

We Said We Loved Him

The Reluctant Interview Subject

In October 1963, a *Newsweek* profile by Andrea Svedburg hit the street; Dylan had hastily pulled the plug on the piece when the questioning veered toward the unexpectedly autobiographical. Now, for all the world to see (including his parents), some of the youthful wanderings he'd foisted on unsuspecting journalists from Robert Shelton to Nat Hentoff to Studs Terkel were revealed to be nothing but tall tales. He'd never run away from home, not even once. It was hard to tell which bits of personal dirty laundry bothered him more: the awful shame of his relatively ordinary background or the reference to the long-debunked rumor of his buying "Blowin' in the Wind" from a New Jersey high-school student.

Although it's enticing to believe this tall tale and wonder how different Dylan's career trajectory might have been had he not written "Blowin' in the Wind," the tale had already been refuted by its teller, Lorre Wyatt, long before the article came out, leaving one to suspect Hedburg's motive for dredging it up.

(Wyatt further tried to set the record straight in the magazine *New Times* in 1973, in which he revealed all the deceitful steps that concluded in his own Dylan-esque tall tale that changed his life. Interestingly, his single claim to later fame was a collaboration with Pete Seeger called "Somos El Barco / We Are the Boat," recorded by Peter, Paul and Mary in 1993 and twenty years later by Seeger, who provided a blurb for Wyatt's website: "I predict that many of Lorre's songs will be sung—humanity willing!—by our grandchildren's grandchildren.")

In any case, Dylan had a platform at least as powerful as *Newsweek*'s. If all it took was a disdainful hotel clerk to inspire his raging anthem "When the Ship Comes In," a disdainful journalist upsetting his carefully constructed house of Guthrie-esque cards should have set the heavens aflame with venom. But although he vented his spleen and defended his life and his love life over five verses and nine takes at Columbia's Studio A on October 31, "Restless Farewell," based on the old Irish folk song "The Parting Glass," was hardly biblical in its vengeance, leaving his retaliation to the last verse, in which he rather softly bids farewell to all of that, preferring to go his own way. Which was, in fact, old news for Bob Dylan, who was already singularly adept at saying farewell.

Even so, Dylan's often-contentious relationship with the press was probably written in stone with that article, and for years after there was never an innocuous interview question he couldn't answer with a scathing or dismissive or absurd joke. If the time was right and his mood was right and the stars were in alignment, he could also be amazingly forthcoming about his beliefs and his working habits.

Much of the time, though, he would use the interview forum he always had available to refute whatever theories were currently blowing in the wind about these beliefs and working habits, if only to maintain the air of mixed-up confusion that has surrounded his every move.

By 1965, Dylan's interviews with the press had become almost as surreally sarcastic as his songs. When asked about his influences by the *Village Voice*, he cited "Hank Williams, Captain Marvel, Marlon Brando, the Tennessee Stud, Clark Kent, Walter Cronkite, and J. Carroll Naish." When asked for some biographical information by the British trade magazine *Disc Weekly*, he snapped, "I couldn't care less what your paper writes about me. The people that listen to me don't read your paper. You're using me. I'm an object to you. It's nothing personal; I just don't want to be bothered with your paper at all. Why don't you just say that my name is Kissenovich, I come from Acapulco, and my father was an escaped thief from South Africa."

Capturing him for a rare sit-down in 1965, *New York Post* reporters Nora Ephron and Susan Edmiston were girding themselves for an epic battle. Ephron—later to achieve significant fame herself, writing for print and for the screen, as a chronicler of her own inner follies, foibles, and demons— had been assigned to do a piece on what was then the talk of the music scene: Dylan going electric. Her cohort at the *Post*, Edmiston, then known as Susan Szekely, the "Teen Talk" columnist who later became a successful writer and editor, snagged the elusive Dylan for the interview at Albert Grossman's office, several days after his Forest Hills concert.

"Nora asked me if she could tag along on my interview," Edmiston told me. "What was striking for me on first seeing Dylan up close was the impression of fragility he conveyed. He was doing his usual clowning in deflecting questions and not giving straight answers. I think the fact that I sort of played along with this—kind of speaking his language—is partly what elicited the responses that we got. Meanwhile, Nora was asking straight questions about folk-rock and his move to electric. I think because there were two of us and we were bouncing around in our questions we got more out of him than others had been able to."

Never one for labels, Dylan scoffed at the term the media had come up with for his music. "What does it mean?" he asked the writers. "Folk-rock. I've never even said that word. It has a hard gutter sound. It's nose thumbing. Sounds like you're looking down on what is fantastic music." He did frankly acknowledge what he felt was the major change in his music, however. "It's very complicated to play with electricity," he said. "You're dealing with other people. Most people don't like to deal with other people, it's more difficult."

Early in February 1966, Edmiston and Ephron broke the story in the *Post* of Dylan's marriage to Sara Lownds the previous November 22—an event he was probably prepared to keep secret a while longer. Not that being married made much difference to the electric bard. Instead of a honeymoon, he was booked for fifty-six concerts in the US and abroad, straight through to the end of May, allowing himself only the month of January off to welcome his son Jesse to the world. Anyway, he'd already been living with Sara and her daughter Maria at the Chelsea Hotel for some time. That was the fabled bohemian meeting ground where he started writing "Sad-Eyed Lady of the Lowlands" for her, as well as the stark and elusive "Visions of Johanna," both of which he wouldn't fully capture until the next month, in Nashville, when the sessions for *Blonde on Blonde* took a strange southern turn.

15

Stuck Inside of Nashville

Blonde on Blonde

ere is where the drugs start to get weird. It was one thing for a solo Bob Dylan, armed with a bunch of acoustic songs, to record an entire album in a single night, as he did with *Another Side of Bob Dylan*. It was something else again for an ill-prepared Bob Dylan, hopped up on speed and psychedelics, to decide to write and record an entire (double!) album in the studio.

Actually, it was two studios, since the whole floating opera picked up its tent, at the suggestion of producer Bob Johnston, to basically start over again in the new year in Nashville, with an entirely different set of musicians, save for Al Kooper, Robbie Robertson, and Mike Bloomfield. Gone were Garth Hudson, Rick Danko, and Richard Manuel of the Band, along with Paul Griffin on keyboards and Bobby Gregg on drums; they were replaced by guitarists Jerry Kennedy, Wayne Moss, and Charlie McCoy; bass players Joe South and Henry Strzelecki; Hargus "Pig" Robbins and Bill Aikins on keyboards; and Kenny Buttrey on drums.

But that's the kind of delusional thinking that began to predominate the music business as speed and weed overcame rational thought in the mid-'60s, making *Blonde on Blonde* a perfect album for its time, containing the most diverse and hilarious imagery of Dylan's life, as if dipping into an acid-expanded mind vision of his personal collected encyclopedia of remembered dreams, wise sayings, wise-ass sayings, poetic gibberish, cultural references, Beatles and Stones references, and, just to keep the peace, an 11:22 tone poem dedicated to his wife, Sara, sitting at home with a newborn baby. At turns ingenious and ingenuous, profound and superficial, several songs on the album deserve their historic slot on the track list merely due to a brilliant line or two, conjured up on the spot, after seventeen takes. Others are among the best Dylan's ever written. But Dylan was determined to rein in that "wild mercury sound" in his head, even if it took all night. Indeed, most of the Nashville regulars he recruited for the 1966 sessions must have felt like they were stuck inside of Music Row with the Bob Dylan Blues as they waited for the master to deliver his latest benedictions.

At least, according to one perhaps apocryphal story, he let them throw a party on the company tab before the sessions were through, allowing them to get wasted on their substances of choice in order to provide the appropriately rowdy backdrop for "Rainy Day Women #12 & 35," even if none of them knew what the hell the title had to do with everybody getting stoned. That the resulting single went to No. 2 on the pop charts tells you as much as you need to know about the drug-soaked sensibilities of the culture at that moment.

The first choice of single from the album was the "Like a Rolling Stone" soundalike "One of Us Must Know (Sooner or Later)," which Dylan spent the last part of '65 failing to complete, ultimately blaming the band if not the entire singles-making process. Making a single, he told radio personality Bob Fass, took him too far away from the album. "Singles just pile up and pile up," he said. "They're only good for the present." Later, he told *Rolling Stone* editor Jann Wenner, "I never did care for singles, 'cause you have to pay so much attention to them."

In January, after several changes in personnel, he finally nailed the song, only to see it fail to reach the Top 100 when released in February. Thus, by the time he came to record "Rainy Day Women," near the end of the final *Blonde on Blonde* session, Dylan and crew were probably far away from thinking "single" and concentrating only on having a rip-roaring good time, artificially aided or not.

Used to tight budgets, a ticking clock, and the glorious confines of the three-minute song, the Nashville cats were stunned to find themselves sitting on their hands as Dylan spent all of February 15 writing the majestic "Sad-Eyed Lady of the Lowlands"—and even more stunned when they finally got to play it at four in the morning, as it passed the eleven-minute mark. The next day was more (or less) of the same, as the musicians waited for him to finish "Stuck Inside of Mobile with the Memphis Blues Again" before wading through fourteen takes to get it right.

The return trip to Nashville on March 8–10 was a lot more cost-effective, with the final nine songs going down with relative ease, including "Just Like a Woman," one of Dylan's best and most covered songs; the aforementioned hit single; and, while the mood was still right, crackling versions of the follow-up Top 20 single, "I Want You," and the deliciously droll "Leopard-Skin

Pill-Box Hat," one of the most astute pieces of social satire Dylan has ever written, and one of his most personal. (An avowed hat devotee ever since he and his friend John Bucklen went scouring the bargain basement at Feldman's Department Store for blue caps like those worn by Gene Vincent's backup band, Dylan's catalog of hats as a statement of identity, from the Huck Finn hunting cap he wears on the cover of his first album to the Amish farmer hat he peeks out from under on *John Wesley Harding* to the country gentleman chapeau he donned in Woodstock to introduce *Nashville Skyline*, is beyond refute or compare. Only for a brief period of time, during his mid-sixties heyday, did he abandon the skillfully chosen and perfectly positioned hat, his wild, spiky hairdo a hat in itself in those days, on which the placing of any other would have been, to quote Dylan on this scathing track, "like balancing a mattress on a bottle of wine.")

The Missing Final Track?

The final mixes for *Blonde on Blonde* wouldn't be complete until late June, when a harpsichord overdub was added to "4th Time Around," Dylan's answer to "Norwegian Wood." Thus it was still technically possible, if he'd been so inclined, to write another song for this already overstuffed album, on the morning or the afternoon, of, say, May 18, which he then might have recorded in Paris or London before leaving for home. It would have to have been born of the same impulses that produced "Restless Farewell" and "Ballad in Plain D" and "Positively 4th Street"—inspired by a particularly gross or painful affront to his personal or artistic integrity. Had he been in that frame of mind, the song he might have written would almost certainly have been entitled "Judas."

Significantly, according to Clinton Heylin, Dylan did attempt three songs with Robbie Robertson in a Glasgow hotel room on May 19, in the aftermath of one of the most famous concert confrontations in rock history, at the Manchester Free Trade Hall on the night of the seventeenth, none of which he completed. "On a Rainy Afternoon" and "I Can't Leave Her Behind," both included on the soundtrack to the documentary he was making of his tour, *Eat the Document*, don't seem to relate to any outside events and may actually constitute two parts of the same song. But the fragment called "What Kind of Friend Is This," the first song they attempted on that rainy afternoon, is an intriguing if unfinished candidate, a bouncy blues number whose first line reads, "What kind of friend is this / Speaking like an awful man."

For whatever reason, Dylan didn't finish the song that day, perhaps thinking he'd eventually dust it off for his next album. But after writing and recording three albums in a little over thirteen months, by the time his next album was released, a year and a half later, that song and a lot of others would be forgotten, and the man who wrote them would be a very different Bob Dylan.

16

One Man with a Guitar

Seven Defining Concerts of the Sixties

The Gaslight, New York City, October 15, 1962

Initially released as a Starbucks exclusive in 2005, *Live at the Gaslight, 1962* documents Bob Dylan's many sets at the legendary basement club in Greenwich Village, his favorite venue (along with Folk City) in the days just before and just after the appearance of his first album. Famous among bootleg collectors since 1973, this ten-song excerpt from his repertoire at the time shows him still bound by tradition, while moving confidently into his own works, typified by an early version of the monumental "A Hard Rain's a-Gonna Fall" and the masterful "Don't Think Twice, It's All Right," both of which would appear on his second album.

With his penetrating performances of warhorses like "Moonshiner," "The Cuckoo," and the timeless "Barbara Allen," Dylan is firmly planted in the roots of folk music growing on MacDougal Street, yet exhibiting his own decidedly unique take on the process. But his days at the Gaslight, among the cognoscenti, would be numbered. Soon his second album would come out, and he'd belong to the world beyond the Hudson River. As Sean Wilenz writes in his liner notes, "Bob Dylan made a leap in a dank, smoke-filled hole-in-the-ground coffeehouse, in the heart of America's last authentic bohemia. The following April, he finished recording *Freewheelin'*. Along the way, he'd become another Bob Dylan. Once he'd done it, he didn't look back."

Town Hall, New York City, April 12, 1963

Columbia Records considered making the tape of Dylan's Town Hall concert—his biggest to that date, given just two weeks before he returned to Columbia studios to radically change the *Freewheelin'* album—part of its official bootleg series, but ultimately decided against it. Thus for many folks the only opportunity to hear these dozen contenders for his second record remains the illegal underground route.

The show featured several exceedingly rare songs, some brilliant, some forgettable, many of them never performed in public again, including "Dusty Old Fairgrounds" and "Hidin' Too Long." Of the twenty-three songs performed, fully a dozen wouldn't appear on any official albums in the '60s.

After concluding the concert on a fierce note with "Hidin' Too Long," "With God on Our Side," and "Masters of War," Dylan had one more ace up his sleeve. Having well established his protest credentials, he neatly dipped into his poetry bag for the eloquently risky and lengthy "Last Thoughts on Woody Guthrie," a rare moment of spoken performance art scheduled to be included on a *Bob Dylan in Concert* album that also never appeared.

Though he'd officially disowned them in the press, Dylan's parents were in attendance for this significant concert, and were joined by Suze and Bob

Bob Dylan always said a lone man with a guitar could change the world.

for dinner after the show. "His mother, especially, was friendly," Suze writes in her memoir, "while his father was more reserved."

Carnegie Hall, New York City, October 10, 1963

The folks at Columbia did release the October Carnegie Hall concert, but only as a frustratingly brief six-song EP, featuring "The Times They Are a-Changin'" and "With God on Our Side," along with the rarely heard "Lay Down Your Weary Tune." Nine other songs were released in Europe only (on vinyl) on *The 50th Anniversary Collection* in 2010.

Having nearly finished his third album a couple of days before this important concert, Dylan played eight of the nine songs written thus far, leaving out only the mild-mannered love song "One Too Many Mornings." In its place he played three songs he'd never played in concert before and would never play again: "Lay Down Your Weary Tune," "Percy's Song," and "North Country Blues," which had only been heard once in public during a songwriter's workshop at Newport the previous July.

This made the concert, like the album he was finishing, a virtual *Bob Dylan Protest Songbook*, featuring "The Times They Are a-Changin'," "With God on Our Side," and "When the Ship Comes In," along with the grim portraiture of "The Lonesome Death of Hattie Carroll," "Ballad of Hollis Brown," "North Country Blues," and "Only a Pawn in Their Game," leavened only by the sad Suze kiss-off, "Boots of Spanish Leather." Surrounding these songs were more topical laments, including "Blowin' in the Wind," "Masters of War," "A Hard Rain's a-Gonna Fall," "Talkin' World War III Blues," "Talkin' John Birch Paranoid Blues," and "Who Killed Davey Moore," as well as the downcast "Percy's Song," "Walls of Red Wing," and "Seven Curses," leavened only by the relatively sprightly Suze kiss-off "Don't Think Twice, It's All Right" and the mellow and totally out-of-place early showstopper "Lay Down Your Weary Tune."

The album may well have reflected the new seriousness of his mood and his elevated sense of purpose as his fling with Joan Baez began to overshadow his troubled relationship with Suze Rotolo, but the way they collided at Carnegie Hall that night in October presented an eerie foreshadowing of events about to explode, inside his world and outside it, over which he had little control.

Probably affected more than he'd care to admit by the Kennedy assassination, Dylan was determined now to leave behind his whole Greenwich Village, protest-writing, voice-of-a-generation phase—a phase he'd just indelibly stamped with the first 90 percent of an album that wouldn't even be released until January 1964. Even if "Restless Farewell" may initially have been an impulsive thumb in the eye to the journalists and purists, intrusive fans and demanding girlfriends who were trying to rule his life, it soon became a creative shield to defend himself against a world turning cockeyed in the aftermath of a cataclysmic event that would forever become a dividing line between reality and absurdity in facing the future.

"They're trying to tell you, 'Don't even hope to change things,'" Dylan told the WBAI radio personality Bob Fass at the time—even while, internally, everything was changing for him.

Newport Folk Festival, Newport, Rhode Island, July 26, 1963; July 24 and 26, 1964

Established in 1959 by George Wein, founder of the prestigious Newport Jazz Festival, the Newport Folk Festival had an impressive board of directors, including Pete Seeger and Albert Grossman. The inaugural lineup featured Seeger, Odetta, Jean Ritchie, and the New Lost City Ramblers. The highlight of the first festival was when Bob Gibson brought out the previously little-known barefoot soprano, Joan Baez, who both hushed and wowed the crowd with "The Virgin Mary Had a Son" and "We Are Crossing the Jordan River." In 1960, John Lee Hooker and Cisco Houston were the must-see performers, along with Ewan McColl and Peggy Seeger. After a two-year hiatus, Baez came back in 1963 to return Bob Gibson's favor to her scruffy protégé, Bob Dylan, who sang "With God on Our Side" during her set. Dylan also participated in the ballad workshop (performing "North Country Blues" and "With God on Our Side") and the topical song workshop ("Who Killed Davy Moore," "Masters of War," and, with Pete Seeger, "Playboys and Playgirls").

A year later, Dylan's message was quite different. At the July 24 topical workshop, he sang the biting "It Ain't Me Babe" (with Baez) and the allusive "Mr. Tambourine Man." Two nights later, he led off his set with "All I Really Want to Do" and performed "To Ramona," "Mr. Tambourine Man," and "Chimes of Freedom," before closing, with Baez, on "With God on Our Side." This time, the elders of the folk community regarded his performance dubiously. Like the stunned audience at his ECLC performance the previous December, these stalwarts felt like they'd received a slap in the face from Dylan, after all the free meals and free couches and traditional melodies they'd bequeathed him. It was like he was a different person now. What else was new? Dylan and his artistic vision were beyond their command.

For Dylan, by far the high point of the festival was meeting and bonding with his country hero, Johnny Cash. Nuzzling with Joan Baez wasn't so bad, either. With Suze Rotolo out of the picture, she was all he had, so he made the most of it, as many photo opportunities attest. They were inseparable, insufferable, like a besotted pair of virtual newlyweds. After the festival they made plans—along with Joan's sister Mimi and her new husband, Richard Fariña, who were now a folk singing duo themselves, signed to Vanguard Records—to spend most of August housesitting at Albert Grossman's farmhouse in Bearsville, just as soon as Dylan got back from an August 1 gig in Waikiki.

(A funny thing happened to Dylan on the way to the gig. Bonnie Beecher was in L.A. at the time. "I drove him to the airport and wound up getting on the plane and spending a week with him in Hawaii," she told Howard Sounes.)

At festivals in Newport and Philadelphia, the new breed of folk singer/songwriters, represented here by Eric Andersen, met and mingled freely with their audience.

Diana Davies, courtesy of the Ralph Rinzler
Folklife Archives and Collections, Smithsonian Institution

Philharmonic Hall, New York City, October 31, 1964

The image of one man standing alone on a stage with his acoustic guitar, attempting to change the world, has always been a powerful one for Bob Dylan, perhaps reaching its apex at this Halloween night concert at Philharmonic Hall. Safe behind his Bob Dylan mask, he ran through a set of songs ranging from the topical to the transcendent. It was similar to his concert at the Royal Festival Hall the previous May, except for his having added the newly penned "It's Alright, Ma (I'm Only Bleeding)" in Philadelphia in September and "Gates of Eden" the week before in Boston. At this show, aside from introducing Joan Baez to his audience—just as she'd introduced him to her audience earlier at Forest Hills—to sing three duets with him ("Mama You Been on My Mind," "With God on Our Side," and "It Ain't Me Babe") as well as her own "Silver Dagger," the only other new wrinkle was his first and only performance of "Spanish Harlem Incident."

From then on, the world Bob Dylan would hope to change was the one inside himself. And from then on, these changes would be accompanied by an electric rock band.

Newport Folk Festival, Newport, Rhode Island, July 24 and 25, 1965

The Newport Festival of 1965 has long since fostered its own grandiose legacy as one of the turning points in musical history. But it is an event whose troubled mythology—like the warring viewpoints about what actually happened—has gone on to become, over the years, as misty, muddled, and contentious as the theories surrounding the Kennedy assassination. Decades and scores of eyewitness accounts later—many of them referenced in Elijah Wald's *Dylan Goes Electric: Newport, Seeger, Dylan, and the Night That Split the Sixties*—it is still a sore point among casual fans and Dylanologists alike as to whether Bob Dylan suffered the wrath of his more bucolic cronies for stabbing them in the back with an electric guitar plug, or instead received hysterical praise for the same brave acceptance of the rock 'n' roll chalice.

As far as Dylan was concerned, the booing never bothered him, at Newport or at his first concert after the event, on August 28 at Forest Hills, where he debuted five songs from the just-released *Highway 61 Revisited*— "Desolation Row," "Tombstone Blues," "From a Buick 6," "Just Like Tom

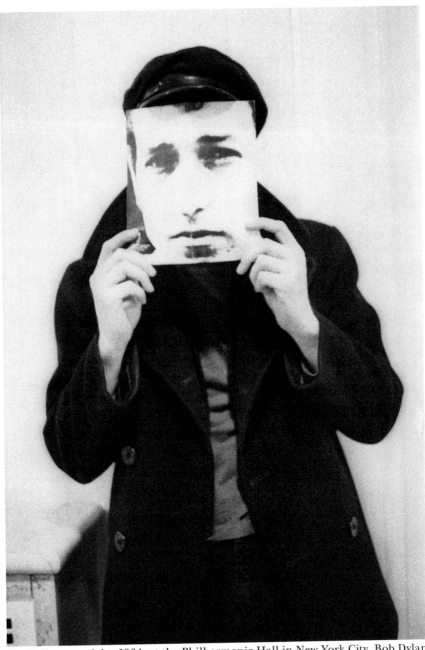

On Halloween night, 1964, at the Philharmonic Hall in New York City, Bob Dylan donned his "Bob Dylan Mask," shown here being worn by Dylan cohort Eric Andersen.
Diana Davies, courtesy of the Ralph Rinzler Folklife Archives and Collections, Smithsonian Institution

From 1963 to 1965, the Newport Folk Festival in Rhode Island was the scene of some of Dylan's most stirring and controversial performances.

Diana Davies, courtesy of the Ralph Rinzler Folklife Archives and Collections, Smithsonian Institution

Thumb's Blues," and "Ballad of a Thin Man"—before closing with "Like a Rolling Stone."

(Aside from his next concert, a few days later at the Hollywood Bowl, Dylan never played "From a Buick 6" live again. But seven of the other eight songs on *Highway 61 Revisited* would remain among his live favorites, with the title track, "Like a Rolling Stone," and "Ballad of a Thin Man," all in his personal Top 10. Which didn't mean he was in a rush to play them all onstage. He waited until his Isle of Wight appearance on August 31, 1969, to perform "Highway 61 Revisited," and until November 11, 1975, to debut "It Takes a Lot to Laugh (It Takes a Train to Cry)" to an astonished audience in Niagara Falls. Were it not for Jerry Garcia's prodding, he might never have unearthed "Queen Jane Approximately" on July 4, 1987, to open the Dylan and the Dead tour at the Meadowlands in New Jersey. He then played it at seventy-five more shows over the course of the next twenty-five years.)

When asked about the booing, Dylan told interviewers Nora Ephron and Susan Edmiston, of the *New York Post*, "I thought it was great. I really did. If I said anything else I'd be a liar." Not averse to lying in interviews, he did veer into a forthcoming comment about his Newport experience. "They twisted the sound," he said. "They didn't like what I was going to play and they twisted the sound on me before I began."

With Pete Seeger in the role of Dylan's old high-school principal at the Jacket Jamboree, attempting to or wanting to pull the plug on his high-octane performance, none of the folks at Newport really got to experience "Like a Rolling Stone" in its proper context. Hampered as usual by his lack of patience with the technical aspects of amplification and presentation, Dylan and his ad-hoc band of Chicago blues musicians probably came close to blowing up the entire festival, with their gear and their volume more suited to a stadium than a pristine pasture. Dylan finished up the set acoustically, humbled by his inexperience, but in no way blown off course.

Free Trade Hall, Manchester, England, May 17, 1966

Considering the onslaught of arena-sized electric rock music starting in the latter part of the 1960s, the gauntlet Bob Dylan faced and endured throughout his fractious tour of America and Europe in 1965–1966 is even more heroic than historic. Though the Beatles and the Rolling Stones would follow him in 1965 and 1966 to venues as spacious as JFK Stadium in Philadelphia, Shea Stadium in New York, and the Hollywood Bowl in Los Angeles, because he was Bob Dylan, his fans felt entitled to use their exalted suppositions to block his path at every turn, and never more so than on the night of May 17.

Apparently, Dylan had been feeling bored by the applause that had become a nightly ritual by 1965. "It was too easy," he told writer Jules Siegel. "Every concert was the same. I'd get standing ovations and it didn't mean anything." Devoting the second half of his concerts to rock arrangements of songs dating as far back as his first album ("Baby Let Me Follow You Down") and his third album ("One Too Many Mornings"), as well as his new full-on rock songs that changed the musical firmament of America forever (i.e. "Ballad of a Thin Man" and "Like a Rolling Stone") completely reversed the situation in 1966, changing the automatic cheers to automatic howls of protest. If Dylan was more satisfied by these results, it was hard to tell.

Surely his band, whose members had been plying their trade in semi-anonymity as the Hawks, backing up the wild rockabilly singer Ronnie Hawkins, were caught entirely unaware. When they hit the road with Dylan in '65 and '66, there was nothing in their lexicon to prepare them for what they faced that fall, winter, and spring on the road. They might have experienced a few beer bottles tossed toward the stage or the occasional bar fight in Canada and the States between floozies dueling with broken pool cues, but in England that spring, they endured an entirely new level of hostility.

As Robertson recalled of that period in an interview I did with him for the magazine *Guitar for the Practicing Musician*, "Everywhere we played, they booed us every night. Threw things at the stage. It was violent. We would listen later on to the tapes that were made during the show and we'd say, 'This isn't terrible music.' When we were recording *Blonde on Blonde*, there was a feeling of, 'This is very fresh. I hope it's not too fresh. I hope this isn't going to be something nobody's going to understand.' So you did feel like you were taking chances, you were trying something, and there was nothing quite to compare it to. A lot of critics wrote, 'This is the worst stuff I've ever heard in my life.' And then the world changed. With time people changed their stories on it, audiences did, critics did, everybody did."

That bit of hindsight did little to help during the last leg of the '66 tour, leading up to the events of May 17, in Manchester, when Keith Butler, a student at Keele University, became the single most famous audience member to interrupt a public event (supplanted in 1978 by Jeffrey Maier at Yankee Stadium) when he cried out "Judas!" during a lull in the proceedings just after Dylan completed a thrilling version of "Ballad of a Thin Man."

Usually indifferent toward his audience, so completely into his performance as to render them invisible and inaudible, Dylan heard the taunt as

Robbie Robertson on lead guitar hit some incredible high notes, and sustained some enduring low moments, during Dylan's frantic tour of England in 1966.

clearly as the rest of the crowd did. Knowing his Bible better than most, he shouted back, "I don't believe you."

By this time, according to his old Minneapolis friend Tony Glover, who wrote the liner notes for Columbia's 1998 release of the concert, "The combination of the hectic schedule and the intense white heat in which Dylan was working were beginning to take their toll. Watching him in the film of the tour, *Eat the Document*, is scary. He has a wired-to-the-bone stoned fragility that makes it look like he might vanish in a burst of flame at any second."

One veteran Dylan-watcher, the pioneering rock critic Paul Williams, describes the tour in his book, *Performing Artist: The Music of Bob Dylan, 1960–73*: "He was literally burning himself out, not to please the audience and certainly not out of obligation, but for the sheer joy of doing it, traveling with intrepid comrades out into unknown aesthetic realms, shining light onto unexplored darkness."

"You're a liar," Dylan continued, before fearlessly directing the band into a scorching, gut-wrenching version of the night's closer—a perfect song of revenge—"Like a Rolling Stone."

As Tony Glover notes, "At bottom what really matters is that one night in 1966 a poet stood on a stage with a band he chose to help him propel his vision and made incredibly powerful music which was utterly unique. He was true to his vision and went right to the edge for it."

17

Howling in the Wind

Dylan's Ten Most Played Songs in Concert . . . and Twenty Forgotten Gems

As a measure of their longevity and popularity, the songs Dylan plays live reflect not only his feelings about them but the feelings of his fans, which he often takes into account when constructing his always-varied playlists for his never-ending concert tours.

The Top Ten

Number of plays calculated through November 1, 2016.

1. "All Along the Watchtower"

First played: January 3, 1974, Chicago Stadium, Chicago, Illinois

Total plays: 2,257

This song is perhaps the first indication relayed back to his fans that Bob Dylan had definitely not been rendered brain-dead by his motorcycle accident of 1966. Impatient, perhaps. Here his imagery is mostly crisp and stark, the music suitably spooky, his hatred steady if contained, and his message typically biblical. The old Dylan might have hit the six-minute mark easily with this cryptic tale, but the new, recovering Dylan found brevity more powerful than length, understatement more conducive to allowing the listener the space to fill in the rest of the story. The musician who filled in the space most productively was the late guitar god Jimi Hendrix, who turned the song into an out-and-out arena-rock classic—which, in effect, Dylan has been covering ever since.

2. "Like a Rolling Stone"

First played: July 25, 1965, Newport Folk Festival, Newport, Rhode Island
Total plays: 2,011

When Bob Dylan sang "the losers now will later . . . win" in "The Times They Are a-Changing" in 1963, the words and music for "Like a Rolling Stone" weren't even specks on his consciousness. He still had a few changes to go through, elders to annoy, girls to needle. Right after his first performance leading an electric rock band since Principal Pedersen rang the curtain down on the Golden Chords in 1957, he knew what he had in his hands, the sound and the message he'd been searching for since that day. In 1965, America was ready for its own revolutionary arrival, having had enough of the twinkly feel of the British Invasion. Earlier in the year, when the Byrds covered "Mr. Tambourine Man," just one verse of a Dylan song had been enough to top the charts; by the summer, when deejays played only half of "Like a Rolling Stone," listeners demanded the full catastrophe. Even the song that kept it from the No. 1 slot, the Beatles' "Help," was Dylan-inspired. At Dylan's induction into the Rock and Roll Hall of Fame, Bruce Springsteen spoke for every loser turned winner within the sound of Dylan's voice that summer and ever since. "That snare shot sounded like somebody had kicked open the door to your mind. He had the vision and talent to make a pop song that contained the whole world."

3. "Highway 61 Revisited"

First played: August 31, 1969, Isle of Wight Festival, Wootton, England
Total plays: 1,796

If Bobby Troup's "Route 66" defined the boogie-woogie era of the '40s, winding out of St. Louis toward Oklahoma City, "Highway 61 Revisited" supremely updated the blues for the rock era, with a comedic touch only a master absurdist like Bob Dylan could provide—and a police whistle only a demented ringmaster like Al Kooper could provide. Memorializing a highway already memorialized by Robert Johnson in "Crossroads," Dylan took a hometown landmark starting in Duluth and following the Mississippi River all the way to New Orleans and populated it with a wild assortment of mythic figures, from God to Abraham to Georgia Sam (aka Blind Willie McTell).

4. "Tangled Up in Blue"

First played: November 13, 1975, Veterans Memorial Coliseum, New Haven, Connecticut

Total plays: 1,556

Dylan often wondered who in the world could appreciate some of the more festering wounds he opened up on *Blood on the Tracks*. Although he would subsequently take great pains to discount any autobiographical intent, it seems a lot of his fans could identify much more with the troubled and lovelorn genius heading for a divorce than they ever could with the happy, sappy father of five trying to sell them homilies while crooning country tunes. Using newly acquired painterly techniques to confuse time and space and gossipmongers, Dylan has rewritten this song several times since its release, spending a lot of energy trying to disguise the real people involved, his favorite version being the one heard on *Real Live*. But his son Jakob knew exactly who this song—as well as the rest of the album—was really about. "That's my parents," he's quoted as saying in Michael Gray's *Bob Dylan Encyclopedia*.

5. "Blowin' in the Wind"

First played: April 16, 1962, Gerde's Folk City, New York City

Total plays: 1,398

Dylan's most famous song, and probably one of the most famous songs in the entire pop pantheon, post–World War II, in the US and around the world. Fittingly enough, it's also his most covered song—one that's been translated into at least ten languages, including Italian, French, Swedish, Romanian, German, Ukrainian, Portuguese, Catalan, Czech, and Bengali. Haunting and universal, its simple, timeless message struck home the first time he played it for Gil Turner one evening at Folk City, prompting Turner to play it for a live audience that night. A few weeks later, Peter, Paul and Mary heard it; more importantly, so did their manager, Albert Grossman, who had ties to the venerable Witmark publishing firm. With a few strokes of the pen, Bob Dylan would never be a complete unknown again.

6. "Ballad of a Thin Man"

First played: August 28, 1965, Forest Hills Tennis Stadium, New York, New York

Total plays: 1,111

As already noted, by the time of the writing of this song, Bob Dylan had amassed a formidable and warranted reputation as something of a difficult interviewee—if, that is, you were fortunate enough to secure an interview at all. When he wasn't outright lying, his answers could be as absurdly confounding as some of his songs. He lied to Nat Hentoff, the well-respected journalist who wrote laudatory liner notes for one of his albums; he even lied to the man whose rave review launched his career, Robert Shelton, in his first interview with the *New York Times* music critic. But those lies were more of the childish sort, Dylan trying to pawn off his childhood as that of Hank Snow or Woody Guthrie, which he eventually outgrew, especially after they were exposed in *Newsweek*. Like the Beatles, Dylan relished the press-conference format, where the reporter from Australia generally asked him, "When are you coming to Australia?" and the reporter from Costa Rica generally asked him, "When are you coming to Costa Rica?" And someone inevitably broached a question along the lines of, "What are you trying to say?" or the equally mundane, "Are you a spokesman for your generation?" After enough of such questions and the eventually exhausting repartee that followed, something was bound to explode. When it did for John Lennon, who claimed in a rare moment of candor that the Beatles were bigger than Jesus, it got him into a lot of hot water with the pope. Bob Dylan resorted to his mighty pen and piano for his rebuke to the know-nothing press (and, by inference, anyone who thought they knew more than they—or he—did). It was a far safer method of revenge, and one that proved almost as durable and popular as "Like a Rolling Stone."

7. "Maggie's Farm"

First played: July 25, 1965, Newport Folk Festival, Newport, Rhode Island

Total plays: 1,051

As Eddie Gorodetsky states in the liner notes to *No Direction Home*, "Here's where it all changes. This is the music that polarized Newport, inspiring a full range of responses from cheers to boos." Indeed, Dylan's most all-purpose protest song was a fitting choice to lead off his historic inflammatory set at Newport '65. It was as if he had a team of advisors backstage and in the days leading up to the performance, warning him not to go electric, or at least not at this venue—or, at the very least, not at this painful volume. True to fashion, he defied them all. "Maggie's Farm" can be seen as a protest against all the wine-swilling businessmen in his life, or commerce itself, or a simple song of freedom, from chains of any kind. Dylan paid the price for his defiance; his inexperience in either the rock band or the Chicago blues formats prevented him from delivering the optimal performance this song deserved. But even his legendary antagonist, Pete Seeger, eventually came around to what is now the conventional wisdom about the event. "You couldn't understand a word because the mic was distorting his voice," he says in *No Direction Home*. "I didn't mind him going electric; I wanted to hear the words."

8. "Rainy Day Women #12 & 35"

First played: August 31, 1969, Isle of Wight Festival, Wootton, England

Total plays: 963

While Bob Dylan may have thought he heard the Beatles singing the words "I get high" in "I Want to Hold Your Hand" in 1964, it wasn't until 1966 that the secret coded language of drugs started appearing with regularity on the Top 40. On April 9, the first attempt to make a song about pot into gold came from the Byrds, whose "Eight Miles High," a Coltrane-inspired ode to liftoff, might have made the Top 10, had it not started getting banned on the radio as soon as those in power were informed of the words. A week later, Bob Dylan's cautionary tale about the necessity and the pitfalls of getting stoned appeared. It was followed a month later by Ray Charles's "Let's Go Get Stoned," written by the team of Nickolas Ashford and Valerie Simpson. In June, the Association didn't fool anyone with "Along Comes Mary," their ode to Mary Jane. In July, the Rolling Stones focused on uppers and downers in "Mother's Little Helper." In August, the Beatles joined the party, with Paul McCartney writing "Yellow Submarine" soon after hearing "Rainy Day Women."

Given the climate of the time, it was thought that "Yellow Submarine" was a type of acid; more likely, a type of acid called Yellow Submarine came on the scene to exploit the song. In any case, when the Beach Boys delivered "Good Vibrations" in November, everyone knew how those vibrations came about. When Donovan answered the Beatles in December with "Mellow

Yellow," the high in question was produced either by a psychedelic banana or a popular ladies' sex toy—or both.

While Dylan may have been kidding when he said "Rainy Day Women" was a protest song, he was surely not kidding when he said he'd never written a drug song, although many a Dylanologist considers at least 50 percent of his songs to be about drugs. Even the widely circulated story that the Nashville cats on the track were stoned while making the record has been believably disputed. But as with anything Dylan put his mind and his pen to, multiple meanings are possible. Given the biblical derivation of the title, and Dylan's own concurrent trials by public stoning, it could very well be his best public service announcement of all time.

9. "Don't Think Twice, It's All Right"

First played: October 15, 1962, the Gaslight, New York City

Total plays: 949

Nurtured by his tumultuous relationship with Suze Rotolo, this anti-love song virtually invented a genre of which Dylan was the undisputed king. Almost everything else about this song has been subject to dispute over the years, from the melody to the arrangement to the accompaniment to some of the lyrics. Though Dylan borrowed said public-domain melody and arrangement and a few lyrics from his pal Paul Clayton, Clayton didn't seem to mind, having taken said melody from an even older public-domain source when making "Who's Gonna Buy You Ribbons When I'm Gone" out of "Who's Gonna Buy You Chickens When I'm Gone." Dylan seems to have had that older song in mind when he set his own lyric in a place where roosters crow at the break of dawn, instead of garbage cans rattling and police sirens wobbling outside the West 4th Street window of the apartment he shared with Suze before she took off for Italy with his heart, but not his soul.

10. "It Ain't Me Babe"

First played: May 17, 1964, Royal Festival Hall, London, England

Total plays: 947

Written to any number of ex- and future ex-lovers, detailing all the ways he couldn't live up to their fantasies, "It Ain't Me Babe" immediately became something of an anthem for the dropout generation of the late

'60s. Whether they were disappointing their girlfriends, their parents, their professors, or their country, young men in this era, taking their cue from their caustic spokesman, were determined to proclaim their freedom from all obligations. Negating the delightful chants of the Beatles ("Yeah, yeah, yeah") with a much more appropriate refrain ("No, no, no"), this particular Dylan song spoke most clearly to the divide in the music audience between the fluff of the mop-tops and the red meat of the acoustic bard. Eventually, most of these men came crawling back to their senses and their demanding women, following their hero to the altar and the civilizing joys of family life, but not before deposing a president and ending a war.

Twenty Great Songs Dylan's Never Played in Concert

Bob Dylan has been remarkably consistent in his rationale for never playing a song in concert. Time and again he's reminded his fans that, in most cases, outtakes for a given album are outtakes for a reason. Of the twenty songs on this list, five were never used on the albums for which they were recorded, or anywhere else, even if fans regarded these songs as gems: "Angelina," "Farewell Angelina," "Foot of Pride," "Up to Me," and the epic "She's Your Lover Now," which climaxed a frustratingly few short lines shy of completion. "Love Is Just a Four-Letter Word" was given to Joan Baez in what Dylan always claimed was an unfinished state. "I'll Keep It with Mine" was reserved for Nico. "I'm Not There" was merely a jumble of words when critics plundering *The Basement Tapes* for gold declared it to be a lost classic.

Although they were recorded, you can easily see Dylan's reasoning for keeping such torturous confessionals as "Ballad in Plain D" and "Dirge" away from unknowing ears. The revelatory "Don't Fall Apart on Me Tonight," featuring a lyric in which Dylan berates himself for burning all his bridges, may have met with the same fate. Given its length, "Sad-Eyed Lady of the Lowlands" might have been too much to expect, although Dylan did perform the epic "Highlands" a few times, and the wordy "Brownsville Girl" once (forgetting many of the words). He's always been honest in proclaiming his confusion about the reason or rhyme behind "John Wesley Harding." And his failure to promote "Sweetheart Like You" can probably be chalked up to his aversion to its release as a single (peaking at No. 55). "Hard Times in New York Town" was sung a couple of times for friends at the home of Eve and Mac McKenzie in 1961 and '62. By then his hard times were ending. And the more recent "Some Enchanted Evening" was just a bad idea best left forgotten.

All of this must mean Dylan has a special aversion to *New Morning*, having failed to play four very serviceable songs from that album: "Day of the Locusts," "Went to See the Gypsy," "Time Passes Slowly," and the very moving "Sign on the Window." Perhaps these songs, written during his period of salvation in Woodstock, belong in the "too painful to revisit" category, as they remind him, respectively, of his strange honorary degree from Princeton, his abortive visit to Las Vegas to meet Elvis, and his time under the thumb of his wife and kids, suffering from domesticity.

The following songs, as of the beginning of 2017, are still in mothballs, awaiting the delirious whoops of the faithful should he ever deign to dust one off.

- "Angelina"
- "Ballad in Plain D"
- "Day of the Locusts"
- "Dirge"
- "Don't Fall Apart on Me Tonight"
- "Farewell Angelina"
- "Foot of Pride"
- "Hard Times in New York Town"
- "I'll Keep It with Mine"
- "I'm Not There"
- "John Wesley Harding"
- "Love Is Just a Four-Letter Word"
- "Sad-Eyed Lady of the Lowlands"
- "Sign on the Window"
- "She's Your Lover Now"
- "Some Enchanted Evening"
- "Sweetheart Like You"
- "Time Passes Slowly"
- "Up to Me"
- "Went to See the Gypsy"

Ten Great Songs Dylan Has Played Just Once

The next ten wonderful songs mysteriously fell out of favor after just one fateful performance. What could have gone wrong?

- "Let Me Die in My Footsteps"—July 2, 1962, Finjan Club, Montreal, Canada
- "Lay Down Your Weary Tune"—October 28, 1963, Carnegie Hall, New York City
- "Percy's Song"—October 28, 1963, Carnegie Hall, New York City
- "Spanish Harlem Incident"—October 31, 1964, Philharmonic Hall, New York City
- "Can You Please Crawl out Your Window"—October 1, 1965, Carnegie Hall, New York City
- "Abandoned Love"—July 3, 1975, Other End, New York City
- "Caribbean Wind"—November 12, 1980, Fox Warfield, San Francisco, California
- "Brownsville Girl"—August 6, 1986, Mid-State Fairgrounds, Paso Robles, California
- "Oxford Town"—October 25, 1990, Ted Smith Coliseum, Oxford, Massachusetts
- "Buckets of Rain"—November 12, 1990, Fox Theater, Detroit, Michigan

18

Subject to Interpretation

Covering Dylan, Dylan Tributes, In-Concert Covers

T hey say no one can sing Dylan like Dylan, but luckily for his catalog, many an artist has failed to heed the warning. In fact, notables ranging from Joan Baez and Judy Collins to Sebastian Cabot and French singer Hughes Affray have recorded entire albums devoted to his work. You can add Odetta to this list, along with the Hollies, the Grateful Dead, Ben Sidran, Maria Muldaur, Johnny Cash, the Byrds, Steve Howe, the Persuasions, Robyn Hitchcock, Earl Scruggs, and McGuinness–Flint, among others. Listed in this section are his ten most-covered songs along with the best-known version of each, as well as my choices for the ten best cover versions of any Bob Dylan song.

The Ten Most Covered Songs

There are few surprises on this list, other than numbers nine and ten. Nevertheless, for the Dylan beginner, it's a pretty formidable sampler.

1. "Blowin' in the Wind," Peter, Paul and Mary
2. "Don't Think Twice, It's All Right," Peter, Paul and Mary
3. "I Shall Be Released," the Band
4. "Mr. Tambourine Man," the Byrds
5. "Like a Rolling Stone," none
6. "Knockin' on Heaven's Door," Guns N' Roses
7. "All Along the Watchtower," Jimi Hendrix
8. "It's All Over Now, Baby Blue," Van Morrison
9. "I'll Be Your Baby Tonight," Robert Palmer and UB40
10. "Quinn the Eskimo" (aka "The Mighty Quinn"), Manfred Mann

The Ten Best Dylan Covers

In covering a Bob Dylan song, as in life, context is everything. Some of the best Dylan covers have been done on tribute albums for various causes, thus providing showcases for a wide variety of musicians to strut their Dylan chops in front of their friends and in honor of the man himself. Obvious choices abound, with Peter, Paul and Mary having a special place of honor for "Blowin' in the Wind" and "Don't Think Twice" and Jimi Hendrix all but turning "All Along the Watchtower" into a Hendrix song. Joan Baez as a muse and a musician has covered dozens of Dylan songs, from the classics to the oddballs. For this list, historical import has been considered, along with good stories.

"I Will Not Go Down Under the Ground (Let Me Die in My Footsteps)," Happy Traum, 1963

Originally included on a compilation album put out by *Broadside* magazine in 1963 called *Broadside Ballads, Vol. 1*, this is one of the first two Dylan songs covered by another artist. The other, also featured on this album, is the New World Singers' version of "Blowin' in the Wind." Taken together, these two songs represent a huge leap forward in Dylan's songwriting prowess. The album also features several lesser Dylan songs: "Only a Hobo" and "Talkin' Devil," performed by Dylan under the name of Blind Boy Grunt; "As Long as the Grass Shall Grow," by Peter LaFarge; and "The Ballad of William Worthy," by Phil Ochs.

Dylan's cogent remarks in this song about bomb shelters and those who would prefer to dwell in them rather than live free in the open air would strike a deep chord with a generation raised "in the shadow of the bomb" to hide under their desks in school during air raid drills. A fellow Greenwich Village folkie, Happy Traum would remain lifelong friends with Dylan, showing up in Woodstock, where he harmonized on three tracks that appear on *Greatest Hits, Vol. 2*: "I Shall Be Released," "Crash on the Levee (Down in the Flood)," and "You Ain't Goin' Nowhere."

"Tomorrow Is a Long Time," Elvis Presley, 1966

Although it would have been a special thrill for Dylan to see Elvis Presley perform this heartfelt ballad to Suze Rotolo in the movie *Spin Out*, in which he's a race car driver pursued by Shelley Fabares, among others, the song was actually added to the slight soundtrack album as a bonus track. Elvis first heard the song on the *Odetta Sings Dylan* album and here delivers it in a sensitive, "Love Me Tender"–style reading. Dylan always claimed that having Presley cover one of his songs was one of his proudest achievements. When the King died in 1977, he was reportedly too shook up to leave his house for several days.

"Just Like a Woman," Richie Havens, 1967

A soulmate from the same basket houses of MacDougal Street, Richie Havens specialized in reinterpreting Dylan's material in his deep and expansive voice. On his debut album, *Mixed Bag*, Havens commits the (perhaps accidental) sin of trying to rewrite one of Dylan's most moving and covered lyrics—something only Dylan is allowed to do. In this case, he adds the word "problems" in describing the curls of the woman, a far too prosaic image for the speed queen in question. If it was originally added in error, Havens was apparently attached to the word, repeating it decades later during his performance of this song during the legendary "Bobfest" at Madison Square Garden, with the great one in attendance. Whether Dylan or anyone else noticed this gaffe has never been reported.

"This Wheel's on Fire," Julie Driscoll with Brian Auger and the Trinity, 1967

Known in England in the late '60s as "The Face," Julie Driscoll started out singing in the band Steampacket with Rod Stewart, who eventually joined a band called the Faces. In 1968, Julie was voted "Best New Female Artist" by the rock press in Britain, after releasing a tigerish version of Donovan's "Season of the Witch." (She further exhibited her fine taste by covering John Sebastian, Laura Nyro, and David Ackles.) Teaming up with organist Brian Auger and his group, she gives a similarly transformative take here on "This Wheel's on Fire," a track brimming with hidden meanings. It hit the Top 5 in Britain, where rock critics considered it the definition of psychedelia; the Band's version on *Music from Big Pink* was considered by stateside rock critics to be the definition of Americana.

"I'll Keep It with Mine," Fairport Convention, 1969

Fairport Convention, the English folk contingent that spawned such greats as Sandy Denny and Richard Thompson, were huge Dylan fans, covering such rare gems as "Percy's Song," "Lay Down Your Weary Tune," "The Ballad of Easy Rider," and "Masters of War" (in its original form, as "Nottamun Town"). On *What We Did on Our Holidays*, Sandy Denny takes the lead on one of Dylan's overlooked masterworks, as written for the ultimate sixties chanteuse, Nico. Years later, Bangles lead singer Susannah Hoffs put her own wistful stamp on it in a one-off Paisley Underground supergroup called Rainy Days (as well as recording the Velvets "I'll Be Your Mirror").

"Love Is Just a Four-Letter Word," Joan Baez, 1969

In Joan Baez's case, when it came to Bob Dylan, love was a five-letter word—blind. Written while on a busman's holiday at Joan's place in Monterey, along with the similarly themed "Farewell Angelina," here Dylan was communicating to his doting hostess in the only way he knew how—through his guitar—that he was not the one she was looking for, babe. Although Baez was unable to hear the words, she did hear the song (even though Dylan claimed it was never finished) and put it out as a single, which spent four weeks on the Top 100 in 1969, with the similarly inspired-by-Joan "Love Minus Zero / No Limit" on the B-side.

"Highway 61 Revisited," Johnny Winter, 1969

Like Jimi Hendrix and his complete domination of "All Along the Watchtower" in 1968, the albino blues-guitar phenom from Texas, Johnny Winter, ripped into this biblical romp with an evangelical fervor that transcended Dylan's more tongue-in-cheek approach. Just as "Highway 61 Revisited" remains one of Dylan's top five concert favorites, Johnny Winter's version entered his set immediately, and was a showstopper for the rest of his career.

"Every Grain of Sand," Nana Mouskouri, 1982

One of Dylan's (many) crowning achievements as a songwriter, this poetic confession was a song he had apparently written with the Greek superstar Nana Mouskouri in mind, having been introduced to her in Los Angeles by

Leonard Cohen in 1979. Mouskouri recorded it in 1982, in an operatic style at the other end of the spectrum from Emmylou Harris's rootsier version. Either way you approach it, the song's timeless honesty shines through. Dylan only occasionally performed this special treasure onstage, but he did break it out of mothballs in 1989, in Greece, presumably in tribute to a world-class singer.

"Foot of Pride," Lou Reed, 1993

Another lost outtake from an *Infidels* album that could have used more good material—unless Dylan had decided, after forty-four takes, that he didn't want to waste too many good songs on any one album—this performance by Lou Reed emerged from the "Bobfest" of 1993. Considering this was a man who had long competed with Dylan, or at least had long ago competed with Dylan, that Reed was there in the first place among Dylan's more devoted legions was a shock in itself. But this particularly inflamed lyric was so perfect for the cynical Reed, and he performed it with such passionate venom that you'd have thought he'd written it himself (even though he had to read the lyrics off a teleprompter).

"Gotta Serve Somebody," Aaron Neville, 2003

A highlight—some would say the only highlight—of Dylan's Christian period, this song survived his performance of it on *Saturday Night Live* in 1979. It survived winning him his first ever solo Grammy, for "Best Rock Vocal Performance," in 1980 (he'd previously won one for taking part in the *Concert for Bangladesh* album). A version by Mavis Staples and Johnny Lang barely survived an audience of dignitaries honoring George Herbert Walker Bush in 2011. Shirley Caesar introduced her cover with a little sermon of her own on the Bob Dylan gospel tribute album *Gotta Serve Somebody* in 2003. But leave it to the sweet soul man Aaron Neville to come up with the definitive version on his 2003 *Gospel Roots* album.

Best Tribute Albums

Nothing brings artists of every conceivable genre together like a tribute to Bob Dylan, usually for a good cause, or sometimes just because Dylan could use the money. In 2015, in honor of his receipt of the MusiCares "Person of the Year" award, the typically incredible and eclectic assemblage of talent who performed a Dylan classic onstage included Beck ("Leopard-Skin Pill-Box Hat"); Alanis Morissette ("Subterranean Homesick Blues"); Jackson Browne ("Blind Willie McTell"); Tom Jones ("What Good Am I"); Crosby, Stills, and Nash ("Girl from the North Country"); Norah Jones ("I'll Be Your Baby Tonight"); and Bruce Springsteen ("Knockin' on Heaven's Door"). But the highlight of the night was Neil Young's incendiary and inspirational closing tribute to "Blowin' in the Wind."

In 2003 and 2004, a couple of wonderfully unique tributes were released: the gospel *Gotta Serve Somebody* ('03) and the reggae *Is It Rolling Bob* ('04). Topped by Shirley Caesar's sensational "Gotta Serve Somebody," the former package includes "Saved" by the Mighty Clouds of Joy, "Are You Ready" by the Fairfield Four, "Solid Rock" by the Sounds of Blackness, and "Saving Grace" by Aaron Neville, in and of itself almost redeeming Dylan's short-lived pure gospel fixation. On the latter set, reggae versions by artists ranging from Toots Hibbert ("Maggie's Farm"), Gregory Isaacs ("Mr. Tambourine Man"), and the Mighty Diamonds ("Lay Lady Lay") to Don Carlos ("Blowin' in the Wind") and Billy Mystic ("A Hard Rain's a-Gonna Fall") may be more of a stretch. But a couple of listens are all you need to realize that nothing is beyond the reach of a Dylan song.

For sheer range and ambition, few tributes can match the 2012 collection for Amnesty International, *Chimes of Freedom*, featuring four discs and seventy-four tracks. How many other artists would have seventy-four tracks worth covering? From the usual suspects—"Blowin' in the Wind" (Ziggy Marley), "Tonight I'll Be Staying Here with You" (Sugarland), "Mr. Tambourine Man" (Jack's Mannequin), "Just Like a Woman" (Carly Simon), and "The Times They Are a-Changin'" (Flogging Molly)—to the more unusual pairings—"Corrina, Corrina" (Pete Townshend), "Simple Twist of Fate" (Diana Krall), "You're a Big Girl Now" (My Morning Jacket), "You're Gonna Make Me Lonesome When You Go" (Miley Cyrus), "Make You Feel My Love" (Adele), "Property of Jesus" (Sinead O'Connor), and "Don't Think Twice, It's All Right" (Kronos Quartet)—it's an amazing tribute. Just when you thought it couldn't get any better, side four's closing six bring down the house, with "I Shall Be Released" (Maroon 5), "Political World" (the Carolina Chocolate Drops), "Tryin' to Get to Heaven" (Lucinda Williams), "Baby Let Me Follow You Down" (Marianne Faithfull), and "Forever Young" (Pete Seeger/Rivertown Kids), topped off by Dylan's own tribute to himself on "Chimes of Freedom."

A Tribute to the "Bobfest"

As good as these tribute are, still the top is one of the first, the love-in otherwise known as the "Bobfest" that took place at Madison Square Garden on August 16, 1993, to honor Dylan's thirty years with Columbia Records: *The 30th Anniversary Concert Celebration*. While not as insanely eclectic as some of the subsequent tributes, and containing only a relatively small sample of his massive body of work (twenty-seven tracks on two discs, with a couple of bonus tracks added in 2014), the performances here—perhaps because they're live, in front of a sympathetic crowd of Madison Square devotees—are uniformly intense and inspired.

Not known as a big Dylan fan during their mutual '60s heydays, Lou Reed nonetheless tears into "Foot of Pride" as if Dylan had written it specifically for him. Ronnie Wood is similarly committed to the otherwise throwaway "Seven Days." Johnny Winter's version of "Highway 61 Revisited" is rip-roaringly definitive. Johnny Cash and June Carter own "It Ain't Me Babe," while Chrissie Hynde matures before our eyes and ears with her stunning version of "I Shall Be Released." It's a pleasure to hear George Harrison on Dylan's Beatles tribute, "Absolutely Sweet Marie." Willie Nelson plays against type in the caustic "What Was It You Wanted." The Clancy Brothers with Tommy Makem turn "When the Ship Comes In" into an Irish drinking song. Roger McGuinn revisits "Mr. Tambourine Man" with Tom Petty and the Heartbreakers, and a truly spine-tingling "My Back Pages" accompanied by Petty, Dylan, Harrison, and Eric Clapton. Longtime Dylan interpreter Richie Havens rises to the challenge with "Just Like a Woman," while Neil Young delivers a double play, with manic versions of "Just Like Tom Thumb's Blues" and "All Along the Watchtower." The trio of Mary Chapin Carpenter, Shawn Colvin, and Rosanne Cash, introduced by Rosanne's father, Johnny, offer a sweet change of pace with "You Ain't Goin' Nowhere," while the O'Jays raise the roof with a sanctified rendering of "Emotionally Yours."

When they all sang "Knockin' on Heaven's Door" together to close the show, some in the audience might have figured, after thirty years, what more could we expect from Bob Dylan, in terms of the kind of output curated here? Little did we know he had at least another twenty years of world-class productivity ahead of him.

Dylan's Ten Most Played In-Concert Covers

By far one of Dylan's least appreciated talents is his singing ability. Combined with his encyclopedic knowledge and memory of a century's worth of popular and roots music, the Dylan concert experience has been magnetized many times over by his choice of the perfect potent cover song. This playlist contains ten of the largely unrecorded covers that have gotten the Dylan treatment most often over the years, some of them lasting in his set only for a tour or two, some revived years later for an unknown but probably profound reason.

1. "Not Fade Away"

First played: February 6, 1986, Royal Park Hotel, Wellington, New Zealand

Total plays: 141

Written by: Charles Hardin (Buddy Holly) and Norman Petty

Recorded by: the Chirpin' Crickets (Brunswick, 1957)

Released as: the B-side of "Oh Boy"

Inducted into Dylan's set a few days after the twenty-seventh anniversary of Buddy Holly's passing, along with two other Holly songs, "Everyday" and "Maybe Baby," this song was given a remarkable performance as an encore on July 3, 1999, at Bayside Festival Park near Dylan's birthplace in Duluth. "I was born right up there on that hill," he told the audience, obviously recalling a night forty years before, when he looked into Holly's eyes from his own front row seat at the Duluth National Guard Armory, just two days before Holly's death. The set itself could have been subtitled "Bob Sings Brill," as it consisted entirely of covers, including several by the Barons of the Brill Building. There were two by Leiber and Stoller ("Poison Ivy" and "Charlie Brown"), one by Singleton and McCoy ("Trying to Get to You," popularized by Elvis Presley), and one by Carole King ("Crying in the Rain," written with Howard Greenfield and popularized by the Everly Brothers). Dylan was accompanied by Tom Petty and the Heartbreakers, with Stevie Nicks singing occasional backup.

2. "Little Moses"

First played: March 21, 1992, Adelaide Entertainment Center, Adelaide, South Australia

Total plays: 98

Written by: Bert A. Williams and Earle C. Jones

Recorded by: the Carter Family (Victor, 1929)

For his second most covered song in concert Bob Dylan dipped into his favorite well of inspiration, the Harry Smith *Anthology of American Folk Music*, for this 1929 Carter Family gospel retelling of the Bible story "Moses in the Bulrushes" from 1905. The composition is credited to one of Vaudeville's greatest black songwriters, Bert A. Williams ("Nobody"), and his sometime writing partner, Earle C. Jones. It has been covered by artists ranging from Ralph Stanley to Joan Baez to the Seekers. Dylan himself attempted an abortive version for *Self Portrait* in 1970. Most memorably, he sang it in Tel Aviv on September 5, 1987, while Israeli aircraft were in the process of bombing Jordan.

3. "Alabama Getaway"

First played: October 6, 1995, Riverview Music Arena, Jacksonville, Florida

Total plays: 87

Written by: Robert Hunter and Jerry Garcia

Recorded by: the Grateful Dead (Arista, 1980)

Bob Dylan started off his touring schedule of 1995 by playing five dates with the Grateful Dead, finishing up on June 25. The death of Jerry Garcia on August 9 hit him hard. By the end of September, he'd worked a couple of Dead songs into his show, "Friend of the Devil" and "West L.A. Fadeaway," as a tribute to his fallen pal, a man he'd called his "big brother." On October 6, he added "Alabama Getaway," the tune that opens the Dead's 1980 album, *Go to Heaven*. For the next year, up to the anniversary of Garcia's death, Dylan and the band played "Alabama Getaway" nearly every night, using it to open their three-song encore. On many nights, "Friend of the Devil" joined the set, too. In 1996, "New Minglewood Blues" was added as another tribute. After 1996, "Alabama Getaway" was retired for a year, until Dylan again played it and "West L.A. Fadeaway" in late August. He brought it out of mothballs in 2003, again along with "West L.A. Fadeaway," at the Office

Depot Center in Fort Lauderdale, when he sat in for three songs with the remaining members of the Dead.

4. "Cocaine Blues"

First played: October 15, 1962, the Gaslight, New York City

Total plays: 73

Arranged by: Reverend Gary Davis

Recorded by: Dave Van Ronk (Mercury, 1963)

Competing with Dave Van Ronk for cool traditional covers in the early '60s, Dylan famously recorded "House of the Rising Sun" in 1961, before Van Ronk got the chance to do so. The Gary Davis arrangement of "Cocaine Blues" was a vital cog in the repertoires of both interpreters, appearing in Dylan's act at the Gaslight in 1962 and on Van Ronk's album *Just Dave Van Ronk* in 1963. Ironically, given his penchant for swiping arrangements and stealing credits, Dylan erroneously credits T. J. "Red" Arnall, author of a different "Cocaine," for this one. But Van Ronk got the composer wrong, too, crediting Luke Jordan. The Reverend Gary Davis claimed he learned the song from a version by a carnival singer named Porter Irving from 1905. Among the many to adopt it were Richard Fariña and Eric Von Schmidt, Ramblin' Jack Elliott, Townes Van Zandt, Stefan Grossman, and Hoyt Axton. Dylan performed it on August 3, 1997, at Loon Mountain in Lincoln, New Hampshire, and played it until 1999. A version performed on August 24, 1997, at Wolf Trap in Vienna, Virginia, appears on *The Bootleg Series Vol. 8: Tell Tale Signs: Rare and Unreleased 1989–2006*.

5. "Across the Borderline"

First played: February 5, 1986, Athletic Park, Wellington, New Zealand

Total plays: 61

Written by: Ry Cooder, John Hiatt, and Jim Dickinson

Recorded by: Freddy Fender (Dot, 1982)

Written for the Jack Nicholson/Valerie Perrine movie *The Border* in 1982 and recorded for the score by country star Freddy Fender ("Before the Last Teardrop Falls"), this poetic picture of immigrants trying to cross the border into the "broken promise land" had been on Bob Dylan's radar since

1983, when he tried it out during the sessions for *Infidels*. It was cowritten by John Hiatt, who in 1985 wrote "The Usual," as recorded by Dylan during his first and last attempt at leading manhood, the 1987 film *Hearts of Fire*. After trying it out for an audience in New Zealand, Dylan brought "Across the Borderline" to America in time for his July 4, 1986, performance at Farm Aid. He last performed it in 1998.

6. "Barbara Allen"

First played: October 15, 1962, the Gaslight, New York City

Total plays: 60

Traditional Scottish ballad

Recorded by: Joan Baez (Vanguard, 1961)

One of the most widely performed and revered songs in the folk canon, "Barbara Allen" is a retelling of the *Romeo and Juliet* theme of star-crossed lovers doomed to death. When Barbara Allen spurns sweet William, he kills himself; when she learns of his death, she returns the gesture. In a surreal romantic twist Bob Dylan could appreciate, out of Sweet William's heart grows a rose and out of Barbara Allen's a briar, which eventually entwine into a "lover's knot." Dylan did an intense eight-minute version of this song in his Gaslight sets in 1962. Over a quarter of a century later, displaying the impatience of middle age, he debuted a four-minute version in Salt Lake City in 1988, and continued to play it that way for the next three years.

7. "Stone Walls and Steel Bars"

First played: May 22, 1997, the Beverly Hills Hotel, Los Angeles, California

Total plays: 41

Written by: Ray Pennington and Roy Marcum

Recorded by: the Stanley Brothers (King, 1963)

Debuted at a $1,500-a-plate benefit for the Simon Wiesenthal Foundation at the Beverly Hills Hotel on May 22, 1997, this song, along with "Masters of War" and "Forever Young," was a tribute both to the famed "Nazi hunter" Wiesenthal and his good works and also to bluegrass pioneer Ralph Stanley, from whose repertoire Dylan learned "Man of Constant Sorrow," which appears on his first album. In 1988, Dylan recorded "Rank Strangers to

Me," another tune associated with Stanley. Later that year, he participated in *Clinch Mountain Country*, a duets album with Stanley, appearing on the tune "Lonesome River." Also featuring on the album are Porter Waggoner, Connie Smith, Kathy Mattea, George Jones, Dwight Yoakam, Rhonda Vincent, and Ricky Skaggs, while Junior Brown performs "Stone Walls and Steel Bars," written by Ray Pennington and Roy Marcum, who wrote the similarly themed "Don't Cheat in Our Hometown," a hit for Ricky Skaggs. Dylan called the experience "the highlight of my career." He never performed "Lonesome River" in concert, but he played "Stone Walls and Steel Bars" sporadically until 2002, debuting it for his regular audience at Wolf Trap in Vienna, Virginia, on August 23, 1998.

8. "Hallelujah I'm Ready to Go"

First played: June 11, 1999, General Motors Arena, Vancouver, Canada

Total plays: 37

Written by: Don Pierce (William York)

Recorded by: the Stanley Brothers (Starday, 1960)

Another tune from the Stanley Brothers gospel catalogue, also known as "Ready to Go," this uplifting hymn was a show opener whenever it was used, the first time to kick off Dylan's tour with Paul Simon in 1999. He kept it at the top of the show until 2002. Starday producer Don Pierce shared Dylan's approach to traditional tunes, often crediting his William York pseudonym for arrangements of songs in the public domain and claiming them as his own. Ricky Skaggs recorded it in 1982.

9. "We Had It All"

First played: June 11, 1986, Lawlor Events Center, Reno, Nevada

Total plays: 33

Written by: Troy Seals and Donnie Fritts

Recorded by: Waylon Jennings (RCA 1973)

It is tempting to read one too many autobiographical implications into Bob Dylan's relationship with this heartbreaking song of a love cut short, considering that he originally attempted to record it with his then girlfriend, Carolyn Dennis, in 1984. They'd been married a week when he debuted it in performance in Reno, Nevada, with Dennis singing backup, and he sang it for that year only. Written by country songwriters Troy Seals and Donnie Fritts, it was a hit for Waylon Jennings, and has since been covered by Willie Nelson, Dolly Parton, Rod Stewart, Conway Twitty, Ray Charles, and Tina Turner. Keith Richards sings it about Anita Pallenburg, who became his ex in 1979. Carolyn Dennis became Dylan's ex in 1992.

10. "Accidentally Like a Martyr"

First played: October 4, 2002, Key Arena in Seattle, Washington

Total plays: 22

Written by: Warren Zevon

Recorded by: Warren Zevon (Asylum, 1978)

As Suze Rotolo has often said, Bob Dylan could always express himself better with a guitar in his hand than while sitting next to you on a couch or across from you at a coffeehouse. No matter how he may have expressed his feelings to or about his songwriting compatriot Warren Zevon to his face in real life (or when playing harmonica on Zevon's "The Factory" in 1987), it couldn't have been more powerful as a demonstration of emotion than when he began to delve into the extensive Zevon catalog in performance throughout his fall tour of 2002, soon after the news of Zevon's diagnosis of incurable cancer became public knowledge. He started his tribute to Zevon on October 4, 2002, covering three songs of his in a set otherwise dominated in the headlines by Dylan's decision to take the stage behind a keyboard rather than a guitar. He was particularly drawn toward the anti-love "Accidentally Like a Martyr" from Zevon's breakthrough 1978 album, *Excitable Boy*, perhaps because it contained the phrase "time out of mind," also the name of Dylan's 1997 comeback album.

For the rest of the year, Dylan would perform at least one Zevon tune, if not two, on every stop of the tour, including "Werewolves of London," "Boom Boom Mancini," and "The Mutineer," which eventually supplanted "Accidentally Like a Martyr" as his favorite—except at two somewhat attenuated sets on November 5, in the Egyptian Room of the Murat Center in Indianapolis, when the audience was denied the chance to hear any Zevon tunes.

19

Killing Him with Salvation

The Recovery Albums

John Wesley Harding

T here must be some way out of here." This is what the joker would say to the thief in the most famous song from *John Wesley Harding*, which did not appear in stores until a year and a half after *Blonde on Blonde*. It's what Dylan had already told himself many times, soon after he got caught in the glare of stardom, most recently on his grueling tour of the US and Britain in 1966. An accomplished escape artist, he was always looking for the trapdoor. When the Kennedy assassination spooked him out of being a protest singer, he used a road trip through America in a beat-up coupe to free himself from that constricting label by writing a couple of interior rambling songs called "Chimes of Freedom" and "Mr. Tambourine Man."

Having created the sound of the sixties with three mind-blowing albums, he now desperately needed to find out how to keep from "going through all these things twice." Dogged by deadlines for his nearly unsalvageable novel, *Tarantula*, and a completely unsalvageable film about his '66 tour of Britain, *Eat the Document*, which he foolishly decided to recut himself for a projected ABC-TV special that never aired, his mind was already on overload when all this hectic activity came to a screeching halt, along with the idea that he would ever again approach the staggering bravado of *Blonde on Blonde*.

On the afternoon of July 29, coming home from a visit with his neighbor, Grossman, and followed in the car by his wife, Sara, Bob Dylan somehow fell off the road, his bike, and the radar, and into the dust of rumors that would cover him for the next year. Had he been crippled and maimed in a horrible accident or given a vision of the trapdoor opening up right in front

Newport Folk Festival, 1965. Is that Dylan's reclusive wife Sara pictured next to Bob?
Diana Davies, courtesy of the Ralph Rinzler Folklife Archives
and Collections, Smithsonian Institution

of him? As with the Kennedy assassination, the truth will probably be buried forever in conspiracy theories. All we know is that instead of spending the rest of '66 on the road, he suddenly found himself with a lot of free time, up in the woods, off the clock, surrounded by family.

It wasn't until early in 1967, with half the generation marching off to Vietnam and the other half marching to San Francisco, that anyone from his inner circle came to call. After approximately five months of woodshedding with the Hawks at Big Pink, and two weeks after learning his idol Woody Guthrie had finally passed away, Bob Dylan decided the time was right to deliver a series of sermons that could well have been entitled *The Gemini Confessions.*

There are twelve tracks on the album, most of which star hardly concealed versions of Dylan himself, as the misunderstood outlaw, the Saint (nearly) put to death by the crowd, the dissolute drifter on trial for his life, the shady cowboy undone by lust, the messenger accused of bringing only bad news, the joker, the thief, the hobo, the man indebted to his landlord, and, finally, the man saved by the love of his wife and family. Five of the seven deadly sins Dylan had been guilty of committing in the recent past are confronted herein: lust, envy, greed, pride, and wrath; or maybe all seven, if you consider his time with Robbie Robertson and the boys whittling away in the basement on songs no one would ever hear sloth (instead of, as others have opined, sheer genius) and the copious amounts of wine and weed consumed gluttony. (He would offer a more humorous spin on this theme some years later, making fun of these same sins in "7 Deadly Sins," written for and performed by the Traveling Wilburys, the band he formed with Tom Petty, Roy Orbison, Jeff Lynne, and George Harrison.)

Discounting his use of sacrificial wine and weed, on this album Dylan comes across more like a self-righteous, reformed addict, saved by the Bible and the love of a good woman, preaching to the degenerates he'd left behind. A brush with death could do that to you. Whether that brush occurred on a nearby dirt road in Woodstock or on his last tour is anybody's guess. With the benefit of hindsight, it could even be said the brush with death was provided by that very same wife and family, leading to the kind of creative death too much satisfaction can bring about in a restless genius often bored by standing ovations and the like.

Nevertheless, these cryptic and haunting songs hung together as a concept album, quite at the other end of the spectrum from his previous *Blonde on Blonde* (to say nothing of the Beatles Technicolor masterpiece, *Sgt. Pepper,* released in June), featuring sin and redemption, as well as "All

Along the Watchtower," which would become his favorite song to play live. Right now, though, he wasn't about to play them anywhere. (Two years later, instead of appearing at the Woodstock Festival, Dylan and family fled to the Isle of Wight, where he debuted "I Pity the Poor Immigrant," "I Dreamed I Saw St. Augustine," and "I'll Be Your Baby Tonight.")

Although he may still have seen himself as the ultimate honest outlaw, Dylan was bent on telling off all the businessmen in his life, probably aiming at one in particular, although he wouldn't admit it to the press. Moreover, in the Bible he had found a supply of characters and themes even more inexhaustible than those found among the Child Ballads, and just as much in the public domain.

Aside from the little joke on the last line, replacing a baby's bottle with a bottle of wine (the only touch of humor on the album), most devout believers found "I'll Be Your Baby Tonight" hard to take (not least Dylan's decision to rhyme "moon" and "June," a pop cliché out of fashion since the '40s). It was so un-Dylan-like; worse, it was just plain uninteresting. At least the other sermons on the album gave you something to puzzle over at the local opium den.

And yet, outside in the world, it was the Summer of Love, so why shouldn't Bob Dylan get his share? Two months before he got on a train bound for Nashville with his Bible and his guitar, San Francisco's Grace Slick was imploring her followers to find "Somebody to Love." The Beatles were at the top of the charts with their defining anthem, "All You Need Is Love." But whereas the Beatles' vision of love was more of the universal, guru-inspired type, and the Jefferson Airplane version was something of a call to recreational promiscuity, the kind of love Bob Dylan was espousing seemed fairly retrogressive for the era, a mindless and chauvinistic love that last existed in the aforementioned '40s (in song, at least), where the ideal woman was perpetually barefoot and pregnant (which, in the case of the Dylans, seemed all too accurate). Worse than the retrogressive country-music style the songs employed, it was their message that troubled Dylan fans the most. They could tolerate his biblical harangues; that had been part of his agenda since the beginning. It was the Disney version of picket fences and pink houses that was truly disturbing.

Dylan was also vocal in his criticism of the Beatles' magnum opus, claiming it was a waste of studio time, an implied gluttony, while the lifestyle of choice was his alone, solemn and severe. But maybe that was the sin of pride resurfacing in the man, or his good old standby, wrath, a belated flashback in response to Lennon claiming he didn't care for "4th Time Around" when

Dylan played it for him in a London hotel room in 1966. Besides, this was about the time Lennon was claiming the Beatles were bigger than Jesus Christ. Dylan, deeply into the Bible now, was surely not about to let that pass.

So maybe those two songs were an aberration. After all, "I'll Be Your Baby Tonight" and "Down Along the Cove" were the last things he did for the album, written in the studio just to take advantage of Pete Drake's pedal-steel guitar. True, they would have both been tossed into the trash had they been written by or for Willie Nelson or Waylon Jennings or Tom T. Hall or Ray Price or Joe South or Dolly Parton, or Johnny Cash. Maybe one day, when he was more fully recovered and finally had enough of playing around with his buddies or the kids or the dog or his wife, he'd return to those hostile harangues that made him so lovable, moralizing at all the Godless hopheads storming his castle walls, or gleefully giving us his masterpiece, an indelible portrait of the late sixties slouching toward Bethlehem as only Bob Dylan could paint it.

Lotsa luck.

John Wesley Harding did very well, considering there were no singles on the album and Dylan did virtually nothing to promote it. His only public appearance was at the memorial honoring Woody Guthrie in the fall of '67. As *Sgt. Pepper* was all over FM radio and the Summer of Love was seducing the media, Dylan was in the basement, doing his best to recapture the Depression era in his living room, and at the cottage just down the road.

The Basement Tapes

Research by several biographers has revealed the creative, career, and spiritual crises the accident as well as Dylan's marriage to Sara Lownds eventually precipitated. After both of these cataclysmic events, he was indeed a changed man. (What else was new?) He probably weaned himself off the hard drugs he'd used to sustain his superhuman momentum through '66, at the cost of certain synapses shutting down, the doors of perception closing on that wild word-slinging epoch. Instead, he lounged around the house, playing acoustic guitar, reading the Bible, nitpicking his contracts with Grossman, and bouncing his toddler on his knee. Soon there would be another newborn. And another. And another. Anna arrived in '67, Samuel in '68, Jakob in '69. He also adopted Maria, Sara's daughter from her short-lived first marriage, during this period.

At the end of that searing decade, with Bobby Kennedy and Martin Luther King in the ground, and the alternate culture's sworn enemy,

Richard Nixon, ensconced in the White House, the war in Vietnam spreading like a California brush fire, rock stars getting busted every other week, Dylan presided over a brood of kids who called him "Pa": eight, four, two and a half, one and a half, and a newborn. He buried his father for real in 1968 and went to his high-school reunion in 1969, where someone picked a fight with him. No wonder he couldn't concentrate. The death of Abe Zimmerman must have hit him harder than he expected, Bob having shut the man out of his life for so long. In Abe's basement, he was probably stunned to discover that his father had followed his prodigal son's career, with scrapbooks and posters and album jackets pasted to the wall. Now it was too late to make amends. He couldn't even muster up a song about his father during the rest of 1968. In fact, bedeviled more than ever by his carelessness at signing away half his publishing rights to Grossman, it was a wonder he could create at all. Of course, creating was all he did—kids and songs—during that fruitful time of salvation, courtesy of Sara.

If Albert Grossman was Dylan's father figure defiled, and Abe was dead at fifty-six, following Dylan's childhood hero, Woody Guthrie, now Dylan was the only father he had left. His mother, Beatty, came to live with them in Woodstock after Abe's death, completing the family circle he'd known when his grandmother moved in with the family in Hibbing. No wonder he needed a place to escape. For a while he found it in painting, but that must have seemed too much like early retirement, white shoes, golf, dinners at 4:00 p.m. The Hawks were still on retainer, and much fun could be had fooling around with the tape recorder on songs no one else would ever hear. When Columbia or Grossman came calling for the tapes, Dylan claimed none of the songs were good or finished or both. The titles tell a tale: "Nothing Was Delivered," "Too Much of Nothing," "Tears of Rage," "I Shall Be Released," and the ever-elusive "I'm Not There." Was he withholding them from Grossman's clutches, or Columbia's clutches, for a reason, perhaps willing to wait until his contracts could be redone?

Freed from record-company deadlines and the worldly concerns of his citified compatriots, Dylan was now very much a country squire, almost Amish or Hassidic in his approach to life, into his wife's home cooking and the Bible. The members of the Hawks were the closest Dylan would come to having foxhole buddies, so he welcomed them into his home and hearth, found them lodgings nearby, and began to develop a comfortable routine, as much to garner them an eventual record deal as to give himself something to do.

For a while they played for the sheer joy of playing, with Dylan happily revisiting the past. Not necessarily the past represented by Harry Smith's *Anthology of Folk Music*, as some have suggested, but a more recent past just before the crimson flames of celebrity started burning up his traditional roadmap. He revisited his roots through songs by the man he opened for on his first paid gig at Folk City, John Lee Hooker ("Tupelo," "I'm in the Mood"), as well as his early folk champions, Pete Seeger ("Bells of Rhymney") and Judy Collins ("Bonnie Ship the Diamond"); his Greenwich Village pal Tim Hardin ("If I Were a Carpenter"); his Cambridge *compadres* Eric Von Schmidt ("Joshua Gone Barbados") and good old Joan Baez ("Wildwood Flower"); and his new friend Johnny Cash ("Folsom Prison Blues"). Mostly he came to a new appreciation for a couple of his dearest friends, the Canadian couple Ian Tyson and Sylvia Fricker. No less than nine songs from their early '60s albums were among the gems he polished with his hired hands, including "Spanish Is the Loving Tongue," "A Satisfied Mind," "Royal Canal (the Auld Triangle)," "Big River," "French Girl," "Song for Canada," "Poor Lazarus," "Big River," "Come All Ye Fair and Tender Ladies," and "Four Strong Winds."

At times, he went even further back: back to his rock 'n' roll roots in the '50s ("Mr. Blue" by the Fleetwoods, "Silhouettes" by the Rays, "All American Boy" by Bill Parsons, aka Bobby Bare). And, of course, to Elvis Presley ("I Forgot to Remember to Forget," "A Fool Such as I"). As he did in Minneapolis, when Bonnie Beecher or Tony Glover manned the tape recorder instead of Garth Hudson, he played these songs with no expectations. Or, rather, expectations entirely untainted by the reality of achieving them.

While the Beatles and the Stones were presiding over the failing American revolution, Dylan stood apart, like Kerouac, defending his house, his family, and his dog against a rising tide of rabid druggies. His relationship with his last surrogate father, Grossman, on the rocks, he began to stockpile songs as well as wine and canned goods against the coming apocalypse. Revisiting a former self locked in a tiny Witmark studio, making demos, the songs he wrote were primarily for his friends: the Byrds ("You Ain't Goin' Nowhere," "Nothing Was Delivered"); Peter, Paul and Mary ("Too Much of Nothing"); Ian and Sylvia ("Quinn the Eskimo"); and the Band ("Tears of Rage," "This Wheel's on Fire," "I Shall Be Released").

The rest he always claimed he wrote for his own amusement, and perhaps for the pleasure of annoying or outlasting his copublisher, Grossman. Critics, the public, and other artists may have found favor and even deep significance in sometimes not-quite-finished songs like "Million Dollar Bash," "Yea! Heavy and a Bottle of Bread," "Please Mrs. Henry," "Don't You Tell Henry," "Acapulco," "The King of France," "Minstrel Boy," "Crash on the Levee (Down in the Flood)," "Lo and Behold," and the near legendary "Sign on the Cross" and "I'm Not There," but Dylan always held fast to the contention that these were never songs he seriously considered among his best, or even among the contenders for his next album.

However, as we know by now from examining the man's outtakes, his assessment of his own material has often been wrong.

Nashville Skyline

Early in '69, Dylan got the chance to compose something for the movie *Midnight Cowboy*. Inspired by the final two country numbers on *John Wesley Harding*, he wrote the harmless ditty "Lay Lady Lay," which Columbia president Clive Davis must have thought was the second coming of "Hey Good Lookin'." But he delivered the song too late for it to be seriously considered, and instead the slot went to his old Village benefactor Fred Neil, whose "Everybody's Talkin'," as sung by Harry Nilsson, was a much more suitable choice anyway, and won an Academy Award.

Still unconvinced of the song's merits, Dylan offered it to the Everly Brothers, but they turned it down. As Phil Everly confessed to me, "It was the stupidest thing I've ever done. Bob came backstage when Don and I were at the Bitter End in New York and I asked him if he had any songs. He showed us one, but he sang so soft, swallowing his words, that I couldn't quite glom the lyrics. It sounded to me like he was singing, '*Lay lady lay / Lay across my big breasts, babe.*' So when he got finished, I said, 'Bob, I don't think we can get away with that.' And we didn't take the song."

"Lay Lady Lay" went on to become Dylan's last Top 10 hit, peaking at No. 7, even if the Nashville regulars who played on it saw it more as folk than country. The *Nashville Skyline* album itself outstripped anything Columbia Records could have predicted, as far as sales were concerned. Who exactly bought the album remains a marketing mystery. Country music fans? Dylan's old-guard folk fans? The electric rock hordes of 1965? Thirteen-year-old Amish girls? Or perhaps hate-buying was already in effect among a Dylan audience ready to grab whatever he put out just to vilify it. Or maybe Paul Nelson bought them all to present them as a gift to Jon Pankake.

"One day the lights went out," Dylan once said, trying to explain to interviewer Jonathan Cott in the November 16, 1978, issue of *Rolling Stone* how he came to have creative "amnesia" around the turn of the decade. "It took me a long time to get to do consciously what I used to be able to do unconsciously."

Judging from the songs he was producing in the basement with the Hawks at this time, the "amnesia" must have started soon after they packed up their money and picked up their tent in February of 1968, to record their own album as the Band, *Music from Big Pink*, taking three of his best songs of the period with them: "Tears of Rage," cowritten with Rick Danko; "This Wheel's on Fire," cowritten with Richard Manuel; and "I Shall Be Released."

If anything, the basement material was unconscious in the best sense of the word, like a basketball player en route to a thirty-five-point night. It was also unmixed, unmonitored, unmoored, uncensored, spontaneous, free-form, and free-flowing. The material on *John Wesley Harding* was a good deal more buttoned-up, almost ancient in its preoccupations, like a pilgrim at the first Thanksgiving. Although accompanied by such Nashville notables as Pete Drake on pedal steel, Norman Blake on dobro, Charlie McCoy on guitar, and Charlie Daniels on guitar and bass, the songs Bob Dylan contributed to *Nashville Skyline* in February of 1969, just a month after Elvis Presley reappeared in Memphis for the first time since his Sun Records days, to begin recording his comeback album, were lighter still—so light they were virtually weightless, the lightweight songs of the former heavyweight champ, pummeled into an extended state of amnesia by "too much of nothing." With lines like "Love makes the world go 'round" and "You can have your cake and eat it too," they were hardly more believable as country-music parodies or winking homages.

This simple-minded album, delivered in a brain-dead country voice, only seemed to confirm the worst of the suspicions harbored by the rock press that Dylan was, in reality, a vegetable now. A variant on the "vegetable theory" was that Dylan was following in the footsteps of another noted cultural contrarian, J. D. Salinger, opting out of the chase at the height of his mystique. Perhaps he'd developed such a disdain for his audience, the vaunted "counterculture," during his arduous touring experience, followed by his horrifying stint as a Woodstock landowner, that he no longer wanted to satisfy their unquenchable needs. The theory that he was withholding his best stuff not from his audience but from his manager, Albert Grossman, preferring to wait until his publishing contract expired, could not be discounted either.

Or maybe, just as he'd followed Woody Guthrie into folk music, now it was his buddy Johnny Cash leading him astray into the fields of country music, a form he had yet to master. Even Dylan's favorite clients, the Byrds, were exploring this terrain in *Sweetheart of the Rodeo*, released six months before *Nashville Skyline*, with songs like "Hickory Wind" and *Big Pink* Dylan covers like "You Ain't Going Nowhere" and "Nothing Was Delivered." A month after *Skyline*'s release, the Byrds came out with "Drug Store Truck Drivin' Man" and "Old Blue" on *Dr. Byrds and Mr. Hyde*, and then "Jesus Is Just Alright," followed by the elegiac theme for *Easy Rider* (written by McGuinn and Dylan), which came out in July, with the Band's "The Weight" featured alongside it on the soundtrack.

Ironically, *Nashville Skyline* garnered praise from none other than Paul Nelson—which he would retract at a much later date. That summer, aided by Dylan's unsmiling appearance on Johnny Cash's TV show on June 6 alongside another notoriously publicity-shy songwriter, Joni Mitchell, it produced the third biggest hit single of his career in "Lay Lady Lay," certainly a victory for the anti-rock forces who still listened to the reactionary playlists of AM radio. The turn to country music by some of rock's elite may have reflected a widespread disenchantment with the drift of all events countercultural in the face of the many tragedies of 1968, including the assassinations of progressive leaders like Martin Luther King in April and Bobby Kennedy in August.

Later that month, the extent of the troubles was revealed on the streets of Chicago, where the self-destruction of the peace movement in front of the eyes of the world led to the election of Richard M. Nixon. The man whose defeat at the hands of JFK arguably gave us the wild mood swings of the sixties in the first place had come back from the living dead to ring the curtain down on the alternate culture. If the anxious rock constituency was waiting for a statement from its former leader concerning this absurd irony, his unconsciousness was hard to tolerate yet easy to fathom. For a man still on the run from rousing the rabble, whose lyrics inspired the naming of the most virulent faction of the left (the Weathermen), amnesia was probably a natural defense, his brain trying to erase nearly everything that happened to him before the accident.

In the face of his ongoing feud with the immigrant landlords who controlled his music and the plowmen who trespassed on his sacred turf, Dylan may have been willing to alienate them all, as he'd done many times before, just to gain a measure of space for himself and his family, as if there could be such a thing for the most famous man in America. What other reason could there be for him to exclude from *Nashville Skyline* some of the wonderful songs he'd written in the basement and tossed away to other people, even some of the quirky stuff he was writing during the same period of time, like "Wanted Man" and "Champaign, Illinois" and "I'd Have You Anytime," which wound up in the repertoires of Johnny Cash, Carl Perkins, and George Harrison, respectively?

In that case, these poor choices could have been the product of conscious calculation rather than "amnesia."

20

A Poet with a Beat

Dylan on Songwriting

Despite his often-contentious relationship to the press in general, and specifically the interview format, over the years Bob Dylan has let his guard down often enough in public to offer a fairly cogent self-portrait of his writing process. Here are some of his most memorable pearls of wisdom on his chosen craft and art.

"I wrote 'A Hard Rain's a-Gonna Fall' when I didn't know how many other songs I could write. I wanted to get the most down that I knew about into one song. It wasn't about atomic rain. I just meant some sort of end that's bound to happen."
—Studs Terkel, radio interview, April 26, 1963

"Anybody that's got a message is going to learn from experience that they can't put it into a song. After one or two of these unsuccessful attempts, one realizes his resultant message, which is not even the same message he began with, he's now got to stick by it."
—Nat Hentoff, Playboy, *February 1966*

"It used to be if I would sing, I would get a verse and wait for it to come out as the music was there, and sure enough something would come out, but in the end I would be deluded in those songs."
—John Cohen, Sing Out!, *October/November 1968*

"I still write songs the way I always did. I get a first line, the words and the tune together, and then I work out the rest wherever I happen to be, whenever I have the time. If it's really important I'll just make the time to finish it."
—John Rockwell, New York Times, *January 8, 1974*

"I write fast. The inspiration doesn't last. Writing a song can drive you crazy. My head is so crammed full of things I tend to lose a lot of what I think are my best songs. I don't carry around a tape recorder."   —*Jim Jerome*, People, *November 10, 1975*

"Almost anything else is easy except writing songs. The hardest part is when the inspiration dies along the way. Then you spend all your time trying to recapture it. I don't write every day. I'd like to but I can't."   —*Neil Hickey*, TV Guide, *September 11, 1976*

"When you're playing music and it's going well, you lose your identity, you become totally subservient to the music. It's dangerous, because its effect is that you believe that you can transcend and cope with anything. But later on, backstage, you have a different point of view."   —*Ron Rosenbaum*, Playboy, *March 1978*

"When I look back on my albums, for me they're just measuring points for wherever I was at a certain time. I went into the studio, recorded the songs as good as I could, and left. I want to play for the people, not make records that may sound really good."
—*Lynn Allen*, Trouser Press, *December 12, 1978*

"I don't know where these songs come from. Sometimes I'm thinking in some other age that I lived through I must have had the experience of all these songs because sometimes I don't know what I'm writing about until years later when it becomes clear to me."
—*Karen Hughes*, Rock Express #4, *April 1978*

"If I wrote a song like 'Masters of War' now, I wouldn't feel I'd have to write another one for two weeks. There's still things I want to write about but the process is harder. The old records I used to make, by the time they came out I wouldn't even want them released because I was already so far beyond them."
—*Mick Brown*, Sunday Times, *July 1, 1984*

"I began writing because I was singing. Things were changing and a certain song needed to be written. I started writing them because I wanted to sing them. It was nothing I prepared myself for. But I did sing a lot of songs before I wrote any of my own."

—*Scott Cohen*, Spin, *December 1985*

"A lot of times people will take the music out of my lyrics and just read them. That's not fair because the music and the lyrics are pretty closely wrapped up. A lot of time the meaning is more in the way a line is sung, not just the line."

—*Toby Creswell*, Rolling Stone Australia, *January 16, 1986*

"The saddest thing is when you get something really good and you put it down for a while and you take it for granted that you'll be able to get back to it with whatever inspired you to do it in the first place. Well, whatever inspired you to do it in the first place is never there anymore."   —*Bill Flanagan*, Written in My Soul, *1986*

"It's not my intention to have love influence my songs, any more than it influences Chuck Berry or Woody Guthrie or Hank Williams. Those are songs from the tree of life. There's no love on the tree of life. Love is on the tree of knowledge, the tree of good and evil."

—*Paul Zollo*, Songtalk, *winter 1991*

"I don't consider myself a songwriter in the sense of Townes Van Zandt or Randy Newman. My songs come out of folk music and early rock and roll. I'm not a meticulous lyricist. I don't write melodies that are clever or catchy. It's all very traditionally documented."

—*Edna Gunderson*, USA Today, *September 28, 1997*

"I'm not about to compare my new work to my old work. It creates a kind of Achilles heel. I mean, you're talking to a person who feels like he's walking around in the ruins of Pompeii all the time. It's amazing to me that I'm still able to do it."

—*Mikal Gilmore*, Rolling Stone, *November 22, 2001*

Working Titles

Though it may not be true for most songwriters, in many cases, a song's title is often the last thing on Bob Dylan's mind when he works on it, especially a song that's only half-finished when he enters the recording studio. For those familiar with his working process, this is a surprisingly large number, since he has been known to prefer the unrelenting pressure of composing lines and choruses and often entire songs on the spot, with the clock ticking and the sidemen playing cards and drinking coffee. In his later years, the luxury of poring over individual sentences (often replacing them with preferable individual sentences lifted from existing works thought to be in the public domain) has been available to him, thus the preponderance of early titles in this collection. Some of these titles seem to be a case of the person entrusted to logging them on the studio sheets simply mishearing Dylan or making the wrong assumption from the lyrics. In other cases, like "Black Dali Rue," "Look at Barry Run," "Alcatraz to the Ninth Power," and "A Long-Haired Mule and a Porcupine Here," the unwritten songs belonging to those titles still tantalize us with their possibilities.

- "Positively 4th Street"—"Black Dali Rue"
- "Lay Lady Lay"—"A Long-Haired Mule and a Porcupine Here"
- "My Back Pages"—"Ancient Memories"
- "She Belongs to Me"—"Dime Store"
- "It Takes a Lot to Laugh"—"Phantom Engineer"
- "Visions of Johanna"—"Freeze Out"
- "She Belongs to Me"—"Worse Than Money"
- "I'll Keep It with Mine"—"Bank Account Blues"
- "Let Me Die in My Footsteps"—"I Will Not Go Down Under the Ground"
- "Ballad of Hollis Brown"—"The Rise and Fall of Hollis Brown"
- "Abandoned Love"—"St. John the Evangelist"
- "Brownsville Girl"—"New Danville Girl"
- "Tomorrow Is a Long Time"—"If Today Were Not a Crooked Highway"
- "Restless Farewell"—"Bob Dylan's Restless Epitaph"
- "Sign on the Window"—"What It's All About"
- "Just Like Tom Thumb's Blues"—"Juarez"
- "Dirge"—"Dirge for Martha"
- "She's Your Lover Now"—"Just a Little Glass of Water"
- "Obviously Five Believers"—"Black Dog Blues"
- "Farewell Angelina"—"Alcatraz to the Ninth Power"
- "Can You Please Crawl out Your Window"—"Look at Barry Run"

- "Talkin' New York"—"New York City Blues"
- "Rock Me Mama"—"Wagon Wheel"
- "The Man in Me"—"A Woman Like You"
- "Simple Twist of Fate"—"4th Street Affair"
- "Solid Rock"—"Hanging onto a Solid Rock"
- "Property of Jesus"—"Heart of Stone"
- "Tight Connection to My Heart"—"Someone's Got a Hold of My Heart"
- "Everything Is Broken"—"Broken Days"
- "Clean Cut Kid"—"Brooklyn Anthem"

Source Material

It's accepted policy for a blues singer or the occasional heavy metal band to dip into the well of public domain for their material and then call it their own. In the realms of folk music, traditional airs abound, mostly dating back to the nineteenth century. But only Bob Dylan has mined such a rich territory of sources for his various tunes, titles, and the odd line or chorus as to draw the attention and often the ire of scholars, musicologists, contemporaries, and disinterested observers. Dating back to his first forays into country music, folk, and blues, which formed the basis of his early repertoire, he often used traditional tunes and arrangements as mere vehicles for his own expression.

"No More Auction Block for Me" gave him his first important song, "Blowin' in the Wind." On his debut album, "Lord Randall" provided the basis for the searing "A Hard Rain's a-Gonna Fall." On his second album, the venerable "Scarborough Fair" morphed into "Girl from the North Country" and "Boots of Spanish Leather." "Bob Dylan's Dream" can be traced back to "Lady Franklin's Lament" and "Masters of War" to "Nottamon Town." On his third album, he continued to utilize this songwriting process, dipping into the Child Ballad "Mary Hamilton" for "The Lonesome Death of Hattie Carroll," the traditional Irish ballad "The Parting Glass" for "Restless Farewell," and the somewhat more contemporary Irish song "The Patriot Game," whose melody comes from the older "The Merry Month of May," for "With God on Our Side."

Criticism of the practice failed to dissuade him from continuing, and in fact he redoubled his efforts to uncover and update forgotten gems, most notably his tribute to the 1857 song "Gentle Nettie Moore" in "Nettie Moore," and "The St. James Infirmary Blues" in "Blind Willie McTell."

Even getting sued or snubbed by certain owners of unique arrangements that he appropriated and then took credit for failed to convince Dylan to abandon the process. As often as not, he celebrated the process in interviews, probably wondering why so few of his contemporaries indulged in it themselves. Certainly none produced the same results.

While a couple of songs, like "Subterranean Homesick Blues" and "Don't Think Twice, It's All Right," may be closely aligned with their sources, "Too Much Monkey Business" and "Who's Gonna Buy You Ribbons When I'm Gone," respectively, more often the connection is oblique and utterly transformed by a genius at work. Later on, he added a bunch of poets to his repertoire of sources, including Robert Burns ("Highlands"), William Blake ("Every Grain of Sand"), Ovid ("Thunder on the Mountain,"), Henry Timrod ("Tweedle Dee and Tweedle Dum"), Arthur Rimbaud ("This Wheel's on Fire"), Jacques Prévert ("The Times They Are a-Changin'"), Allen Ginsberg ("Desolation Row"), Berthold Brecht ("When the Ship Comes In"), and Junichi Saga ("Floater (Too Much to Ask)").

Soon, whatever was on his bedside reading table would be absorbed into the bloodstream of his songs through dreams and re-imaginings, from the short stories of Anton Chekhov ("Shooting Star") to novels by Mark Twain ("Lonesome Day Blues"), Nathanael West ("Day of the Locust"), and F. Scott Fitzgerald ("When I Paint My Masterpiece"), as well as a best-selling book of Christian prophecy, *The Late Great Planet Earth*, by Hal Lindsay ("Slow Train," "Ye Shall Be Changed," and "License to Kill").

During his overtly Christian phase in the late '70s and early '80s, the Bible, in addition to Lindsay, became his main source of inspiration. According to one of the ultimate Dylanologists, Clinton Heylin, a Bible scholar as well as a preeminent musicologist, at least ten books of the Bible directly informed Dylan's songs of the period.

Matthew
- "Gotta Serve Somebody"
- "Gonna Change My Way of Thinking"
- "Do Right to Me Baby (Do unto Others)"
- "Solid Rock"
- "Are You Ready"
- "Under the Red Sky"

Romans
- "Dead Man, Dead Man"
- "When You Gonna Wake Up"

Corinthians
- "Precious Angel"
- "Saved"
- "I Believe in You"
- "Saving Grace"

Genesis
- "Man Gave Names to All the Animals"
- "Pressing On"
- "Spirit on the Water"

Revelation
- "When He Returns"

Jeremiah
- "Covenant Woman"

Ephesians
- "What Can I Do for You?"

John
- "In the Garden"

Psalms
- "Trouble in Mind"

Deuteronomy
- "Ring Them Bells"

In Dylan's more recent output, the influence of his radio show cannot be discounted. He scoured the entire previous century of blues, folk, country, rock, and pop music for magical and mystical connections, leading to songs influenced or inspired by Bukka White ("Po' Boy"), Muddy Waters ("Rollin' and Tumblin'"), Sleepy John Estes ("Someday Baby"), Charlie Patton ("High Water (for Charlie Patton)"), Big Joe Williams ("Workingman's Blues #2"), the Stanley Brothers ("Ain't Talkin'"), Billie Holiday ("Bye and Bye"), and Gene Austin ("Sugar Baby").

Indeed, listening to Bob Dylan these days, whether on the radio (until he retired his show in 2007) or onstage or on record, is like taking a graduate course in the history of the popular song, put through the blender of a master craftsman.

21

I Might Have a Few Songs Left

Dylan's Twenty-Five Best Songs Since (at Least) *Blonde on Blonde*

Much to his dismay, one of the consistent tropes of Bob Dylan's career has been to label the odd stellar song dotting his albums since his '60s heyday as "his best since *Blonde on Blonde*." Ten years later, this would later change to "his best since *Blood on the Tracks*." In either case, what's hardly mentioned is that Dylan has continued to produce high-level songs well into his seventh decade—a monstrous achievement for a popular songwriter, placing him up there with Irving Berlin. (Leonard Cohen and Paul Simon also continued working.) Listed below, in alphabetical order, are the best of these songs, even if some of them were originally outtakes, not deemed ready for mass consumption, at the time the album deadline rolled around.

When it comes to compiling any sort of "best of" list from Bob Dylan's massive body of work, all the usual disclaimers apply. Some minds may differ; there's no accounting for taste, one man's meat is another man's poison, it's a free country, etc. And if any given fan, from the serious to the casual, would have a different list, imagine Dylan's list, in the solace of a privacy he can never have? Or, if empirical evidence is more of a qualifier, consider how Dylan values the list of songs below in performance. Six of these songs he's never played live even once (five if you want to discount his performance of "Abandoned Love" at the Other End on July 3, 1975). Another he played nine times over a two-year span before retiring it in 2001. At the other end of the spectrum, he's played one of these songs almost 750 times, including at least once in 2016. Four others he's played at least 200 times.

But you have to hand it to Dylan, anyway, to be a democratic ruler over his catalog. Of the twenty songs on this list that he's attempted live, he's done eleven of them within the last five and a half years: one in 2011, five in 2012, one in 2013, one in 2014, two in 2015, and one thus far in 2016. "I Shall Be Released" was last performed in 2008, and "You're a Big Girl Now" in 2007, so it wouldn't be out of the question for him to dust off either or both of them one of these years, provided he keeps living and touring until he's at least eighty, which is not out of the question either.

In any case, if the typical fan will want to dispute the appearance of some of these songs on the list, Bob Dylan most certainly would throw out at least a couple. He's on the record as saying he despises all outtakes, and several of these songs never made it onto the album for which they were originally recorded. Luckily for us, "Mississippi" and "Brownsville Girl" were rescued from purgatory to appear on future albums; "Abandoned Love," "Up to Me," and "Blind Willie McTell" never were. And although "Up to Me" was never performed in concert, and the great "She's Your Lover Now" was never finished, Dylan has at least acceded to critical and audience pressure to make the mournful and elegiac "Blind Willie McTell" a regular part of his set.

For the purposes of this discussion, we can also excuse Dylan for putting the lengthy and complex "Highlands" into mothballs so quickly. Even a song as delightfully twisted as "Brownsville Girl" he could only get up for once, and according to reports he forgot many of the words. And from his productive Wilbury period, which he's rarely dipped into onstage—either out of respect for the others or because he'd prefect to block it out—the epic "Tweeter and the Monkey Man" certainly deserved a better fate.

There are three songs here from Dylan's Basement Period—which was more like a Garage Period, even if Dylan may have thought of it as a Garbage Period—that he donated to the Band and the Byrds for their albums. But he put "When I Paint My Masterpiece," "You Ain't Goin' Nowhere," and "I Shall Be Released" on his *Greatest Hits, Vol. 2* album and continued to perform them, although the final revised lyrics for "Masterpiece" may still be undetermined. A couple of other gems emerged from his Woodstock residency, too: "This Wheel's on Fire," which found his favor on the road, and his ultimate restless farewell, "Sign on the Window," which absolutely did not. And though he may or may not have written his personal masterpiece, he did write an Oscar-winning masterpiece, "Things Have Changed," for the similarly brooding movie *Wonder Boys*.

Of all the great songs from *Blood on the Tracks*, I've chosen "Shelter from the Storm" and "You're a Big Girl Now," because of how closely and nakedly they adhere to real life (even more so than "Tangled Up in Blue"), although the very similar "Up to Me" is also about as revealing as Dylan gets, and a lot more fun than most of his songs that made the album. While Dylan has gone out of his way to deny the autobiographical elements in that album, when he provides us with the image of the girl in "Shelter from the Storm" giving him a "lethal dose" of salvation, and the girl in "You're a Big Girl Now" sending a corkscrew up his heart, you know he's telling a bitter truth, whether he meant to or not.

I'd say my most offbeat choice here is the melancholy "Nettie Moore," which certainly fits well with his late troubadour period. Like the rousing "Mississippi," the roots of this song are in the Deep South. Like the mournful "Dark Eyes," it could have been written during the Civil War. In "Mississippi," he raids the Alan Lomax songbook for an old slave tune; in "Nettie Moore," he stands at the crossroads of the Southern and the Yellow Dog (railroads), in Moorehead, Mississippi, lamenting fate, as W. C. Handy had before him in 1903, with the ghost of Robert Johnson a mere hundred miles further south, in Jackson.

"Every Grain of Sand" is a song that seems to have come to Dylan fully realized, as if in a dream you usually forget upon awakening. To many, it's his best pure poem, and the most palpable and palatable expression of his religious beliefs. It's also one of his few great songs that he seemed to be able to translate in the studio without wanting to kill either himself or his producer. And yet even this perfect finished song went through a lyrical change from the demo to the album, resulting in Dylan sometimes singing the lyrics from the demo in concert, although since garbled, changed, or forgotten lyrics are part of the typical Bob Dylan live experience, many fans probably didn't even realize it. On the same album, and in a similar theme, "Trying to Get to Heaven" presents Dylan's religious journey in its most sympathetic light.

Several of these songs have made the list due to their being among the best two or three on a given album, Dylan's latter-day quota from the late seventies through the eighties. But the two from *Street-Legal*, the hard-charging "Changing of the Guards" and the dazzling and revealing "Where Are You Tonight (Journey Through Dark Heat)," lead me to believe that album may have been severely underrated. Elsewhere, Dylan had to be convinced by his fans to include "The Groom's Still Waiting at the Altar" on *Shot of Love*, and even then he performed it rarely and dropped it out of his set quickly. The same fate would have met the mystical "Dark Eyes" were it not for another fan, Patti Smith, who caused him to briefly reconsider it.

The blazing "Caribbean Wind" was sadly left to molder until the *Biograph* set came along.

Of the five songs included from his late-innings renaissance of the last twenty years, some may be indifferent ("Things Have Changed"), some may be bleak ("Nettie Moore"), and some may be more accepting ("Mississippi," "Highlands"). "Not Dark Yet," which kicked off the renaissance in 1997, with Dylan in his mid-fifties, still sums them all up with age-appropriate wistfulness.

Playlist

- "Abandoned Love," *Biograph*
- "Blind Willie McTell," *The Bootleg Series Vol. 1–3: (Rare and Unreleased) 1961–1991*
- "Brownsville Girl," *Knocked Out Loaded*
- "Caribbean Wind," *Biograph*
- "Changing of the Guards," *Street-Legal*
- "Dark Eyes," *Empire Burlesque*
- "Every Grain of Sand," *Shot of Love*
- "The Groom's Still Waiting at the Altar," *Shot of Love*
- "Highlands," *Time Out of Mind*
- "I Shall Be Released," *Bob Dylan's Greatest Hits, Vol. 2*
- "Mississippi," *Love and Theft*
- "Nettie Moore," *Modern Times*
- "Not Dark Yet," *Time Out of Mind*
- "Shelter from the Storm," *Blood on the Tracks*
- "She's Your Lover Now," *The Bootleg Series 1–3: (Rare and Unreleased) 1961–1991*
- "Sign on the Window," *New Morning*
- "Things Have Changed," *The Essential Bob Dylan*
- "This Wheel's on Fire," *The Basement Tapes*
- "Trying to Get to Heaven," *Shot of Love*
- "Tweeter and the Monkey Man," *The Traveling Wilburys*
- "Up to Me," *Biograph*
- "When I Paint My Masterpiece," *Bob Dylan's Greatest Hits, Vol. 2*
- "Where Are You Tonight (Journey Through Dark Heat)," *Street-Legal*
- "You Ain't Goin' Nowhere," *Bob Dylan's Greatest Hits, Vol. 2*
- "You're a Big Girl Now," *Blood on the Tracks*

22

A Troubled Mind

Deconstructing Dylan's Major Themes

It's common knowledge that Bob Dylan has always had a problematic relationship with his albums. At times he's gone so far as to say that, without contractual obligations, he might not record at all. Other times he's stressed that he writes songs and records albums only to give himself something new to play on the road.

Some of this is a pose he puts on for the press, a strange kind of reverse modesty from a man who's created and recorded some of the most influential albums and songs in rock history. But in real life, he has expressed much the same feelings to friends. He's also suggested that the songs contained on his recorded albums—many of them thrown together or finished off in the studio—are really no more than blueprints to be developed, rearranged, and often rewritten on the spur of the moment onstage, in a dank hotel, or sitting in the back of his tour bus.

Those who complain that in a typical Bob Dylan concert he is prone to mangle some of his greatest hits beyond recognition, miss the point. To Dylan, the album versions of these songs are little more than place-markers meant to indicate a stolen moment in time, never to be duplicated. It's just as likely that a given song is the harried four-in-the-morning choice out of sixteen previous similar takes, recorded over the course of three chaotic sessions (and, to connoisseurs, always the wrong one).

Given this penchant for the destructive deconstruction of his catalog, there needs to be a way to put Bob Dylan's prodigious output of magnificent songs into a perspective outside of the norm of singles, albums, and concert performances. The following six playlists, covering nearly a hundred songs, are meant to capture the essence of Dylan's massive catalog by putting them in the context of his most familiar themes.

This approach may fly in the face of Dylan enthusiasts who prefer returning from an album or a concert in a state of utter frustration. It may fly in the face of professional Dylan-compilation producers who are advised to adhere

During a time of low inspiration, Dylan turned to his old Greenwich Village friends Ian Tyson and Sylvia Fricker for pleasure.   *Diana Davies, courtesy of the Ralph Rinzler Folklife Archives and Collections, Smithsonian Institution*

to strict chronological boundaries when putting together their packages. It may certainly fly in the face of Dylan himself, who would never consciously agree to be pigeonholed, and who would do everything he could to deny whatever category in which a given song was placed.

"'Like a Rolling Stone?'" I can hear him saying. "That was actually my first children's song."

Anti-Love Songs

Bob Dylan was typecast early as a "protest" singer. But by far the kind of protest that resonated most deeply with his audience of disaffected young men (and the girls who tried to love them) was that contained within his catalog of anti-love songs. More than any of his other early works, these songs shaped the attitude of a generation seeking to break free of the traditions of love and marriage held most dearly by their parents, as well as the

Tin Pan Alley–based traditions of respectable behavior into which rock 'n' roll had fallen by 1961. While "Don't Think Twice, It's All Right" is a bit more cynical than your typical anthem of unrequited love, and the later "I Don't Believe You (She Acts Like We Never Have Met)" a bit too droll to take seriously, it was "It Ain't Me Babe" that really broke the mold, with its chorus of "no, no, no" a direct threat to the complacent and compliant "yeah, yeah, yeah" offered by the Beatles in "She Loves You."

By the time the excoriating "Like a Rolling Stone" came along to put a stamp on Dylan's brand of personal freedom of expression (which today might be called "verbal abuse"), he'd already torn himself and his previous lover to shreds in "Ballad in Plain D" and "It's All Over Now, Baby Blue." The sadly abandoned "She's Your Lover Now" might have been the self-righteously wrathful follow-up to "Like a Rolling Stone" he'd been searching for. But he had to settle for "One of Us Must Know (Sooner or Later)," which was pretty dire in its own right. Often mistaken for love ballads, "She Belongs to Me" and "Just Like a Woman" are far too wickedly sarcastic (the former) and condescending (the latter) to ever be sung on bended knee.

If you thought Dylan might mellow with age, then you weren't following his life or his work too closely. In 1974, *Blood on the Tracks* offered the songwriter in the throes of extreme pain and suffering. Just listen to the word "oohh" on "You're a Big Girl Now," or to the entirely of any of the several existing takes of "Idiot Wind." Although cloaked in admiration for his domestic keeper (aka his wife), "Shelter from the Storm" sums up his imprisoned mood during his marriage on far gentler terms than the intemperate "Dirge."

Divorced for a second time, by 1997 Dylan was still speaking for the generation he taught the new rules of romantic (dis)engagement. Perfectly summing up the ambivalence of a life lived on the razor's edge of domesticity and desire, he introduced "Love Sick" in a commercial for the ladies' lingerie line Victoria's Secret.

Playlist

- "Don't Think Twice, It's All Right," *The Freewheelin' Bob Dylan*
- "It Ain't Me Babe," *Another Side of Bob Dylan*
- "I Don't Believe You (She Acts Like We Never Have Met)," *Another Side of Bob Dylan*
- "Ballad in Plain D," *Another Side of Bob Dylan*
- "It's All Over Now, Baby Blue," *Bringing It All Back Home*

- "She Belongs to Me," *Bringing It All Back Home*
- "Like a Rolling Stone," *Highway 61 Revisited*
- "She's Your Lover Now," *The Bootleg Series 1–3: (Rare and Unreleased) 1961–1991*
- "Sooner or Later (One of Us Must Know)," *Blonde on Blonde*
- "Just Like a Woman," *Blonde on Blonde*
- "Most Likely You Go Your Way (And I'll Go Mine)," *Blonde on Blonde*
- "You're a Big Girl Now," *Blood on the Tracks*
- "Shelter from the Storm," *Blood on the Tracks*
- "Idiot Wind," *Blood on the Tracks*
- "Dirge," *Planet Waves*
- "Love Sick," *Time Out of Mind*

City Songs

As a further way of denying he was ever in the business of writing "protest" songs, Dylan claimed the output of his coming of age in Greenwich Village instead comprised "city songs." They were words and chords he unconsciously absorbed while walking down West 4th Street toward Sheridan Square for a hotdog and a chocolate egg cream. If not, they were valentines to his first city girlfriend, Suze, who was much more attuned to the news of the day and the atrocities of the moment; songs written for her approval.

"Talkin' New York" is certainly based on his experiences arriving in the Big Apple with nothing but his guitar, his cap, and his Woody Guthrie fixation. "Let Me Die in My Footsteps (I Will Not Go Down Under the Ground)," an early classic, may have been tailor-made for publication in the folk magazine *Broadside*, but that couldn't take away from the obvious passion behind his feelings about bomb shelters and a life lived out in the open. "Blowin' in the Wind" did emerge from the frenzy of songs and songwriters he'd stumbled into at Folk City and the Gaslight—a group he'd later repudiate in "Positively 4th Street," which also could have been about 4th Street in Dinkytown. One of his saddest city songs is "Boots of Spanish Leather," written as his dream of a life with Suze was crashing against the reefs of reality during her prolonged stay in Italy. If "The Times They Are a-Changin'" seemed to be another written-to-order anthem, its writer would do some serious rethinking of the whole process after the Kennedy assassination, resulting in "My Back Pages." His later city songs, typified by the surreal masterpiece "Visions of Johanna" and the cutting gem "Leopard-Skin Pill-Box Hat," would reflect a different Bob Dylan as celebrity sightings of him alongside Allen Ginsberg and Edie Sedgwick would begin to prepare him for taking on the world past 4th Street—a world he acknowledges in the last of these songs, the optimistic "Up to Me," and the more pessimistic "Abandoned Love," sung once at the Other End in Greenwich Village before an audience he was getting ready to once again abandon for the lure of the road and the sound of rolling thunder.

Playlist

- "Talkin' New York," *Bob Dylan*
- "Let Me Die in My Footsteps," *The Bootleg Series Vol. 9: The Witmark Demos: 1962–1964*
- "Blowin' in the Wind," *The Freewheelin' Bob Dylan*
- "Masters of War," *The Freewheelin' Bob Dylan*
- "The Times They Are a-Changin'," *The Times They Are a-Changin'*
- "Boots of Spanish Leather," *The Times They Are a-Changin'*
- "Can You Please Crawl out Your Window," *Biograph*
- "My Back Pages," *Another Side of Bob Dylan*
- "Spanish Harlem Incident," *Another Side of Bob Dylan*
- "Subterranean Homesick Blues," *Bringing It All Back Home*
- "Just Like Tom Thumb's Blues," *Highway 61 Revisited*
- "It Takes a Lot to Laugh, It Takes a Train to Cry," *Highway 61 Revisited*
- "Positively 4th Street," (non-album single)
- "Leopard-Skin Pill-Box Hat," *Blonde on Blonde*
- "Visions of Johanna," *Blonde on Blonde*
- "Stuck Inside of Mobile with the Memphis Blues Again," *Blonde on Blonde*
- "Up to Me," *Biograph*
- "Abandoned Love," *Biograph*

Real People

Some of Bob Dylan's most controversial songs are those about real people, ripped from the headlines (probably by Suze). If "Song to Woody" was a true homage, based on a beloved Woody Guthrie tune, by the time he got around to writing "The Lonesome Death of Hattie Carroll," about an unfortunate black woman who died of a heart attack after being struck by a privileged white man, the needs of his narratives were beginning to displace an absolute loyalty to the rigors of good journalism.

To fill the "new material" void, Columbia Records recapped Dylan's first decade.

(In a few years, the rigors of good journalism would themselves come under attack by a number of newspaper and magazine writers, including Tom Wolfe and Hunter S. Thompson, who would become major characters in their own stories, ushering in a brief heyday of creativity in this restrictive genre. But Dylan's songs were hardly a forerunner of New Journalism; they were further evidence of his rather problematic relationship to the truth. Probably the same problematic relationship that has caused him, over the years and in many subsequent interviews, to insist that there was a real "Mr. Tambourine Man" upon which that famous song was based, citing none other than Bruce Langhorne, the noted session guitarist, who also apparently owned a magnificent tambourine.)

"Hattie Carroll," based on a cursory reading of a news story riddled with even more factual lapses than Dylan's song, worked far better as a narrative than it did as journalism, eventually leading Dylan to reconsider his attraction to the genre—but not before committing "Hurricane" to publication in 1974. Based on the life and crimes of Rubin "Hurricane" Carter, his slanderous original lyrics had to be rewritten at the suggestion of lawyers. Even so, one Penny Valentine, who appears by name in the song, wound up suing him for defamation of character. The suit was eventually thrown out of court.

Definitely attracted to outlaws, Dylan preceded that song with "George Jackson" in 1971, about a particularly violent member of the Black Panther party who was shot to death by prison guards at San Quentin while trying to escape (a fact not revealed in the song). Thankfully burdened with few real details, the George Jackson of "George Jackson" was, according to Dylan, being held in prison for a seventy-dollar robbery (a charge for which he'd actually served a year before being imprisoned again). Nowhere in the account is Jackson's murder of a prison guard mentioned.

Preceding that troubling song, Dylan's 1967 portrait of "John Wesley Harding" is similarly devoid of factual veracity, right down to the misspelling of the title character's name. For one thing, Hardin was never a friend to the poor. He was known to have cheated many an honest man. Most of the charges against him were proven, resulting in a lengthy jail sentence. And, finally, he never did take a stand in Chaynee County. He'd never been to Chaynee County. There is no Chaynee County. Dylan himself maintained he eventually got so confused by what he was trying to say in the song that he decided to name the album after it and make it the opening track, although he never performed the song in public.

He also attracted a lot of grief for his overly glamorous portrait of the mobster "Joey" Gallo, a few years later, on *Desire*, which he deflected by claiming the lyrics were written by his collaborator at the time, Jacques Levy. An outlaw of a different sort, Lenny Bruce, suffers from Dylan's criminal abuse of the English language in the song bearing his name. In one verse he places himself in a taxicab with Bruce in a ride that covers a mile and a half but inexplicably "seemed like a couple of months."

This probably explains why Dylan never identified the specific Mr. Jones of "Ballad of a Thin Man," although many have come forward like camels to claim the title. It also may explain his indignation when people assumed the song "Sara" was about his first wife, just because she happened to have the same name as his first wife, and the same astrological sign (Scorpio) as his first wife, and is referred to in the lyric as "mystical wife." And while Blind Willie McTell is prominently name-checked and extolled in the song that bears his name in the title, at least one critic has come forward to claim that Dylan was really referring to another blues singer entirely, one Blind Willie Johnson, whose out-of-print catalog unfortunately failed to receive the same bump as that of McTell.

Finally, Dylan's lengthy John Lennon tribute, "Roll on, John," was only played twice in public, both times within earshot of the subject's birthplace.

Playlist

- "Song to Woody," *Bob Dylan*
- "Who Killed Davey Moore," *The Bootleg Series Vol. 6: Bob Dylan Live 1964: Concert at Philharmonic Hall*
- "The Lonesome Death of Hattie Carroll," *The Times They Are a-Changin'*
- "Ballad of Hollis Brown," *The Times They Are a-Changin'*
- "Mr. Tambourine Man," *Another Side of Bob Dylan*
- "Ballad of a Thin Man," *Blonde on Blonde*
- "John Wesley Harding," *John Wesley Harding*
- "George Jackson," (non-album single)
- "Hurricane," *Desire*
- "Joey," *Desire*
- "Sara," *Desire*
- "Lenny Bruce," *Shot of Love*
- "Blind Willie McTell," *The Bootleg Series Vol. 1–3: (Rare and Unreleased) 1961–1991*
- "Roll on, John," *Tempest*

My Apocalypse or Yours?

Fairly early in his career, Bob Dylan discovered he had a knack for writing long, image-drenched songs about the end of the world. He'd been reading the French poets, smoking pot with the Beat poets, listening to the songs of Berthold Brecht with his girlfriend, and possibly recalling the anarchic rants of his possibly fabricated Village roommate Ray Gooch. When "A Hard Rain's a-Gonna Fall" came pouring out of him during the lead-up to the Cuban Missile Crisis in 1962, it contained enough verses for several songs and enough stark images colliding with each other for several songwriters' careers. On his fourth album, Dylan's apocalypse was more internal, with the early 1964 "Chimes of Freedom" written for "every hung-up person" in a generation whose visions of the future had just been rendered surreal by the events in Dallas, 1963. Dylan carried these surreal visions to impossible extremes during the next few years, with the post-apocalyptic "Gates of Eden" and the all-inclusive "It's Alright, Ma (I'm Only Bleeding)" appearing on the same album.

Barely drawing a breath, he next composed the ultimate surrealist freak show: the eleven-and-a-half-minute "Desolation Row." After he suffered his own apocalypse in Woodstock a year later, where his life may have flashed before his eyes as he slipped off his motorcycle, "All Along the Watchtower" offered a more subdued vision, ironically turned apocalyptic by Jimi Hendrix's guitar-heroic cover.

In later years, Dylan has been no less transfixed by the end. Even if you disregard his "Christian" period (too painful and obvious a playlist to include here), songs like "The Groom's Still Waiting at the Altar," "Changing of the Guards," "Foot of Pride," "Jokerman," and "When the Night Comes Falling from the Sky" should put the fear of God into even the most devout of non-believers. On the other hand, even as he acknowledges that "Everything Is Broken," the blissful and beautiful "Every Grain of Sand" (recorded with his dog nearby) and the "Chimes of Freedom" follow-up "Ring Them Bells" seem to reflect Dylan's final coming to terms with his spiritual vision. As he stumbles toward his eternal reward, Bob Dylan still sees death and destruction all around, invoking blues singer Charley Patton's "High Water Everywhere," in "High Water (for Charley Patton)," a song concerning the great Louisiana flood of 1927, about which Randy Newman has also written eloquently ("Louisiana, 1927").

Playlist

- "A Hard Rain's a-Gonna Fall," *The Freewheelin' Bob Dylan*
- "Chimes of Freedom," *Another Side of Bob Dylan*
- "Gates of Eden," *Bringing It All Back Home*
- "It's Alright, Ma (I'm Only Bleeding)," *Bringing It All Back Home*
- "Desolation Row," *Highway 61 Revisited*
- "All Along the Watchtower," *John Wesley Harding*
- "Foot of Pride," *The Bootleg Series Vol. 1–3: (Rare and Unreleased) 1961–1991*
- "The Groom's Still Waiting at the Altar," *Shot of Love*
- "Every Grain of Sand," *Shot of Love*
- "Changing of the Guards," *Street-Legal*
- "Jokerman," *Infidels*
- "License to Kill," *Infidels*
- "When the Night Comes Falling from the Sky," *Empire Burlesque*

- "Everything Is Broken," *Oh Mercy*
- "Ring Them Bells," *Oh Mercy*
- "High Water (for Charley Patton)," *Love and Theft*

Tall Tales

In the BBC documentary *Getting to Dylan,* Dylan would submit to the interviewer Christopher Sykes that he didn't write story songs. "My songs are more like short-attention-span things that happen in a crowd of people, that go down very quickly so the normal eye wouldn't even notice it," he said. Considering his longstanding attitude toward lying to the press, this statement, as convoluted as it is, is shockingly truthful, even if it seems to describe his drawing style (he was drawing a portrait of the interviewer as he said it) more than his songwriting style. For as far back as when he was singing "Barbara Allen" at the Gaslight in 1962, or even before that at Bonnie Beecher's Minneapolis apartment, he's been drawn to the ballad form, to endless repetitive stanzas describing fantastical occurrences that beguile the audience, transporting them back to a magical time.

While many of his early songs take their structure and melody from seventeenth-century ballads, "Bob Dylan's Dream" (based on "Lady Franklin's Lament") stands out as the one of the first times he attached a contemporary story to the existing framework. Not as fantastical as his later tall tales, Bob Dylan's dream is heavily laden with sentimentality, as he seeks to glamorize his early years in Hibbing, antagonizing the local audiences with his Little Richard imitations. Then again, old friend John Bucklen is on record as claiming his sister's house on Pergilly Road was the place where everyone hung their hats by the old wooden stove before jamming on old folk songs.

After leaving the ballad form aside for half a decade, Dylan returned to it with an old-fashioned Western, about a couple of gamblers, one of them named Judas Priest, a cowboy oath uttered in the 1941 movie *They Died with Their Boots On.* This particular Judas Priest died with his boots by the side of the bed, at the brothel where he briefly found paradise before fatally overdoing it. Almost twenty years later, he returned to the form with the epic "Brownsville Girl," cowritten by Sam Shepard and costarring Dylan and Gregory Peck. This is one eleven-minute song that could easily run for twenty minutes without losing any of its colorful detail, merging the Old West of Peck's *The Gunfighter* with the New West of Dylan and Ruby and the rest of the cast wrangling through the night in a beat up Ford. Another

Western, "Lily, Rosemary, and the Jack of Hearts," suffers by comparison, offering a story that fails to support its length.

"Isis" comes straight out of *Indiana Jones* territory, giving Dylan the chance to wear another hat: that of the action movie hero. Hearing him gleefully shout "Yes!" at the end of a Rolling Thunder performance caught live in Montreal on December 4, 1975, is a particular revelation, coming from the man who was much more famous for declaring "no, no, no" in "It Ain't Me Babe" and elsewhere. He puts the hat on again in "Where Are You Tonight," like the slinky "Isis" and the wicked "Angelina" a mystical tale of love found and lost, in which he's heard to utter the most nakedly honest line of his career, "I can't believe I'm alive." Despite the plethora of detail offered in "Tempest," about the sinking of the Titanic, Dylan's most fully realized dramaturgy can be found in something he tossed off in an afternoon with the guys in the Traveling Wilburys, "Tweeter and the Monkey Man." Multiple Springsteen references notwithstanding, this is a Martin Scorsese film-noir classic waiting to happen.

Playlist

- "Bob Dylan's Dream," *The Freewheelin' Bob Dylan*
- "The Ballad of Frankie Lee and Judas Priest," *John Wesley Harding*
- "Simple Twist of Fate," *Blood on the Tracks*
- "Lily, Rosemary, and the Jack of Hearts," *Blood on the Tracks*
- "Isis," *Desire*
- "Caribbean Wind," *Biograph*
- "Angelina," *The Bootleg Series Vol. 1–3: (Rare and Unreleased) 1961–1991*
- "Señor (Tales of Yankee Power)," *Street-Legal*
- "Where Are You Tonight (Journey Through Dark Heat)," *Street-Legal*
- "Tweeter and the Monkey Man," *The Traveling Willburys, Vol. 1*
- "Brownsville Girl," *Knocked Out Loaded*
- "Tempest," *Tempest*

Don't Shoot the Troubadour

In his later years, Dylan has begun to increasingly resemble his favorite French artist, the actor and singer of morose songs, Charles Aznavour. But Dylan had been partial to the wily wiry Aznavour way back when he was a struggling young poet in Greenwich Village, enamored of the early '60s

Francois Truffaut film *Shoot the Piano Player*, which stars Aznavour as a shy and withdrawn musician recovering from the death of his wife by playing piano at a seedy bar. The description offered by critics of the Aznavour character "hiding from his shattered life while doing the only thing he knows how to do, while remaining unable to escape the past" eerily evokes Dylan at various low points in his personal and professional life, as well as the character he seems to have settled into from the mid-'90s on, desolately plodding an endless road to salvation.

But it was as far back as "Tomorrow Is a Long Time," another song written in the early '60s in response to Suze's absence, that he first revealed his tender, moody side. As an incipient rock star on the rise, hobnobbing with poets and Beatles, it was a side he chose not to feature, calling it "too soft," which may be why he left the song off several albums and performed it rarely. Others didn't see it that way, among them men's men like Rod Stewart and Elvis Presley, who did fine covers. Later on, Dylan himself would come around to it in performance, as life began to wear away his James Dean facade.

Recuperating from his electric bard period in Woodstock with friends and family all around—inescapable—led Dylan into a contemplative state, wondering in "Sign on the Window" if this "must be what it's all about." In the '70s, he considered family again in "Forever Young," mortality in "Knockin' on Heaven's Door," and his legacy in "When I Paint My Masterpiece." After confronting some heavy choices mid-decade, he spent an interlude on the road as his marriage dissolved, eventually finding Jesus Christ at the end of the line at the end of the '70s. Thrashing through the '80s in search of his soul and in search of a sound, he was haunted by the acoustic sound and soul of "Dark Eyes." Though his Christianity was no longer so apparent, inside he was still consumed by "Tryin' to Get to Heaven." Self-loathing and self-doubt permeate *Oh Mercy*, with "What Was It You Wanted" and "What Good Am I" dominating his thoughts.

After a seven-year drought, *Time Out of Mind* solidified that vision, with the staunch "Not Dark Yet" and the doleful "Highlands" casting him as someone determined, like the man he didn't take his name from, Dylan Thomas, to "rage against the dying of the light."

He has continued to plunder the same turf in the new century. While the chance to write "Things Have Changed" for the movie *The Wonder Boys* brought him out of himself, if only slightly, in further works he began to evince an acceptance of his life and career and his partial comeback in "Mississippi," while the semi-darkness of "Not Dark Yet" had "turned black" before his eyes in "Nettie Moore." As late as his 2015–2017 albums of pop standards, *Shadows in the Night, Fallen Angels*, and *Triplicate*, and their accompanying tours, the troubadour was still "hiding from his shattered life while doing the only thing he knows how to do, while remaining unable to escape the past," like an American Aznavour, closing each night in 2015 with a poignant prayer he could have written himself, "Stay with Me," from the 1963 movie *The Cardinal*. In 2016, the first single from *Fallen Angels*, "Melancholy Mood," entered the set in an upfront slot, proceeding to make the dour and stately "Stay with Me" seem in retrospect like a Virginia reel.

Playlist

- "I Shall Be Released," *Bob Dylan's Greatest Hits, Vol. 2*
- "Tomorrow Is a Long Time," *Greatest Hits, Vol. 2*
- "When I Paint My Masterpiece," *Greatest Hits, Vol. 2*
- "Sign on the Window," *New Morning*
- "Forever Young," *Planet Waves*
- "Knockin' on Heaven's Door," *Pat Garrett and Billy the Kid*
- "Dark Eyes," *Empire Burlesque*
- "Tryin' to Get to Heaven," *Shot of Love*
- "What Was It You Wanted," *Oh Mercy*
- "What Good Am I," *Oh Mercy*
- "Not Dark Yet," *Time Out of Mind*
- "Highlands," *Time Out of Mind*
- "Things Have Changed," *The Essential Bob Dylan*
- "Sugar Baby," *Love and Theft*
- "Mississippi," *Love and Theft*
- "Nettie Moore," *Modern Times*
- "Stay with Me," *Shadows in the Night*
- "Melancholy Mood," *Fallen Angels*

23

What Was Delivered

The Writer's Block Albums

Looking in the Mirror, Forty Years Apart: *Self Portrait* and *Another Self Portrait*

Almost as soon as he'd gotten done writing "The Times They Are a-Changin'," and then immediately attempting to disown it, Bob Dylan began to develop a very distinctive relationship with his fans.

They terrified him.

And never more so than when they started to invade his space in Woodstock in 1969, in anticipation of his rumored appearance at the upcoming festival bearing its name. "It was like a wave of insanity breaking loose," he once told *Rolling Stone* magazine. "You'd come in the house and find people there, people coming through the woods at all hours of the day and night. It was as if they were sucking your very blood out. I said, 'Now wait, these people can't be my fans. They just can't be.'"

In hindsight, buying a townhouse on MacDougal Street, in the heart of Greenwich Village, where most of his followers still camped out, may not have been wisest way to ensure invisibility for the man or his family. It was in an effort to get these monkeys off his back, he said, that the idea of *Self Portrait* was born. "I wanted to do something they can't possibly relate to," he continued. "They'll listen and they'll say, 'He ain't sayin' it no more. He ain't giving us what we want.' And they'll go on to somebody else. But the whole idea backfired."

With his fifth kid on the way and his mother in the house, it was all Dylan could do to amuse himself playing other people's songs. If he wasn't an outlaw anymore, or a savior, a hero, or a poet or a hobo or a (Luke the) drifter, at least he could still croon "Blue Moon." In mid-August of 1969, on the first night of the fabled Woodstock Festival, at which it was widely rumored that neighborly Dylan would appear, he was headed off to London with his wife and kids, there to vacation lavishly and jam with the Beatles (*sans* Paul and Ringo) in his suite at Foreland Farm, before giving a lackluster one-hour performance at the Isle of Wight Festival at the end of the month.

Finally, after one too many mornings of arriving home to find hippies in his garden or his living room or his bed, Dylan's view of the Woodstock Nation was somewhere on the dark side of Jack Kerouac's. But moving his family back to New York City in 1969, back to his Greenwich Village proving grounds, was more than a mere foolish romantic gesture. Although it surely *was* foolish and romantic, and perhaps meant to salvage his sanity and save his marriage, it was also meant to light a torch under his dormant creativity by reuniting him with the places and faces that sparked so many nights of musical pleasure and mayhem. But if Dylan wasn't the same as he was in 1965, neither was the Village.

It wasn't only Bob Dylan whose writing suffered during the early years of the reign of Richard Nixon. "The election of Nixon in 1968 was a turning point," Dave Van Ronk told me. "Everyone who was involved in folk music certainly felt it. The whole left-wing wave had passed. Thermidor had arrived." By 1969, the folk wave had peaked and long since crashed out to sea. "A lot of things started to happen," Van Ronk recalled. "The rock 'n' roll revival cut into business. When political protest moved over to rock 'n' roll; I think we lost a lot of our constituency. You had that business around Saint Marks Place—the Fillmore East, the Electric Circus. I think the most important thing was the raising of the rents. Suddenly all those little dustbins on Bleecker and MacDougal started to look like gold mines to the landlords, and they would jack up the rent literally every month. But in a club, there's just so much you can charge for a cup of coffee, especially when the wave you're depending on is petering out anyway."

On the other hand, when the *Self Portrait* album was released, Dylan defended it by saying that history would vindicate his explorations and experiments and new directions. Which in an odd way it did, some forty-four years later, when *Another Self Portrait* emerged. Containing many of the same songs, albeit in different versions, and more tightly produced and sung, the set generally received favorable press, compared to the howls of complaint that greeted its predecessor. But the concept was the same: the noodling troubadour rifling through the Great American Folk songbook, acknowledging his mentors and paying tribute to his friends.

Of the twenty-four songs on the first *Self Portrait*, including two takes of "Little Sadie" and two versions of "Alberta," nine are duplicated on the second *Self Portrait*: "Alberta #3," "In Search of Little Sadie" and "Little Sadie," "Minstrel Boy," "All the Tired Horses," "Wigwam," "Days of 49," "Copper Kettle," and "Belle Isle." In the original *Portrait*, as on *The Basement Tapes*, Dylan recognizes (even if only barely) some of his Greenwich Village cohorts, among them Paul Simon ("The Boxer"), Paul Clayton ("Gotta Travel On"), and Gordon Lightfoot ("Early Morning Rain"). He trots out his love of Elvis ("Blue Moon"), the Everly Brothers ("Let It Be Me," "Take a Message to Mary"), and traditional country music ("I Forgot More Than You'll Ever Know" by the Davis Sisters, "Take Me as I Am (or Let Me Go)" by Ray Price). Similarly, on the sequel, his choice of material reflects his return to Greenwich Village midway through the sessions, with several tunes either written by or associated with Gaslight-era pals, including Tom Paxton ("Annie's Going to Sing Her Song"), Eric Andersen ("Thirsty Boots"), Dave Van Ronk ("I Buyed Me a Little Dog," aka "Tattle O' Day," and "Tell Old Bill," aka "This Evening So Soon"), Jean Ritchie ("Pretty Saro"), Ramblin' Jack Elliott ("Railroad Bill"), and Ian and Sylvia ("Spanish Is the Loving Tongue")—the latter of which is also found on the extended *Basement Tapes*.

A bonus feature, of a sort, on the first *Self Portrait* was the inclusion of three tracks from the notorious Isle of Wight concert Dylan gave in August of 1969, instead of kowtowing to the hordes at Woodstock: "Like a Rolling Stone," "The Mighty Quinn," and "She Belongs to Me." With a road-rusty Dylan having performed in public a grand total of three times since May '66, the concert is not generally regarded as among his finest work. Nonetheless, he debuted eight songs there, including "Highway 61 Revisited" and "Rainy Day Women #12 & 35," and gave his one and only performance of the basement curiosity "Minstrel Boy." This performance of "Highway 61 Revisited," as well as the debut of "I'll Be Your Baby Tonight," eventually appeared forty-four years later on *Another Self Portrait*.

The entire concert is included as a part of the deluxe edition of that latter package, which is otherwise notable mostly for the inclusion of several outtakes from *New Morning*, the album Dylan was recording at the same time: two versions of "Went to See the Gypsy," two versions of "Time Passes Slowly," and alternate takes of "If Dogs Run Free," "New Morning," "Sign on the Window," and "If Not for You." Easily the most revelatory track on the set, considering the songwriter's daily battles with his fans and his muse and his "amnesia," would have been the poignantly self-deprecating "When I Paint My Masterpiece." However, that song had already appeared some forty-three years earlier, on *Greatest Hits, Vol. 2*, released a year after *New Morning* in November 1971.

Released in June of 1970, *Self Portrait* received some of the worst reviews of Dylan's career. Two months before, the entire counterculture had taken a symbolic as well as actual bullet in the chest when four students were shot and killed during an antiwar rally on the campus of Kent State University in Ohio, and "Blue Moon" was his response? No less a Dylan-esque figure than Neil Young had immediately issued a protest song called "Ohio," recorded with his musical brothers David Crosby, Steven Stills, and Graham Nash, while even the less politically inclined were affected. A true believer in the hippie ideal, Peter Tork of the Monkees, called the Kent State shooting "the end of the flower-power era. That was it. You throw your flowers and rocks at us, man, and we'll just pull the guns on you."

Not usually attuned to public criticism of his work, but especially vulnerable during this period of loss, Dylan was back in the studio recording tracks for his next album before the ink was dry on the first negative review of *Self Portrait*. He has always claimed the chronology was coincidental. "I didn't say, 'Oh my God, they don't like this, let me do another,'" he told writer Larry Sloman, in his book *On the Road with Bob Dylan*. "The *Self Portrait* album laid around for a year. We were already working on *New Morning* when *Self Portrait* got put together. Some of that stuff was left over from *Nashville Skyline*."

Columbia's Revenge: *Dylan*

Interestingly, on *Dylan*—released by Columbia in November 1973 during Dylan's brief flirtation with Asylum Records, and widely renounced by the artist himself—the same formula holds true, with Jerry Jeff Walker's Greenwich Village classic "Mr. Bojangles" receiving the cover treatment, as well as Joni Mitchell's "Big Yellow Taxi" and Peter LaFarge's "The Ballad of Ira Hayes." "Spanish Is the Loving Tongue" gets another reprise. There are two nods to Elvis ("Can't Help Falling in Love" and the basement-era "A Fool Such as I").

There are also two traditional songs on *Dylan* that may have stemmed from his very first public recording, at the St. Paul home of one Karen Wallace: "Mary Ann" and "Sarah Jane." However, the quality of these widely bootlegged tracks is so terrible that many have disputed whether it's even Bob Dylan singing. Listed by *Time* magazine as one of his ten worst songs, "Sarah Jane," which clocks in at around thirty seconds on the St. Paul tape, may well have become a different, quite autobiographical song by 1970, when he sang, "I got a wife and five little children" (his fifth child, Jakob, was born in December 1969). Similarly, the Wallace tape was also probably not the source for this version of "Mary Ann," a widely recorded calypso number that had turned up on the 1965 album *Come My Way* by none other than "Miss Lonely" contender Marianne Faithfull.

A (Rude) Awakening: *New Morning*

Noted Greenwich Village lurker and self-appointed Dylan chronologer and acolyte, the late David Blue (né Cohen), wrote as his signal legacy the jaunty song "I Like to Sleep Late in the Morning," a defining anthem of those lazy, hazy days of hippie splendor. It's safe to say, though he might want (us) to believe otherwise, that from mid-1966 through 1972, Bob Dylan rarely got to see a sunrise unless he "didn't get to sleep last night." Thus his purported *New Morning* undoubtedly took place during the midafternoon. Neither did dawn break on his slumbering muse to any great extent, although when compared to the trifles on *Nashville Skyline* and the atrocities perpetrated on *Self Portrait*, one or two of the songs on *New Morning* might qualify as minor masterpieces (although not when compared to the gems he was coming up with daily and throwing away in the basement in 1966), including the mournful "Sign on the Window."

Typical of Dylan's addled way of thinking, following the departure of his steady anchors, the Hawks, was his decision to move himself and his family back to New York City in the desperate hope of finding his departed muse in a hidden doorway on Grove Street. What he found instead were picket lines in front of his MacDougal Street townhouse, demanding his immediate return to pre-accident form.

There are indications that Bob Dylan could sympathize, even if many of the songs he was writing evoked a false-hearted nostalgia for the joys of living in the country not indulged in since his *Freewheelin'* days, when he extolled a Hibbing youth he'd been all too eager to escape and erase. At least he tested his limits by putting himself in front of real musicians like David Bromberg (guitar and dobro), Buzzy Feiten (electric guitar), Harvey Brooks (bass), and Billy Mundi and Russ Kunkel (drums). And he tested himself even more by submitting to one or several meetings with the seventy eight-year-old poet Archibald MacLeish, ostensibly to talk over a project in potential need of a few Dylan originals.

As with when he dropped in on Carl Sandberg, or when Joan Baez dragged him off to meet her esteemed neighbor Alan Marcus, Dylan was probably overwhelmed by the three-time Pulitzer Prize–winning poet, author, and playwright (and graduate of Yale and the Harvard Law School). That this college dropout was himself about to receive an honorary degree from Princeton must have seemed a laughable irony when compared with this towering figure who'd hung around the Left Bank in Paris in the twenties with the likes of Hemingway, Fitzgerald, Cocteau, Picasso, Dorothy Parker, and Cole Porter. They were there to discuss MacLeish's new play, a reworking of *The Devil and Daniel Webster* called *Scratch*. But it's his previous play, *J.B.*, that would truly have been in Dylan's wheelhouse. In it, God and Satan in a circus tent concoct a wager for the soul of a millionaire, killing off his children, destroying his property, and wiping out his fortune, until he finally finds solace with his devoted wife, Sarah, with whom he builds a new life. Written in 1959, the play was hardly found wanting for its lack of music, winning both the Pulitzer and a Tony Award. But it does sound a bit like a rough draft for *Blood on the Tracks*—except for the part about Dylan and Sara getting back together.

Dylan dutifully worked on some of the titles given him by MacLeish, including "New Morning" and "Father of Night," but both of them soon realized he was in way over his head. Meanwhile, songs like "If Not for You," "One More Weekend," and "The Man in Me" continued to tread the same well-worn path of domestic bliss he was still trying to talk himself into in songs like "Sign on the Window" and "Time Passes Slowly." "Went to See the Gypsy," probably about seeing Elvis perform in Las Vegas, has some energy, but not enough to inspire Dylan to ever play it live. And not enough to inspire him to meet the King—at least not in his "Fat Elvis" incarnation. "Two or three times we were up in Hollywood and he had sent some of the Memphis Mafia down to where we were to bring us up to see him," he told Douglas Brinkley in *Rolling Stone* in 2009. "But none of us went. I don't know if I would have wanted to see Elvis like that. I wanted to see the powerful mystical Elvis."

His honorary graduation from Princeton on June 9 was another experience that he found painful enough to immediately write about. It took him two months to finish the song, but that was about as fast as Dylan worked during this period. Another last-minute addition à la "Ballad in Plain D," "Day of the Locusts" was also another song he would never play live. In all, he only played four songs from the album on tour ("The Man in Me," "New Morning," "If Not for You," and "If Dogs Run Free"), none of them in any great hurry; he waited eight years to debut "The Man in Me," which remained his favorite.

As for Dylan's work habits, by far the most interesting developments in his career at this time revolved around the severing of his relationship with Albert Grossman. Their management deal ended in July 1970. By late 1971, Grossman was also out of his publishing pocket. Nevertheless, no new albums would emerge in 1971, which made his appearance as the old Bob Dylan at the two concerts for Bangladesh at Madison Square Garden that August all the more astonishing. But not as astonishing as the single he released around the end of the year, "George Jackson," which evoked an even older Bob Dylan. It was a genuine protest song in the mode of "Hattie Carroll," about a renegade Black Panther who was shot by prison guards that summer in attempting to escape from San Quentin. Not letting any of the facts get in the way of his theme, Dylan channeled much of his pent-up frustration and rage into this prison drama, making it a weird sequel to the much more moving "I Shall Be Released." Produced by Leon Russell, "George Jackson" cracked the Top 40, but would not appear on any US Dylan album. It does appear on the 1978 Japanese collection *Masterpieces*, the audience for which undoubtedly had no clue as to who George Jackson really was.

The only albums of Bob Dylan material released in '71 or '72 would be comprised mainly of classics.

The Best He Could Do: *Greatest Hits, Vol. 2*

In addition to his one true hit of the period, "Lay Lady Lay," and his previous single, the Leon Russell–produced "Watching the River Flow," which nearly cracked the Top 40 in June 1971, these four sides contain an eclectic and informed choice of classics, including "All Along the Watchtower," "My Back Pages," "Stuck Inside of Mobile with the Memphis Blues Again," "It's All Over Now, Baby Blue," a 1963 performance of "Tomorrow Is a Long Time," and the revelatory "When I Paint My Masterpiece."

The last three songs on side four are the basement-era gems "I Shall Be Released," "You Ain't Goin' Nowhere," and "Crash on the Levee (Down in the Flood)," newly rerecorded with longtime compatriot Happy Traum on banjo, bass, and vocals. "As I relisten to the CD today I can still hear the informal, home-style picking that so many listeners have told me they like about those particular performances," Traum recalled. "There's a relaxed intimacy there that I like to think is partly due to our friendship, and to the many occasions in which we sat around the house playing the old songs. Of course, much of it was due to Bob's studio technique at the time: establish a good feel, play the song as if you really mean what you're singing about, and get it in one or two takes."

Since the actual *Basement Tapes* wouldn't be widely available until 1975, the inclusion of versions of Dylan singing these songs was extra special. Fans acknowledged as much, making this the best-selling album in Dylan's entire catalog.

A Surprise Appearance: Concert for People of Bangladesh

All it took was a phone call from George Harrison to pry Bob Dylan out of his fortress under the watchful glare of his prime tormentor, garbologist A. J. Webberman, and into a more forgiving public eye for the first time since August 1969. For everyone encamped on MacDougal Street and elsewhere around the world wishing for Dylan's return to active performing, if not activism itself, this was a major coup.

Appearing for free at both shows on a card that included Harrison, Ringo Starr, Eric Clapton, Billy Preston, Leon Russell, and Ravi Shankar, Dylan did not disappoint. Gone was the Bible-toting country squire, the happily married father of five, the purveyor of platitudes and crooner of clichés. In his place was the real thing, the long-ago acoustic folk singer of "A Hard Rain's a-Gonna Fall" fame, the electric bard of his generation. Although initially reluctant to unearth "Blowin' in the Wind," having not played it live in eight years, Dylan was reported to have said he'd do so only if Harrison would play "She Loves You" or "I Want to Hold Your Hand." But, as Harrison pointed out, he didn't write those songs; he played his own material, but did give a nod to Dylan by opening his set with one of their collaborations, "I'd Have You Anytime," and later playing another, "If Not for You." This was apparently significant enough a concession to allow Dylan to win over the crowd with powerful renditions of "Mr. Tambourine Man" and "Just Like a Woman." The ensuing live album went on to win a Grammy for "Album of the Year" and set the model for future superstar benefit concerts, like Live Aid and Farm Aid.

But if anyone thought it would lead Dylan into a renaissance of songwriting and performing excellence, they would be sorely disappointed during the rest of '72 and on into '73. And in 1974, when one of those people, Phil Ochs, called upon Dylan to join his Friends of Chile benefit at the same Madison Square Garden, on May 9, the results would be even more dismal. Along with Pete Seeger, Arlo Guthrie, Dave Van Ronk, Mike Love and Dennis Wilson of the Beach Boys (!), and Melanie (!!), Dylan literally slogged through the motions.

My college friend Les Erickson was among the audience. "I squatted between the first row and the stage, with Dylan's shoes sniffable from my perch," he commented. "On my left was Daniel Ellsberg and on my right my first wife. There was a jug of Gallo red wine on the stage. A disheveled, bipolar Phil Ochs clutched Dylan's armpits from time to time in order to steady himself it seemed, as Arlo Guthrie, Pete Seeger, and many more sang protest songs to honor the victims of Kissinger's and Nixon's Chilean *coup d'état*." To Erickson, the best moment was also the most inappropriate, when the apolitical Beach Boys sang "California Girls" to much booing and hissing. "A voice in the back screamed out, 'Get out, lumpen.' Ah, sweet memories."

Scoring a Film for (Dis)pleasure: *Pat Garrett and Billy the Kid*

As well as giving him another arrow in his quiver, doing the soundtrack for a movie (and trying to act in it), turned out to be a good way for Bob Dylan to get his family out of New York City for a while. The creatively starved artist was still more concerned during this period with finding a place to put down roots than living the life of a rock star, a poet, or even a musician. So the Dylans left town, much to the delight of their immediate neighbors, who resented the improvements he'd made to the property, in hopes of walling himself off from the disaffected fans who loitered in front of his pad daily, urging him to resume his abandoned role of generational spokesman.

Out west in new homes in Arizona and California, Dylan felt equally isolated from both the present and the past. After the debacle in Durango, they finally settled in the hills of Malibu. But life at Point Dume was complicated by the endless remodeling of his hideaway castle, a Gemini house, the changes seeming to mirror the splits in Dylan's personality.

Meanwhile, segueing from the intimidating figure of the cultured poet Archibald MacLeish to the even more intimidating figure of gruff director Sam Peckinpah took Dylan way beyond the outer edges of a comfort zone now almost seven years in the construction. With his role in the film minimal, and his scoring coming under constant criticism, the potential learning situation soon deteriorated into a struggle for survival. "Time started to slip away," he told Cameron Crowe in the *Biograph* liner notes, "and there I was trapped deep in the heart of Mexico with some madman ordering people around like a little king. I was sleepwalking most of the time and had no real reason to be there."

In terms of Dylan's catalog, "Knockin' on Heaven's Door," the song that emerged from the film and went on to become a Top 10 single, was reason enough.

But apparently not enough for Columbia Records. When Clive Davis, Dylan's champion there, was let go before Dylan's new contract with the label was signed, Dylan saw the indifference as a clue that it was time to take his business elsewhere.

Once again, his comfort zone (and Sara's) would be stretched to the limit, this time by the demands of a new label and, inevitably, a new tour just up the road.

24

Put Some Bleachers in the Sun

Back on the Road

S till in the throes of an emotional and creative (and marital) crisis, Bob Dylan chose at this moment to sever ties with Columbia Records and sign with David Geffen's new label, Asylum, prior to beginning work on *Planet Waves*. Having given him four babies in four years, by this time Sara was likely in no shape or mood to be a muse anymore. He would write "Forever Young" for one of his kids and "The Wedding Song" for Sara, but the keynote songs of the period were "Watching the River Flow" and the wistful, wishful "When I Paint My Masterpiece"—among the very few songs he'd done since 1967 that were anywhere up to his standards.

Where would he find the muse now? Was the road the muse? Were the nameless taunting audiences the muse? The inevitable girls at the backstage door? Apparently, Dylan had been sexually faithful for the first time in his life, at least for a few years. So was infidelity the muse, the secrets and lies of the double life essential nourishment for the wandering Gemini? He was still wary of the troubadour role, the spokesman role, the sheriff role, but also the saved family-man role. Must this be what's it's all about?

What would Elvis do?

What would Jesus do?

More importantly, in this instance, what would the Rolling Stones do?

Watching the back door slam as her husband left with the Band to tour behind *Planet Waves* for a couple of months in 1974, Sara could probably see the remains of their troubled marriage blowing away in the wind.

1974

With a new album to promote, and a new label owner to impress, the idea of going on the road after such a long layoff represented a major challenge

Leon Haggarty, Bobby Dylan and the Sheik of New York

by Bruce Pollock

The summer I was fourteen I made my living hawking ice cream at Coney Island. My buddy down on Bay Twenty-three was this kid name of Leon Haggarty, five-one, a hundred and six pounds of hustle, week after week- the leader in Sales, who held down two paper routes in the winter, on opposite sides of Brooklyn.

So anyway, time goes on, the summer ends in a blaze of fall, the old ladies with their stockings halfway rolled down desert the sand for the safety of the boardwalk and the nursing homes thereon. I return to my deteriorating high school career in Flatbush, Leon hustles back to his paper routes in Canarsie. We drift apart, then lose touch completely.

Now it is fourteen years later. I am writing for a large metropolitan music rag, high into my Sheik of New York phase, attending all the rallies, where shakers move and movers shake; Kevin Sanders of ABC-TV News and I have developed a nodding acquaintance. I attend Mets playoffs games and root for the Knicks courtside courtesy of some good friends high up. It is the fourth quarter of a Knick runaway and who do I spot coming down the aisle, but Leon Haggerty! He is fourteen years older, maybe five-six, a hundred and seventy-one pounds, but I'd recognize that voice anywhere.

"Hey cold beer! Getcha cold beer here!"

"Leon Haggerty!" I cry, jumping up from my seat.

"Leon Haggerty!" I cry, jumping up from my seat.

"Down in front!" shout a chorus of rabid Knick fans.

"Brooklyn Slim—as I live and breathe!"

Anyway, we reunite by the loading ramp back of Gate Fourteen, regale each other with high and low times, and get good and sick on Sabrett's finest hotdogs. It seems that good old Leon is now the head hawker at the Garden.

You may wonder what all this has to do with Bob Dylan returning to New York City last month. Well, the connection will dawn on you presently. I mean, don't tell me about Dylan: I was there. I was there in 1964, third balcony at Philharmonic Hall. I was there at Forest Hills when he got booed off the stage. There a couple of months later when he was cheered by the same crowd at Carnegie Hall. I mean, I saw him live at the Gaslight Cafe in the Village, previewing songs from Bringing It All Back Home. I was so close I got hit with the spray as he spat out "It's All Right Ma," for the first time. So, don't tell me about Dylan.

When news of his concert began trickling into these offices toward the end of last year, I trembled with anticipation. Quickly I phoned Columbia Records to find out if I'd have any trouble getting tickets. (Me? The one and only? Trouble?) I found out I might have some trouble. Columbia wasn't even sure if Dylan was still on the label. I phoned Elektra/Asylum, the rumored choice for Dylan's new label; they weren't admitting anything. The long wait was on.

Eventually I got a number to call for tickets and was put on a preferred list. I mean, all right! If I can't get tickets for Dylan, then what's the point of it all; what's the point of all those free passes to see the New York

Dolls and Blue Oyster Cult, if, when The Man arrives I have to scrounge for scalper seats like the rest of the rabble? I mean, justice does exist somewhere in this world, doesn't it?

Friends, I am here to tell you it does not!

The day of his opening concert came around and I was still without a ticket. After a series of phone calls, each more frantic and desperate than the next, to a variety of parties, all of whom denied final responsibility for dispensation of the tickets, it dawned on me that not only would I miss opening night, but there was the distinct, crushing possibility that I would not get to see either of Dylan's last two shows the next day. How could this happen to me?

So that night, as everyone else who is anyone in the world is listening to Bob sing his lungs out at the Garden, I am seated atop my slum tenement slugging rotgut with a few of the neighborhood winos ... when, at the edges of my panic I hear a small voice calling out to me. On the sultry, smog-encrusted New York breeze I hear it calling ... Leon Haggerty! Leon Haggerty!

The next day I awake around noon and put in a phone call to my man. "Leon," I shout into the phone, "it's me—Brooklyn Slim. You've got to get me into that concert today."

"Concert? You mean the one for the folksinger?"

"That's the one, man—can you get me in?"

"Gee, I don't know—I hear it's all sold out."

"Leon, you've got to do it—I'll be your best friend!!!"

There is a long, engulfing silence. I can hear the FBI men crawling through the wires. Finally Leon speaks up. "Say, listen Slim, I think I may be able to help you—"

"Leon, you're a doll!"

"But you might have to stand ..."

* * *

"Hey beer! Get your beer here, ice cold beer!" I am standing on the Garden floor in a white pith helmet, white monkey suit, a case of beer strapped to my shoulders. I've heard of reporters going to any lengths for a story, frenzied fans trekking to the ends of the earth to see their idols—but this is absurd.

"Cold beer, folks, let's go, get it while it's hot ..."

Most of the punks in this crowd aren't even old enough to drink beer. They're the same crew who'd show up for Alice Cooper in glittery gowns, now dressed down for Dylan in shabby overalls. I wonder what kind of feeling they could possibly have for him. Except that, perhaps, he was the next must concert on the list.

I mean I am from the generation that grew up with the guy, who scuffled the same Village streets in search of inspiration, who dropped acid and saw not God but Dylan. A generation left stranded on the road to Woodstock in a failed attempt to crash with Bob and the Band at Big Pink, and feed off their sainted vibes to make up for the lack of our own. All those who are now complaining about Dylan selling out, are really jealous

As a crusading rock journalist, I had a front-row view of Dylan's Madison Square Garden comeback performance in January 1974.

to Bob Dylan's stultifying status quo after being cooped up at home for so long. Prior to '74, he could count his public appearances in the last seven years on the fingers of one hand and still have a middle finger left over for his audience—the audience that kept buying his lackluster records: one for Woody Guthrie in '67; one at the Isle of Wight, for the folks expecting him to show up at Woodstock, in 1969; one day/night doubleheader for his friend George Harrison at Madison Square Garden, and nominally for the starving people of Bangladesh, in 1971; and one for the Band on New Year's Day 1972, in Champaign, Illinois, just because he felt like it. While friends and commentators said he'd never seemed more centered and content as he walked his daughter to the school bus each morning and vacationed in the summer on Fire Island with the rest of the glitterati, he knew very well what he'd lost.

As he often said to journalists—sometimes from the depths of his soul, sometimes facetiously just to throw them off the scent of the truth—performing in front of an audience was what always drove his writing. If there was no audience, he had no reason and no desire to write. He'd already written enough for a dozen songwriters' lifetimes. As he proved during the basement era, he wasn't attached to even some of his best songs; he probably couldn't differentiate at first between a good song, a great song, and an immortal song. Probably it was something that only emerged in the studio or in front of an audience, and studio musicians were a notoriously tough crowd. He'd always preferred the challenge of a concert audience—even a concert audience turned against him. His albums, once they were finished, were always disappointing to him, never quite capturing the sound inside his head. They never interested him much, except in the context of providing him choices for a future set list.

Unlike the growing chaos of his family life in 1974, the road probably offered Dylan the kind of security he could no longer find at home. There was a place you had to be every morning, a place you had to leave every night. If there was a stalker to be dispatched, he had a Bobby Neuwirth or a Victor Maymudes to fend them off. If there was a groupie to be groped, these same functionaries could be counted on to discreetly usher them into his chambers. Hotel meals may have been uninspired, but the menus were always changing with the venue, the venues and the accommodations changing with the scenery and the seasons as the country whipped by through an airplane, bus, or limousine window. If the road was your home, it was constantly being remodeled in the style favored by Nebraska or New Mexico. At that point in his life, the controlled bedlam of the road had to seem like a breeze.

A Really New Morning

Opening up the 1974 tour that was to be the first day of the rest of his life at Chicago Stadium in Chicago, Illinois, on January 3, Dylan was finally ready to confront his audience, face-to-faces, and to talk to them in song. At the first concert, he chose to open with the semi-obscure "Hero Blues," written in 1962, about a girl, probably Suze, who wanted him to be a hero, and who he had to set straight, noting that heroes generally had a short lifespan. In other words, he was telling his audience to lower their expectations, otherwise "you can shout hero all over my lonesome grave."

By the time he reached the Spectrum, in Philadelphia, two nights later, he'd had enough of "Hero Blues" and chose instead to open with "Hollis Brown," a song about a man who kills his wife and family (of five kids). This song may have had too much of a symbolic meaning only for Bob and Sara Dylan, so he dropped it as the opener the next night in favor of "Rainy Day Women #12 & 35," in which everybody is either stoned or getting stoned. This interesting conceit lasted until the second night at Maple Leaf Gardens in Toronto on the 10th, when it was replaced by the song that would open the show for the rest of the tour: the comically confrontational "Most Likely You Go Your Way (And I'll Go Mine)."

After a little trial and error, as usual, Dylan had come up with the perfect note.

As one of the lucky few to attend the concert at Madison Square Garden on the afternoon of January 31, due to my exalted position as staff writer at the distinguished tabloid *Rock* magazine, I can attest to the rarefied vibes in the air as we waited for the deposed king to reclaim his throne at the "World's Greatest Arena." As I wrote at the time, it was by far the best Garden crowd I'd ever witnessed—and I'd been there that night in '72, when the Knicks scored the last nineteen points of the fourth quarter to beat Abdul-Jabbar and the Milwaukee Bucks by one point. During "Like a Rolling Stone," there was such pure and beautiful bedlam that even Dylan cracked a smile (though I am told he cracked a smile in several other key cities on the route).

Ten minutes after his last encore, the crowd was still roaring, unwilling to leave. The ovation was bigger by a ton than the one that greeted Willis Reed when he hobbled onto the court for the seventh game of the championship series against the Los Angeles Lakers in 1970. Bigger even than that. Ten minutes, fifteen minutes. On it went, until, after nearly twenty minutes, Dylan reappeared, without his guitar, without his sunglasses, wearing a New York Rangers jersey, which came down to his knees. "Cupping the

Dylan took his trusted Woodstock companions the Band on the road with him in 1974.
Hugh Shirley Candyside/Wikimedia Commons/Public domain

microphone in his hands," I wrote, "you can see the ovation had reached him. We're not your average stalker, hiding underneath his bed. There's something lovable about us. Into the microphone he then says, clear and loud, 'See ya next year . . . ' and spins and walks off."

That was it. Nothing more. The crowd was pulverized into silence. It was a knockout blow so sudden and unexpected that no one knew how to react. Did he mean it? Another full-scale tour? Or just a New York gig? Maybe a week at Shea Stadium or the UN? But this tour was so well-planned, not a word wasted or out of place, that it was impossible not to believe the words were a product of the high emotions of the afternoon, perhaps a little wishful thinking, but indicative nonetheless of the crowd's effect on Dylan, an effect he would always choose to deny. "You say you love me . . . but you could be wrong."

In fact, though he did not make the same offer after the evening concert, Dylan would return to the Garden in 1975, on December 8, at a benefit concert given to support his latest cause, the boxer Rubin "Hurricane" Carter. It was at the end of the first leg of the fabled Rolling Thunder tour, which would keep him busy through the spring of '76.

The Rolling Thunder Tour, 1975–1976

Back in New York City, at the same studio where he'd recorded many of his '60s classics, Dylan finished *Blood on the Tracks* in September 1974, only to redo most of it in Minneapolis at the end of the year. Released in January 1975, the album was a spectacular critical and commercial success that pointed to another creative growth spurt (about which more details later), perhaps followed by another stint on the road. But if he was to get back on that particular wild horse, the method and madness behind touring again would have to be unveiled to him in an intuitive moment.

Such a moment occurred on June 26, 1975, when Dylan, after attending a Rolling Stones concert at Madison Square Garden, dropped in on the latest "new Bob Dylan" at the Other End, the sexy New Jersey poetess Patti Smith, one part Bruce Springsteen, three parts Mary Weiss of the Shangri-Las, and her scruffy band of brothers, including eminent rock scribe Lenny Kaye on guitar and Jay Doherty on drums.

As it did in the mid-'60s, word of Dylan in the neighborhood brought an electric charge of energy to the street, even to a stagnant scene on the brink of rebirth. Word of Dylan in the building was even more incendiary. Onstage at the Other End, Patti caught the vibes and gave an especially inspired performance. Backstage, the meeting of the two was as anticlimactic as similar Dylan confabs with Henry Miller, Leonard Cohen, Jerry Lee Lewis, and often John Lennon, the blistering geniuses shyly circling each other with epic small talk. "They didn't seem to have that much to say to each other," an unnamed Columbia exec recounted. "She was happy and he was smashed, so it all worked out very well."

Dylan was at the Other End the next night and the next, studiously taking notes on Patti's backup band, in preparation for his own form of musicianly camaraderie. In order to have something new to play, if the road was to be his destiny, Dylan only needed to turn the corner, where Jacques Levy had a loft in walking distance from the Other End. A director who had made his name and his notoriety directing the nudie musical *Oh! Calcutta!*, Levy had also collaborated with Dylan's old friend and recent Malibu hoops buddy Roger McGuinn on a bunch of songs meant for a Broadway play that never happened, including "Chestnut Mare." His collaboration with Dylan started with the epic "Isis" and ended in East Hampton, later in the summer, with "Sara," and the hectic sessions in late July that produced "Romance in Durango," with Eric Clapton on guitar.

"No one knew what anyone was doing," Clapton confessed to *Rolling Stone*. "It ended up with twenty-four musicians in the studio all playing these incongruous instruments. Dylan was racing from song to song. I had to get out in the fresh air because it was just madness in there."

A few nights later, with a much smaller ensemble, most of the tracks that would comprise *Desire* were completed. Thus, if the Greenwich Village of old wouldn't come to Bob Dylan, the wheels were already in motion for Bob Dylan to bring those long-ago half-imaginary vibes to the rest of America, across the Jersey line.

"It was the end of July 1975 and I was living in Los Angeles," the rock singer Cidny (then known as Cindy) Bullens told me. Her friend Bob

Neuwirth had sent her a ticket to New York to perform at the Other End. Dylan was going to be there, he told her, along with Mick Ronson, Ramblin' Jack Elliott, T Bone Burnett. "I was basically part of the backup band and we all sang songs together for a week an out of that came the seeds for the Rolling Thunder tour."

(Cindy backed out of her backing role at the last minute to take a similar slot working with Elton John, never regretting her decision for a minute. Well, maybe for a minute. "I never felt I made the wrong decision," she recalled. "I just have felt over the years regretful that I couldn't have done both. I ended up doing three concerts with Rolling Thunder. I did have some moments backstage, in the hotel room, and on the bus with Allen Ginsberg, but I wasn't involved in the whole subculture on a daily basis.")

That subculture descended *en masse* on Folk City near the end of October, to celebrate club owner Mike Porco's sixty-first birthday. Starring Dylan and costarring Joan Baez, this was a triple A–list bill straight out of 1964, including Dave Van Ronk, Eric Andersen, Phil Ochs, David Blue, Roger McGuinn, and Buzzy Linhart, as well as a couple of ascendant bohemian superstars, Patti Smith and Tom Waits, and the incomparable (if incongruous) belter Bette Midler.

Dylan's Rolling Thunder tour of 1976 was a traveling tribute to his folk roots. The last stop was at the University of Southern Mississippi.

Ticket stub courtesy of Dcurbow/ Wikimedia Commons/Public domain

Among the many members of Dylan's extended musical family that accompanied him on the road in 1975, perhaps the least excited was his embattled wife, Sara, whose feelings were decidedly mixed about seeing her wandering husband submit to the temptations of the road again. "Well, it's just another one," tour diarist Larry Sloman reported her telling a member of the entourage, speaking of the upcoming tour at a listening session for *Desire*, just before Dylan introduced "Sara" to the assemblage.

Dylan's collaborator, Jacques Levy, thought Sara was stunned by the honesty and the plea inherent in the song; Sloman saw her as "impassive." At the beginning of her stay on the road, Sloman took special note of her appearance, calling her fragile, enigmatic, quietly charismatic, and stunning. Meeting him, he writes, in *On the Road with Bob Dylan*, "she smiles wanly and offers a delicate hand."

Or perhaps she was just exhausted by her husband's recent transgressions, starting with his previous summer on the farm in Minnesota, where he was accompanied by Columbia Records employee Ellen Bernstein—apparently one of the perks offered him when he re-signed with the label in August.

At the time, Dylan blamed his faltering marriage on his two-month residency with his new painting teacher, the seventy-four-year-old Norman Raeben, whose intuitive approach to painting seemed to perfectly mirror Dylan's similar approach to songwriting, especially the concept of merging past, present, and future in his songs, leaving him and them, as he'd predicted in "Stuck Inside of Mobile," with "no sense of time." From that point on, he suggested, he could no longer explain himself to Sara—who nonetheless hung on for another three years (and a costarring stint in his upcoming magnum fiasco, *Renaldo and Clara*) before filing for divorce.

The Rolling Thunder traveling caravan barnstormed through the northeast in two buses, Dylan in whiteface, starting at Plymouth Rock on the night before Halloween, and ending with the benefit for "Hurricane" Carter at Madison Square Garden on December 8, with a regular cast including Rob Stoner on bass; Howie Wyeth on drums; David Mansfield, T Bone Burnett, Steven Soles, and Mick Ronson on guitars; and Scarlet Rivera on violin, along with whichever superstars were able to jockey their schedules to join them. Joni Mitchell, Arlo Guthrie, Kinky Friedman, and the trusty Allen Ginsberg performed guest sets, backing Dylan as he opened each of the shows with "When I Paint My Masterpiece" (except, inexplicably, the November 29 show in Quebec City, for which the lead-off spot was taken by "It Ain't Me Babe"), and joining hands at the rousing closer, "This Land Is Your Land." Preferring not to play in Quebec City, Leonard Cohen entertained the performers at his modest cottage in Montreal. Declining to play without his E Street Band, Bruce Springsteen came backstage in New Haven to pay his respects, resulting in another stilted meeting of the titans, the interminable small talk interrupted only by Springsteen's girlfriend, who asked Dylan why he was wearing makeup.

"I saw it in a movie once," was Dylan muffled response.

Earlier in the day, Dylan even claimed not to know who this "Springfield" cat was, even though, just a week earlier, Springsteen's face had been featured on simultaneous covers of *Time* and *Newsweek* as not only the latest "New Dylan" but also "the future of rock 'n' roll."

By the time of Dylan's 1976 TV performance for the *Hard Rain* special, the good vibes of the tour were gone.   *NBC-TV/Wikimedia Commons/Public domain*

Perhaps the high point in this extended nostalgia trip for Dylan occurred in mid-November, when his old Camp Herzl pal Larry Kegan, long crippled from a swimming accident, arrived in his specially appointed van to spend a week on the tour. Dylan even included him in some scenes for *Renaldo and Clara*, where he chases his old friend down the hall in his chair.

The second leg of the Revue picked up in April, at the Civic Center in Lakeland, Florida, after another benefit performance for the "Hurricane" in January 1976 at the half-filled Astrodome in Houston. (Carter was released on bond in 1977, only to be convicted again, and then have that conviction overturned in 1985; the single peaked at No. 33 early in 1976.)

After Dylan gave his only live performance of the epic "Lily, Rosemary, and the Jack of Hearts," the festivities lurched to a close at the Salt Palace in Salt Lake City, Utah, on May 25, the day after Dylan turned thirty-five. The previous night's performance in Colorado, in a rainstorm, with his wife and children and mother looking on, was historic, however, as captured on the live album *Hard Rain*. But for the most part the mystical mythical vibes and camaraderie had long since disappeared. The set list became a shambles, with only the closing song on most nights, "Gotta Travel On," cowritten by old Dylan rambling buddy Paul Clayton, carrying any significance. (Ironically, Clayton had years before sold off his share of the publishing rights.)

The magic and the music, as well as the shambles, would be captured in at least three books and one epic failure of a movie, into which Dylan poured tons of his ego and an equal amount of his money.

Renaldo and Clara

In her memoir, *And a Voice to Sing With*, Joan Baez is fairly contained and controlled in her reflections, offering a measured voice of reason and composure and self-deprecating humor, especially when dealing with her complicated and tortured relationship with Bob Dylan. Except when it comes to her depiction of Bob and Sara on the Rolling Thunder tour, captured for posterity (although seen by relatively few) by the rolling camera eye of *Renaldo and Clara*. Dylan might have originally conceived it as the sequel to *Dont Look Back* and *Eat the Document* as rewritten by Fellini. Or the movie version of his mashed-up novel, *Tarantula*. Or a home-movie confessional to his estranged wife and estranged girlfriend. Or, more likely, if only for a minute, his masterpiece.

For Joan, it was the final humbling chapter in a virtual *War and Peace* of their time together and their time apart. "I wondered what I was doing in this monumentally silly project," she writes. Yet many moments of truth emerged on the tour and in the film, as duly noted in Joan's book. In one scene in a bar in Springfield, Massachusetts, Joan starts improvising, asking Bob why he never told her about Sara and speculating about what would have happened had they married in the sixties. In the film, she says it wouldn't have worked out because he was too much of a liar. "And he just stood there with his hand on the bar smiling and embarrassed because he didn't know what else to do," she writes.

As the tour wound on through its desultory second leg in the spring of '76, Joan began to realize that "musically, spiritually, politically, and in every other way I was limiting myself severely."

To Baez, the defining moment of the tour, and perhaps Dylan's unraveling marriage, occurred when Sara arrived again during the late stages, scattering her husband's groupies in her wake. Later, Joan happened upon an unrehearsed scene of Sara on a straight-backed chair, with Bob down on one knee in front of her in whiteface and eyeliner, enduring her recriminations. She bonded with Sara then, and sang "Sad-Eyed Lady of the Lowlands" for her that night.

Sara may or may not have been in the audience to hear it, having decided the carnival atmosphere of the tour, along with Dylan's role as King of the Gypsies, with a concubine in every port, was not ideally suited to her fragile position as his reigning wife. In her absence, Dylan tore into "Idiot Wind" with particular venom.

Summing up her feelings about her life "being wasted in a madhouse," Baez closes her chapter with a personal note to Bob, written from a distance, filled with diamonds and rust and rue. "I thought maybe I shouldn't write all this stuff about you but it turns out it's really all about me anyway, isn't it? It won't affect you. The death of Elvis affected you. I didn't relate to that either."

The award-winning playwright Sam Shepard, who was invited to join the Rolling Thunder troupe by Dylan, ostensibly to write the script of *Renaldo and Clara*, lost faith in the project way before it was completed. "The organization of the film has fallen into smithereens till it has no shape or sense," he writes in his diary of the experience, *Rolling Thunder Logbook*. "No way of planning a day's shooting. Everything is at the mercy of random energy." Long before that, he continues, they'd "abandoned the idea of developing a polished screenplay or even a scenario type shooting script. So there's no chance of directing the scene or even stopping long enough to make adjustments in camera angles. Nothing to do but let it roll and hope there'll be something in the can that looks as good as it feels."

With interminable stretches dominated by Dylan acolyte and imitator David Blue, few scenes resonate as much as the music, which is probably why the Dylan/Baez encounter at the bar stands out. It was brought up in an interview Dylan did to promote the film with Ron Rosenbaum of *Playboy* magazine, who notes, "Baez turns to you at one point in the film and says, 'What if we had gotten married back then?'"

"Seems pretty real, doesn't it?" the ever-elusive Dylan replies, before deftly segueing out of autobiographical danger. "Just like in a Bergman movie, there's a lot of spontaneity that goes on. Usually the people in his films know each other, so they can interrelate. There's life and breath in every frame because they know each other."

The critical consensus, however, was that there was not enough life and breath in Renaldo and/or Clara to sustain a motion picture.

The "Alimony Tour," 1978

The final dissolution of Dylan's marriage to the former Shirley Noznisky was a stunning tableau of passive aggression, occasionally spilling over into actual aggression. The divorce proceedings reveal domestic violence on Dylan's part, kidnapping on Sara's part. As in the past, Dylan, unable to make the definitive move to break up a relationship, kept piling abuses on Sara until she was forced into being the one to file for the divorce. At one point, shortly after the Rolling Thunder tour ended, Sara was surprised if not humiliated when she found his latest girlfriend seated with the children at the kitchen table in their Point Dume mashed-up mansion. When Dylan refused to tell her to leave, Sara left instead. The first person she visited was David Geffen, who recommended she call the noted divorce attorney Marvin Mitchelson, who was soon to become fully acquainted with the collected works of Bob Dylan, especially the ones composed between the years of their marriage, 1965 to 1977, and their monetary value.

Because Mitchelson was so adept at his job (and because Dylan was also way over budget on his movie, and way overextended on Point Dume redecorations), the forthcoming so-called "Alimony Tour" of 1978 became a financial as well as an emotional necessity.

Getting about as far away from his home and his marriage as he could, Dylan also got about as far away from his previous image as a solo folkie turned electric folk-rock bandleader as possible, signing with Neil Diamond's management company and adopting the Diamond mode of theatrical excess along with its requisite fashion statements. Thus, dressed in ridiculous Las Vegas–style costumes, Rolling Thunder graduates Rob Stoner, Steven Soles, and David Mansfield were joined by Billy Cross, a guitarist who'd played in the musical *Hair!*; Ian Wallace, an ex–King Crimson drummer; Alan Pasqua, a keyboard player from the fusion group the Tony Williams Lifetime; Bobbye Hall, a female percussionist from Motown; Steve Douglas, a saxophone player from the Phil Spector stable; and three black backup singers, Jo Ann Harris, Debi Dye-Gibson, and the young and inexperienced Helena Springs, who would go on to cowrite a number of songs with Dylan during their extended alone time. While this created a bit of dissension among the backup singers, it was nothing compared to the friction that ensued between Helena and another black woman, Mary Alice Artes, when she joined Dylan on the road early in the tour.

The uneasy troupe began their eight-month, 114-date trek across four continents with two weeks in Japan, opening up three nights in Tokyo with the ironic choice of the blues tune "Empty Bedroom." Three nights in Osaka preceded another five in Tokyo. By the time they moved on to eleven concerts in Australia in March, uncovering rabid fans in Brisbane, Adelaide, Melbourne, Perth, and Sydney, "Love Her with a Feeling" had become Dylan's blues of choice, usually following a rousing opening of "A Hard Rain's a-Gonna Fall."

During a three-month hiatus back in Los Angeles, Rob Stoner was replaced by former Elvis Presley bassist Jerry Scheff, and Debi Dye-Gibson was replaced by young gospel singer Carolyn Dennis, whose mother once sang with Ray Charles. (In the '80s, both Dennis and her mother would sing with Dylan on tour. Dennis and Dylan were secretly married in 1986, had a secret child named Deserie in the same year, and were secretly divorced in 1992.) It's safe to say that the triumvirate of Springs, Dennis, and occasionally Artes kept Dylan up to his ears in soul food and sex as the tour wound down toward the end of the year.

In June, Dylan put in a solid week at the Universal Amphitheater in Los Angeles, playing basically the same set every night, featuring mostly '60s classics and only a few from the '70s. These included "Going, Going Gone" from *Planet Waves*, "Shelter from the Storm" and "Tangled Up in Blue" from *Blood on the Tracks* (along with the revelatory outtake "You're a Big Girl Now"), "One More Cup of Coffee (Valley Below)" from *Desire*, and two new songs, "Baby Stop Crying" and "Señor (Tales of Yankee Power)," which would appear on *Street-Legal*, the album he put together during a week in April, filling with songs he'd previously written on the farm in Minnesota, to which he again escaped just after Sara filed for divorce, this time accompanied only by his new girlfriend, his children's former nanny, Faridi McFree, a free spirit of Middle Eastern descent.

A month in Europe consisted of a week at Earl's Court in London, a week in Germany, including a gig in Nuremburg where he sang "Masters of War," and five nights in Paris, before swinging back to the Blackbushe Aerodrome in Camberley, England, where the opening acts included Joan Armatrading, Graham Parker and the Rumour, and Eric Clapton, and the crowd at the abandoned airfield numbered upward of 165,000 people.

The desultory North American leg of the tour started in September in Augusta, Maine, and covered sixty-five dates in thirty-five states (plus three Canadian provinces) in eighty-eight days. As opposed to the lavish accommodations during the Far Eastern and European parts of the tour, the latter stages of 1978 were typified by the night before Thanksgiving, when Dylan and the band stayed at a Howard Johnson's in Norman, Oklahoma, within walking distance of a bowling alley. A circulating flu virus didn't help anyone's mood. By this time, Dylan's mood was probably more determined by his girlfriend(s) than by his audience.

A Religious Epiphany

In much the same way as his early girlfriends had helped him turn his country and blues obsessions into folk music, and his later girlfriends had given him their political theories to try on for size, and his wife had eased him into the life of a Bible-reading family man, now the African American trio of Helena Springs, Carolyn Dennis, and Mary Alice Artes—most likely in separate consultations—were urging Bob Dylan to pray. At the same time, close touring friends and members of his band, among them T Bone Burnett, Steven Soles, and David Mansfield, were all recent converts to Christianity. Even his Malibu basketball buddy Roger McGuinn had turned to Christianity in 1977, in the midst of his third divorce and a failed Byrds reunion. "I said, 'Oh God, how can I keep feeling like this?'" McGuinn told me of this low period. "And I got this sort of . . . not a loud voice or anything: 'Well, you could accept Jesus.' So I said okay, and I felt good again."

Shortly after starting to wear a cross that someone had thrown onstage in San Diego on the night of November 17, Dylan had a similar vision of Jesus appearing before him in his hotel room. He soon translated this vision into the song "Slow Train Coming," which he would demo in Nashville in December and debut on the road a year later.

By that time, Christianity had nearly overtaken his life. He became part of the Vineyard Fellowship, having been led there by Artes. He spent the first three months of 1979 in Bible classes in Reseda, accepting Christ and getting baptized in the ocean. Just as significantly, this conversion opened up an entirely new area of music with which to become infatuated. While he was no stranger to biblical imagery and the occasional apocalyptic tone poem, the Christian music that saturated his next three albums, *Slow Train*, *Saved*, and *Shot of Love*, were less poetic and inspired than dogmatic and clichéd. Much like his flirtation with commercial country music on *Nashville Skyline*, devoted fans and music lovers who might have been able to live with Dylan's new forays into gospel music simply couldn't abide Dylan's unsubtle attempts to conquer this traditional form.

His Christianity phase would get a lot worse before he evolved past it. If his old folk fans were offended by electricity and his folk-rock fans offended by country simplicity, they'd all rallied to his side after *Blood on the Tracks* and *Desire* reaffirmed his genius. So he'd raised their hopes again, only to lead them off a cliff into the music of eternity. To all but confirmed Christians, a Bible-reading Bob Dylan was one thing; a Bible-toting televangelist Bob Dylan was quite another. This is not to mention those of the Jewish faith who felt doubly betrayed.

But betrayal and controversy seemed to be Dylan's cup of meat, as he endured several years of audiences at the top of the '80s that were even more contentious than those that greeted him in the United States and England in 1965 and 1966. As in his previous experience with deep relationships and family life, it seemed that, once the going got smooth, he felt the need to make it rough. Not for him the calming waters of mass (or personal) acceptance; his other self (one of many) craved the excitement of nothing less than a new and hostile world to conquer.

As Dylan told Larry Sloman, "These attacks don't do nothing to me, because, to me, I'm always going on to the next thing. They expect something else. They're still looking in the same mirror. They're looking in the mirror and they don't realize they're seeing somebody different from who they saw ten years ago."

25

Living Outside the Law

Seven Famous Bootlegs

I t is a thankless as well as meaningless task to attempt to name Dylan's "best" bootleg releases. For one thing, virtually all of his concert performances and almost all of his plethora of outtakes exist in some form or fashion on a bootleg available for purchase. But let the buyer beware. Sound quality varies widely and wildly. As do the tastes of the compilers. In many cases, you simply had to be there, and even if you were, your memory of the event may have been colored by any number of extraneous circumstances and soft drugs. It is also something of a bottomless pit in that any given song may have been performed wonderfully or terribly on any given night, so in order to have the ultimate set of the 100 or 500 best Bob Dylan performances of each song, you may have to get hold of 100 or 500 separate concert tapes. In the murky outtake arena, experts' views differ as to whether take seventeen of a particular song is actually better than the released version, while the four other takes available in four different officially sanctioned products totally miss the mark. This too varies depending on which expert is holding the floor.

A Wonder of Wonders

The eventual marketplace for all things Dylan was started in 1969, with *Great White Wonder* (issued on the TMQ—Trademark of Quality label). Containing performances that go all the way back to Minnesota in 1961 and all the way forward to a 1969 straight-to-TV rendition of "Living the Blues" on *The Johnny Cash Show*, the album's major claim to fame, other than its mere existence, was the inclusion of seven songs lifted off the basement floor of Dylan's rehearsal space with the Band in West Saugerties, New York: "The Mighty Quinn," "This Wheel's on Fire," "I Shall Be Released," "Open the Door, Homer," "Too Much of Nothing," "Nothing Was Delivered," and "Tears of Rage."

Vol. 2 appeared in 1970, featuring six more basement songs: "Million Dollar Bash," "Yea! Heavy and a Bottle of Bread," "Please, Mrs. Henry," "Lo and Behold," "Tiny Montgomery," and "You Ain't Goin' Nowhere." When FM stations in L.A. started airing tracks from the package, and *Rolling Stone* magazine started demanding these great songs be officially released, Columbia Records had to respond; in due time came the official release of the woefully inadequate *The Basement Tapes* in 1975, leading eventually, a quick forty years later, to the release of *The Basement Tapes Complete*.

Dylan's Best Boot?

The collection generally considered the finest and most wide-ranging bootleg offering is *Ten of Swords*, issued in 1985, and featuring 134 previously unreleased tracks from 1961 to 1966. It seems obvious this ten-LP set led directly to the creation of *The Bootleg Series* by Columbia Records, starting the following year with *Biograph*, which would redistribute these tracks into at least five different boxed sets. *Ten of Swords* came with a booklet written by Paul Cable, author of *Bob Dylan: His Unreleased Recordings*, which was originally published in 1978 and reissued by Schirmer in 1980, while credit for the compilation itself was (probably) facetiously given to "Carla Rotolo, Chairman of the Board, P.S.A. (Parasite Sisters Anonymous)."

Amazingly, the collection pulls together random existing bootlegs into a much better-sounding chronological and contextual entity, with sections including "The Minnesota Hotel Tapes," the Leeds and Witmark demos, some nights at the Gaslight, Dylan's early Town and Carnegie Hall performances, outtakes from his first seven albums, and a final side devoted to his infamous confrontation with the man who cried "Judas" in England. Cable has interesting observations about all of it, even if some of his notes are factually lacking. What may be more telling is how, even back then, those close enough to the material to have a respected opinion felt some of Dylan's best songs were left off his first album, including "Hard Times in New York Town," "Worried Blues," and "I Heard That Lonesome Whistle Blow." The inclusion on that album of "Black Cross," which finds Dylan giving a fairly serious reading of the legendary satirist Lord Buckley's work, would definitely have drawn the attention of hip scholars.

The sections for Leeds Music and Witmark Music show Dylan beginning to take songwriting seriously as he prepared himself for his second album.

The legendary *Ten of Swords* bootleg collects many of Dylan's best performances from the sixties.

"Ballad for a Friend" is generally considered the best of the meager Leeds output. "Tomorrow Is a Long Time," a *Freewheelin'* outtake, stands out as the peak of his early Witmark years, alongside "Mr. Tambourine Man," which closes out side twelve, and "Blowin' in the Wind," which is also on the package. On the other hand, the chapter on the Gaslight features Dylan singing "No More Auction Block for Me," the tune "Blowin' in the Wind" was based on, as well as a superior version of "The Moonshiner." And the *Freewheelin'* section has the other three tracks that got the axe when the album was withdrawn, ostensibly to remove "Talkin' John Birch Paranoid Blues": "Rambling, Gambling Willie," "Rocks and Gravel," and the truly worthy "Let Me Die in My Footsteps."

"Seven Curses," "Mama You've Been on My Mind," and "Percy's Song" get the nod as tracks worthy of being on *The Times They Are a-Changin'*. Of the twenty tracks recorded on June 9, 1964, for *Another Side of Bob Dylan*, the two unissued cuts that most deserved a place on the album are "Lay Down Your Weary Tune" and "I'll Keep It with Mine." Cable is particularly fond of the latter.

Sides sixteen and seventeen are primarily of interest only to the most severe of Dylanologists keen to compare the outtake versions of some songs from *Bringing It All Back Home* and *Highway 61 Revisited* to the official versions. Of considerably more interest are the sessions with the Band on side eighteen, especially "She's Your Lover Now," about which Cable is quite vociferous in his praise, stating that the song perfectly symbolizes the entire '65–'66 period, with lyrics easily as vicious and cunning and clever as "Like a Rolling Stone." He speculates that there may be a completed take in existence somewhere, and tape of a phone conversation between Dylan and Bob Johnston in which Johnston mentions Columbia's plans to release the track as a single. "Anyhow, all this brilliant material was not given an official release. What was Columbia up to? Putting something aside for a rainy day?" he writes. (The nineteenth and last known take of "She's Your Lover Now" was ultimately released in 1991 on *The Bootleg Series Vol. 1–3: (Rare and Unreleased) 1961–1991*, while the entirety of Dylan's studio adventures in '65 and '66 occupy three different versions of *The Bootleg Series Vol. 12: The Cutting Edge 1965–1966*, released in 2015 as a two-CD set, a six-CD set, and a whopping eighteen-CD set.)

Finally, sides nineteen and twenty contain eight songs from the famed "Albert Hall" concert of 1966 that actually took place a few nights earlier at the Free Trade Hall in Manchester, England, including the rousing outtake "Tell Me Mama," and the vicious concert closing "Like a Rolling Stone."

Five More to Boot

Of the myriad choices available, perhaps the easiest to envision gaining a legitimate commercial life one of these years is *Nashville Sunset* (Cream of the Crop), which contains every known Dylan and Johnny Cash duet from February 1969, except for "Blue Yodel #4," which can be found on the import-only *The Dylan Cash Sessions*.

Folk Rogue (Wild Wolf) documents Dylan's 1964 and 1965 appearances at the Newport Folk Festival, a time during which he was moving out of his political protest phase into a more revealing type of personal protest music, accompanied by electric instruments (and, by 1965, a Chicago blues band). The set includes two songs from a September 3 concert at the Hollywood Bowl ("Tombstone Blues" and a second stab at "It Ain't Me Babe"). Also available is *From Newport to the Ancient Empty Streets in L.A.* (Dandelion), which has the same lineup of Newport tracks (except for "It Ain't Me Babe") and the entire Hollywood Bowl concert, including "She Belongs to Me," "To Ramona," "Gates of Eden," "It's All Over Now, Baby Blue," "Desolation Row," "Love Minus Zero," "Mr Tambourine Man," "Tombstone Blues," "I Don't Believe You," "From a Buick 6," "Just Like Tom Thumb's Blues," "Maggie's Farm," "It Ain't Me Babe," "Ballad of a Thin Man," "Like a Rolling Stone," and an alternate studio take of "Tombstone Blues."

Then there is *The Other Side of the Mirror*, a commercially available DVD that covers the same territory, adding some performances from 1963.

Another important bootleg represents Dylan's first major concert outside of Greenwich Village, at *Carnegie Chapter Hall*, an event produced by Izzy Young where only fifty or so people had the prescience to catch this pre–*Bob Dylan* Bob Dylan. Of the twenty-two songs he performed that night, seven have long been available on the bootleg market. Seven more surfaced in 2004 and 2008. "This Land Is Your Land," which appears on the *No Direction Home* soundtrack, is not included. Having taken place more than fifty years ago, the contents appear now to have lapsed into the public domain, prompting several labels to issue this material in a more-or-less legal context.

Finally, but by no means the last word on the subject, there is *Alias: The Complete Sideman Story* (Diamonds in Your Ear), released in 1998, which documents Dylan's very considerable activity as a studio hand on harp and vocals (and sometimes keyboards) throughout his career. Disc one features the voices of the folk and blues stalwarts who hired him, like Carolyn Hester, Jack Elliott, Pete Seeger, Big Joe Williams, and Victoria Spivey. On disc two you can sample his work behind Doug Sahm, David Blue, Booker T. and Priscilla Jones, Kinky Friedman, Leonard Cohen, and Eric Clapton. Disc three offers the dubious pleasure of hearing Dylan rap with Kurtis Blow, harmonize with Brian Wilson and Willie Nelson, and play harmonica behind Warren Zevon. Disc four offers the same eleven Dylan/Cash duets featured on *Nashville Sunset*, with the addition of three more: "Blue Yodel #5," "One Too Many Mornings," and "I Walk the Line." The set concludes with a revelatory set by Allen Ginsberg.

26

The Idiot's Revenge

The Breakup Tapes

Planet Waves: Seeking Asylum on the Road

Having just ended one long-term marriage (to Columbia Records) and with another (to Sara) about to face its biggest challenge, Dylan wrote all about his turbulent feelings on *Planet Waves*, surely his most contradictory album to date. There are, for instance, two versions of one of the first songs he wrote for the album, the somber, hymn-like "Forever Young" and the jaunty backwoods version of the same song. Rather than saving one to exhume from the vaults twenty years later, the warring Gemini within him chose to include them both on the LP. "Tough Mama" and "You Angel You" represent women from opposite sides of the tracks—although another reading of "You Angel You," which Dylan always suggested wasn't finished, makes it more appealing as a song of a father to a child (who has a tendency to keep him up at night). "Something There Is About You" has the two Bob Dylans inside the same song—actually the same verse—where on the one hand he swears to the woman he loves that she has the key to his soul, but in the next two lines takes it back, saying she can't expect him to be faithful, because it "surely would be death." In "Never Say Goodbye" he presents a picture of himself having nothing but time, while in "Going, Going, Gone" he's got one foot on the ledge, about to push off into space. But this is nothing compared to the last two songs he wrote for the album, in the studio, while work was winding down, with two of the many sides of Bob Dylan revealed on the venomous and important "Dirge," in which every nerve in his body is exposed as he confronts his needs, and the (slightly) more hopeful "Wedding Song," wherein he tries to convince himself that his love and his marriage are beyond the reach of whatever temptations lie ahead.

Now completely on his own, stripped of the comforts of his first record label and of recording in New York City and Nashville, Dylan clung to his few remaining links with the past, joining up once again with his fellow travelers in the Band (Robertson, Manuel, Helm, Hudson, and Danko), with whom he was last seen in Woodstock in 1967 making music for eternity. Now the stakes were higher and lower at the same time: to make music for his audience, or what remained of it. To do that would require a lot of his attention. Much to displeasure of his wife—the mother of five children, four of them under the age of seven—he left them in a rented house in Malibu for three weeks while he returned to New York to write without distractions.

What proved to be a big distraction was provided, when he came back to Malibu, by an offhand comment in the studio from a visitor. Dylan has never been a fan of criticism, whether from Phil Ochs or John Lennon or the generic "Mr. Jones"; the girlfriend of his old Minneapolis pal Lou Kemp had no idea what she'd stepped into when she remarked upon hearing the slow version of "Forever Young" that perhaps Dylan was getting soft in his old age. Had she not been listening to his recent works? Nevertheless, as unqualified as she was, Dylan took her feelings to heart, and was ready to toss this version of "Forever Young" from the album in favor of a less mushy take. When producer Rob Fraboni stuck up for the original, Dylan compromised by putting them both on the album. Over the years, Fraboni's judgment would trump that of Lou Kemp's opinionated girlfriend. The mushy version was the only song from *Planet Waves* to survive the tour, going on to gain favor among several new generations of fans who were not at all offended by this softer side of Bob Dylan.

The album was completed in November and set for release on January 3, to coincide with the beginning of his first tour since 1966. Unfortunately—or perversely—at the last minute Dylan decided the album needed some of his trademark liner notes, thus delaying its release until the 17th.

The tour went on as scheduled, opening in Chicago, with "Tough Mama," "Something There Is About You," and "Forever Young" the only three songs in the set to represent the album. If Dylan's new label owner, David Geffen, wasn't pleased by the delay to the album's release, which affected sales, he also must have been having second thoughts about signing this mercurial artist when he learned he'd played so few songs from the album at the first show. Although things didn't improve as the tour went on—the only other song Dylan added from the album was "Wedding Song," which he played sporadically—Geffen couldn't have been too upset by the album becoming Dylan's first to top the important *Billboard* album chart.

On the other hand, among the tunes conspicuously missing from live sets was the only single from *Planet Waves*, "On a Night Like This," which peaked at No. 44 on the still somewhat important singles chart.

Hard Rain: A Tour Souvenir

If Bob Dylan had been, as he claimed, "bored" by the automatic standing ovations that greeted him in 1965, and shell-shocked but galvanized by the boos that greeted him in 1966, the audience response to his 1974 tour with the Band might have sent him back to the woodshed to create another batch of songs no one would ever hear, or respond to, or certainly not light matches after hearing. Despite the critical raves, it's no wonder Dylan has gone on record with a relatively dismissive attitude about this series of performances.

"It was all sort of mindless," he told Cameron Crowe, in the liner notes to *Biograph*. "What they saw wasn't what they would have seen in '66 or '65. That was a much more demanding show. This was an emotionless trip."

Including only three major new songs ("All Along the Watchtower," "Knockin' on Heaven's Door," and "Lay Lady Lay") and none at all from his *Planet Waves* (even though he played "Forever Young" at every stop), *Hard Rain* was basically a "greatest hits" set. Perhaps Dylan was still conflicted about "Forever Young" being too soft for a rock setting, both in sentiment and arrangement. In any event, it would only be featured on one live album, 1979's *Bob Dylan at Budokan*, where most of the audience undoubtedly knew none of the words.

Other than the appearance of the Band on eight of the twenty-one songs, the track list for *Bob Dylan at Budokan* offered no surprises, opening with "Mr. Tambourine Man," which shortly became his regular opening song (sometimes doubling as his closing song), and closing with what became, midway through the tour, his regular finale of "Highway 61 Revisited," "Like a Rolling Stone," and "Blowin' in the Wind." Many of the segues are the ones most often heard on the road, making the record, at the very least, an accurate reflection of this particular candlelit tour. If Dylan was at times a little too strident, and the Band at times a little too intrusive, this can be attributed to his pent up nervous energy of seven years on the sidelines, gathering moss.

Drawing *Blood on the Tracks*

Confirming his wife's worst fears, Dylan's first extended adventure outside the house in seven years resulted in an ill-disguised affair. While Sara, knowing she had married not only a rock star but a virtual rock god, might have been willing to accept her husband having a few casual flings on the road, as any traveling salesman who came of age during the Summer of Love might, this was not Dylan's way. Just as he'd done while he was in a committed relationship with Suze Rotolo years before, he got himself so seriously involved with another woman as to destroy what he'd been building with the person he loved for nearly a decade.

But he did get a bunch of great new songs out of it.

These songs he started writing while living at his farm in Minneapolis, perhaps at Sara's suggestion, in July of '74, with his new girlfriend at his side. The one song apparently dedicated to this new girlfriend was the relatively upbeat kiss-off "You're Gonna Make Me Lonesome When You Go." So much for this new affair.

As much as the writing on this album represented a return to a level of songcraft and wordplay that Dylan had not consistently approached since *Blonde on Blonde*, perhaps the most touching and revealing aspect of its creation was how much of it he shared with his brother, David. While he'd always gone to great lengths in the early days to disown his parents and his past, the fact that he had a younger brother went almost unnoticed. Biographers rooting around in Hibbing for clues to his former existence as a Zimmerman found David, when they found him at all, rather uncommunicative. That the guy who'd shared a room with the future spokesman of his generation refused to open up about their mutual past implied a great rift between them, a pain of omission too much to contemplate, certainly to bare in print. But since Dylan wrote these new songs in Minneapolis, it's reasonable to assume that David knew of them in their formative state. Even if not, once the album was supposedly wrapped, he took the acetates back to Minneapolis to play them for David and to ask his brother for his opinion.

Generally, when he asked someone for their opinion of a work in progress, he didn't really want an honest answer, or at least an answer that went against his own feelings. But in the case of *Blood on the Tracks*, he was definitely in a questioning mood, playing the completed New York tapes to a variety of musician friends and even a couple of cousins. Had he perhaps opened up too much in this painful song cycle? Should he rein in the feelings a notch? That he should finally turn to David—a successful music man on the local level—not just for an opinion but to help him overhaul half the album, proves the childhood bonds they shared still meant something to him after all.

David's opinion was that the New York album was too spare and severe (an opinion not shared by everyone who'd heard both versions, including noted producer Phil Ramone, who'd engineered those sessions). Enlisting guitarists Kevin Odegard and Chris Weber, bass guitarist Billy Peterson, keyboard player Gregg Inhofer, and drummer Bill Berg, David and his Minnesota crew redid five tracks, including the album opener and single, "Tangled Up in Blue," the two most nakedly emotional songs, "You're a Big Girl Now" and "Idiot Wind," the cinematic "Lily, Rosemary, and the Jack of Hearts," and the wistful "If You See Her, Say Hello."

Critics subsequently called the production and the musicianship on the album "trash," "incompetent," and "shoddy"; others have lauded it as Dylan's most perfectly realized album. Unquestioned is the lyrical mastery Dylan regained in song after song, attributed by Dylan to several months of therapeutic painting sessions (leave it to Dylan get himself psychoanalyzed by a painter rather than a shrink). Justifiably proud of the songs on this album—although he has compulsively rewritten many of them over the years—he has gone to great lengths to deny any autobiographical or confessional elements. Indeed, many of the last-minute Minnesota rewrites were specifically intended to conceal rather than reveal the bitter truths. And yet, one listen to his vocals on "You're a Big Girl Now" and "Idiot Wind," even in their supposedly muted new versions, renders all of his denials moot. And "Shelter from the Storm" is one of the greatest anti-love songs of his career.

Collectors and theorists, however, remain united in their thus far unrequited quest to find the original New York sessions of those five songs revised in Minneapolis by Bob and David (who, coincidentally or not, was never again utilized on any Dylan recording), envisioning the ultimate double album of both sessions side by side. This is par for almost any Dylan album, of which multiple alternate takes if not alternate universes exist in which the great Bob Dylan could have been an even greater Bob Dylan, had he just been paying more attention.

Reclaiming His Desire

If ever there was an album title that could sum up the resurgence of the beaten down baby-boom generation in the '70s, it was Bob Dylan's *Desire*, which also sums up his time on the streets of Greenwich Village, recapturing the vibes of his youth, while Sara remained in Malibu with the kids. Rekindled desire ran rampant on those streets in the wake of the ending of the war in Vietnam and the ending of the draft in 1973, and Nixon's downfall at Watergate in 1974. The man whose election in 1968 signaled the empire striking back on the heads of the alternate culture was eventually pardoned by his appointed proxy, the same Gerald Ford who tried to deny lending funds to a New York City in need, evoking the famous headline in the *Daily News* of October 30, 1975: "Ford to New York City: Drop Dead." Of course, Ford never actually said that, and he wound up bailing out New York City anyway, but who was going to quibble with a few small facts? Certainly not Bob Dylan, whose massive misguided narratives on the guilt or innocence of boxer Rubin "Hurricane" Carter and the virtuous character of mobster "Joey" Gallo, written in the summer of '75, formed the centerpiece of *Desire*, and, in the case of the Hurricane, the basis for his upcoming tour, which would result in Carter's release (before he was convicted again, and then eventually pardoned).

At the end of 1976, the progressive, Dylan-quoting Jimmy Carter was elected president. He invited Dylan to the White House, where Dylan seemed to have a Dinkytown flashback. "He never initiates conversation," Carter said of their epic meeting, "but he'll answer a question if you ask him."

In 1975, on the eve of his thirty-fourth birthday in May, Dylan paid a visit to a gypsy king in Saintes-Maries-de-la-Mer in Provence, France, the one-time artists' colony favored by Van Gogh, Picasso, and Hemingway, which produced the song "One More Cup of Coffee (Valley Below)" and a vision for much of the album's gypsy-influenced sound. With the remains of his marriage down there in that valley, he spent the summer of '75 with Roger McGuinn's former collaborator, the theater director Jacques Levy, writing a series of lengthy dreamscapes at Levy's Village apartment and later spending a busman's holiday with him finishing it up in the Hamptons.

In the meantime, like many of the men of his generation, Dylan was thirty-four attempting to be twenty-two again, haunting the streets he knew so well, listening to music, reuniting with old friends like Jack Elliott, Dave Van Ronk, Phil Ochs, Bobby Neuwirth, and David Blue at the Other End and Folk City. He found his gypsy violinist Scarlet Rivera on those streets, capturing her with the pickup line of all time: "Hi, I'm Bob Dylan. You want to play on my next album?" After going through a bunch of other musicians, most notably Eric Clapton, he finally found what he was looking for in Rob Stoner (bass), Howard Wyeth (drums), and Steve Soles (guitar). Here was a band he could take with him on the road, along with a supporting cast of all the ghosts from his past, including the perfect right-hand lady to help ease him out of his currently painful relationship: Joan Baez, who'd been there, done that.

With a few typically elliptical nods to a troubled marriage ("Isis," "Romance in Durango," "Oh, Sister") Dylan really comes out of the emotional closet into the clear light of autobiographical scrutiny on the album's closer, "Sara," echoing other album-closers like "Wedding Song," "Restless Farewell," and "Ballad in Plain D"—songs he would write in haste and soon reconsider. He was even heard to claim the song, a naked plea to a girl named Sara to take him back, wasn't particularly autobiographical. "Just because of the title?" he snorted, when asked about it by Bill Flanagan. "It couldn't be about anyone else? I don't write confessional songs. Well, actually I did write one once and it wasn't very good and I regret it."

Nevertheless, the singer emerged from the song a chastened figure, which aligned him perfectly with the audience that sent the album to the top of the *Billboard* charts, humbled a bit by life, embarrassed by their drug-induced pronouncements, their free-love indiscretions, painfully aware of their shortcomings, but ready to begin again, to turn the rest of the '70s into something of a million-dollar bash at places like Plato's Retreat and Studio 54, opened in 1977, and full-frontal Broadway shows like Levy's own *Oh! Calcutta!*, revived in 1976.

Coming up on 1976, America was on the brink of celebrating a rebirth and for the battered renegades of the alternate culture there was an exhilaration in the air not felt since the Summer of Love. His verbal and performing powers restored, Bob Dylan only needed to figure out how to take advantage of it.

Rolling Thunder, *Hard Rain*

As a tour, the Rolling Thunder Revue was historic. For the entire fall of '75, it was a journey through the past in dark paisley. All the jugglers and the clowns in Dylan's entourage had their moment in the hot spotlight, one more time for all time. As an album trying to capture the event, *Hard Rain* was a historic swing and miss, acknowledged twenty-five years later with the *Bootleg Series* release *Bob Dylan Live 1975: The Rolling Thunder Revue*, by and large a much more representative set. For some perverse and never explained reason, *Hard Rain* chose its tracks from two 1976 performances at the burned-out end of the tour and everyone's patience. Dylan's wife had become part of the entourage, at the suggestion of the moviemakers along for the ride, and she put a definite damper on the frat-party, out-of-control atmosphere.

The film of the event, *Renaldo and Clara*, had long since spun out of control, too. The lightning captured in a bottle in '75 had turned to so much nervous energy. With only one night left before they all could go their separate ways, a miserable rainy night at Hughes Stadium in Fort Collins, Colorado, with his family in attendance, prior to his thirty-fifth birthday the next night, Dylan seemed to make one last desperate plea to Sara, to save what was long ago lost in the flood. Although he'd been showcasing songs from *Desire* throughout both legs of the tour, on the second leg more and more songs from the much more revelatory *Blood on the Tracks* came creeping in, culminating, on the night of the twenty-third of May 1976, with five, of which three are included on *Hard Rain*, all on side two: "Shelter from the Storm," "You're a Big Girl Now," and the epic "Idiot Wind," which follows the poignantly placed "I Threw It All Away," recorded in Fort Worth a few nights earlier. None of these songs gained anything from the blustery conditions or Dylan's own frazzled emotional weather.

The mangled classics that lead off the first side, including "Maggie's Farm," "One Too Many Mornings," and "Stuck Inside of Mobile," have no such external or internal excuse, although "Stuck Inside of Mobile," as well as "Oh Sister" and "Lay Lady Lay," were also recorded in Fort Worth. They are all disheartening reminders of what casual fans regularly discover at a Bob Dylan concert: his disdain for the original melodies and arrangements—and sometimes lyrics—of the treasured songs that most in the audience have come to hear.

The belated corrective is much better, featuring twenty-two songs from four different concerts in November and December 1975, none of them duplicating the nine songs on *Hard Rain*. Although ten songs come from one show—the second set at the Boston Music Hall, on November 21—only three of them duplicate the sequence in which they were played: "One More Cup of Coffee (Valley Below)" into "Sara" into "Just Like a Woman." The closing "Knockin' on Heaven's Door" is taken from the Harvard Square Theater performance the night before, while the lead-in, "Hurricane," comes from the nineteenth at Memorial Hall in nearby Worcester. Four songs come from the December 4 performance at the Forum in Montreal, two nights before the tour wrapped up.

If *Hard Rain* made any statement at all, it was that Bob Dylan was determined not to be a nostalgia act. By the time it came out (along with the widely panned TV special of the Fort Collins show), he was already on to the next thing. In this case, the next thing would be almost three years in coming. By then, the breakup would be complete, if not its lingering, debilitating aftereffects.

Kicked to the Curb

Street-Legal is the first Bob Dylan album where you can get the best clues as to his motives and overall direction simply by looking at the credits.

His basic intention here, as on almost all of his albums, was to avoid the dread notion of "going through all these things twice." In his post-accident career thus far, he'd messed around with traditional forms with the Band (*The Basement Tapes*), written a series of folk parables (*John Wesley Harding*), tried his hand at a country album (*Nashville Skyline*), collaborated with a couple of theater people (Archibald MacLeish on *New Morning*, Jacques Levy on *Desire*), dabbled in pop and folk covers (*Self Portrait*), attempted movie-scoring (*Pat Garrett and Billy the Kid*), ventured into hard rock (*Planet Waves*), and proved he could compete with the best of the confessional singer/songwriters (*Blood on the Tracks* and *Desire*). In performance, he'd conquered arena-rock (*Before the Flood*) and the more intimate gypsy-caravan (Rolling Thunder Revue) aspects of touring. While many of these experiments were failures, they echoed his earlier musical changes from blues interpreter to folk songwriter to protest balladeer to blues-rocker to electric bard.

With his life in the toilet, his marriage broken up, his costly home under endless renovations, and his costly home movie virtually unsalvageable, the only constant in his life in the late '70s was his need to continue the experimental process with his music, no matter how risky. What he came up with for his next tour and for his long-gestating next album was a cross between the Motown Revue and Elvis in Las Vegas. Toward that end he hired a couple of musicians with extensive Elvis experience, bass player Jerry Scheff and sax player Steve Douglas. To help with the R&B feel, he included a trio of black female backup singers, Helena Springs, Jo-Ann Harris, and Carolyn Dennis (whose place on the first leg of the tour, in Japan and Australia, was taken by Debi Dye).

After a two-month break following his return from Sydney, Dylan spent the rest of April recording the songs for *Street-Legal* and getting to know his backup singers—often in the biblical sense. With Springs he wrote several songs, including "Walk out in the Rain," which was recorded by Eric Clapton. With Dennis he had a child in 1986; they married that year and divorced in 1992. Also buried in the credits for the album is another black woman named Mary Alice Artes. In addition to being a vague and all-encompassing "Queen Bee," Artes is credited as the person who brought Dylan to Jesus; like Sara before her, she was literally his salvation.

Like the tour that surrounded it, *Street-Legal* was reviled by critics incensed at another change of direction for the mercurial Gemini. They didn't like the horns, the new arrangements, the costumes, the backup singers. They accused Dylan of trying to emulate his prime emulator, Bruce Springsteen, by adding a saxophone to the mix. This in particular irked Dylan no end. "The saxophone thing was almost slanderous," he complained to Cameron Crowe. "His saxophone player couldn't be spoken of in the same breath as Steve Douglas, who'd played with Duane Eddy and on literally all of Phil Spector's records. I mean no offense to Clarence, but he's not in the same category. Anyway, people need to be encouraged, not stepped on and put in a straight jacket."

While clearly not a major album, especially when compared to his recent work, *Street-Legal* would usher in a new era of appreciating Dylan—one that would last for the next twenty years. Instead of expecting a (well-produced) work of cohesive genius, with stunning lyrical turns throughout and a masterpiece every third track, for now the bar he'd established in the sixties (and reached again only on *Blood on the Tracks*) would have to be set a bit lower. The random stirring couplet had to be considered a happy surprise; the occasional return to epic form a cause for tearful celebration, no matter how badly Dylan mangled said song in the studio or on the road (or neglected to put it on an album or perform it at all). One or two performing perennials, or "greatest hits" candidates, was all that you could reasonably hope for on any new album in this era.

With *Street-Legal*, the performing perennial was "Señor (Tales of Yankee Power)," which some critics have dubbed (perhaps in retrospect) the first indication of his impending religious conversion. Most of the songs on *Street-Legal* he hasn't played since 1978; "New Pony" and "No Time to Think," he's never played live at all. (For some odd reason known only to its author, the rarely played "We Better Talk This Over" suddenly appeared during the second of two shows at the Sun Theater in Anaheim, California, that kicked off his 2000 tour on March 10, sandwiched between "Country Pie" and "Things Have Changed" in the middle of the set.)

By and large, the songs on *Street-Legal* have the feel of being driven by a compulsive search for internal rhymes within tortuous medieval adventures. To Dylan's probable satisfaction, the occasional confessional image passes fleetingly, like a town viewed from a train going west. A lot of folk glommed on to the lyric from "Is Your Love in Vain" about his needing a woman who can cook and sew (while Neil Young's "A Man Needs a Maid" went by without drawing picket lines). Considering Dylan's likely state of mind at the time of the writing, I'm willing to give him a pass. To me, aside from the stirring but ultimately unrevealing "Changing of the Guards," the real return to form on *Street-Legal* is "Where Are You Tonight (Journey Through Dark Heat)," which sounds a lot like "Like a Rolling Stone" as written by a man scarred by events and no longer riding so high on his chrome horse, grappling with his Gemini nature, "the enemy within." When he cries out at the end of the song, "I can't believe I'm alive," it's probably the most confessional statement he's ever made on record.

Maybe this vulnerability caused him to lose faith in this song, as well as the others on the album. Or maybe his faith was being directed elsewhere, toward another style of music and showmanship he'd yet to try on for size.

Turning Japanese: Live at Budokan

For this "greatest hits" show, taped during his first ever visit to Japan for twelve nights in February 1978, Bob Dylan gave his hosts what they asked for (in writing), as only he could provide it. Thus, though the song titles may have been the ones requested, the performances are barely recognizable; likewise the high-gloss stage show, complete with horns and backing vocalists. Distributed later in the year in Australia, where Dylan also played five cities, *Bob Dylan at Budokan* got a stateside release only when imports started flooding the American market. American reviewers did not take kindly to the twenty-two–song record, which may have bothered Dylan a bit, but it didn't stop him from continuing to take further and even more drastic liberties with his catalog. The Elvis/Neil Diamond–inspired stage show did not return, however. By the time the album came out, Dylan was already on to a new and even more polarizing thing.

27

The Holy Trinity

Dylan's Christian Period

Nobody complained when Elvis put out a gospel record as early as 1957 (*Peace in the Valley*). Nobody complained when Little Richard put out a half-dozen gospel albums in the early '60s (although no one bought them). Original rockers like Little Anthony and the Imperials and Dion found Christian music after their rock 'n' roll careers had stalled—Dion, his faith intact, returned to secular music late in the '80s. From as early as 1959 up through 2004, Johnny Cash was no stranger to spirituals. George Harrison's guru-inspired songs inspired many. Even Jimmy Page's dabbling in the occult or Mick Jagger's sympathy for the Devil failed to affect their superstardom. But when Bob Dylan found Jesus Christ at the burned-out end of a 1978 tour, all of his old fans took up arms against him.

Maybe it was because these were no ordinary, time-honored, feel-good hymns he was singing. Like the apocalyptic folk songs he dared to write in the early '60s, enraging the traditionalists, these were clearly Dylan songs, the work of a man who unabashedly found himself rewriting the Bible in his own unforgiving terms.

By all accounts, Dylan's conversion began at end of '78, when he had a vision of Jesus appearing before him in a hotel room in Tucson, Arizona. An early draft of "Slow Train," written at the time, did not begin to hint at the well of creativity this vision would unearth over the course of the next couple of years, when he immersed himself in the Bible (as well as the Hal Lindsay screed *The Late Great Planet Earth*) and seemed to take on the persona of someone who'd been saved onstage and off, to the exclusion of normal conversation. Following the lead of touring band-members T Bone Burnett, Steven Soles, and David Mansfield, Dylan turned to the Vineyard Fellowship, a small California congregation, having been brought into the fold by close friend Mary Alice Artes, who was also a recent convert. After spending four days a week for three months at the top of 1979 taking a discipleship course, he was ready to plunge into writing. Convinced his previous songs were the work of the Devil, he was intent on creating enough new material to fill out his set list for the rest of 1979 and beyond.

Enlisting the Great Jerry Wexler

Two of the three albums that comprise Dylan's "Holy Trinity" (*Slow Train Coming* and *Saved*) were produced at the famed Muscle Shoals Studio by the legendary producer Jerry Wexler, along with Barry Beckett. The third was mainly done at Dylan's Rundown Studios, aided by Chuck Plotkin and, on one track ("Shot of Love"), Bumps Blackwell, Little Richard's original producer (although not for his gospel material). They also made (limited) use of stellar sidemen, including Mark Knopfler, Spooner Oldham, Ron Wood, Ringo Starr, Donald "Duck" Dunn, Benmont Tench, Fred Tackett, and Steve Douglas.

It was all for naught. The three albums rose or fell on one's toleration for the lyrics.

The songs he wrote for *Slow Train Coming* are certainly Dylan-esque. Their mission is to change the world, in this case by Bob Dylan reminding everyone of the need to accept Christ as a hedge against the apocalypse. Even an ostensible love song like "Precious Angel" is laden with fearful prognostications and hate-filled lyrics, all of it directly based on his rewriting of various passages from the Bible, much as he'd started out in musical life rewriting ancient folk songs. While the album was reviled by old fans, "When He Returns" and "I Believe in You" were considered classics by Christian music devotees, who flocked to Dylan during his 1979 and 1980 tours as if he were the messiah. The usually taciturn performer rewarded their faith by introducing many of his songs with fiery sermons as if he were the second coming of Daddy Grace. "Gotta Serve Somebody" won a Grammy; the album won a Dove Award, the Christian music version of a Grammy.

Saved is more of the same, although Dylan's focus seems to shift a bit in songs like "Pressing On," "In the Garden" (not to be confused with Van Morrison's lush number of the same name), and "Saving Grace" toward merely trying to save himself. It did less well, failing to make the Top 20 on *Billboard*, although "In the Garden," "Solid Rock," and "Saving Grace" became concert staples.

Listening to Bill—Not Billy—Graham

By the time Dylan started work on *Shot of Love* a year later, he'd moved from trying to save himself to trying to save his career, even allowing a few non-Bible-related songs into his set lists. In concert, from November 1979 through the spring of 1980, he had exclusively played Christian material for approximately seventy-four shows in a row, aside from one inexplicable lapse at the Stanley Theater in Pittsburgh, on May 15, when somehow "Lay Lady Lay" crept into the set. In the down period between May 21 and November 9, when the tour started up again for twelve nights at the Warfield Theater in San Francisco, he began mixing secular hymns like "Mr. Tambourine Man" and "Like a Rolling Stone" into the set (reportedly at the urging of concert

Dylan didn't fully appreciate the power of this song—originally released as the B-side to "Heart of Mine," from the *Shot of Love* album—until his Christian phase petered out.

promoter Bill—not Billy—Graham), a practice he'd continue until, by the end of '81, he was singing at least half of his old catalog, inspired either by the Devil or else the wrath of Graham. However, he would usually start each show with "Gotta Serve Somebody" or "Saved," and by the time he was back in the USA in the fall, after touring Europe in the spring, he was closing with "Knockin' on Heaven's Door."

Oddly enough, the two best songs from *Shot of Love* were rarely heard live during Dylan's Christian phase. He played the fiercely rocking "The Groom's Still Waiting at the Altar"—originally the B-side of "Heart of Mine," until it was belatedly added to the album later in '81—only five times, all at the end of 1980. And he waited until the last night of his 1981 tour in Lakeland, Florida, to perform the gorgeous "Every Grain of Sand." No less devotional and heartfelt, this song was truly a poem, with a universal meaning almost anyone could relate to, especially fans of great songwriting. Longtime friend and chronicler Paul Nelson compared it to "Chimes of Freedom" and "Mr. Tambourine Man" in his review for *Rolling Stone*: "For a moment or two, he touches you, and the gates of heaven dissolve into a universality that has nothing to do with most of the record."

Although it did become a concert favorite in later years, instead of immediately pursuing this direction, Dylan being Dylan seemed to say, "The hell with it." After the last of his 1981 shows, he stopped touring for almost three years.

28

His Career in the Balance

A Troubled Decade

After getting off the road in 1981, Dylan played sparingly until 1987. After a three-month European tour in 1984, he gave only two public appearances in 1985: his problematic stint at Live Aid in July, and his more favorably received set at Farm Aid in September.

About a year later, he teamed up with the heavily Dylan-influenced rockers, Tom Petty and the Heartbreakers, in Australia in February and March, and then again in the summer in the American West and Midwest, joined on some of those dates by the Grateful Dead. Mostly, it was a great learning experience . . . for Petty and his band. "You had to be pretty versatile," Petty explained to Andrea Rotondo, in the book *Tom Petty: Rock and Roll Guardian*, "because arrangements might change, keys might change, there's just no way of knowing what he wants to do each night."

Translation: the band-members were generally befuddled and bewildered each night by the relentless shifts of repertoire and direction of their mercurial bandleader.

Dylan and the Dead: A Disaster That Led to an Epiphany

Dylan wouldn't be back on the road for another year, this time bringing his loose, jangly style to a band he figured to be more accustomed to improvising on the fly: the very same Grateful Dead.

The tour was an unmitigated disaster.

Yet it marked a turning point in Bob Dylan's professional career.

When he opened the first set in Foxboro, Massachusetts, on July 4, with "The Times They Are a-Changin'," after a few weeks of sloppy rehearsals, neither Dylan nor his audience could have foreseen how much was about to change, in both the man and his mission. Aside from bringing "Queen Jane

Approximately" into the live arena for the first time, the changes wrought by his close proximity to the Grateful Dead, and especially their charmingly spacey leader, Jerry Garcia, were more internal than external.

"Listening to him perform with Tom Petty's band the year before had whetted our appetites," Phil Lesh reveals in his memoir, *Searching for the Sound*. "We had always wanted to play behind him like the Band did in the '60s. We were very pleased that Bob found this agreeable."

In May of '87, Dylan came out to the Dead's studio, Club Front, to rehearse for the tour. In short order, Weir compiled a notebook filled with chord sequences and lyric cues for about fifty songs. All they had to do was make sure Dylan gave them a set list each night before the show. Good luck with that. "At least twice," Lesh writes, "Bob threw in a song we hadn't rehearsed, and more than once he left us slack jawed in confusion as he switched songs in midstream."

The performances on the six dates were mostly lackluster at best, but it wasn't Dylan's quirkiness that undid the tour; the shifty habits of an indecisive Gemini that were more or less his trademark. It was rather the harrowing presence of a man twisting in the mangled synapses of his own mind.

At the age of forty-six, maybe for the first time in his life, Bob Dylan had begun to doubt himself, his performing ability, and his entire catalog. He pretty much thought his performing career was over, as he told interviewer David Gates for *Newsweek* in 1997. He could no longer summon the internal fire necessary to light under himself onstage. The lyrics made no sense to him. He was beginning to think the unthinkable for any artist. "Maybe it's like what all these people say, just a bunch of surrealistic nonsense."

The impervious, impenetrable Bob Dylan, believing the worst of his critics? This was surely the start of a creative nervous breakdown of mythic proportions—more severe even than his Woodstock comedown of '66, when at least there was a wife and family around to distract and support him, and then the Band to provide comfort and company as he buried himself in the roots of his craft and the roots of his soul with daily music sessions and readings from the Bible.

On the other hand, some said it may have been that he was still in the character of Billy Parker, the role he was called on to portray in *Hearts of Fire*, the dud of a film he'd spent several months working on, six months prior to joining the Dead. A washed-up one-hit rocker living in well-deserved, drunken obscurity on a chicken farm, Parker's career was about as far from Dylan's as you could imagine . . . unless you were Bob Dylan, in the throes of an artistic and critical and performing dry spell. Wandering, as Packer, into the creative maelstrom that was the Grateful Dead operation, Dylan might well have felt lost, a completely different person. As he told Gates, in

Dylan rarely toured during the mid-'80s, but he graced Barcelona, Spain, with one of his best set lists of the decade on June 28, 1984, including ten of his top twelve in-concert favorites along with the early "Girl from the North Country" and the later "Every Grain of Sand." *F. Antolín Hernández/Wikimedia Commons/Public domain*

his best Gemini fashion, "I change during the course of a day. I wake up and I'm one person and when I go to sleep I know for sure I'm somebody else. I don't know who I am most of the time."

In any event, at this time of crisis, the comfort and support he needed came from none other than Jerry Garcia, a man known for his deep understanding of psychology and physiology borne from over a thousand acid trips and a similar amount of free-form concerts. When Dylan sat down with Garcia during one of these informal therapy sessions—when he couldn't remember his lyrics, or why he wrote them, or, probably, the sound of his own name—he found Garcia to be the embodiment of the ultimate devoted fan; and, moreover, one that didn't live at home with his mother and six thousand bootlegs of every Dylan concert forever on rewind in his skull.

Garcia was perhaps the only human being, let alone the only musician, capable of relating to Dylan on this astral plane of common knowledge since his legendary compadres in the Band, who'd mostly fallen on hard times in recent years. Not only was Garcia a vast resource of Dylan trivia, a bottomless vault of Dylan covers, a man who drank from the same well of traditional music, and in his own way a deeply spiritual being; the Grateful Dead was an outfit long accustomed to life on the road, the ever-expanding set list of expectations and gratifications derived from cultivating a loyal if not rabid fan base for the near term and the long haul.

As Dylan told *Newsweek* ten years later, Garcia had said, "'Come on, man, this is the way it goes.' And I'd say, 'How's he gettin' there and I can't get there?' And I had to go through a lot of red tape in my mind to get back there."

Apparently, Garcia's intense intervention, probably occurring during the break between the East Coast leg of the tour and beginning of the West Coast leg, did the trick, at least as far as the first concert in the west, in Eugene, Oregon, which critics have singled out as the best of a weak menu, especially the inspired intro and performance of "Queen Jane Approximately."

Long after the tour was a distant memory, Dylan acknowledged his debt to Garcia. "To me he wasn't only a musician and a friend," he wrote in a eulogy, after Jerry died in August of 1995, "he was more like a big brother who taught and showed me more than he'll ever know. He was there for me when nobody was."

When Dylan returned to action in 1987, playing a series of dates in Europe with Petty and his band that fall, he was once again a changed man.

And the biggest change was just up the road.

A Tour of Europe Under Threatening Skies

Before playing an outdoor concert on a windy and foggy Monday, October 5, at the Piazza Grande in Locarno, Switzerland, site of a famous film festival since 1973, Dylan and his backup band had already done two dates in Israel, seven in Italy, seven in Germany, three in Scandinavia (Finland, Sweden, and Denmark), a previous date in Switzerland (Basel), and one in the Netherlands (Rotterdam). Up ahead were shows in France and Belgium, and three nights at the International Arena in Birmingham, England, before the last four nights at Wembley Arena in London, which closed down the tour and the year on October 17.

Right from the start, the tour was not without its share of high drama, even if Dylan himself might have been unaware of it. Backstage at the opening concert in Hayarkon Park in north Tel Aviv (his first ever concert appearance in Israel), his old friend and new tour-manager-in-training, Victor Maymudes, was confronted by an Israeli general who advised him of an impending curfew. When Dylan was still singing with Tom Petty at the 10:00 p.m. witching hour, the general threatened to shut down the show. Maymudes attempted to improvise, in order to buy time.

The general was not to be swayed. "We're bombing Jordan right now, this instant, and we're afraid of retaliation," he said, as soldiers with machine guns began to surround the stage. "This concert is too good of a target to let sit on this beach."

But by the time Maymudes stopped talking, Dylan was done with his startlingly appropriate concert closer, "Go Down Moses," and bedlam was averted.

The next night, after the concert in Jerusalem, Dylan and his faithful squire got a tour of the Old City with "the head of hostage negotiations for the Israel Defense Forces, who showed up with an Uzi strapped to his back and a pistol attached to his leg," along with an agent with the Israel Ministry of Tourism.

According to Maymudes, Dylan and Petty pretty much traveled separately. "The relationship didn't exist behind the curtains like it did onstage," he notes in his book, *Another Side of Bob Dylan*.

Maymudes also writes of how the historic show at the Treptower Festwiese in East Berlin on October 17 was a spontaneous addition to the tour, selling some 120,000 tickets in a couple of days. "When the show started you couldn't see the edge of the crowd. They had to put up a fence but they didn't have a fence big enough, so it didn't matter who had tickets by the time the show started."

Someone may or may not have shouted (in German), "The Bob Dylan show at the Treptower Festwiese is now a free concert!"

The Piazza Grande, Locarno, Switzerland, October 5, 1987: "I Am Determined to Stand"

On what was dubbed the "Temple in Flames" tour, the temple in question was neither a specifically Jewish or Christian edifice. Rather, the temple was inside Bob Dylan's head: the temple of his sanity, his creativity, his ability to face himself and his audience as the miles started to pile years onto his thin frame. Later on, he'd disavow his Christian phase, as well as his speculated return to Judaism, claiming he found all the spirituality he needed inside his songs, the ones he wrote and the ones he covered.

In order to keep his head straight and his priorities straight, even if it drove Tom Petty and his band crazy, Dylan incessantly tinkered with his set list, probably inspired by his time with the Grateful Dead. Sometimes a song that ended the show one night would begin the show the next. Others would disappear for a week, only to be brought back in another country. During his two concerts in Israel, he sang thirty different songs, not duplicating any of them, although many of these songs were ones he'd previewed in the States with the Grateful Dead the previous summer. A few nights later, in Basel, Switzerland, he added a dozen more. Every night he debuted at least one new song (perhaps to the surprise of his backing band), sometimes three or four. It was almost as if he was sifting through the back pages of his catalog, looking for one specific song, something he'd already sung a hundred times, which on one particular night, in one particular remote spot on the map, might remind him of who he'd been, and who he still was if he could will himself into the mind that created these gems once upon a time.

In reading the comments of the greatest of all Dylan scholars, Paul Williams, in *Mind out of Time: Bob Dylan Performing Artist, 1986–1990 and Beyond*, I believe the inspiration Dylan was searching for was found in "Tomorrow Is a Long Time," a song he'd originally written for and about Suze Rotolo in 1962, during her sojourn in Italy. He'd sung it once during his six shows with the Dead, at the Meadowlands in New Jersey, on July 7, before retiring it, only to sneak it back into the set on September 25, in Sweden. From then on, he played it at ten of his last seventeen concerts, never as movingly as he did in Locarno, on the night of October 5, in a performance Williams called "showstopping."

Backed only by Mike Campbell on guitar and Benmont Tench on piano, Dylan offered a new arrangement of the song that made it "more romantic and (in the best sense of the word) nostalgic and dramatic than if Dylan were singing the song alone, accompanying himself on harmonica and acoustic guitar. These 1987 performances speak of the present, including Bob Dylan's relationship with his audience and with the endless highway and crooked trail of the performance artist."

The song takes on even more mystical import when considered in the context of what happened to Dylan during that concert in Locarno. Much like the incident in the Southwest in 1978, when the voice of Jesus came to him in his hotel room, onstage in Locarno he had a similar visitation. It was almost like he heard a voice saying, "I'm determined to stand, whether God will deliver me or not." "All of a sudden things just exploded," he told *Newsweek* in 1997. That's when he knew it was his mission to play these songs on all of the stages of the world, until the end of his days.

For a man who, a few short months before, couldn't understand his own words, or the sound of his own voice, or, for that matter, see his own reflection in the water, now "Tomorrow Is a Long Time" was opening up a new path in front of him: an endless highway, leading to a Never Ending Tour, one that would last for as long as he could stand and deliver. One that would carry him deeper into his relationship with the music and the muse than ever before.

29

A Falling Star

A New Recording Low

In the musical dry spell that was the '80s—for himself and for much of the rock community—Bob Dylan suffered from what I call Woody Allen/Michael Jackson syndrome. People confused the artist with his work. His various domestic misdeeds in the '70s during the course of his divorce, along with his escape into a messianic sort of religious upheaval in the early '80s, turned many away from his music on principle alone. Which would have been a shame, had he been producing really great or even good music during this period. But he wasn't.

Although he attempted to make use of virtually every working sideman and superstar in New York City and Los Angeles (with Britain, Detroit, and New Orleans thrown in for good measure), his historic inability or refusal to capture what was inside his head in the studio, along with his perverse pleasure in withholding his best songs from the given album in progress, resulted in a string of mediocre products unbefitting his name. In other words, there was hardly a *Thriller* in the pack; and even Woody Allen produced *Zelig* and *Broadway Danny Rose* during this culturally barren epoch.

Dylan continually sabotaged himself with side projects, including a shelved duets album with Clydie King, the time he spent offering input into the career-spanning *Biograph* set, two albums with the Traveling Wilburys, and the awful movie *Hearts on Fire*. Every year from '86 on, he hit the road. Moreover, his personal life was a confusing mess. In '86, he married his backup singer, Carolyn Dennis, and fathered her child (not necessarily in that order). They got divorced in 1992. During that period, according to his biographer, Howard Sounes, he was also involved with several other women. Like the teenager in Hibbing, leading a double life, the Gemini superstar was now living a quadruple life, with a surrogate wife in every house he owned. Like his idol, Robert Johnson, he was able to keep many of these relationships secret, not only from the public but from the other women involved. No wonder his focus during this time was not on music.

In the six albums (as well as *Real Live*) released between 1983 and 1990, he often seemed to be not even trying, to the dismay of some of the most talented and expensive musicians on the planet. From 1986 to 1988, during the first years of his marriage to Dennis, he used a total of fifty-one musicians on the albums *Knocked Out Loaded* and *Down in the Groove*; only Ron Wood appears on both, playing guitar on one album and bass on the other. He used thirty backup singers, with only two—his wife and his mother-in-law, Madelyn Quebec—appearing on both albums. Playing behind him on various tracks were Tom Petty, Mike Campbell and Benmont Tench of Petty's Heartbreakers, Dave Stewart of the Eurythmics, Eric Clapton and Mark Knopfler, Carlos Santana, Mick Jones and Paul Simonon of the Clash, Jerry Garcia, Bob Weir and Brent Mydland of the Grateful Dead, the great Motown bass guitarist James Jamerson, as well as Nathan East, Robbie Shakespeare, and eight others, including Kip Winger from the hair metal band of the same last name. Oh, and the drummers—so many drummers—fourteen of them, including Sly Dunbar, of course, and Clem Burke of Blondie fame, and the New York regular Anton Fig.

COLUMBIA 47401	BOB DYLAN The Bootleg Series Volume 3

BOB DYLAN
The Bootleg Series Volume 3
(Rare and Unreleased) 1961-1991

Side One

1. IF YOU SEE HER, SAY HELLO
2. GOLDEN LOOM
3. CATFISH
4. SEVEN DAYS
5. YE SHALL BE CHANGED
6. EVERY GRAIN OF SAND
7. YOU CHANGED MY LIFE
8. NEED A WOMAN
9. ANGELINA

Side Two

1. SOMEONE'S GOT A HOLD OF MY HEART
2. TELL ME
3. LORD PROTECT MY CHILD
4. FOOT OF PRIDE
5. BLIND WILLIE McTELL
6. WHEN THE NIGHT COMES FALLING FROM THE SKY
7. SERIES OF DREAMS

Promotional Copy - Not for Sale
Copyright 1991 Sony Music Entertainment Inc.

With his output dwindling, Dylan finally agreed to look back at his career. The 1986 *Biograph* set was but a prelude to a long-awaited raiding of the vaults.

And to what purpose? Mainly collaborations and cover songs. *Knocked Out Loaded* includes songs by the blues singer Little Junior Parker, playwright Sam Shepard, country icon Kris Kristofferson, rocker Tom Petty, gospel composer J. B. F. Wright, and, most randomly of all, pop craftsman Carole Bayer Sager. *Down in the Groove* features only two songs solely written by Dylan (one of them from *Hearts on Fire*), two collaborations with the Dead's Robert Hunter, two country classics, two R&B classics, one pop classic, and the traditional "Shenandoah." Coincidentally, the mix of selections evokes his *Self Portrait* years, when marriage and family and the stiffing of Albert Grossman took precedence over maintaining the quality of his work.

Really, he could have just put out an extended single of "Brownsville Girl" and gone back to changing diapers, and nobody would have complained. As it was, he spent much of '86 touring Australia, Japan, and the United States. It was only on August 6, the last day of the tour, at the Mid-State Fair in Pasa Robles, California, that he treated the crowds to a somewhat truncated performance of his one true masterwork released in the decade, as part of a twenty-five-song set. Typically, he never played "Brownsville Girl" live again. He was in Europe in '87, and in June through October of '88 he toured the US again, in a tight rock unit headed by G. E. Smith, opening every night with "Subterranean Homesick Blues." So much for changing diapers.

Best Since *Blood on the Tracks*?

Bookending Dylan's '80s output were his two most highly regarded albums of the decade, both of which invoked the phrase "his best since *Blood on the Tracks*." Which was not necessarily the highest of praise. At least they had somewhat consistent songwriting and committed performances, if not any enduring classics, although "Jokerman," the first single from 1983's *Infidels*, and "Ring Them Bells," from 1989's *Oh Mercy* did make it onto his *Greatest Hits, Vol. 3* collection. But if "greatest hits" meant live favorites, neither of these songs makes the grade.

From the earlier album, "I and I" is the song Dylan performed the most; from the later album, "Man in the Long Black Coat," "Everything Is Broken," and "What Good Am I" saw a lot of action on the boards. He failed to play three songs from *Infidels* at all onstage, including, of course, the second single, "Sweetheart Like You," for which he appeared in his first MTV music video. The song peaked at No. 55 on the *Billboard* charts.

Although there were few overtly religious songs on either record, Dylan's return to secular protest seemed to annoy fans and critics just as much. Maybe his protests on *Infidels* in favor of Israel ("Neighborhood Bully") and against unions ("Union Sundown") and space travel ("License to Kill") weren't *their* protests anymore. That the once angry young man had grown into a cranky old coot was the defining complaint against the songs on *Oh Mercy* that dared to comment on events ("Political World," "Everything Is Broken"). Most of Dylan's complaining on this album is focused on himself ("Most of the Time," "What Good Am I," and "What Was It You Wanted").

Just as Dylan followed *Infidels* with the markedly inferior *Empire Burlesque*, the underwhelming *Under the Red Sky* depleted any critical capital he might have accrued after the relative success of *Oh Mercy*. *Empire Burlesque* was merely mediocre. Despite the appearance of sidemen like Slash; Elton John; Jimmie Vaughan and his brother, Stevie Ray; George Harrison; David Crosby; and Bruce Hornsby, *Under the Red Sky* sounds (and reads) more like a deranged children's album ("Wiggle Wiggle," "2x2," "Handy Dandy," "Cat's in the Well"). This would have actually made sense in that children's music was one area Dylan had yet to infiltrate (and even Woody Guthrie recorded at least a couple of kids' albums). But Dylan has yet to reveal his motives behind this very slight album, although on his 1990 tour he did proceed to open up shows in Oklahoma City; Dallas; Charleston; and Carbondale and Normal, Illinois, with "Ol' MacDonald."

With *Empire Burlesque*, recorded over the course of a year at five different studios, Dylan left famed disco engineer Arthur Baker to clean up the mess. "I'm not too experienced at having records sound good," he explained, stating the obvious, to Toby Creswell in the Australian edition of *Rolling Stone* in 1986. "I just went out and recorded a bunch of stuff all over the place, and then when it was time to put it together, I brought it all to [Baker] and he made it sound like a record." A disco record at that, apart from the album's closer, the acoustic stunner "Dark Eyes," which he performed only once in 1986, cutting the song short before it was finished. He was reminded of this beauty in 1995 by another beauty with dark eyes, Patti Smith, who had begun performing it. For a while, the two performed it as an odd duet, before it was retired to the shadows once again. The other track of note, "When the Night Comes Falling from the Sky," suffered from overproduction by Baker and overthinking by Dylan, as he rejected a truly smoldering take, aided by guitarist Miami Steve Van Zandt and keyboard player Roy Bittan of Bruce Springsteen's E Street Band. "The alternate take has such an undeniably raunchy attitude," critic Tim Riley writes in his book *Hard Rain:*

At this house on Sonia Street in New Orleans, Bob Dylan and producer Daniel Lanois continued the arduous process of recording *Oh Mercy*.   *Charliedylan/Wikimedia Commons/Public domain*

A Dylan Commentary, "you wonder why Dylan stuck with the lifeless take that makes *Empire Burlesque* drift off on side two."

Such misguided opinions and poor choices dominated Dylan's '80s output during these lost years, when probably the most significant songs of the era were the ones he abandoned, like "Foot of Pride," "Series of Dreams," and the majestic "Blind Willie McTell," claiming they were unworthy, unfinished. It was almost like he seemed to delight in passing over quality material.

Even the epic "Brownsville Girl" suffered this fate in its earlier incarnation as "New Danville Girl" in 1985. "When we first recorded it we made a cassette," said Ira Ingber, one of the players on the session, "and he took it out and started playing it. He came back the next day we were working and said, 'Yeah, a lot of people like this thing.' And then he didn't do anything with it. It's like he was doing it to spite people who were all liking it, and he just held on to it."

As if to underscore the fragility of the artistic process—especially as it applies to recording music in the studio, or at least as it applies to Bob Dylan—these occurrences eerily evoked shades of "Like a Rolling Stone" and "Visions of Johanna," in which the recorded takes seem more and more to be the product of pure chance.

After all his travails in the studio, trying to capture his best new songs on tape, it's no wonder Dylan decided to cut his losses on his next two albums—by not supplying any.

30

I and I

Collaborating with Dylan

For an artist as singular and singularly gifted as Bob Dylan, he has participated in a surprising number of collaborations, dating back to his first forays into songwriting in 1957, when he wrote some words to an instrumental by Monte Edwardson, his lead guitarist in the Golden Chords, called "Big Black Train," which Edwardson eventually recorded as an instrumental at Kay Bank studios in Minneapolis with his next group, the Rockets.

While convalescing from his motorcycle accident in 1966 and '67, Bob wrote some songs in the basement with Rick Danko ("Tears of Rage") and Richard Manuel ("This Wheel's on Fire") of the Hawks, soon to be the Band. And when George Harrison dropped by in November of 1968 to spend several days with Bob and Sara and the kids, before long they brought out their guitars and the host supplied the bridge for "I'd Have You Anytime," which opens George's first solo album, *All Things Must Pass*. (The next time Dylan got together with Harrison, it resulted in "If Not for You," which was a hit for the ex-Beatle as well as for Olivia Newton-John.)

Down in Nashville early in 1969, hanging out singing duets with Johnny Cash, Dylan donated the unfinished "Champaign, Illinois," to Carl Perkins, who was in Cash's band at the time. Perkins put the finished song on his 1969 album *On Top*. Later in the year, Roger McGuinn of the Byrds prevailed upon his old friend to add a bridge to a song he was writing for the movie *Easy Rider*. Dylan didn't like the movie much, so he asked that his name be taken off the credits for "Ballad of an Easy Rider," which was the Byrds' biggest hit in two years, spending six weeks on the *Billboard* singles chart.

In 1975, with his marriage on the rocks, Dylan bonded with Roger McGuinn's pal, Jacques Levy. Although Dylan was coming off his comeback album, *Blood on the Tracks*, he and Levy had a rousing time writing most of the lengthy and dramatic songs for *Desire* together out on Fire Island in the summer of '75. In 1978, slogging through the winter in Japan, New Zealand,

and Australia, he wrote a few songs in Brisbane with his backup singer and perhaps potential new girlfriend, Helena Springs, among them "Walk out in the Rain" and "If I Don't Be There By Morning," which Eric Clapton included on his 1978 album *Backless*.

But the bulk of Dylan's later collaborations arose out of more dire and needy circumstances, in the decade from 1985 through 1995, when his future as a songwriter and recording artist—to say nothing of his career as a performing artist—seemed to hang in the balance. What else can explain his indiscriminate promiscuity in flitting from the sublime ("Brownsville Girl" with Sam Shepard) to the ridiculous ("Under Your Spell" with Carole Bayer Sager), with a special local stop at just plain incomprehensible ("Street Rock" with rapper Kurtis Blow)? As had been the case with Harrison and McGuinn, Dylan occasionally entertained collaborators closer to his own exalted level, including U2's Bono ("Love Rescue Me," from *Rattle and Hum*), and Tom Petty ("Jamming Me," a Top 20 single for Petty in 1987; and "Got My Mind Made Up," which Dylan recorded on *Knocked Out Loaded* in 1986). He also worked with the Grateful Dead's resident lyricist Robert Hunter on "Silvio" and "The Ugliest Girl in the World," from 1988's *Down in the Groove*, and they would collaborate on nine more songs for 2008's *Together Through Life*. More desperately, he had an audience with the undistinguished rock journeyman Michael Bolton (albeit at the height of Bolton's fame), resulting in Bolton's 1992 hit "Steel Bars," which spent twenty weeks on the rock charts.

Typical of Dylan's later collaborating process was his work with Danny O'Keefe, the fine singer/songwriter known for the hit "Good Time Charlie's Got the Blues" and "The Road," which was covered by Jackson Browne. Their song "Well Well Well" was recorded by several artists, including Maria Muldaur. According to O'Keefe, it wasn't much of a true collaboration: someone from Dylan's publishing company sent him a demo.

As with most things Dylan, much was left up to O'Keefe's interpretation. "It sort of made me think that Bob had recommended that I try to write something to it," O'Keefe told me. "But whether Bob actually did or not, we may never know. Bob had done the demo, but there were only two words on it, 'Well, well,' that he was using as a cue to let the band know he was going to change chords." O'Keefe saw the whole situation as comical. "I appreciated the humor, and I thought that Dylan would, too. Although I don't know if he did. So I just added another 'well' and made it a song about groundwater."

O'Keefe never heard from Dylan, but he assumed the song was okay, as it was sent to Maria Muldaur, who cut a great version with Mavis Staples.

The song was also cut by David Lindley, as well as by Ben Harper with the Blind Boys of Alabama.

A New Generation Discovers Dylan

In the case of two contemporary alt-country bands, the Old 97s and the Old Crow Medicine Show, collaboration worked the opposite way. The Old 97s took "Desolation Row" and transformed it into "Champaign, Illinois," which is a different song from the Carl Perkins tune. After performing it in their set for a number of years, they finally got up the nerve to ask for permission to record it in 2010, for the album *The Grand Theater, Vol. 1.* Amazingly enough, Dylan said okay.

The Old Crow Medicine Show's Ketch Secor first heard what would become "Wagon Wheel" as an outtake from the *Pat Garrett and Billy the Kid* soundtrack called "Rock Me, Mama." According to Secor, it was "not so much a song as a sketch." He added verses to it while at Phillips Exeter Academy, during the height of his Bob Dylan fixation. "I listened to Bob Dylan and nothing else for four years. It was like schooling. Every album and every outtake of every album and every live record I could get my hands on and every show I could go see live." In the meantime, after performing the song for a number of years, he too bit the bullet and asked for Dylan's approval. They signed a fifty-fifty contract on the song, which came out in 2004 on the album *Old Crow Medicine Show.*

In 2013, a box of handwritten Dylan lyrics emerged, written during the basement era. Much in the way Billy Bragg and Jeff Tweedy got their hands on some unrecorded Woody Guthrie lyrics (in his memoir, Dylan says he was offered them first) and turned them into *Mermaid Avenue,* released in 1998, with a second volume following in 2000, these rare Dylan lyrics were put in the custody of Dylan's trusted cohort T Bone Burnett. Burnett then reached out to Elvis Costello, Rhiannon Giddens, Taylor Goldsmith, Jim James, and Marcus Mumford to supply melodies, and the twenty-track *Lost on the River: The New Basement Tapes* was released in November 2014.

Perhaps Dylan's most rewarding collaboration personally, if not artistically, was in 1995 with Gerry Goffin, the former Brill Building hit-maker once married to Carole King, which resulted in two songs that appeared on Goffin's album *Backroom Blood,* "Tragedy of the Trade" and "Time to End This Masquerade," which Dylan coproduced. A meeting of the lyrical minds, it may have been the closest thing to fun he'd had in the song-making process since his epic collaboration with George Harrison, Tom Petty, and the boys in the Traveling Wilburys in 1988 and 1990.

This was a true supergroup that I like to call . . .

Dylan's Beatles: *The Traveling Wilburys, Vol. 1* and *3*

Many were the benefits reaped by Bob Dylan when he allowed his friend George Harrison the use of his home studio at Point Dume in Malibu in April of 1988 to record a European B-side for his single "This Is Love." At the cost of a few hotdogs for the expanding crew, which ultimately included Jeff Lynne, Roy Orbison, and Tom Petty, Dylan got to take part in a musical experience that recalled his deliciously free flowing Woodstock heyday with the Band, while bringing him face-to-face (to-face-to-face) with his long-standing fantasy of having what the Beatles had: a creative brotherhood of trust and complicity, with the joys multiplied by five and the burdens shared.

When the resultant single, "Handle with Care," completed inside of five hours with all five musicians sharing in the workload, was deemed too good for a B-side by George's label (actually, it was a C-side, since they added "All Those Years Ago" and Hoagy Carmichael's "Hong Kong Blues" to the German single), another significant benefit of being part of this group took effect, even though the group was not at this point officially a group. But had this been a Bob Dylan composition for a Bob Dylan session for a Bob Dylan album (the dismal *Down in the Groove* was already done and about to be released, with the only Harrison on the credits Wilbert Harrison, composer and originator of the opening track "Let's Stick Together"), it's an even-money bet a song this good might have wound up on the outtake reel, consigned to the private collections of the bootleg crowd. Instead, with George Harrison and Jeff Lynne at the helm, the song became the basis for a group called the Traveling Wilburys and the lead single on an album that wound up selling upward of three million copies—far more than any previous solo Dylan album.

Dylan had just gotten done plundering the depths of aging country fare like "Rank Strangers to Me" and "Shenandoah," collaborating with Robert Hunter on deathless tunes like "The Ugliest Girl in the World," and meandering through his own mordant "Death Is Not the End." Surrounded by upbeat fellows like Petty and Lynne, a well-centered fellow like Harrison, and the beautifully broken-hearted Orbison at Dave Stewart's studio for a two-week period in May, he was able to escape from his worldly and other-worldly concerns.

Dylan's "Dirty World" and "Congratulations" were hardly soft-shoe dit-ties, and "Tweeter and the Monkey Man," tossed off in a wild and wicked improv session with Petty at his side and Bruce Springsteen on his mind, was perhaps his sharpest story song to date, filled with some unsubtle references to Boss titles the Boss had yet to release. (Name-checked in the lyric, "Lion's Den" was a *Born in the USA* outtake, while "Paradise" didn't come out until *The Rising* in 2001. In what was perhaps his own return tribute to Dylan in 1990, Springsteen recorded a song called "Part Monkey, Part Man" and used it as the B-side to "57 Channels (and Nothin' On).")

With Harrison supplying the hooks in "Handle with Care" and "End of the Line," and Lynne supplying Orbison with his high note in "Not Alone Anymore," the album was an unquestioned collaborative triumph, with liner notes by one of George's Monty Python friends, Eric Idle. Not that the critics were in agreement, with many deeming these aging hippies (along with one aspiring aging hippie in Petty) over the hill and out to pasture, like the supergroup concept itself, which in their collective mind peaked with Derek and the Dominos. But the album clicked with the public, even if it may have resembled Bob Dylan in the watered-down Byrds more than it did Bob Dylan in the watered-down Beatles.

Although the Wilburys didn't tour in support of the album, Dylan did. Perhaps it was the small group camaraderie he'd just left behind in Dave Stewart's kitchen that impelled him to ditch his backup singers and the Neil Diamond Vegas approach in favor of a tight, three-man unit for his next series of dates. With G. E. Smith on guitar, Kenny Aaronson on bass, and Christopher Parker on drums, he lit out for Concord, California, with a new spring in his step, taking his own '50s-style rocker "Subterranean Homesick Blues" out of the closet for the first time to open up the show for the duration. In St. Louis, home of Chuck Berry, Dylan broke out "Nadine" in honor of the man who inspired it.

The playful early rock 'n' roll spirit may not have carried over into his work with Daniel Lanois on *Oh Mercy* in 1989, but Dylan's time in a commu-nal group setting may have been on his mind when he implored his friend Jerry Garcia to let him join the Grateful Dead. Luckily for all concerned, the Dead turned him down. But there was a second Traveling Wilburys album in the offing, if only to cash in on the goodwill of the first, with Michael Palin, another Python alum, hired for the liner notes.

The intentionally mistitled *Vol. 3* was nowhere near as successful as its predecessor, though it still went platinum. Recorded early in 1990, it suf-fered from, among other things, the untimely passing of original member

Roy Orbison. Dylan's contribution was also muddled by his work on the exceedingly strange *Under the Red Sky* around this time. And yet "Inside Out," "The Devil's Been Busy," and the doo-wop send-up "7 Deadly Sins" could have replaced almost any track on that album. As Dave DiMartino remarked in *Musician*, "I think Bob's 'If You Belonged to Me' is better than anything on his *Under the Red Sky* album, even 'Wiggle Wiggle.'"

Phil Sutcliff in *Q* agreed, especially regarding Dylan's participation. "His enthusiasm for rock 'n' roll without the burdensomely enigmatic responsibilities of 24-hour-a-day Bobness is even more apparent than on *Vol. 1* and stokes the fire for the whole album.'"

As sung by Tom Petty, the marriage-breakup anthem "Poor House" also probably reflected, in retrospect, Dylan's state of mind better than most of his other recent work, in that Dylan had received notice in August that his second wife was filing for divorce.

With his "Beatles" moment now having passed, he next submitted to a painful journey back to the heart of the blues in 1992 and 1993. But first, the weary and world-weary troubadour made one more unscheduled detour, recording a children's song for Disney with the telling title "This Old Man."

31

The Back Pages

Unearthing the Outtakes

Like the second coming, the idea that there were mind-blowing lost and unreleased and unfinished tracks in the Bob Dylan archives was regarded as a life sustaining fable to some, plain rubbish to others, and the gospel to believers. While Dylan routinely pooh-poohed the idea, as the years went on eventually a bootleg industry sprang up, right around the time of *The Basement Tapes* in the late '60s, to roundly disprove him. According to those in the loop who had access to these treasures, unreleased tracks not only existed in vast quantities, but many of them were better than anything the man had put on record, and included probably some of the best songs he'd ever written, known only to the cognoscenti and as unlikely to fall into the hands of your average fan on the street as a bag of Acapulco Gold tossed off an East 10th Street rooftop.

Once the bootleg industry started gaining traction in the underground economy, no sooner would a Bob Dylan album come out than the accompanying bootleg would appear, filled with the markedly superior tracks unaccountably left off the album. This angered the faithful, especially as the quality of the released product began to dwindle at different points in Dylan's career. They started to harbor suspicions that Dylan had left certain excellent tracks off his albums on purpose, in order to alienate his fans. And if it was not Dylan's fault, then it was his label, Columbia, hoarding these tracks against Dylan's inevitable early death (if not at age twenty-seven, then certainly at age forty-two). At which point they would release two or three gems at a time on otherwise routine repackaging collections, to thus squeeze every penny out of his legacy (otherwise known as the Elvis Solution).

Now add to this quandary the notion that the artist was constantly second-guessing himself, not only in the studio but also on the road, changing lyrics, melodies, and arrangements at the whims of mood, band, and geography. Possessing, for instance, the original version of "Visions of

Johanna," as it appeared on *Blonde on Blonde*, in no way guaranteed that you had the best version of the song Dylan had ever done, or even the current version. The best version may have been the second, third, ninth, or the fifteenth take, to which only the true insiders were privy. Or, the actual best version may have been the one performed on November 6, 1990, at the Chick Evans Field House in DeKalb, Illinois, to which only extremely devoted or extremely deranged fans or board-tape collectors were privy. Leaving as a hopeless dream the idea that one would ever fully appreciate the magnitude of any given Bob Dylan song, aside, perhaps, from the album version of "Like a Rolling Stone."

This all changed, however, with the release of the *Biograph* set in 1985, just as Dylan was entering one of his steepest declines. Whereas he had previously refused permission to issue any similar collection comprised primarily of outtakes on the principle that this would necessarily cause critics and fans to assume he was now washed up and willing to rest on his laurels, Dylan's fury at the bootleggers gaining so much business at his expense now finally trumped his ego.

"The bootleg records are outrageous," he told Cameron Crowe, in the notes that accompanied the five-record (later three-CD) set. "I mean, they have stuff you do in a phone booth. If you're just sitting and strumming in a motel, you don't think anybody's there, and then it appears on a bootleg record. With a cover that's got a picture of you that was taken from underneath your bed and it's got a striptease type title and it cost thirty dollars. Then you wonder why most artists feel so paranoid."

Selected and sequenced by Jeff Rosen, the man who runs Dylan's publishing empire, the collection spans twenty years, from an early *Freewheelin'* outtake, "Baby I'm in the Mood for You," to a version of "Every Grain of Sand," sung with Clydie King. The tracks are not in any kind of chronological or conceptual order, although sides seven and eight of the original set contain the most unreleased tracks, including three major finds, "Caribbean Wind," "Abandoned Love," and "Up to Me," as well as an alternate take of "You're a Big Girl Now"—but not the particular alternate take most fans crave, the original New York City version, from before it was rerecorded in Minneapolis. And there may also be a better take of "Caribbean Wind" floating around somewhere. You're not likely to hear a board tape of "Abandoned Love" from an obscure concert recording, because Dylan never did it live, except for one time at the Other End just before the Rolling Thunder tour—a performance now readily available on YouTube.

Other than these, the most coveted outtakes are "I'll Keep It with Mine," which he has never performed, and "Lay Down Your Weary Tune," which was only heard by the audience at his Carnegie Hall concert in October 1963. There is a live version of "Visions of Johanna" from his first Royal Albert Hall concert in London on May 26, 1966, but whether this compares to the version from the Field House in DeKalb, Illinois, or perhaps somewhere else, is subject to ongoing debate. Aside from some otherwise unavailable singles ("Mixed-Up Confusion," "Can You Please Crawl out Your Window"), the overwrought "Percy's Song," and a demo version of "Forever Young," the rest of the collection is pretty much a sampler from some perhaps overlooked albums, including "You Angel You" and "On a Night Like This" from *Planet Waves*, "Señor (Tales of Yankee Power)" from *Street-Legal*, "I Believe in You" and "Gotta Serve Somebody" from *Slow Train Coming*, and "Solid Rock" from *Saved*.

The Official *Bootleg Series* Begins

Six years later, heading into the bleak '90s, *The Bootleg Series* was a much more illuminating effort, comprised of three lengthy CDs, arranged chronologically. These go back to Dylan's earliest days in Minnesota and feature mainly unreleased tracks, including "House Carpenter"—but apparently not the definitive "House Carpenter"—and "No More Auction Block for Me," upon which "Blowin' in the Wind" was based. The second CD recollects "I'll Keep It with Mine" and "Subterranean Homesick Blues," but throws in the rare "Farewell Angelina," the very rare "Angelina" (probably not the same girl), and the even rarer "She's Your Lover Now." A New York version of "Idiot Wind" is featured, but not the highly sought-after New York version. On CD three there's a demo version of "Every Grain of Sand," complete with barking dog (Hercules?). "Foot of Pride" and "Seven Days" would appear in scorching versions at the 30th Anniversary concert, as covered by Lou Reed and Ronnie Wood, respectively. The much treasured Steve Van Zandt and Roy Bittan version of "When the Night Comes Falling from the Sky" is also here, along with "Series of Dreams," which would also show up on *Greatest Hits, Vol. 3*. By far the biggest get of the entire collection is the criminally misperceived (by Dylan) epic "Blind Willie McTell." The version selected here, however, is the acoustic one, not the even more sought-after electric band version.

Three years later, the vaults opened up again, to produce Dylan's third *Greatest Hits* album, with the "greatest" label loosely defined as anything that was released as a single from 1973–1995. The biggest hit was "Knockin' on Heaven's Door," which peaked at No. 12. "Gotta Serve Somebody" peaked at No. 24. "Tangled Up in Blue" and "Hurricane" hit the Top 40. "Dignity," which Bob featured in his *MTV Unplugged* performance, only charted in the UK; "Silvio," his collaboration with Robert Hunter, hit No. 5 on the Rock Tracks chart. "The Groom's Still Waiting at the Altar" was the B-side of "Heart of Mine." "Brownsville Girl" was the B-side of "Got My Mind Made Up." "Changing of the Guards" and "Jokerman" failed to chart at all.

With Dylan's late-'90s comeback underway, the vaults stayed closed until 1998, when the famous "Royal Albert Hall" concert was released. This was followed in 2002 with the first leg of the Rolling Thunder tour. In 2004 came the 1964 concert he gave at Philharmonic Hall in New York City. In 2005, the famed director Martin Scorsese got to peek inside the vaults for an extended period of time so he could put together the soundtrack to the documentary *No Direction Home.* This set goes even further back into Dylan's childhood with a 1959 recording of "When I Got Troubles," followed by several more Minnesota rarities, including "I Was Young When I Left Home" and Woody Guthrie's "This Land Is Your Land." Disc two is mostly derived from the tumultuous tour of England in 1966, climaxing with the legendary "Judas" performance of "Like a Rolling Stone," which is also featured on the "Albert Hall" recording but actually taken from the performance a few days earlier in Manchester. Leading off the disc, "Maggie's Farm" is taken from his equally tumultuous Newport performance of '65.

In 2008, for *Vol. 8* of this now seemingly endless income stream, we got to peek inside Bob Dylan's painful process in the studio during the 80s and 90s for multiple versions of tracks that eventually appeared on his albums, most notably three presentations of one of his greatest new works, "Mississippi." This look behind the mask was taken to an unheard-of extreme in 2015, with the multiple-CD set *The Cutting Edge, '65–'66*, which gives an entire disc to the twenty takes "Like a Rolling Stone" necessitated before take number seven was given the nod. Six takes of "Visions of Johanna" should be more than enough to satisfy almost anyone, while four takes of "She's Your Lover Now" still leave unanswered the question of why this venomous song couldn't have been finished in time to become one of his greatest hits. It's a fascinating, if costly, look at the nuts and bolts of rock's greatest songwriter going through a historically intense creative period.

32

Can You Repeat the Past?

The Acoustic Sets

After coming off a period of time in the mid-to-late '80s when his entire identity as an artist was called into question (by Dylan himself, among others) in front of thousands of people, it's not surprising that he would seek to rediscover that identity by occasionally playing a series of surprise gigs at small, out-of-the-way venues. By their nature, these off-the-cuff, off-the-radar gigs would necessarily put him in touch with his roots, both as a performer and as a struggling artist playing in people's living rooms (with said people soon drifting out of earshot into the kitchen). In close quarters with his audience and his repertoire, these might be the gigs he feared the most, but the risky artist was always ready to face his fears. And as much as they may have been therapy for him, several dates in the 1990s were apparently just what the doctor ordered for his wavering audience.

Toad's Place, New Haven, Connecticut, January 12, 1990

Legendary as the tiny but extra-loud rock club just up the block from Yale University in New Haven where the Rolling Stones launched their 1989 US tour with a surprise performance of hits like "Start Me Up," "Tumblin' Dice," "Honky Tonk Women," "Brown Sugar," and "Jumpin' Jack Flash," in front of 700 lucky souls who just happened to be listening to the right radio station at the right time for tickets, Toad's Place burnished that reputation five months later by playing host to an impossible-to-fathom night of four sets by Bob Dylan and his Never Ending Tour band, featuring G. E. Smith on guitar.

Kicking off a tour that would find him spending the winter in Paris, London, and Brazil; the spring in such exotic locales as Sioux Falls, South

Dakota, and Bismarck, North Dakota; and the summer in Iceland, Finland, Denmark, Belgium, and Germany, before winding up in Detroit at the end of November, the Toad's gig may have simply been a rehearsal stop for Dylan, but for fans it was a fifty-song dream come true. Over the next few days, students at Penn State and Dylan's honorary alma mater Princeton would get an attenuated version of this historic set when he played forty-two songs over two nights, duplicating only four.

The sets were a mix of hits and obscurities and the occasional well-chosen cover, ranging from Joe South's "Walk a Mile in My Shoes" to Bruce Springsteen's "Dancing in the Dark." He even took requests, including the never-before-played Traveling Wilburys song "Congratulations" and a lengthy tribute to the mobster "Joey" Gallo. He finished up with brilliant versions of "Highway 61 Revisited" and "Like a Rolling Stone," closing the show at approximately 2:30 a.m.

"Dylan's tendency of late has been to toss this material off with an apathy bordering on disdain," a critic wrote in the March 8, 1990, issue of *Rolling Stone*, "but these versions were rich and impassioned, full of the humor and bite that he seemed to have lost . . . Dylan is only one year away from his fiftieth birthday and his thirtieth year as a recording artist. Yet here he was, in close contact with his fans once again, still experimenting with new songs, still working on numbers he has been playing for decades. It was an awe-inspiring performance, as close to a comprehensive retrospective as Dylan is ever likely to offer onstage."

The Supper Club, New York, New York, November 16 and 17, 1993

On Tuesday and Wednesday the 16th and 17th of November, 1993, Dylan closed out his year of touring with four sets over two nights at one of Manhattan's poshest venues, the Supper Club at 240 West 47th Street, where the opportunity to see the electric bard up close and personal at such an intimate space had people lining up in front of Tower Records on West 4th Street and Broadway as early as Sunday night, with the first thousand gaining free tickets on Monday morning. Others ponied up as much as $150 a ticket to scalpers for the remaining seats at the 500-seat establishment.

There, Dylan was ably backed by his current road band—John Jackson on guitar, Bucky Baxter on slide and pedal steel, Tony Garnier on bass, and Winston Watson on drums—who'd also played on his last two albums of blues covers, *Good as I Been to You* and *World Gone Wrong*, from which he introduced some songs, alongside favorites from the '60s through the '80s. In the first of his two sets on the Tuesday night, he laid into ten songs, starting off with "Absolutely Sweet Marie" and "Lay Lady Lay" before segueing into the blues classic "Blood in My Eyes." Most of the shows featured a final four of "I Want You," "Ring Them Bells," "My Back Pages," and "Forever Young." "Queen Jane Approximately" was featured in all four sets. The performances were also filmed for a later TV special and DVD.

Dylan was apparently so pleased by the results of Tuesday night that he allowed the press to cover the Wednesday performances, Ira Robbins of *Newsday* among them. "While the concept of Dylan performing in this intimate, egalitarian setting upped the emotional ante considerably," Robbins wrote, "seeing this incalculably larger-than-life icon singing just a few yards away gave him a degree of real-world humanity larger-scale events by artists this famous always prevent. But it is emblematic of this cryptic genius' mesmerizing power as an artist that he remains just as inscrutable up close as in our dreams."

Just as cryptically enigmatic was Dylan's decision to shelve the whole video project, even though the expense of recording it had come out of his own pocket. Judging from his past decisions about which tracks to include on an album and which were inferior, it's a safe bet the resulting commercial DVD would have been awesome—as, now, only those who own the bootleg copies have the pleasure of affirming. Instead, a year to the day later, he allowed MTV to capture him in a semi-acoustic setting, over the course of two nights, for its *MTV Unplugged* series, with much the same band, along with Brendan O'Brien on organ, resulting in a performance and a CD that was neither fully unplugged nor particularly noteworthy. It did sell well in 1995, though, reaching No. 23 in the US and No. 10 in the UK. "Dignity," produced by O'Brien, became a single. The event also spawned a bootleg called *Completely Unplugged*, assembled from all the outtakes.

Tramps, New York, New York, July 26, 1999

As a tune-up for his big Madison Square Garden concert the next night, and three other local gigs over five days to follow, Bob Dylan showed up at Tramps, the noted rock club on 21st Street in Manhattan, for a performance of nineteen songs in front of a capacity audience approaching 1,000 people, most of whom started arriving for tickets on this hot summer day as early as 11:00 a.m.

In a year when he'd played Atlantic City and Las Vegas in the same week, it was a refreshing act of reassurance that Dylan was still Dylan, capable of blowing minds and electric sockets whenever the spirit moved him. By the end of the year, Son Volt would be headlining the last show at Tramps, but Bob Dylan kept moving, hitting thirty cities in twenty-one states before winding up the year on November 20 at the University of Delaware's Bob Carpenter Center.

"It was without a doubt the best show I've seen Bob do since the Supper Club," reviewer Peter Stone Brown wrote on the Boblinks website. "Stellar versions of 'Visions of Johanna' and 'Every Grain of Sand' were topped only by the more recent 'Not Dark Yet,' where the audience went nuts at the line 'I can't even remember what I came here to get away from.' After several encores, including a wild harp solo during 'It Ain't Me Babe,' Bob brought out Elvis Costello as a special guest on the final number, 'I Shall Be Released.'"

"What's the word for beyond magnificent?" asked reviewer Andrew Klewan, reporting on the same show for the same site. "There were moments last night when he looked like Bob Dylan 1966—wild shock of hair, raised eyebrows, bouncing on his toes. But this was a man appreciative of the welcome he received from us and willing to give it all back a thousand fold. Last night was quite simply the greatest Bob Dylan concert I've ever seen."

Echoing these sentiments, another Boblinks reviewer, Carsten Wohlfeld, said, "The setlist was something like a dream come true." Among the highlights for this reviewer were a pair of acoustic tunes, the antiwar "John Brown" and "Visions of Johanna," which morphed midway into "Visions of Madonna," which was either a slip of the lip or a tip of the cap or something else entirely. Wohlfield was the only one to note some of the technical problems leading to forgotten lyrics that nevertheless failed to mar the experience of seeing Dylan in this setting. "Despite the bad, bad sound it was a fun show, even though it was a minor disappointment that he probably didn't do one single song where he got all the lyrics right."

Bob the Bluesman

When I asked fellow poet Leonard Cohen about the question of longevity in songwriters, he was typically thoughtful in his response. "There are a number of things that bear on that," he said. "You can burn yourself out, for one. The late teens and twenties are generally the lyric phase of a writer's career. If you achieve enough fame and women and money during that period, you quit, because that's generally the motivation."

With tons of money and probably three too many girlfriends at any given time, Bob Dylan could have been excused for burning out long before his dry spell of the '90s. But nearing the end of his most recent recording contract, and facing another huge divorce settlement in 1992, he was in need of a way to supply the label with material, even though he had no new songs. Fully aware of the outcries that greeted previous albums of his that contained covers, he nevertheless proceeded to deliver *Good as I Been to You*, an acoustic album devoted to his first love: songs by the masters of traditional folk music, country music, and the blues.

While it may have seemed earth-shattering at the time to a generation of acolytes when Bob Dylan went electric in 1965, Bob Dylan going acoustic in 1992 was a good deal less of a global concern to what was left of his aging fan base. For one thing, he'd always devoted part of his live show to an acoustic set. For another, he'd been filtering the kind of blues, folk, and traditional oldies he was raised on into recent tours. In 1988, he started played "Barbara Allen," a staple of his set as far back as '62, when it was captured for *Live at the Gaslight*. "Man of Constant Sorrow" from his first album often traded places with it. In 1989, "Pretty Peggy-o," another tune from that debut, joined his occasional set list. In the years leading up to 1992, you might have heard "The Water Is Wide," "Dark as a Dungeon," "In the Pines," "Wagoner's Lad," "Rank Strangers to Me" and "Shenandoah" (both of which were featured on *Down in the Groove*), or "Trail of the Buffalo" at one of his shows.

For the first of his two acoustic albums, *Good as I Been to You*, Dylan included none of these crowd favorites, and nothing he'd been playing in the living rooms of Dinkytown or fooling around with in the basement in upstate New York. Instead, he chose a mix of well-known roots classics ("Sittin' on Top of the World," "Step It Up and Go," "Diamond Joe," "Little Maggie," "Blackjack Davey," "Froggie Went a-Courtin'," and Stephen Foster's "Hard Times") and more obscure story songs ("Frankie and Albert," "Jim Jones," and "Arthur McBride"). His own favorite of the bunch was probably "Tomorrow Night," originated by blues guitarist Lonnie Johnson and covered by Elvis Presley. Dylan performed it onstage until 1998.

For his follow-up acoustic album, *World Gone Wrong*, he included the song "Two Soldiers," which he'd been performing live since 1988. He didn't mince words when describing it in his liner notes for the album, writing that it was about "America before Charlie Chaplin, before the Wild One, before the insane world of entertainment exploded in our faces—before all the ancient & honorable artillery had been taken out of the city."

"Delia" is from his earliest days, going back to a tape he made for Karen Wallace in St. Paul in 1960. "Stack a Lee" is from the handy *Anthology of Folk Music*, as done on that record by Frank Hutchinson. "Blood in My Eyes" and "World Gone Wrong" are from the repertoire of the Mississippi Sheiks. "All of their songs are raw in the bone & are faultlessly made for these modern times (the New Dark Ages)," Dylan writes. Of Blind Willie McTell's "Broke Down Engine," he notes, "It's about revival, getting a new lease on life."

At any rate, "Tomorrow Night" and "Two Soldiers" aside, he never played any of the songs from these two albums again after 1993. He also began to phase out traditional and rootsy material from his live set. And he didn't record any old folk tunes on an album until 2006. Instead, continuing his '90s writer's block, he let bits and pieces of lyrics and tunes pile up, on his desk, and in his head, until they finally exploded into an album for the ages in 1997.

33

He's Very Well Read

Dylan, the Renaissance Man

The Novelist: *Tarantula*

Anyone aware of and particular to Dylan's liner notes for his early albums should find the writing in *Tarantula* familiar, if not entirely or even mainly intelligible. In fact, the whole book, put together in various surges from 1966 through 1971, could be construed as liner notes for a dozen or so unwritten (and never-written) albums or rough drafts for twenty or thirty unwritten (and never-written) songs. Like the famous thirty pages of vomit directed at a specific target that resulted in "Like a Rolling Stone," *Tarantula* is 135 pages of manic literary diarrhea directed all over the place, in order to meet a deadline.

The book nevertheless shines a fascinating light on Dylan's creative process in those years, definitively showing how crucial the songwriting and performing discipline was to his eventual finished product (with an unhealthy admixture of speed and psychedelics thrown in). Even "Like a Rolling Stone" had to be rescued several times, by his inner critic and a few other more impartial ears, first from the twenty-nine pages of vomit surrounding it and then from the endless takes Dylan and the boys did in the studio after they'd nailed it, still not sure of what they had. In *Tarantula*, these thirty pages would have been left more or less as is for the reader to deconstruct and decode.

Much as Dylan aspired especially during his electric bard period to join the ranks of Ginsberg and Ferlinghetti, if not Rimbaud and Prévert, as linear poets, *Tarantula* proves his modest protests during the same period that he was "only" a songwriter to be much closer to the mark, with the framework of songwriting and the notion of performance necessary to turn his random words into the powerful and life-changing (for Dylan and for his audience) songs they became.

Seen in this light, consider these lost Bob Dylan classics: "Ape on Sunday," "Mouthful of Loving Choke," "Sand in the Mouth of a Movie Star," "Prelude to the Flatpick," "Pointless Like a Witch," "Cowboy Angel Blues," "A Punch of Pacifists," "Mae West Stomp," "A Blast of Loser Taking Nothing," and "Roping Off the Madman's Corner." Outtakes from *The Basement Tapes*? The transcriber having a bad day? No, these are just some of the delightful chapter headings that lead nowhere in particular in *Tarantula*, like the working titles he would affix to some of his songs off the top of his head. But what a head he had in those days, as the prose in this slim volume confirms, filled as it is with nonsense rhymes, lines from old folk songs, tropes from pop culture, attempted Beat poetry, a skewed view of politics—his hero is Barry Goldwater—and even an alarmingly serious and moving section on page 109 about his childhood dreams in Hibbing, easily the best writing in the book.

The Memoirist: *Chronicles*

If, on the other hand, all you know of Dylan the prose writer is *Tarantula* and/or his liner notes, you're apt to be blown away by the heartfelt clarity and seeming honesty of what passes for his memoir, *Chronicles*. Just don't expect any major or even minor or but the briefest of possibly accidental revelations. And don't expect them to be revelations. More like interesting word choices or errors of omission, revealing only to those of us who have spent the last forty years reading everything written and said about and sung by the almost mythic Dylan.

Again, as in *Tarantula*, the reference to Barry Goldwater as his favorite politician is at once hard to swallow and yet perfectly plausible if you see Bob Dylan in his Woodstock years as a haunted recluse on the order of the later Jack Kerouac. But Bobby Zimmerman in his Hibbing years may have been just as straight-laced and conservative, as hinted at in his reference to a desire to attend West Point and his assertion that his first idol was not really Buddy Holly or Hank Williams but the wrestler Gorgeous George. Of course, one hopes these tidbits were thrown in by a devious mind all too aware of the burden of the perfect liberal legend he carries like a magic hump on his back.

Not especially eager to cast off any of his other more personal burdens in this forum (or anywhere else, for that matter), the author skims over his relationships with women, calling the crucially formative Echo Helstrom "his Becky Thatcher," and the even more important Bonnie Beecher "an old friend." He gives a lot of deserving ink to his first live-in girlfriend, Suze Rotolo (even going so far as to name her), but, having learned the lessons of "Ballad in Plain D," glosses over their breakup, aiming most of the venom he once bestowed on her sister Carla at her mother, Mary, instead. While Joan Baez is cited mainly for the mystery and mastery behind her singing voice, the relatively obscure Greenwich Village caretaker Camilla Adams earns a far more loving portrait. Hardly anywhere to be found is Shirley Nozniski, a.k.a. his first wife, Sara, who is never mentioned by name. Referring to her only as his wife, he is, however, kind enough to comment, on page 127, that she is "one of the loveliest creatures in the world of women."

Perhaps he left his book-length sections on Echo and Bonnie and Suze and Joannie and Sara for the as-yet-unpublished *Vol. 2* (or, if he wanted to be whimsically Wilbury about it, *Vol. 3*) of these highly selective memoirs.

Somewhat attempting reparations with the ghost of Dave Van Ronk (who died in 2002), Dylan pays lengthy and appropriate homage to the man whose uncredited arrangement of "House of the Rising Sun" on *Bob Dylan* caused Van Ronk much consternation, here claiming that half of that album owed a debt to Van Ronk (though not a monetary one). Though he does not take the opportunity to thank Paul Clayton, too, for the inspiration as well as the arrangement for "Don't Think Twice, It's All Right," he does paint a thoughtful picture of the underappreciated folk singer; here, it seems the most important role Clayton played in the young Dylan's life was in introducing him to his most frequent host, the working-class rebel Ray Gooch, at whose loft on Vestry Street Dylan would have you believe he spent most of his free afternoons absorbing the greatest works of fiction, poetry, and history—especially Civil War history—while admiring Ray's gun collection and ogling his live-in lady, Chloe. Surprisingly, this allegedly major figure in Dylan's coming of age, who allegedly died in 1993, goes unmentioned in previous lengthy biographies of Dylan by Howard Sounes, Clinton Heylin, Robert Shelton, and Bob Spitz. Dylan chat site theories abound as to whether Gooch was real or fabricated or a composite creation.

Concering his Dinkytown days, Dylan has a lot of tongue-in-cheek fun sparring with Jon Pankake (while leaving out Paul Nelson entirely), giving some solid clues as to why he indeed might have stolen several of Pankake's rare records one night when Jon was out of town, seemingly just because he felt he wanted (needed, deserved) them more than his overbearing nemesis.

The most telling part of the section of the memoir concerning working with producer Daniel Lanois on the 1989 album *Oh Mercy*—aside from reiterating in truly painful detail what a major struggle he has had in the studio for the past twenty or thirty years—is what seems to be a totally tangential sequence when Dylan and his new wife go motorcycle riding through the outbacks of New Orleans. As with Sara before her, in this section too the wife in question goes nameless. Given that the most thorough biography of Bob Dylan, written in 2001 by Howard Sounes, had already revealed for the first time his previously secret marriage to Carolyn Dennis from 1986 to 1992, the author's coy refusal to name her here implies perhaps a desire for the reader to forget his earlier messy divorce and assume it's Sara and not Carolyn he's talking about. In any event, this glimpse into the private life of Bob and Carolyn is a rare peek "behind the shades," as it were, before Dylan pulls the curtain.

Another moment Dylan glides alongside of, only to leave it behind in a cloud of dust, is his famous "I'm determined to stand" epiphany on tour one night in Switzerland, where his destiny as a performer was revealed to him as if by the hand of God. Rather than muddying up the memoir with anything too personal, or overtly religious, he almost immediately veers into a mathematical discussion of musical technique that is as confusing as it is emotionally distancing.

Drawing a Blank: The Painter

As a nonverbal art, the act of painting would seem to the observer the perfect opportunity to gain an extra-musical window into Dylan's guarded soul. Unschooled and inexperienced in this form, he would perhaps have fewer chances to cover his tracks in the ways he's been so adept at with his words.

No such luck.

Dylan credits Suze Rotolo for helping him learn how to draw and introducing him to the greats. In addition to the usual classic characters like Goya, Reubens, and Picasso, Dylan was particularly taken with one of Suze's contemporary favorites, Red Grooms, calling him "the Uncle Dave Macon of the art world."

Born in Nashville, Tennessee, in 1937, Charles Rogers Grooms perfected a kind of citified pop art that was crammed full of cartoonish color and humor. Critic Judith Stein, who curated a Red Grooms retrospective at the Pennsylvania Academy of the Arts in 1985, would praise his "absurdist streak, full of the impetuous energy and preposterous puns of the Marx Brothers."

"Grooms' stuff spoke volumes to me," Dylan writes in his memoir. "What the folk songs were lyrically Red's songs were visually, all the bums and cops and lunatic hustle, the claustrophobic alleys—all the carnie vitality. I loved the way Grooms used laughter as a diabolic weapon. Subconsciously, I was wondering if it was possible to write songs like that."

In this context, among all his other deserved accolades, you would have to say Bob Dylan fulfilled that vision, easily becoming the Red Grooms of twentieth-century songwriting.

Convalescing in Woodstock, with his currency as a genius safely in the bank, he would return to the joys of creating art on his own terms, both with the Band, in the relative obscurity of Big Pink, and with another painter down the road, Bruce Dorfman, in the complete obscurity of Dorfman's studio. According to biographer Sounes, Dylan especially appreciated the fact that Dorfman wasn't impressed by his neighbor's musical resume. When he wanted to learn about Monet or Van Gogh, Dorfman was more than happy to instruct him. While these artists interested him, it wasn't until he encountered the work of Marc Chagall that he fell head over heels. "It was perfect, because you had all these multilayered images, things flying, things walking, clocks flying, rabbits with green faces," Dorfman told Sounes. "It was all there. Chagall was it. He made the connection."

The evolution of Bob Dylan the painter proceeded in fits and starts, with no expectations, a painting for the cover of the Band's first album *Music from Big Pink* here, a self-portrait for the roundly reviled *Self Portrait* there. Upon escaping from Woodstock in 1970 for the relative obscurity offered by East Hampton, he started doing landscapes, the baby artist already in his dotage, while indulging in idyllic scenes of family life. It wasn't until he started taking semiprivate lessons from Norman Raeben in his studio above Carnegie Hall in New York City that the painter's eye in Bob Dylan began to fully emerge, eclipsing his marriage in the process, but at least giving him a new vision for his songwriting process in return, resulting in *Blood on the Tracks* and *Desire.*

Although none of his actual work from this period gained much attention or favor—or any kind of indication that he'd one day rank up there with such future rock painters as David Bowie, Robert Smith, Patti Smith, John Lennon, Paul McCartney, Ronnie Wood, Janis Joplin, or Grace Slick, who found a particular niche and release in the sedentary joys of the easel and the drawing pad—attention and favor, it could be argued, were never what Bob Dylan was all about as an artist. What he was all about, as an artist and as a person, was finding the edge and then seeing how far out he could go on that edge and still get away with it.

Besides, by then he was already back on the road, as a way of life, where he could flirt with the edge every night just by reinventing his repertoire and rewriting his sacred texts in front of disbelieving ears and unknowing eyes.

Sometime in the '80s, Dylan began doing sketches before and after shows, as a way of unwinding, in hotel rooms, coffee shops, and on the tour bus, much as he used to compulsively scribble lyrics wherever he could find a pad and pencil. In 1994, a collection of ninety-two of these pencil and charcoal sketches formed the first book of his work, *Drawn Blank*. With disarming honesty, he noted in the introduction that he didn't expect many or any of these drawings to ever see the light of day as real paintings. However, fourteen years later, 170 of these former sketches vividly rendered in watercolors and gouaches were shown at the famous Kunstsammlungen Chemnitz art museum in Germany, and were subsequently published as *The Drawn Blank Series* in 2008.

Featuring a Dylan's-eye view of life on the road, a life apart, drifting through endless, nameless neighborhoods from Buffalo to Miami Beach, Reno to D.C., Stockholm to Brussels, these transformed drawings hardly strike at the heart of the real or secret Bob Dylan any more than they strike at the heart of the real or secret Buffalo, New Bedford, or Dallas. Although "South Dakota Landscape" and "Train Tracks (white)" may resonate with those who already know his roots and childhood fixations, and "Chicago Back Alley," "New Orleans Walkway," "Freret Street, New Orleans," "Bicycle," "Dad's Restaurant," "Trailer," and "Amagansett" are also notable, "Desktop," "Guitar Player," and "Cityscape" are missed opportunities. "Girl on North Miami Beach" is probably the closest the painter will ever come to "Girl from the North Country," and "Woman in the Red Lion Pub" the closest he may dare to approach the Boston waitress in "Highlands." Meanwhile, a visual representation of "Visions of Johanna" remains an impossible dream (while, on the other hand, the ghostly "Dreamgirls" is very disturbing). To me, the most poignant painting of the bunch is the tiny and empty "Motel Pool," a sanctuary on a summer's afternoon the artist himself was unlikely ever to have the necessary anonymity to enjoy.

Following the success of this exhibition, Dylan moved into full production mode. In 2010 *The Brazil Series* came out, featuring one hundred acrylic paintings, followed in 2011 by the controversial *The Asia Series*, a set of paintings that wound up drawing similar complaints of authorship and accreditation up to and including plagiarism that dogged his musical output from the early '60s through the turn of the century and beyond. Ostensibly a visual diary of his tours through the exotic Far East in 2010 (South Korea and two weeks in Japan) and 2011 (stops in Singapore, Shanghai, Beijing, and his first ever performance in Vietnam's fabled Ho Chi Minh City), the paintings were soon revealed to be copies. According to cultural blogger Greg Allen, "Whether the source was as famous as Henri Cartier-Bresson, as prominent as a new Magnum photo (licensed, apparently, after the fact), or as anonymous and obscure as a collection of nineteenth century, hand-tinted lantern slides scanned and uploaded to Flickr, they had two things in common: 1) they were entirely unacknowledged, and 2) they were thoroughly and inevitably trackable."

Undaunted, Dylan next produced *Revisionist Art* (2013), which contains thirty silkscreen renderings of popular magazine covers from *Life* to *Playboy* to *Rolling Stone* to *Archeology Today*, with fake covers and cover lines provided by the jovial Dylan. One of the best is the fake *Sports Illustrated* cover featuring a topless model purporting to be baseball's first female third-base coach, but it makes more satirical sense as a comment on *SI*'s annual everything-but-topless "Swimsuit" issue. Among the standout cover lines, "Face Lifts for Babies" for *Baby Talk* magazine tops the list. Continuing his exploration of the form, *Face Value* came out in 2014, featuring twelve pastel portraits.

Many of the books produced from Dylan's exhibitions contain the kind of critical evaluations of his paintings the artist himself would probably scoff at, far outdistancing in excessive verbiage and obtuse fawning the type of theoretical analyses the best (and worst) of his songs routinely draw. Yet some of the verbiage in *The Drawn Blank Series* manages to make sense, typified by this comment from Frank Zollner, a professor of art history at the University of Leipzig. "Whereas in classical central perspective the center is all, the majority of Dylan's drawings of interior spaces have no such center. These interiors, which traditionally communicate a feeling of peaceful duration or of *time brought to a standstill* (my italics) offer no resting point for the eye of the viewer. This is the gaze of a passer by."

A bit more fawning, perhaps, is this from the essay by Diana Widmaier Picasso—granddaughter of the great Pablo, no less. "By assimilating poetry, music and drawing, not only has he rejoined Baudelaire, for whom colors, perfumes and sounds correspond, but above all he has manifested in his way the superior will of the artist to reproduce the illusions of a real world for the sole purpose of reaching out to, and sometimes touching, the ideal, the unknown, the beautiful."

Reviewing the book for the *New York Times*, Marisha Pesci was similarly touched (or gulled, as the case may be). "Seemingly unworried about how something looks, he's not after artistic perfection but something larger, a moment, a feeling," she wrote. "The true joys of Dylan's art derive from his bird's-eye view of our world . . . underscoring an interconnectedness that most of us, without the help of an artist, will never fully recognize."

On the other hand, I'd have liked to see a whole lot more Red Grooms.

Bob the Deejay: Theme Time Radio Hour

Having grown up listening to the music that would infuse his life with meaning the way most kids did in the early '50s—on the radio, late at night, covertly, through the static—Bob Dylan must have felt a profound sense of satisfaction in becoming a late-night deejay himself, dispensing his wit and wisdom in the service of a similar aural vision. In his spot on satellite radio, the only thing missing would have been the static. And the danger. And the idea that someone at the crossroads of accident and coincidence was on a programming mission from out in the vast invisible ether, directly to your personal earlobes. Ideally, one would have stumbled onto *Theme Time Radio* while in search of *The Jack Benny Program* or Kasey Casem or *The Goon Show* or *The King Biscuit Flower Hour* or Wolfman Jack or Jean Shepherd, and remained transfixed by the music and the host, having no idea in the world who this Bob Dylan was, or if that was even his real name.

Actually, the show itself was almost certainly the programming mission and vision of Dylan's music-loving friend Eddie Gorodetsky, who had once lured his pal into a delightful cameo performance as himself on an episode of the sitcom *Dharma and Greg*, for which Gorodetsky was one of the writers. Earlier in his career, Eddie G. was a deejay on the pioneering FM station WBCN in Boston, where he could be heard croaking behind a similar set of ingenious segues called *The Saturday Night Hi-Fi Party* in the late '70s, before such visionary radio was replaced by computers.

Satellite radio precludes all but the experience of the show itself, a continuing unraveling of the deep mystery of life music contains, as narrated if not selected by a weathered, craggy voice only fifty years on the stages of the world and a pack-a-day habit could produce; a slinky, sinister, Raymond Chandler–meets–Allen Ginsberg, all-knowing voice meant for a protracted after-midnight session of the soul.

Dylan had described the voice himself, in an interview he did in *Playboy* long before the idea of a radio show was on the horizon, while talking about discovering the New York deejay Rosko. "It was radiant feeling, coming across it on the radio," he said. "His voice was that of the inner voice of the night."

Theme Time was based on universal themes like money, cars, the weather, fathers, mothers, coffee, jail, baseball, and drinking, filled with brilliant segues through a history of twentieth-century music. It was broadcast from May 2006 through April 2009. A sample show, "Friends and Neighbors," complete with segues, was included as a second disc on *Together Through Life* in 2009, and is listed below. For a more complete listening experience, go to Themetimeradio.com or Notdarkyet.org.

Friends and Neighbors

- "Howdy Neighbor"—Porter Waggoner and the Wagonmasters
- "Don't Take Everybody to Be Your Friend"—Sister Rosetta Tharpe
- "Diamonds Are a Girl's Best Friend"—T Bone Burnett
- "La Valse de Amitie"—Doc Guidry
- "Make Friends"—Moon Mullican
- "My Next Door Neighbor"—Jerry McCain
- "Let's Invite Them Over"—George Jones and Melba Montgomery
- "My Friends"—Howlin' Wolf
- "Last Night"—Little Walter
- "You've Got a Friend"—Carole King
- "Bad Neighborhood"—Ronnie and the Delinquents
- "Neighbors"—The Rolling Stones
- "Too Many Parties and Too Many Pals"—Hank Williams
- "Why Can't We Be Friends"—War

The A&R Man: Egyptian Records

Bob Dylan had been threatening to launch his own boutique record label since 1967. He finally got around to it in 1997. Headed by the man with the greatest job in the world, Jeff Rosen, who also runs Dylan's publishing company, Special Rider Music, Egyptian Records (distributed by Sony) put out its first release on August 19, 1997. It was an obvious labor of love for his boss—as was the second. Using Dylan's extensive Rolodex, as well as his deep knowledge of roots music, an all-star lineup was assembled, with liner notes written by Dylan himself.

Jimmie Rodgers Tribute

"Jimmie Rodgers was a performer without precedent," Dylan writes, "with a sound as lonesome and mystical as it was dynamic. His is a thousand and one voices yet singularly his own. The artists on this compilation all have one thing in common—all have been amazed, moved, and enormously affected by Jimmie like no other."

Track Listing

- "Dreaming with Tears in My Eyes"—Bono
- "Any Old Time"—Alison Krauss
- "Waiting for a Train"—Dickey Betts
- "Somewhere Down Below the Mason Dixon Line"—Mary Chapin Carpenter
- "Miss the Mississippi (and You)"—David Ball
- "My Blue Eyed Jane"—Bob Dylan
- "Peach Pickin' Time down in Georgia"—Willie Nelson
- "In the Jailhouse Now"—Steve Earle and the V-Roys
- "Blue Yodel Number 9 (Standing on the Corner)"—Jerry Garcia, David Grisman, John Kahn
- "Hobo Bill's Last Ride"—Iris Dement
- "Gambling Bar Room Blues"—John Mellencamp
- "Mule Skinner Blues"—Van Morrison
- "Why Should I Be Lonely"—Aaron Neville
- "T for Texas"—Dwight Yoakam

The Lost Notebooks of Hank Williams

Dylan must have been so moved by the artistic success of the Jimmie Rodgers project (if not the actual sales) that he waited a mere fourteen years to allow his label to get behind another similar project, which was finally released on October 10, 2011.

As far back as 1967, Dylan had been approached by Columbia A&R executive Mary Martin with a rare find, dubbed "the lost notebooks of Hank Williams." Like Dylan, Williams was a compulsive scribbler who used to carry around bound notebooks filled with half-finished lyrics in a leather briefcase. It was Martin's idea to have Dylan complete these songs, but Dylan was otherwise engaged in making music with his friends and neighbors that Albert Grossman would never get near.

In 2004, Dylan was finally ready to tackle this project in the same way he'd tackled the Jimmie Rodgers project: by finding suitable artists to give new melodies to these old lyrics (while obeying the rule that they couldn't rewrite any of the lyrics) and put them on record in Hank's style. And this is exactly what artists ranging from Norah Jones to Alan Jackson and from Jack White to Holly Williams (Hank's granddaughter) did. A further rarity finds Dylan and his son Jakob on the same disc! The liner notes are by Michael McCall from the Country Music Hall of Fame and Museum.

"The history of Hank's notebooks is as complex as the legend himself," McCall writes. "Yet, in the end, what matters most are the songs, and these new works rise from the ether with ghostly relevance. Hank wrote songs the way he drank whiskey; like there was no tomorrow. As with his many standards, these new recordings tap straight into the soul of man. This is songwriting at its most artful and most powerful."

Track Listing

- "You've Been Lonesome Too"—Alan Jackson
- "The Love That Faded"—Bob Dylan
- "How Many Times Have You Broken My Heart"—Norah Jones
- "You Know That I Know"—Jack White
- "I'm So Happy I Found You"—Lucinda Williams
- "I Hope You Shed a Million Tears"—Vince Gill and Rodney Crowell
- "You're Through Fooling Me"—Patty Loveless
- "You'll Never Be Mine Again"—Levon Helm
- "Blue Is My Heart"—Holly Williams
- "Oh, Mama, Come Home"—Jakob Dylan
- "Angel Mine"—Sheryl Crow
- "The Sermon on the Mount"—Merle Haggard

Adding a further irony to the whole project, it was around this time that a cache of lost Bob Dylan lyrics surfaced, written circa 1967, which T Bone Burnett was eventually given the task of finding musicians to complete. But for some reason *Lost on the River: The New Basement Tapes* wouldn't become the third release on Dylan's Egyptian Records. Probably not enough time had gone by. Instead, the honor went to Capitol Records.

On Broadway: *The Times They Are a-Changin'* by Twyla Tharp

Like most of his other artistic translations into realms outside of songwriting

When choreographer Twyla Tharp tried to put Dylan's music and lyrics into a modern/contemporary dance format, the critics shrugged.

and performing, the arrival of Bob Dylan's music on Broadway via the world of dance, as envisioned by Twyla Tharp, one of the visionaries of the form, was a resounding disappointment, artistically and financially. The show started life at the Old Globe Theater in San Diego on February 9, 2006, before opening at the Brooks Atkinson Theater on Broadway on October 26; the principals involved had high hopes that the circus-themed theater-of-the-absurd production could elevate the jukebox musical form past the traditional song-and-dance patter of Leiber and Stoller's *Smokey Joe's Cafe* into the same ethereal plateau occupied by Dylan's songs. Or at least it would equal Tharp's previous triumph in *Movin' Out*, set to the more earthbound music and lyrics of Billy Joel.

In fact, that honor would go to the same season's *Jersey Boys*, based on the life and music of the Four Seasons, which also had its roots in San Diego and officially opened a week after the Bob Dylan fiasco (although Dylan's actual role in the fiasco was probably limited to licensing the music). While *Jersey Boys* went on to critical success, sold-out houses, and eventually a disappointing movie, *The Times They Are a-Changin'* thankfully crashed and burned after twenty-eight performances (plus thirty-five previews).

The show was touted in *Playbill* as "a tale of fathers and sons, of men and women, of leaders and followers, of immobility and change," and "used prophecy, parable, metaphor, accusation and confession like the Dylan songs that comprise it to confront us with images and ideas of who we are and who it is possible to be." Closer to its murky and mangled execution is the review that appeared in the *New York Times*, which summed up the magnitude of its missed opportunity. "Most of Mr. Dylan's best songs tingle with ambivalence, mystery, and a knowing sense of the surrealism of so-called reality. If Ms. Tharp had seen fit simply to keep us wandering through a shifting dreamscape, set to Mr. Dylan's music, *The Times* might have passed muster as a really cool head trip."

The Movie Actor: *I'm Not There*

The vaults containing Dylan's image are among the most zealously guarded in the history of celebrity. Whether it's a photo shoot for a magazine or an album cover or a music video, no organization has a tighter grip on the image of its prized client than the one controlling Bob Dylan. Which makes it all the more confounding whenever that image turns up on a movie screen, usually in the service of some mangled version of himself. I blame it on Tommy Sands, who announced to the public on *The Les Crane Show* in 1965 that Bob Dylan was the second coming of James Dean.

In his unfortunate bit-part as Alias in the roundly reviled movie *Pat Garrett and Billy the Kid*, Dylan comes across more like the second coming of Michael J. Pollard in *Bonnie and Clyde*. In recent years, that film experienced a critical reevaluation when Sam Peckinpah's original director's cut finally surfaced. Dylan's performance in it has not received a similar reappraisal, although the song that emerged from the soundtrack, "Knockin' on Heaven's Door," became a big hit and a concert favorite, making the experience (for fans at least) something of a cosmic wash.

Though Dylan was purportedly Chaplin-esque onstage in his early years, by the time we saw him playing himself in the 1968 D. A. Pennebaker documentary about his 1965 British tour, *Dont Look Back*, he had honed his comic timing at press conferences in front of clueless older people in suits and ties to a vicious pitch more befitting of Don Rickles on crack. In Dylan's own quasi-documentary *Eat the Document*, about his return to face the wrath of his British fans a year later, he was a drugged-out blob, hardly able to control his own bodily functions, much less the press and his defecting fan base, to say nothing of the editing of the film itself. On the other hand, the scenes of Dylan developing music with Robbie Robertson are riveting, especially on the song "What Kind of Friend Is This," which was apparently written in a Glasgow hotel room the day after the infamous "Judas" concert in Manchester.

As a fictional character, Dylan fared best when played by seven other actors, although it's hard to imagine anyone being able to follow the storyline of *I'm Not There* without a spreadsheet containing all the arcane references to his life and career made use of by writer Oren Moverman and director Todd Haynes. Admittedly, the movie is a marvel at placing those references into a context the devout Dylanologist is sure to pick up on, and Cate Blanchett's Academy Award–nominated turn as Dylan during his electric bard period is worth the price of admission alone (although Richie Havens's cameo, singing "Tombstone Blues," is where I'd put my own money).

Dylan's 1987 foray into leading-man territory, *Hearts of Fire*, was more than just your average misfire. Having in the solitude of his private confessional written such enduring gems by this time as "Every Grain of Sand" (1981), "Blind Willie McTell" (1983), "Dark Eyes" (1984), and "Brownsville Girl" (1986), he was nonetheless ready to risk (and achieve) humiliation before the cameras once again, saddled with a love interest, a bad makeup job, a lot of bad dialogue, and an earring.

Much more convincing is 2003's vastly underrated *Masked and Anonymous*, in which Dylan had a hand in the writing, under the name Sergei Petrov. In my opinion, this is a cult classic waiting to blossom, in the same league as *The Big Lebowski* with which it shares bravura performances by Jeff Bridges and John Goodman (Goodman is also a stoned smash in the

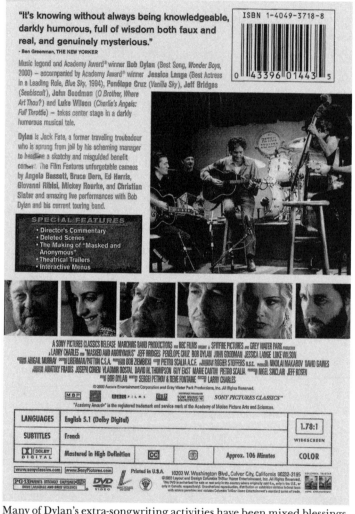

Many of Dylan's extra-songwriting activities have been mixed blessings. His home movie of the *Rolling Thunder* tour, *Renaldo and Clara*, was a massively expensive dud. But his portrayal of Jack Fate in *Masked and Anonymous* (which he cowrote) helped make the film a cult classic.

Dylan-era reimagining *Inside Llewyn Davis*). If *I'm Not There* captures the essence of the many sides of Bob Dylan from 1960–1980, *Masked and Anonymous* gives a stunning portrait of the latter-day wizened and grizzled troubadour in his sixties, a man of few but inevitably mysteriously powerful and provocative words ("I might have a few songs left"). Dylanographers should pay particularly close attention to the appearance of the omnipresent Eddie Gorodetsky early in the film.

The DVD of *Renaldo and Clara* is a rarity even on the bootleg market.

Apart from the inherent historic or prurient interest value of his semi-fictional Rolling Thunder tour diary, *Renaldo and Clara*, an epic dud of a home movie, and Martin Scorsese's much more well-received nonfictional account of Dylan's rise to stardom, *No Direction Home*, the musical value of these cultural artifacts cannot be underestimated. Yet for depth and breadth of artists connected to fascinating song choices (among them "Stuck Inside of Mobile with the Memphis Blues Again" by Cat Power, "Pressing On" by John Doe, "Dark Eyes" by Iron and Wine and Calexico, "Highway 61 Revisited" by Karen O and the Million Dollar Bashers, "Ring Them Bells" by Sufjan Stevens, "Can You Please Crawl out Your Window" by the Hold Steady, and "Knockin' on Heaven's Door" by Antony and the Johnsons), the *I'm Not There* soundtrack has to rank among the best of all the tribute albums as well.

From the opening credits of *Dont Look Back*, where Dylan and his best comic foil, Allen Ginsberg, hilariously invent and send up the music video format with their shenanigans in "Subterranean Homesick Blues," to the new and especially powerful version of "Blowin' in the Wind" used at the end credits of *Masked and Anonymous* to the use of certain legendary basement-era outtakes (the song that gives the movie its title, for instance, as performed by Dylan and the Band) in *I'm Not There*, Dylan the singer and songwriter for the most part far outclasses Dylan the actor or subject.

34

Song and Dance Man

Top Ten TV Performances and Music Videos

Ten Best TV Appearances

Though he has been a galvanizing presence on the club, theater, or arena stage, the TV screen has never been a particular friend to Bob Dylan. Here, his nervous energy comes across only as nerves. His put-on patter seems like stage fright. Worst of all, he's got to talk. As has been proven time and again, it's a dangerous proposition to let Bob Dylan go unscripted. Here, then, in chronological order, are his ten most memorable TV performances.

The Steve Allen Show (February 2, 1964)

After famously walking off *The Ed Sullivan Show* in 1963 in protest over CBS censors not allowing him to perform the relatively toothless "Talking John Birch Society Paranoid Blues," Dylan would not make his first major TV appearance until February 2, 1964, on *The Steve Allen Show.* The bespectacled Allen was at the time revered in hip literary circles as an erudite cross between Jack Paar and Mort Saul. He'd already had Lenny Bruce on his show. Crucially, as far as Dylan should have known, he'd almost made Elvis Presley cry back in 1956, when he had him sing his newly recorded "Hound Dog," dressed in top hat, tuxedo, and tails, to the loving audience of a sad-faced bassett hound. Years later, Elvis was still fuming about the episode. "It was the most ridiculous appearance I ever did and I regret doing it," he said. This is the same Steve Allen who once thought it the height of humor to quote the song "Be-Bop-a-Lula" as an example of "the poetry of rock 'n' roll."

With his old high-school principal Pedersen in mind, Dylan not only agreed to do the show but also chose to sing the problematic "The Lonesome Death of Hattie Carroll" in the bargain. Instead of quoting some of Dylan's lyrics that would have eloquently made the case he was trying to squash in the '50s, Allen decided to let Dylan do the talking. Did he know that some of the facts in this supposedly true story were altered to fit Dylan's dramatic purposes? That the song was true only in the sense that movies based on true stories are often altered in the same way? Was this an attempt to get Dylan to own up to his journalistic lapses?

In any event, though Allen seemed courteous enough, to forestall further grilling Dylan mumbled that they should let the song do the talking—a wise choice, even if it led to the subsequent six-minute harangue. Later, Allen would get the last word on Dylan's future with this withering understatement, given to Robert Shelton, "It struck me that he was somehow not suited to television."

The Les Crane Show (February 17, 1965)

Whether he was persuaded to swear off television after the *Steve Allen* performance, or whether he simply had better things to do (or both), it was a year before Bob Dylan returned to the talk-show format, this time gracing Les Crane with his presence on a program that featured two other singers, the Italian chanteuse Caterina Valente and the Bobby Darin wannabe Tommy Sands. I saw this show myself when it first aired, and for the last fifty years, in my mind, its high point has been an exchange between Dylan and Sands, in which Dylan hilariously skewers the pretentious Sands as if in preparation for his encounter with Donovan in England a few months later. (Since no footage of the show in question exists, I was only able to read the quote in the transcript.)

Dylan does come off a lot cooler in his bantering with Crane than during the previous Allen fiasco. Crane, at times a figure of ridicule among TV cognoscenti for his confrontational style, is in this instance more than game for Dylan's byplay. In fact, he seems to impress Dylan on several occasions, such as when he mentions that Dylan's friend in the audience, Odetta, is scheduled for an upcoming appearance on his show, and later, when he talks of how Allen Ginsberg had proselytized for the legalization of marijuana when he was on the show. When Dylan talks about buying a Maserati with his songwriting royalties, Crane offers the example of James Dean crashing to his death in a Porsche as a warning to the young antihero.

Here the pompous Sands steps in. "He does remind me of Jimmy Dean," he says, obviously feeling his recording of "Let Me Be Loved" from the 1957 biopic, *The James Dean Story*, qualifies him as an authority. "I think I recognize talent," he continues, "and as big and as successful as Bob Dylan is as a singer and writer of folk songs, I think he has a tremendous future as an actor."

While *Renaldo and Clara* was at this point a distant dream, Dylan does reveal, with a somewhat straight face, that he and Allen Ginsberg are concocting a "cowboy horror movie" in which Dylan is to play his own mother.

Still taking him seriously, Tommy Sands then ventures into the segment now lost in the mists of time.

"May I ask you a question, Bob?" he says. Bob probably shrugs. "So many of the [folk] artists seem to do the same thing as the country artists, yet they seem to have a wider appeal. Why is that?"

It may have been this deeply philosophical question, so reminiscent of those tossed at him during his press conferences of the era, that Dylan found so vexing. In the transcript, all he says in response, after a long pause, is "I don't know."

Of course, with Dylan, it is always more than just the line that got the laughs: it's the phrasing, the expression, the timing. In this case, I'm pretty sure all of that was captured on TV, although not for eternity.

The Johnny Cash Show (June 7, 1969)

Having totaled his motorcycle, along with his touring career, a year or so after *The Les Crane Show*, Dylan wouldn't appear on television again until 1969. At the height of the Woodstock Nation's much-touted revolt against conservative rock 'n' roll, the news that Bob Dylan was going to be on a country-music show hosted by that noted reactionary, Johnny Cash, would have been a lot more shocking had he not already released his controversial ersatz country-music album, *Nashville Skyline*, a couple of months earlier.

Still, seeing him live on TV would offer the unconvinced definite proof that Dylan was not, as had been rumored, a walking zombie, even if, to some diehards, his ersatz country-music album was proof enough.

Dylan was used to performing in front of hostile audiences; the crowd at the Grand Ole Opry in Nashville, though bemused by the idea of Bob Dylan attempting to join their ranks, was hardly Newport '65 or Manchester '66. However, though it wouldn't change anyone's opinion about *Nashville Skyline*, doing *The Johnny Cash Show* turned out to be a very cool move on Dylan's part, not least of all because of Cash's future stature as an American icon, and the show's format of being virtually wall-to-wall music.

Not hurting the show's pop-cultural credibility was the appearance of Joni Mitchell, the lady who would soon write Woodstock's title song, in the leadoff slot, singing "Both Sides Now" and, in a duet with Cash, "I Still Miss Someone." Dylan's duet with Cash, on "Girl from the North Country," is a tense affair, lacking the crucial final verse. Though Cash was clearly no Joan Baez, they both persevere, with Dylan almost cracking a smile when it was over. Similarly grim but confident was his performance of "I Threw It All Away," his choice for the first single from the album, which barely dented the charts. (The choice for the second single went to label president Clive Davis, and "Lay Lady Lay" duly hit the Top 10.)

The John Hammond Tribute (December 13, 1975) and Saturday Night Live (November 20, 1979)

Through the 1970s, Dylan rarely appeared on TV; several projects went down the tubes before they even aired. Thus, it was an event when it was reported he'd agreed to take part in a TV tribute to his original mentor and producer, John Hammond, the man who'd signed him to Columbia Records, burnishing a résumé that already included Bessie Smith, Billie Holiday, Benny Goodman, Aretha Franklin, Leonard Cohen, and, more recently, Bruce Springsteen. On the occasion of Hammond's retirement, Dylan performed three tunes he was preparing to take with him on the road with the Rolling Thunder contingent, backed by Rob Stoner on bass, Howie Wyeth on drums, and Scarlet Rivera on gypsy violin—"Hurricane," "Oh Sister," and "Simple Twist of Fate"—in front of a small audience, before disappearing into the night so swiftly he forgot to thank Hammond for the memories and the leg up in the music business.

When told of his *faux pas*, Dylan immediately telexed his regrets. "For all John Hammond's done for me, it was worth staying late," he said.

Dylan's next TV cameo, four years later, was much more dramatic. In the months leading up to it he'd found religion, and where else but on the subversive four-year-old comedy show *Saturday Night Live* could Dylan find such a tailor-made audience of baby-boom liberals to tick off? Once again, he was not required to talk or take part in a skit, but his songs spoke volumes: "Gotta Serve Somebody," with a gospel quartet behind him and a nifty Fred Tackett guitar solo; a somber "I Believe in You"; and the more emphatic "When You Gonna Wake Up," which, on inspection, is probably less accusatory than epics like "Gates of Eden" and "It's Alright, Ma (I'm Only Bleeding)."

With the audience not necessarily tuned in to Dylan's inner life, the response was a lot more respectfully tepid than that which greeted him on the road in 1980. And the industry's response, as witnessed by the Grammy won by "Gotta Serve Somebody" for "Best Rock Vocal Performance," was even more confusing. Anyway, after playing "Bob Dylan" for several tours in the mid-'70s to rousing acclaim but scant creative satisfaction, this version of Bob Dylan was probably in the right frame of mind for a little more "Judas" and a lot less rock 'n' roll.

Coincidentally, another guest on *Saturday Night Live* that night was comedian/wrestler Andy Kaufman, who also had a knack for confounding and confusing his audience every chance he got.

Late Night with David Letterman (March 22, 1984)

Although Dylan's performance on the then three-year-old *Late Night with David Letterman* was considered a highlight not only of Letterman's career to that point but also of Dylan's (in the TV division, at least), to Dylan the highlights were getting to mingle with Liberace backstage and meeting the sad-sack comedian Calvert DeForest (aka Larry "Bud" Melman).

Having initially committed to only one song—unless things went especially well—both Dylan and Letterman were so hyped by his opening number and warning, the Sonny Boy Williamson blues "Don't Start Me Talkin'," that Letterman immediately requested another.

"Mr. Dylan and the band will be back for perhaps two more songs?" he asked.

Dylan said okay.

"I'm almost sure it's gonna happen," Letterman responded.

Backed by the members of the L.A. roots-rock band the Plugz, with whom he'd been rehearsing for at least a day, he then tore into "License to Kill" and "Jokerman," prompting Letterman to offer him a standing invite for every Thursday night. But it would be eight years before he returned.

The peripatetic Eddie Gorodetsky, who was working for Letterman at the time, may have played a role in booking Dylan. As noted elsewhere, the former Boston deejay turned comedy writer would cross paths with his friend again, more than once.

Live Aid (July 13, 1985) and Farm Aid (September 22, 1985)

Perhaps buoyed by his success with a couple of minimal ad libs on the Letterman show, Dylan decided to wing it in front of 1.9 billion people watching in 150 nations, as he performed "Ballad of Hollis Brown," the first of his three-song set at JFK Stadium in Philadelphia, backed by the impromptu guitars of Keith Richards and Ron Wood, to close out the all-day Live Aid benefit concert for the starving people of Ethiopia.

In retrospect, it was a bad idea.

After partying backstage for several hours with Richards and Wood, who seemed particularly lost in front of the curtains, Dylan may have overly identified with the ballad's beleaguered farmer, Hollis Brown, who murdered his wife and family in frustration over his failure to feed them, when he suggested to the audience of 100,000, "I hope that some of the money that's raised for the people in Africa, maybe they could take just a little bit of it and use it to pay the mortgages on some of the farms that the farmers here owe to the banks."

The people cheered.

The event's organizer, Bob Geldof, was not so charitable. "Saying something so simplistic and crowd-pleasing was beyond belief," he said. "He displayed a complete lack of understanding of the issues raised by Live Aid. Live Aid was about people losing their lives. There is a radical difference between losing your livelihood and losing your life."

Dylan's further contribution to the cause wasn't helped any by the generally disheveled performances that followed of "When the Ship Comes In" and the closing "Blowin' in the Wind," during which he broke a string on his guitar and had to borrow Ron Wood's instrument, leaving Wood literally twisting in the wind.

Of course, anyone familiar with Dylan's penchant for putting his foot in his mouth whenever he opened it in a live setting (especially after a few drinks) will recall his (thankfully untelevised) remarks in reference to Lee Harvey Oswald when accepting the Tom Paine Award at the Bill of Rights dinner in December 1963.

While certain commentators were aghast, Live Aid promoter Bill Graham hardly noticed. "In terms of the artists who volunteered their time that day, I doubt that very many of them really understood the situation in Ethiopia," he writes in his memoir. "I know I didn't."

What Dylan's comment did accomplish was to spark the idea of Farm Aid, which became an annual series of concerts organized by Willie Nelson, John Mellencamp, and Neil Young, to benefit American family farmers, which started two months later, at the University of Illinois Memorial Stadium in Champaign, in front of 80,000 people and a vast national TV audience. Much better prepared this time, Dylan was backed by Tom Petty and the Heartbreakers for six songs. "Shake," "I'll Remember You," and "Trust Yourself" were aired on TV, while his opener, "Clean Cut Kid," and two fine closers, "That Lucky Old Sun" and "Maggie's Farm" (with Willie Nelson on acoustic guitar), were not. Nothing upsetting or slanderous was heard.

Thirty years later, Dylan would sing "That Lucky Old Sun" on his 2015 album *Shadows in the Night*.

Getting to Dylan (September 18, 1987)

Widely considered one of the finest interviews with Bob Dylan to appear on TV in the '80s (and, at the same time, listed as tied for second in "The Ten Most Incomprehensible Bob Dylan Interviews of All Time" by the culture blog Vulture.com), *Getting to Dylan* was conducted in 1986 by the British journalist Christopher Sykes in Dylan's trailer on the set of the film *Hearts on Fire*. It would air in the UK on the BBC as part of the *Omnibus* series on September 18, 1987 (but never in the US). Some of the accompanying documentary deals specifically with the film; the final thirty minutes or so comprise the interview, one of the most revealing aspects of which is its demonstration of just how hard it is to interview Bob Dylan.

Presumably agreed-to in advance by the elusive subject, the interview even so starts with him saying today's talk will just be a test run, to see if a real interview might take place sometime in the future. Nothing like a superstar potentially backing out to make a journalist's blood run cold and tongue go dry. Add to that Dylan's off-putting decision to use this "pre-interview" as a means to practice his drawing technique, sketching a portrait of the interviewer even as Sykes searches for his sheet of questions (which are conveniently found under Dylan's drawing pad). When an interviewer has to resort to his prepared questions, any hopes of a rewarding conversation are out the window (or in this case, the trailer door).

Nevertheless, Sykes perseveres with hardly a quaver in his voice, not intimidated, it would seem, by Dylan's evasive tactics. Under the circumstances, it may not be a coincidence that his first question concerns how Dylan decides whether to do an interview or not. Sketching away, Dylan regards the first few questions as he might the opening of a concert, getting his sea legs under him before activating his concentration. He doesn't really become engaged until Sykes brings up someone's complaint in the press that Dylan never said hello to the audience of extras assembled in an earlier scene to watch a performance by Dylan's character in the movie.

There follows a heartfelt but certainly not revealing diatribe about the price of fame; how he can never do enough to satisfy everyone, how things change when he walks into a room, how people are stalking him around the clock and around the globe, the true meaning of the word fan, and how he only performs because he's good at it.

And then, stopping sketching for a moment, he proceeds to tell Sykes that none of this really bothers him; he's far beyond it, and life's too short for such petty concerns.

Which is a revealing way of (not) looking at it.

While his eventual portrait of the interviewer is far more faithful to its subject than the interviewer's portrait of Dylan, the most poignant part of the documentary comes at the end, when Dylan confronts a few "fans" in the parking lot and, against all odds, seems to have a genuine interaction with them. Here you see him drop his mask and act like you'd hope he'd act if you were brave enough to approach him in a parking lot (assuming the whole thing wasn't prearranged). He hugs a couple of women, and you can see their knees buckle. He hugs the fat bearded guy they're with like a long-lost war buddy. Then he gets into his car and is driven to the next outpost, the next encounter, back inside his shell until another moment from real life comes to intrude on his isolation.

The Grammy Awards (February 20, 1991, and February 25, 1998)

By far Bob Dylan's most legendary (if not defining) TV moments occurred at the Grammy Awards, the first in Los Angeles, the next in New York City. In 1991, Jack Nicholson was on hand to deliver some scripted comments about the honoree before handing him the appropriately heavy "Lifetime Achievement" award.

After spinning around, desperately looking for the exit, Dylan finally steps up to the podium as an anxious nation holds its breath.

"My father once told me," he starts out, in time-honored "Lifetime Achievement" fashion, as if having learned the previous hard lessons of improv. But then the old Bob Dylan invades his brain. "He told me so many things," he says after a pause, drawing a hearty laugh from the relieved audience. Then comes the remark that will probably rank, as far as poetic ambiguity, alongside the best of his lyrical couplets. "He said it's possible to become so defiled in this world that your own mother and father will abandon you. If that happens, God will always believe in your ability to mend your own ways."

Cut to commercial.

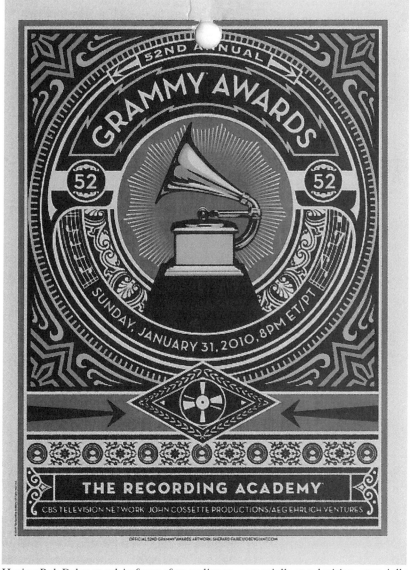

Having Bob Dylan speak in front of an audience—especially on television, especially at the Grammy Awards—is a psychodrama not to be missed.

Something of a family reunion, the 1998 ceremony, held at Radio City in New York, saw Dylan's *Time Out of Mind* win Grammys for "Album of the Year" and "Folk Album of the Year," and "Cold Irons Bound" win for "Best Rock Vocal," while his son Jakob's group, the Wallflowers, took home prizes for "Best Rock Song" and "Best Rock Performance with a Duo or Group" for "One Headlight." Dylan's acceptance speech was thankfully brief, evoking the ghost of Buddy Holly in a nice tribute.

It was earlier in the show, during his otherwise innocuous performance of "Love Sick," that trouble reared its ugly head (and slithering body) in the form of a performance artist who had slipped through security (some say it was planned in advance) to wriggle in front of Dylan, with the inscrutable words "Soy bomb" scrawled on his chest. If the abject weirdness of this act seemed hardly to faze Dylan, the spastic dance itself evoked shades of the infamous streaker who invaded the Academy Awards in 1974, just as David Niven was about to introduce Liz Taylor to the audience. Taking it in without missing a beat, the suave Niven ad-libbed, "Well, ladies and gentlemen, isn't it fascinating to think that probably the only laugh that man will ever get in his life is by stripping and showing off his shortcomings?"

While a line like that may well have occurred to Dylan during this criminally prolonged interlude, it is to his everlasting credit that he let only his dazed expression do the talking.

Dharma and Greg, "Play Lady Play" (October 12, 1999)

To the uninitiated, Bob's Dylan's appearance in a three-and-a-half-minute scene in the goofy sitcom *Dharma and Greg* may have seemed like just the kind of impenetrable move the quixotic performer has become justly famous for, like granting an interview to a high-school newspaper somewhere in middle America while leaving the mainstream press dangling. But once the gnomic presence of writer/producer Eddie Gorodetsky is revealed as the probable behind-the-scenes instigator of this coup, the *modus operandi* if not the motive for the move becomes a little bit clearer.

In the scene, Dharma (Jenna Elfman) is trying out as a replacement drummer for Dylan's band, which includes T Bone Burnett and Tony Gilkyson on guitars, John "Strawberry" Fields on bass, and Joe Henry on keyboards. As opposed to the faux-keyboard playing by Charlie Sheen on *Dharma and Greg* creator Chuck Lorre's subsequent hit *Two and a Half Men*, Jenna really does attack the drums here as Dylan and the band wade through a blues, a polka, and a rock riff. His reaction to her untutored playing is highly empathetic. To help with his performance, he may have been tapping into an old memory of a particularly sloppy gig in Toronto in 1990. Backstage after the gig, when he asked rockabilly great Ronnie Hawkins what he thought of the show, Hawkins responded, "In my long career, Bob, I have had guitar players in my band that are as bad as you are. But you're the only one of them making a living."

What also makes this one of Dylan's most likable TV performances is his truly pained reaction when Dharma asks him if she made the band. It's as if he's got to turn down one of his own daughters. "Well, we don't know yet," he hedges.

When Dharma then asks him if he and his band can help her pack up her drums in her van, he responds with a genuinely surprised chuckle, as if he'd never heard the line before.

Judging from previous Dylan experiences on various sets, he probably hadn't.

60 Minutes (December 5, 2004)

On the occasion of his memoir *Chronicles* topping the book charts, Bob Dylan begrudgingly sat for an unprecedented chat with Ed Bradley on the CBS News show *60 Minutes*. From the look on his face throughout, you'd think he was having several impacted molars removed from his mouth without anesthesia, a living, breathing version of the man in "Up to Me" who had only smiled once in the past fourteen months "and didn't do it consciously."

By the end of the appointed twenty minutes, Bradley is almost pleading with Dylan to look at his career on the bright side. After all, hadn't *Rolling Stone* magazine just voted "Like a Rolling Stone" the greatest rock song of all-time? "It's a pat on the back," Bradley notes.

Hard-pressed to deny it, Dylan merely suggests, with a grimace, how transitory such acclaim can be.

Bradley might then have mentioned, just to cheer him up, that this transitory state of being heralded far and wide had so far lasted more than forty years. But Dylan wouldn't have wanted to hear that. With a mostly curmudgeonly scowl, sometimes undercut with a droll smirk he can't quite conceal, he reprises a number of old themes. People have him all wrong. He certainly isn't a spokesman for anybody but himself. He has no idea how he wrote most of his classic songs—and, anyway, he has no illusions that he could ever write like that again (this in the aftermath of a particularly fertile decade of creativity that produced some of his best work, including *Time Out of Mind* and *Love and Theft*).

Basically, he feels people saw him as "a threat to society," yet he can't walk into a restaurant without being hustled into a political conversation. His visit to the Wailing Wall in Israel when he turned thirty, he says, was just a stunt to change people's perception of him. Anything was better than being thought of as a messiah, even being thought of as Elvis Presley. The one time he cracks a full smile is when Bradley follows up on Dylan's notion that he only kept touring because of a bargain he'd made a long time ago.

"A bargain with who?" Bradley asks.

"The Chief Commander," says Dylan, "on this earth and of the world we can't see."

One of the two most interesting tidbits to come out of the interview is that Dylan is planning to write volumes two and three of his memoirs (we're still waiting). The other is this moldy chestnut about lying to the press. "The only person you have to think about lying twice to is either yourself or to God," he says. "The press isn't either of them. I just figured they're irrelevant."

His Ten Best Music Videos

One of the more unlikely characters pressed into the service of the video age ushered in by MTV, Bob Dylan has generally been fairly uncomfortable in front of the camera, especially when playacting, as anyone who has seen his various movies and TV appearances will attest. Despite having a worthy array of story songs that would be ideal for a video treatment, most of his work in this arena has been in the live-performance mode. Easily fifty years of his live performances, in all sorts of venues and in all sorts of hats, can be seen in one form or another via the Internet, from an early "Blowin' in the Wind" on TV to a 1970 duet with George Harrison on "Gates of Eden," to any number of his classic and throwaway songs from this year's, or any year's, tour. Several of his official videos are live clips, including an excruciating five-minute close-up of him in whiteface from the Rolling Thunder era, singing "Tangled Up in Blue." And then there's the strange, bearded Civil War figure he cut for "Across the Green Mountains," his song for the movie *Gods and Generals*. Suffice it to say, he is much more appealing in his various cameos in *The Wonder Boys*, for which he wrote the Oscar-winning "Things Have Changed."

While hardly having conquered music videos as he has conquered songwriting, performing, memoir-writing, and radio hosting—and while the jury is still out on the video form itself as a worthy pop cultural artifact—Dylan has on occasion found himself thrust into a number of fairly interesting scenarios, which I present below in descending order of interestingness.

10. The Nash Edgerton Collection: "It Must Be Santa Claus" (2009), "Duquesne Whistle" (2012), "The Night We Called It a Day" (2015)

In his later years, Bob Dylan has come to terms with the video format, much as he's come to terms with life, presenting himself as a wizened, grizzled, curmudgeonly, crazy but lovable uncle figure. As directed by Nash Edgerton, this persona comes across best in "It Must Be Santa Claus," wherein we find Dylan reliving the joys of his childhood in the land of the midnight polka band, accompanied by an accordion player. Safe to say, the holiday gathering taking place in this video is meant to show that Dylan's not in Greenwich Village anymore; he's back home among the fun-loving good folks of the country he calls the Midwest. But wait, toward the end of the proceedings it seems as if someone's spiked the eggnog, as one of the revelers starts to party like it's 1969, ending up going straight through the window while Bob (and Santa) can only watch in wizened, grizzled bemusement.

Much the same treatment is given to the otherwise upbeat "Duquesne Whistle," which takes place on the streets of downtown Los Angeles, where a kind of all-American doofus is stalking a lovely actress/model, occasionally with stolen roses. While the actress takes this in stride, only whipping out the pepper spray when absolutely necessary, the local florist and Bernie Sanders lookalike is a good deal less forgiving. Suddenly, while Dylan and the unlikeliest entourage he's ever been surrounded by look on, the poor sap is kidnapped. Later, beaten but unbowed, he's deposited back to the same street where the actress lives, apparently still in the grip of his unattainable fantasy. When last we see him, the lad is stretched out on the street in a bloody pulp, as Dylan and his motley crew jauntily step over him, presumably on their way to a gig.

In the third of the Edgerton trilogy, "The Night We Called It a Day"—a song that was introduced by Dick Powell in the 1944 B-movie *Sing a Jingle* and later was the title of a D-movie based on Frank Sinatra's experiences in Australia called *All the Way*—Dylan goes all the way noir in a send up of Bogey and the boys. Here he drops the lovable uncle figure for a more menacing ladies' man type—a not altogether believable twist in which he comes off more like Woody Allen than Humphrey Bogart. At any rate, by the time of the final shots (and gunshots), no one will be contemplating Frank Sinatra.

9. "When the Deal Goes Down" (2006)

Like Woody Allen, Bob Dylan must have a certain fascination for Scarlett Johansson, who dominates the screen in this wistful home movie set in Minnesota. Unlike Allen, Dylan prefers not to appear in this video. A wise choice. As in many of his best songs, faux-autobiographical hints abound. In one shot, Johansson is seen holding a copy of *Bound for Glory*, the story of another influential Woody, Woody Guthrie. In another, a seminal Hank Williams album is pictured. The grainy and wobbly home-movie effect gives the impression all the extras in the video are really part of Dylan's Minnesota family—or else Johansson's New York City family—though it's extremely doubtful that Dylan, even for a fast buck, would subject anyone close to him to such sentimental scrutiny.

8. "Cold Irons Bound" (1997)

Taken from his period "in a cowboy band," this is one of Dylan's best live-performance videos, shot close up in a honky-tonk setting. As opposed to the more rocking versions that exist elsewhere, this performance is the essence of control. It's apparent, at least in this instance, that Dylan has fully achieved his lifelong desire to carry himself like his idols, specifically Hank Williams. One of the joys of this video is that you can almost see this recognition dawning on him. As the song fades out, the impenetrable bandleader allows himself just the hint of a smile.

7. "Like a Rolling Stone" (interactive version, 2013)

Directed by Vania Hegmann, this video interpretation of Bob Dylan's most classic '60s song would seem to be a dream come true for those who always felt MTV came along a decade too late to offer them anything of substance. Indeed, the idea of seeing not just this but gems like "Mr. Tambourine

Man," "Ballad of a Thin Man," "Desolation Row," and so many other creatively challenging songs is still a proposition a certain demographic would undoubtedly pay good money to see on a channel entirely devoted to re-imagining Dylan in the video context. (However, if it's anything like Twyla Tharp reimagining Dylan in a dance context—*The Times They Are a-Changing*—or Todd Hanson reimagining Dylan in a film context—*I'm Not There*—perhaps some dreams are better left to the bed stand.)

In this case, the most significant part of the (interactive) video is its technological achievement. Something like the equivalent of Bruce Springsteen's tepid "57 Channels (and Nothin' On)," the video gives us a clickable cable network menu of food, gossip, sports, game shows, news, talk, and movies featuring a wide array of talking heads, all lip-syncing the lyrics to this iconic song. Though it's hardly a reimagining, it does make the perhaps accidental point that the song is by now so ingrained in American pop-cultural history that everyone from sportscasters to weather girls to game-show hosts know the lyrics to it—even if none of them knows what any of them are worth.

6. "Sweetheart Like You" (1983)

Bob Dylan finally joining the ranks of the MTV corporate machine with this video was kind of like the last rent-control tenant surrendering his apartment to the wrecking ball of progress, MTV being the builder of the projected new condo, Bob Dylan's career being the apartment, "Sweetheart Like You" being the wrecking ball. Much has been made of the condescending tone of Dylan asking the sweetheart in question what she's doing in a dump like this, but in the video the question takes on a certain poignancy, as the sweetheart in question is a somewhat older female custodian at a recording studio, consigned to mopping floors after Dylan and the band are done running down the number. Bearing a definite resemblance to him—maybe even being Dylan in drag, or his mother, or at least a mother figure—this hardly nubile sweetheart surely does deserve a house in the suburbs, underwritten by her superstar son.

Of particular note are some of his sidemen in the video, who seem to be playing his real-life sidemen of the era, including the great reggae bassist Robbie Shakespeare, a lovely young girl who seems to take a nifty guitar solo (played on the record by Mick Taylor), and a female backup singer who gazes adoringly at the singer throughout the song, as if she knows she'll someday marry him (Carolyn Dennis?), or at least write some songs with him (Helena

Springs?), or at the very least cut an unreleased album of duets with him (Clydie King?).

5. "Love Sick" (1997)

This video's inclusion on this list is made possible by the involvement of the good folks at Victoria's Secret, who used a minute of it to promote something called "Angels in Venice." Knowing the expense budgets of the corporate world, for the use of this song, Dylan was probably rewarded with a trip to Venice on Victoria's tab and his choice of a supermodel (or three) with whom to spend the lonely evenings over the course of the shoot. While the naysayers were out in force, protesting the dubious integrity of the former protest singer, Dylan was undoubtedly laughing all the way to the bank (and/or the bed).

4. "Things Have Changed" (2000)

Another Woody Allen tribute—this time to *Zelig*, the movie in which Allen is craftily inserted into key moments in history. In this video, Dylan is inserted into key moments in the classy movie *The Wonder Boys*, alongside Michael Douglas, Katie Holmes, Robert Downey Jr., and Tobey Maguire.

Dylan's involvement with a film about a college professor with terminal writer's block turned out to be the height of symmetry. While he'd just come from battling a huge writer's block throughout the early '90s, the arrival of *Time Out of Mind* in 1997, followed by this song a few years later, put an end to his creative doubts, while also winning him an Academy Award for his troubles. While the message of the song is that Bob Dylan couldn't care less, it's obvious he cared deeply, which is what makes the song so affecting. The video? Not so much, especially the need for Dylan to be lip-syncing all the time. When he occasionally morphs into Michael Douglas, mouthing the words, the effect is unsettling.

3. "Subterranean Homesick Blues" (1965)

Easily Dylan's most natural and penetrating performance, captured in his first celluloid appearance, in D. A. Pennebaker's documentary *Dont Look Back*, this is Bob's flip answer to the Beatles' *A Hard Day's Night*. Which makes him the natural antithesis to the Beatles that the Rolling Stones were always hyped up to be but never were. With the legendary Beat poet and friend of Corso and Kerouac, Allen Ginsberg, as his comedic foil, manning the cue cards, Dylan prances through the motions of the yet-to-be-invented video form with the casual disdain of a rock James Dean—a pose he would maintain throughout the 1965 movie, and throughout his subsequent 1966 tour, which produced the lesser *Eat the Document*, right up until the moment his career, to say nothing of his life, hit a literal bump in the road.

2. "Series of Dreams" (1995)

This has all the elements of what a Bob Dylan video should be: great song, great concept, great images. As directed by Chris Austopchuk, Nicky Lindeman, and Meiert Avis, it's a video you could watch many times in succession and find something new each time. It's a video where you want to hit the pause button and rewind and freeze on an image or some poetic lines. It's a video where you wish you could collect the entire set of stills for five dollars apiece so you could have them to rifle through at your leisure— although given the nature of Dylan's latter-day business model, if such a set existed, each still would probably go for more like $500 apiece.

Like a series of dreams itself, the video is a dreamscape of Bob Dylan's entire career, featuring moment upon moment of iconic splendor, perfectly capturing not only the song but also Dylan's import as a figure of monumental luminosity in the galaxy of the twentieth century and beyond. Charting the artist's journey through this incredibly well chosen series of images is charting the journey of a generation still fascinated by this character's every move, movement, twitch, and grimace, from his earliest days at the Gaslight to his triumphant tour of England to his later-years fall from grace, skulking around the outskirts of the city in a hoodie. Among the many real gems that emerge on the fourth or fifteenth viewing, check out the scene at Jack Kerouac's gravesite and the picture of Bob in a taxi next to a life-size still of Lenny Bruce.

1. "Like a Rolling Sex Machine" (1976)

Once you finish marveling at the concept and laughing hysterically at the result, you still have to sit back and be amazed at the magnitude of this cultural artifact—and doubly amazed that it was put together in 1976 for the short-lived *Wolfman Jack Show*, which likely never came close to duplicating this sterling feat—although, I have to admit, having not seen any episodes of the program, that this is only an educated guess. But who could top this marvelous mash-up of two of rock's most influential and mercurial figures, intermingling two of their most treasured and important songs? Here, a James Brown performance of "Get Up (I Feel Like Being a) Sex Machine" is intercut with a Bob Dylan performance of "Like a Rolling Stone," to absolute perfection. When Brown cries "Take it, Bobby" (referring to his own band member, Bobby Byrd) and Bobby Dylan rips into the chorus of "Like a Rolling Stone," the two titans join forces to make video history.

35

Information Highway 61

Best Websites

f the countless amateur and professional sites devoted to one aspect or another of Bob Dylan's amazing career, I've singled out a few that render most of the others redundant.

The Official Site (www.bobdylan.com)

This is the official and definitive site for anyone from the casual fan to the Bob obsessive. It's straightforward, cleanly and purposefully presented, and filled with facts. In other words, everything the real Bob Dylan is not. There are clickable links to (almost) every set the man has performed: the date, the city, the venue, and which songs were performed. Given Dylan's performing style, the lyrics section of this site is particularly revealing and valuable. If you want to know how many times he's played San Diego, you can find out through this site. If you want to know when a given song from *Street-Legal* appeared on the tour, how many times it was played, and when it disappeared from the tour, this site will keep you transfixed for hours. You can sort his entire catalog of songs alphabetically, by the number of times he's played them, or by the date they appeared in a show. And, given that it's the official site, you can also buy any or all of his albums, individual songs, and even his collected artwork. There's also a huge archive of interviews, news, and videos, which is always being updated.

Searching for a Gem (www.searchingforagem.com)

This is the comprehensive site for Dylan collectibles and rarities, which turn out to be so numerous as to contradict the term. Just for starters, nearly every 45 and CD single released in a given territory with its own alternate B-side is accounted for, in a yearly index. You'll find album versions specific to certain countries. As a special treat, there's a massive list of all Dylan songs featured in movies, whether they made the soundtrack album or not. And a list of unreleased songs, whether they're finished or not.

Expecting Rain (www.expectingrain.com)

The most ambitious of all Bob Dylan sites, this one was established by Karl Erik Andersen in 1994 and is still going strong. Among its other unique attributes is an ongoing discussion board, making social media history out of one of pop culture's most antisocial artists. If you want to communicate with likeminded or simply well-versed fans on subjects ranging from favorite tour moments to his radio show to anything else Dylan-related (and even some more general topics), this is the place to be. The news page covers every conceivable aspect of Bob's career. Here are some sample headlines from a given day in 2015:

- "Bob Dylan, Innovator or Historian: Sean Wilentz and Christopher Ricks Take sides"
- "Dylan Still Has a Story to Tell with *Shadows in the Night*"
- "Roadie Report '72 by Camilla McGuinn—54 Trains, 61 Hotels, and 2 Voyages"
- "'Bob Dylan' at Bay Street in Sag Harbor March 21! The Complete Unknowns"
- "Knockin' on Dylan's Door" (audio)
- "Bob Dylan: Saratoga Springs, NY, 2000" (video)
- "2014 Duluth Salute to the Music of Bob Dylan—John Bushey Magic Houdini and Dylan" (video)
- "Letters: Popular Plagiarism—Beyond the Horizon/Red Sails in the Sunset—Royalty Was Paid"

Particularly fascinating is the "Bob Dylan A–Z" section, which sums up the contributions to the Dylan oeuvre by everyone from Brigitte Bardot and Ellen Baker to David Zimmerman and William Zantzinger. There's even a section of fan-supplied artwork.

The Bob Dylan Bootleg Museum (www.bobsboots.com)

Put together over a decade ago by Craig Pinkerton and now drawing over two million hits a month, this site is a massive catalog of all available Bob Dylan bootleg recordings, which may comprise every concert the man ever gave at which someone in the front row (or the back row) had access to a tape recorder. It also contains chat sites, want lists, and other commentary, but at the heart of the site are the bootlegs—a practice about which Pinkerton goes to great lengths to defend and to distance himself.

"This section is not meant to romanticize the obviously illegal practice of intellectual property theft, rather to put it into perspective," he writes. "For the most part, we are talking about recordings that would never see the light of day any other way. The only alternative to bootlegs is for the performances to be forever lost. Looking back to the roots of blues, jazz, country, and rock music, there are multiple thousands of lost performances and artists that we will never hear. Thank God for the handful of bootleggers that did preserve the recordings that we now view as true treasures of the history of music, and therefore, the history of mankind."

Words Fill My Head / Still on the Road (www.bjorner.com)

This is the site for one of the world's premier students of Bob Dylan, Olaf Bjorner, who has published thirteen volumes on the man in performance and in the studio. This massively detailed site has everything from song, performance, and studio-musician databases to a list of almost every known (and a few complete unknown) Dylan covers. There are at least forty-five downloadable concerts, dozens of rare interviews, and a special section devoted to his poetry, featuring such early scribblings as:

- "Go Away You Bomb"
- "For Dave Glover"
- "Lonesome Christmas"
- "The Kennedy Poems"
- "A Message from Bob Dylan"
- "A Letter from Bob Dylan"
- "Six Poems"
- "Letter to Larry"
- "Dear Mummy"

Also essential is Olaf's list of links, including: the first Dylan site, Bringing It All Back Home (www.punkhart.com/dylan); the unfortunately titled fanzine *Isis* (www.bobdylanisis.com); the self-explanatory Bob Dylan Ticket Stub Archives (www.dylanstubs.com); and Bob Links (www.boblinks.com), started by William Pagel, your virtual street map to Dylan's presence on the information highway, which has had about thirty-six million visitors.

Off Road: The Dylan Museums

Bob Links creator William Pagel definitely ranks high among Dylan collectors. He is the owner of the Central Hillside duplex that is Dylan's childhood home, as well as the highchair the young poet sat in as a baby. In 2016, he brought his twelve-plus tons of memorabilia to Duluth, for a museum exhibit at the Karpeles Manuscript Library, "Einstein Disguised as Robin Hood." According to a report in the *Duluth News Tribune* by Christa Lawler, the lists of exhibits includes, among other items of interest: the official Hibbing District Court document from August 9, 1962, marking his change of name from Zimmerman to Dylan; a photograph of Dylan at the age of three; pictures of his synagogue; and shots of him and his buddies at Camp Herzl.

By the Time You Get to Tulsa

In a bid to make Tulsa, Oklahoma, the roots-music capitol of the United States, the University of Tulsa's Helmerich Center for American Research, in association with the Gilcrease Museum, landed the jewel in the crown. After snaring the Woody Guthrie Archives in 2011, before putting them on display at the Brady Arts District in 2013, the George Kaiser Family Foundation shelled out upward of fifteen million dollars to acquire from Bob Dylan more than 5,000 handwritten lyrics, rare photographs, private letters, and contracts, as well as audio recordings and videotaped concert footage. Exhibit curator Michael Chaiken told the Associated Press, "I think there's something endearing about it going to Tulsa and not to an Ivy League school."

For the apprentice Dylanographer, there are lyrics to "Chimes of Freedom" on stationery from the Waldorf Hotel in Toronto, an early draft of "Visions of Johanna" on a yellow legal pad, a typewritten draft of "Subterranean Homesick Blues," and two notebooks from the *Blood on the Tracks* period. Even more eye- and ear-opening are the complete sessions for all of Dylan's albums, dozens of professionally filmed shows, and perhaps thousands of soundboard tapes, previously only the province of the severe underground aficionado. Others may find pleasure in perusing the outtakes from *Dont Look Back*, *Eat the Document*, and *The Rolling Thunder Revue*. Of particular interest may be Dylan's old address book, containing then-current phone numbers for Johnny Cash, Nico, Lenny Bruce, and Allen Ginsberg. If for nothing else, I'd punch my ticket to see footage of

Dylan and Tiny Tim cavorting in Woodstock, or, most fascinatingly of all, the 1978 postcard from Barbra Streisand, thanking Dylan for sending her flowers (obviously in response to her complaints in her duet that year with Dylan's then management stablemate, Neil Diamond, "You Don't Send Me Flowers").

36

He's Been Around the World

The Never Ending Tour

One of Bob Dylan's strangest accomplishments has been to render most of his albums superfluous. Many times, they capture tortuous journeys through the dark heat of the recording studio, where he was (and probably still is) generally underprepared and overmatched, resulting in some of his discarded outtakes becoming among his most treasured and highly regarded achievements. At the same time, it has also been Dylan's penchant to render his individual songs superfluous by rewriting them after the fact and rearranging them in concert.

Thus it is only in concert, say his followers, that you get the true experience of Bob Dylan's greatness—even if, often enough, Dylan has (seemingly) gone out of his way to render his performances superfluous by the wide range of his inconsistency, from night to night, city to city, year to year, decade to decade.

Nevertheless, the truly diligent Dylanographer's primary mission in life and consummate joy is to wade through dozens if not hundreds of individual performance tapes to get to the definitive night when the definitive version of the definitive song was played. Sometimes this will be the only great performance given on that night (or that tour). Often it will bear no resemblance to the song as captured on the album it came from, instead lifted to the heavens by virtue of some divine inspiration (or divine body undulating in the front row). From this lofty vantage point, known only to rabid collectors, a particularly compelling "Under the Red Sky" could supplant a temporarily vapid reading of "Like a Rolling Stone" on the holy scroll of great Dylan songs (or great Dylan moments).

It is in the quest of chasing those moments—indeed, living for those moments—that Bob Dylan has cultivated an international fan base willing to follow him on his "Never Ending Tour," even while the performer himself has claimed he hates these obnoxious front-row dwellers. And, besides, there no longer is such a thing as a never-ending tour. "There was a Never Ending Tour but it ended in '91 with the departure of guitarist G. E. Smith," Dylan writes in the facetious liner notes to the *World Gone Wrong* album. He proceeds to name some of the more memorable tours since then, including:

- The Money Never Runs Out Tour (fall of '91)
- The Southern Sympathizer Tour (early '92)
- The Why Do You Look at Me So Strangely Tour (Europe, '92)
- The One Sad Cry of Pity Tour (Australia and the West Coast of America, '92)
- The Principles of Action Tour (Mexico/South America, '92)
- The Outburst of Consciousness Tour ('92)
- The Don't Let Your Deal Go Down Tour ('93)

Further research has come up with several more delightfully evocative tour names:

- The True Confessions Tour ('86)
- The Temples in Flames Tour ('87)
- Interstate 88 ('88)
- The Fastbreak Tour ('90)
- The Paradise Lost Tour (late '95)
- The South of the South Tour (early '08)
- The Americanarama Tour (summer/fall 2013)

The Dylan Map

Since Dylan has spent upward of half his life since 1989 out on the road, in some years gigging for as many as ten months of the year (although he's cut back to six or seven months since 2009), it must be said, regardless of his dismissive comments, that the performer himself lives for these tours—and lives during these tours—as much as his most obsessed fan. A glance at the mythical Bob Dylan Map will reveal his own obsession with scouring the globe, pulling some of the most obscure towns and venues out of his hat, if only to say, "Been there, done that." What other reason on earth would he have to play the Buffalo Chip Campground in Sturgis, South Dakota (aside from the opportunity to hook up with some biker chicks), or the Houston Livestock Show and Rodeo, or the Ice Palace in St. Petersburg, Russia?

Indeed, when Bob Dylan sings a line on the order of, "I've been all around the world, boys," he's one of the few performers who can back it up, from the Neumann Outdoor Field in Fargo, North Dakota, to the famed Pantages Theater in Los Angeles, founded in 1930 and the home of the Academy Awards presentations from 1950 to 1959. In 2002 and 2008, Dylan played Pimlico, site of the Preakness Stakes horse race. In 1982, he played the Rose Bowl. In 1994, he played Roseland. In 2010 and 2012, he played at the East Room of the White House, at the request of President Obama. In 1994, he finally played Woodstock. In 2004, he played Bonnaroo. In 1976, he played the Troubadour in L.A. (singing a couple of songs as a guest of Roger Miller and Larry Gatlin) and Winterland in San Francisco (helping to close the place in the film *The Last Waltz*). In 1975, just before ending the first leg of the Rolling Thunder tour, he played a raucous seven-song set at the Correctional Institute for Women in Clinton, New Jersey (where "I Shall Be Released" was particularly well received). In 1990 and '94, he played the Eisenhower Hall Theater at West Point. After recording *The Johnny Cash Show* at the legendary Ryman Auditorium in Nashville, home of the Grand Ole Opry, in 1969, he returned to the venue four more times. In 1987, he hit Sun Studios in Memphis to record "Love Rescue Me" with U2. In 2010, it was over to Greyhound Park in Post Falls, Idaho.

Not surprisingly, his favorite city is New York, where he favors almost equally the great, vast Madison Square Garden and the cozier confines of the Beacon Theater. But he usually finds a spot on his schedule, every few years or so, for the Jones Beach Summer Theater. In his second favorite city, Los Angeles, he has no clear-cut favorite, dividing his visits between the spacious Forum and legendary theaters like the Pantages, the Wiltern, and the El Rey. The Greek and the Community in Berkeley hold fond memories of Dylan performances, as does the Fox Theater in Atlanta, the Academy of Music in Philadelphia, and the Orpheum Theater in Boston. In Atlantic City, Dylan has preferred the Borgata; in Vegas, it's the Joint. At the bottom of the list are such low-density, high-mileage locations as Hawaii, as well as Wyoming, Idaho, and Delaware. The only state he's never played is Alaska. He has, on the other hand, played Iceland in 2002, Turkey in 2003, Lithuania in 2008, South Korea in 2010, Vietnam in 2011, and Costa Rica in 2012.

Woodstock Revisited for the First Time: August 14, 1994

In a year that offered a pop-cultural bonanza, ranging from the Major League Baseball strike that stole the World Series, the Rangers winning the Stanley Cup for the first time since 1940, the Tonya Harding–Nancy

Kerrigan scuffle at the Olympics, the marriage of Michael Jackson and Lisa Marie Presley, and O. J. Simpson's white Bronco, nothing could upstage Bob Dylan's return to Woodstock, twenty-five years after the fact. Like the original event, the three-day twenty-fifth-anniversary concert on Winston Farm in Saugerties, New York, was covered in mud, attracted a huge crowd, and featured an amazing lineup, from Blues Traveler, Collective Soul, Sheryl Crow, and the Violent Femmes on Friday to Joe Cocker, Nine Inch Nails, Metallica, and Aerosmith on Saturday to the Allman Brothers, Green Day, the Red Hot Chili Peppers, the Neville Brothers, and Santana on Sunday. Though Dylan was clearly a highlight, Peter Gabriel had the honor of closing the show on Sunday night.

Dylan took the stage just as the clouds broke at sunset on the last day. "We waited twenty-five years to hear this," said the announcer. "Ladies and gentlemen, Mr. Bob Dylan."

"It's on the North Stage today that Woodstock is finally redeemed," Andrew Mueller wrote in the October 1994 issue of *Vox*. "He's fired up for tonight, delivering 'It Ain't Me Babe,' 'It's All Over Now, Baby Blue,' and 'Masters of War' with chilling conviction. Up on the monitors during 'I Shall Be Released,' his face looks transported and tear-struck, as if looking for escape from his myth in the raging red sky above us. Good to know that, after all these years, Dylan, of all people, can still sing it like he means it."

The Year of Our Dylan, 1997

Inspecting the list of bootleg concerts from the Never Ending Tour available to the obsessed Dylan fan, and the comments they draw, it's clear that for every highlight, when Dylan sang it like he meant it, and the band played it like they knew all the changes, there was a corresponding set of glorified mumbles, when nobody in the audience (or the band) could be sure of what the set list contained until it was posted on his website the following morning. In some cases, these praises and complaints were directed toward the same night. Many were the debates between those who were there and those who only heard the recordings (along with those who did both) as to what was Dylan's ultimate performance of a given song during a given tour, or if indeed such a concert had taken place.

In this context, by far the most perspicacious collection available has to be 1997's *Bathed in a Stream of Pure Heat*, for which the compiler selected the best twenty-two songs from thirteen different concerts, from a February 24 performance of "Viola Lee Blues" in Sapporo, Japan, through a May 21 performance of "Stone Walls and Steel Bars" taken from a benefit for the Simon Wiesenthal Center, given at the Beverly Hills Hilton. Although the set is light on classics, containing only a New Jersey version of "Desolation Row" and a Portland, Maine, version of "A Hard Rain's a-Gonna Fall," it does sport "This Wheel's on Fire," "You're a Big Girl Now," and the ineffable "Every Grain of Sand." Three shows in April may have been especially notable—the 9th in Bangor, Maine, the 17th in Providence, Rhode Island, and the 19th in Hartford, Connecticut—in that two songs were extracted from each night. By that logic, the best concert of the early part of 1997's epic touring season had to be his show at the Fisher Auditorium in Indiana, Pennsylvania (only sixty miles east of Pittsburgh), from which "Pledging My Time," "Wicked Messenger," and "Shooting Star" all make the cut.

Five Nights at the El Rey in Los Angeles, December 1997

Bob Dylan's five-night stand to wrap up 1997 at the El Rey on Wilshire Boulevard, Los Angeles, drew a host of celebrities, including Ringo Starr, Joni Mitchell, Dennis Hopper, Danny DeVito, Andre Agassi, Jack Nicholson, and Gregory Peck. Although it's true that regular devoted fans consistently and constantly differ on what constitutes a great Bob Dylan show as opposed to a monumental Bob Dylan show, and have their personal Top 50 set lists in their back pockets and several dozen bootleg tapes in their backpacks, ready to prove their point, the first and only time Dylan would play this onetime art deco movie theater built in 1936, and in business as a rock venue since 1994, would certainly be a highlight for most of them, especially considering how the man himself had spent six weeks in bed earlier in the year suffering from a rare and debilitating heart disease.

Each night featured a different opening act. On the first night, Beck dubbed the proceedings "the Bob Dylan festival," and there was no denying it. Jewel, Sheryl Crow (twice), and Willie Nelson took the honors over the next four nights, during which Dylan played a total of forty-two different songs, with the recurring regulars being "Maggie's Farm," which opened every night, and "Rainy Day Women #12 & 35," which closed every night. His first encore each night was "'Til I Fell in Love with You," usually followed by "Highway 61 Revisited." Most nights he inserted seven songs that hadn't been played the night before. On the night of the 18th, he performed "Blind Willie McTell" for only the eighteenth time, having debuted it in August, at the Du Maurier Stadium in Montreal.

Of all the celebrities in attendance that week, perhaps the only one who really meant anything to Dylan was Gregory Peck. Having been prominently name-checked in "Brownsville Girl," the cinematic extravaganza Dylan wrote with Sam Shepard, Peck had repaid the favor when he presented Dylan as a Kennedy Center honoree just two weeks before the show with a beautifully crafted speech. "The first time I heard Bob Dylan I thought of him as a kind of nineteenth-century troubadour, a maverick American spirit," Peck said. To top off the speech, Peck gave a nod to the Dylan epic inspired by *The Gunfighter*. "All through that movie, the townspeople kept telling my character to get out of town before the shooting starts. Bob Dylan's never been about to get out of town before the shooting starts."

Bob Dylan at the Key(s): Seattle, October 4, 2002

You'd think that at the age of sixty-one, Bob Dylan would be done making changes, if not to his personal life then at least to his performing career. But the man who shocked the world when he added an electric guitar to his act (twice, in fact, but his Newport '65 performance had more far-reaching implications than his Hibbing High performance in 1957), and shocked the world again when he became a barnstorming rock 'n' roll preacher in 1979, now shocked a somewhat lesser contingent of his loyal fans at the beginning of his fall 2002 tour, when he took the stage at the Key Arena in Seattle on October 4 with no guitar at all, determined instead to stand behind a little electric keyboard for the first five songs of his set: "Solid Rock," "Lay Lady Lay," "Tombstone Blues," Warren Zevon's "Accidentally Like a Martyr," and "I'll Be Your Baby Tonight." Later that night, he returned to the keyboard for "It's Alright, Ma (I'm Only Bleeding)," "Honest with Me," "High Water (for Charlie Patton)," another Zevon cover, "Mutineer," and "Floater (Too Much to Ask)." To honor the terminally ill Zevon, he also covered a third tune of his, "Boom Boom Mancini," that night. Furthermore, to rebut Mick Jagger's claim that Bob Dylan could never sing "Satisfaction," he tore into "Brown Sugar."

During the next couple of weeks, as word of this new kind of blasphemy spread across the chat boards of the Internet, Dylan would provide a virtual new album's worth of standards in piano/vocal format, including "Maggie's Farm," "Stuck Inside of Mobile with the Memphis Blues Again," "A Hard Rain's a-Gonna Fall," "Tangled Up in Blue," "Just Like a Woman," and "You Ain't Goin' Nowhere." During the next few years, almost everything guitar-led in his repertoire could now be heard in concert with the guitarist on piano (and sometimes grand piano), including the revered trilogy of "Highway 61 Revisited," "Like a Rolling Stone," and "All Along the Watchtower."

The 2002 shows were captured on a four-CD bootleg with the evocative title *Looking for Maurice Chevalier's Passport in America*. In most other cases, bootleg titles have had something to do with the time (*Summer of Zero*) or the place (*A Dark Night on the Spanish Stairs*), or made use of a particularly memorable lyric (*Don't Talk to Strangers*). This one sounds more like a discarded chapter title from *Tarantula*. It nevertheless fits the bill, with "Solid Rock" and "Boom Boom Mancini" representing that historic night in Seattle. "Friend of the Devil" from the next night in Eugene, Oregon, typified a year of magnificent covers, including "Brown Sugar," Neil Young's "Old Man," Don Henley's "The End of the Innocence," and more Warren Zevon—"Lawyers, Guns, and Money," "Mutineer," and "Accidentally Like a Martyr"—topped off by "Something," an emotional tribute to George Harrison at Madison Square Garden on November 13.

Twenty-First-Century Dylan

While Dylan was dismal the last two times I saw him, at Foxwoods in 2005 and the Harbor Yard in Bridgeport in 2007, with new songs indistinguishable from the old, he did wind up ending 2005 with five sellout nights at the Brixton Academy in London, where, as was typical, not only did his performance and set list vary from night to night, but his overall persona shape-shifted as befitting his mood, according to the ad copy for the bootleg of this concert, "from the troubadour to the jokerman" and from "serious to lackluster." Sprinkled through the five nights was the occasional welcome surprise, from "Every Grain of Sand" to "Mississippi" to the first ever unveiling of "Million Dollar Bash" on the second night. And, having recently worked with Mick Jones and Paul Simonon of the Clash, who were in the audience, Dylan played what he could remember of "London Calling" on two separate nights, to much astonishment and applause.

The essence of this experience, as well as my own, which is the essence of seeing Bob Dylan in the twenty-first century, was admirably captured by Stephen Moss, writing in the *Guardian*. "Critics of Dylan gigs—twangy, nasal voice; wonderful songs deconstructed to the point of indecipherability; efficient band overwhelming the anonymous artist at the centre—miss the point. We are here to touch the hem, give thanks, confirm that we may still be alive. This is more religious ritual than concert."

Still going strong at sixty-five, Dylan took to the keyboards at the New Orleans Jazz and Heritage Festival in 2006. "Positively 4th Street" was a highlight.

Paparazzo Presents/Wikimedia Commons/Public domain

As reported by Neil McCormick, the music critic for the London *Daily Telegraph*, Dylan was still going strong on his fourth ever visit to the Royal Albert Hall in October 2015. "Dylan shows have long been notorious, even with his most devoted fans. Following his own internal compass, he has been prone to playing rambling set lists so chewed up as to be barely recognizable, growling and barking unintelligible lyrics, altering vocal melodies and rhythm until, by some invisible alignment of stars, a song will come into magical focus. Now . . . every lyric unfolds with clarity, melodies roll out gently, and these extraordinary songs come fully alive."

For a rare view of Dylan's own opinion on his performing style, this nugget captured in an interview with Bert Kleinman and Artie Mogull, which ran on the Westwood One radio network in 1984, says volumes, even if it predates the never-ending phase of his touring life, and even if his answer concerns his feelings about the Arabic singer Om Kalthoum, who died in 1975 but whose records still sell a million copies a year around the world: "In a live show it's not all about the lyrics. It's in the phrasing and the dynamics and the rhythm. Om Kalthoum was one of my favorite singers of all time—and I don't understand a word she sings. She'd sing one song—it might last for forty minutes, same song, and she'll sing the same phrase over and over and over again, but in a different way every time. I don't think there's any Western singer that's in that kind of category . . . except possibly me."

37

Gentlemen, Don't Get Up

Songs of the Endgame

B ob Dylan in the '60s was an unstoppable force. Unaccountably and magically, Bob Dylan in his sixties would again become an unstoppable force. Starting up his engines in 1997, at the wise old age of fifty-six, he released eight albums over the next nineteen years, regaining the favor of the *Billboard* charts and the almost unanimous praise of the critics who had written him off for the last time at the end of the '80s, and winning a boatload of Grammy nominations and awards in the process. Where once his muse was Suze; and then Joanie; and then Sara; and then his rabid, disapproving audience; then the Band and the Bible; then Sara and the kids and country music, the romance of the road, the divorce and his lost youth, his backup singers one-two-three; and then God for a couple of years, followed by the blues, and perhaps even a new appreciation of his catalog, his muse now—his last muse—was mortality, physical decay, and the impending death of the body as well as the planet, due to the End Times predicted in the scriptures and given a secular voice by, among others, Hal Lindsay in *The Late Great Planet Earth*. While these end times were mainly kept in the background during his prolific late-innings output, his message of life's small triumphs and larger travails, as processed through whatever he was reading and set to a roiling stew of roots and pre-war pop music, continued even into his not-so-homey rendering of Christmas songs and his poignant attacks on the Great American Songbook.

Bob Dylan was back, even though, as usual, you might not like his message or his delivery. Or his working methods. Of great concern among the musicologically literate, as the first three of these eight albums emerged, was the way Dylan had returned to the past, not only to the source of his formative inspirations, but to his habit of sourcing those sources for his own ends, usually without credit. When he did this during one of his biblical periods, who was going to come after him? John the Baptist? When he did this to the citizens of Harry Smithville (Greil Marcus's name for the crusty rustics who reside in the mythic community whose sound and soundtrack is Harry Smith's *Anthology of American Folk Music*), there were enough devotees with access to computers and prestigious publications who were able to identify the original artifacts and showcase their findings before a national audience to arouse complaint, at least among a certain coterie of purists.

But Bob Dylan went even deeper and wider in his extravagant pilfering. With his early reputation untouchable, and his current reputation already in the toilet, he may have felt he was at a point where he had nothing to lose by going way over the top with his cavalier handling of the public domain. He surely felt no shame in what he termed was "moving the line" in his approach to songcraft. He explained it over and over to inquiring journalists, most explicitly to Robert Hilburn of the *Los Angeles Times* in 2004. "My songs are either based on old Protestant hymns or Carter Family songs or variations of the blues form. I'll take a song I know and simply start playing it in my head. At a certain point, some words will change and I'll start writing a song."

Love and Theft

Although he never replied in public to the concerns of the critics (which took nothing away from their admiration for the final products), his answer was as plain as the title of his 2001 album *Love and Theft*, which was itself the title of an existing work of social scholarship published in 1993, *Love and Theft: Blackface Minstrelsy and the American Working Class* by Eric Lott, reissued in 2013 with an introduction by none other than Greil Marcus and a new afterword by the author "that extends the study's range to the twenty-first century," undoubtedly with a nod to Dylan for the free publicity.

Less obvious to the uninitiated were the purloined lines and thoughts throughout the album from such wildly and sometimes comically and often brilliantly disparate works as F. Scott Fitzgerald's *The Great Gatsby* and Junichi Saga's *Confessions of a Yazuka*. Throw in the Civil War poet Henry Timrod; one of Dylan's favorite blues singers, Charlie Patton; the country duo Johnny and Jack; the great alley-dweller William Shakespeare; the Marx Brothers; Mark Twain; Virgil's *Aeneid*; the Carter Family; and the legendary crooner Bing Crosby, and you've basically got the undisguised lineup of "Desolation Row" rattling around in the brain and showing up in the lyrical couplets of the one-time college dropout with an honorary degree from Princeton.

The rekindled love of theft was more cinematic than literary or musicological on 1997's *Time Out of Mind*, which may be one of the reasons a masterful song like "Mississippi" failed to make the cut, only to show up in a supposedly lesser version on *Love and Theft* four years later, where its clever use of its source material (the early '30s prison song "Rosie") made it a seemingly perfect fit. In actuality, most of the reason behind it being left off the former album was due to Dylan's unresolved conflict with his producer, Daniel Lanois, over the song's presentation and importance. Certainly, its world-weary message was right in line with the other downcast tomes on the earlier album, including "Love Sick," "Cold Irons Bound," "Not Dark Yet," and the epically melancholy "Highlands," in which, after escaping from a brief (but hilarious) encounter with a Boston waitress, Dylan is able to notice the sun shining down on him, but not like it used to shine, much as in "Mississippi," where he talks about his ability to make a comeback, but "not all the way." Some said the song was just another victim of Dylan's historic and chronic ambivalence toward the recording studio. "It's very difficult for me to think that I'm going to eclipse anything I've ever done before," he told *Guitar World*. "I lose my inspiration in the studio real easy, and my mission, which starts out wide, becomes very dim after a few failed takes."

While claiming time had passed him by, that youth was gone forever, and beyond that it was getting dark outside may not seem the ideal way to court a new audience, these sentiments definitely spoke to Dylan's core of weathered hippies facing the prospect of entering the pearly gates "against their will." His resultant comeback precipitated by this album did in fact go all the way, beyond the pop charts to the president and the pope. Dylan, who'd recently fought off a grave illness, certainly appreciated getting the prizes and the tributes and the official pats on the head while he was still alive and well enough to enjoy them, even the long overdue and duly controversial 2016 Nobel Prize for Literature, which he took his sweet time in acknowledging, eventually sending Patti Smith to Sweden to accept it on his behalf.

Dylan the Modernist

Debuting at No. 1 on the *Billboard* album chart, 2008's *Modern Times* continued Dylan's dabbling in music that was anything but modern and themes that were as timeless as Charlie Chaplin's 1936 comedy of the same name, about a mystery tramp displaced in the mechanized world. Right back to the beginning of his performing career, Dylan was characterized more as Charlie Chaplin than Woody Guthrie, although at this point, with his cowboy hat and boots, he seemed to be trying for a cross between two of country singer Don Williams's favorite non-relatives, Hank and Tennessee, as name-checked in his 1982 country hit "Good Old Boys."

Ironically, the artist the Bob Dylan of the twenty-first century most closely resembled, both in stature and point of view, was French. Where in his youth he may have modeled himself after a magnificent burnout like Arthur Rimbaud, in his later life it was the diminutive Charles Aznavour,

In his later years, Bob Dylan has become a living embodiment of Charles Aznavour's troubled troubadour from *Shoot the Piano Player*. Aznavour's possible attraction to Dylan's first dream girl, Brigitte Bardot, only adds to the mystique.   *Wikimedia Commons/Public domain*

singer and cowriter of such melancholy classics as "Yesterday When I Was Young," who continued to speak to him and through him, much as he did in his bravura performance in one of Dylan's favorite movies, *Shoot the Piano Player*, from 1960. (Dylan himself paid tribute to Aznavour in an amazing performance of the Frenchman's "The Times We've Known" at Madison Square Garden on November 1, 1998.)

One of the oddest name-checks on *Modern Times* (ranking right alongside Erica Jong in "Highlands" and Gregory Peck in "Brownsville Girl") is that of current R&B diva Alicia Keys in the opening song, "Thunder on the Mountain," which is otherwise a tribute to blues legends Ma Rainey and Memphis Minnie, whose influence on Keys was subliminal at best. Muddy Waters, Sleepy John Estes, Lightnin' Hopkins, Willie Dixon, Big Joe Williams, and Howlin' Wolf come in for the Dylan co-optation method here, along with classic pop tunes "Red Sails in the Sunset" and "Where the Blue of the Night (Meets the Gold of the Day)."

Stretching the point even further, pundits from New York City to New Zealand were eager to link random lines in Dylan's work to the Civil War poet Henry Timrod and the first century Roman poet Ovid. The best two songs on the album take a bit of their choruses from existing works recorded approximately one hundred years apart: "Highway of Regret" by the Stanley Brothers informs "Ain't Talkin'," and "Gentle Nettie Moore," cowritten in 1857 by the co-author of "Jingle Bells," was Dylan's starting point for his own poignant "Nettie Moore," one of his last great songs.

True to form, and very wisely, the songwriter kept silent on the issue. But he did avoid that particular controversy with 2009's *Together Through Life*. The controversial aspect of this album is that it contains only one original solo composition, "This Dream of You." The other nine were written in collaboration with Robert Hunter, whose previous employer was Jerry Garcia of the Grateful Dead (although he'd moonlighted for Dylan before, coming up with "Silvio" and "The Ugliest Girl in the World," among others). Dylan's generally jaundiced mood can be summed up by the album's opener, "Beyond Here Lies Nothing" and its closer, the viciously satirical "It's All Good," which certainly wasn't.

Remaining on this familiar ground, the keynote song on his next album, *Tempest*, released in 2012, is the fourteen-minute title tune, all about the sinking of the good ship Titanic almost exactly one hundred years before—a mere twinkling of an eye in Dylan's musical chronology. Slightly more current, though no less dour, is his song about John Lennon, "Roll on John." The idea that the high points of the album are a lengthy ballad about a sinking ship, a tribute to a dead crony, and a song about divorce called "Long and Wasted Years" probably sets up the kind of listening experience Dylan intended, although he never played "Tempest" live and only played "Roll on John" twice, both times as special encores: once on November 24, 2013, at the Blackpool Opera House, fifty-five miles north of Lennon's Liverpool birthplace, and two days later at that most holy of venues, the Royal Albert Hall in London.

Dylan the Crooner

When Dylan did finally choose to take on the repertoire of a crooner, *mano a mano*, after battling a bunch of Christmas tunes more or less to a draw on *Christmas in My Heart*, it was not the aforementioned Aznavour, nor was it Bing Crosby, who had turned up favorably in his previous research, although the Christmas album may well have been a nod to *Der Bingle*, the acknowledged benchmark when it came to Christmas crooners. (It was also a nod to the omnipresent Eddie Gorodetsky: way back in 1990, impressed by his pal's knowledge of Christmas songs, Dylan was influential in the Columbia Records release of the eclectic *Christmas Party with Eddie G*, featuring tracks ranging from "Winter Wonderland" by Byron Lee and the Dragonaires to "Mr. and Mrs. Santa Claus" by George Jones and Tammy Wynette. Not only would this compilation serve as a forerunner to the kind of radio show the two of them would concoct a decade later for Sirius Satellite, it most likely formed the template for *Christmas in the Heart*, too.)

Instead, for *Shadows in the Night* (2015) and *Fallen Angels* (2016), Dylan turned his attention to Frank Sinatra. "When you start doing these songs, Frank's got to be on your mind, because he is the mountain," he explained to John Pareles of the *New York Times*. "That's the mountain you have to climb, even if you only get part of the way there."

Sinatra never covered a Bob Dylan song, although his daughter Nancy did twice ("It Ain't Me Babe" and "Blowin' in the Wind"), and Dylan recounts a very pleasant encounter with Frank Jr. in his memoir, *Chronicles*. Sinatra Sr.'s favorite Dylan song was reportedly "Restless Farewell," Dylan's closest thing to "My Way," which he sang for Frank when he was invited to perform at Sinatra's eightieth birthday bash, billed as Eighty Years My Way, at the Shrine Auditorium in L.A. in 1995, among such incomparable luminaries as Tony Bennett, Bruce Springsteen, Steve and Eydie, Little Richard, Don Rickles, and Bono. (The song was appropriately misidentified in the coverage of the event by the *Los Angeles Times* as "Reckless Forever.")

Aside from once in 1964, the only other time Dylan played this song live was exactly a week after Sinatra died, on May 21, 1998, at the nearby Pauley Pavilion in Los Angeles, where it showed up as a poignant encore, and a fitting tribute.

To Pareles, the first of the two-album cycle was a fitting tribute as well, standing firmly alongside the best of Dylan's later output, as well as the best of Frank. "Even when it falters, *Shadows in the Night* maintains its singular mood: lovesick, haunted, suspended between an inconsolable present and all the regrets of the past."

It's a past Bob Dylan had been spending most of his adult life coming to terms with. "Look, you get older," he told Bob Love, the editor of *AARP Magazine*. "Passion is a young man's game. Young people can be passionate. Older people gotta be more wise. I mean, you're around awhile, you leave certain things to the young. Don't try to act like you're young. You could really hurt yourself."

Part of the pleasure derived from *Shadows in the Night* is that Dylan seems to have developed the kind of rapport with his long-time stalwart band-members—George Receli on drums, Tony Garnier on bass, and Donnie Herron on pedal steel—that he had long ago with the Band, with Stu Kimball and Charlie Sexton playing the role of Robbie Robertson. Another joy is that he doesn't hurt himself either physically or image-wise, which is definitely a fear longtime listeners would have had before previewing the record. With that out of the way, the concept begins to pale after the fourth or fifth song. Recorded during the same sessions, most of the songs on *Fallen Angels* pale right out of the gate.

Sure, he can sing just about anything he puts his mind to; sure, he can find songs to fit the limited parameters of his current voice; and a resounding yes that, on *Shadows in the Night* at least, he makes several of these songs his own. Perhaps after a few bottles of wine, an enterprising interviewer might even get Dylan to admit he wished he could sum up his feelings of self-worth and faith as tersely and as poignantly as lyricist Carolyn Leigh did for "Stay with Me," one of the album's several highlights. (Leigh also wrote the lyrics for Sinatra's "Young at Heart," which pops up on *Fallen Angels*.)

Plunging further, the appearance of "Autumn Leaves," at first just another moldy chestnut on aging, becomes something else entirely when it's discovered that the original French composer is none other than Jacques Prévert, one of Dylan's more obscure but incredibly important influences from back in his French poet days. Nods to Irving Berlin ("What'll I Do") and Rogers and Hammerstein ("Some Enchanted Evening") have less

Dorian Gray had nothing on the Nobel Prize–winning Dylan.
Stefan Kahlhammer/Wikimedia Commons/Public domain

symbolic or contextual import, but Dylan recovers at the end with a brilliant "That Lucky Old Sun," on which he actually does almost hurt himself.

Nothing so dire occurs on *Fallen Angels*; in fact, for much of the time Dylan and the band seem to be going through the motions, as if they're trying out for a new career, once Bob gets off the road, as a high-end wedding band. Nonetheless, of the twelve songs on the album, only two have lyrics profound and relevant enough to Dylan to have potential for further development in performance.

"Maybe You'll Be There," written by Rube Bloom and Sammy Gallup (born in Duluth), was a hit for Gordon Jenkins in 1948. In more recent times, it's been covered by Gene Pitney, and by Lee Andrews and the Hearts. With its narrator constantly prowling the empty midnight streets in search of a lost love, it's right in Dylan's current wheelhouse (since 1975 or so).

"Melancholy Mood" was the B-side of Sinatra's very first single, "From the Bottom of My Heart," which flopped in 1939. Written by Walter Schumann, better known for his Christmas music, and Vick R. Knight, not known for anything else, it's the find of the album, containing a lyric so grim, you wonder what kind of melancholy mood Sinatra must have been in to choose to record it. The song makes trifles like "Not Dark Yet" and "Nettie Moore" sound like rave-ups. On the record, Dylan hardly does it justice. But maybe, after ten or fifteen concert performances, he'll turn it into another poignant portrait of the artist as an old man.

38

His Cowboy Bands

Road Bands, Opening Acts, Guest Stars

As much as Bob Dylan has had an uneasy relationship with his albums, from the process of recording them to the finished product, for much of his career he's had just as problematic a relationship to the bands he's brought with him on the road. As he once said to journalist Nora Ephron, "It's very complicated to play with electricity. You're dealing with other people. It's more difficult." Dylan's forte has never been dealing with other people, especially in a musical setting. His first bandleader, Chicago blues-guitar master Michael Bloomfield, who led the troops at the recording of *Highway 61 Revisited*, and with whom Dylan threw down the gauntlet for the musical revolution at Newport, in 1965, certainly agreed. "As far as I can remember, I never saw any communication between Dylan and the band—ever," he told Jim Delahunt of *Hit Parader*, when asked to recall those formative sessions.

Since the road became Dylan's home in 1988, keeping a band together has been a challenge. For the first ten years of the Never Ending Tour, he went through ten guitarists and five drummers, with only Minneapolis native Tony Garnier, who replaced original bassist Kenny Aaronson in June of 1989, remaining constant. Replacing Hall and Oates and *Saturday Night Live* guitarist G. E. Smith proved especially messy, as Dylan auditioned Steve Bruton, Miles Joseph, Steve Ripley, his guitar tech Cesar Diaz (who had also worked for Keith Richards and Stevie Ray Vaughan), and John Staehely alongside Smith during successive weeks in the summer and fall of 1990, before Smith finally stepped aside in October, in favor of Staehely and Diaz. Three months later, Nashville guitarist John Jackson replaced Staehely and when a new tour started up in April, Diaz was gone. Jackson's run went uncommonly well, until the fall of 1996 when he displeased his boss in Dallas, perhaps during a performance of "Alabama Getaway," and as punishment was replaced for a couple of shows by Austin gunslinger Charlie

Sexton. When the 1997 touring season commenced, Woodstock regular Larry Campbell was in the starting lineup in Jackson's spot.

In 1992, Bucky Baxter, who'd played with Steve Earle, came aboard on slide guitar and pedal steel. Baxter did a fairly good job, until the night of April 30, 1999, when he crossed Dylan during a version of "Trying to Get to Heaven" in Vienna. After two more gigs, Charlie Sexton was back in the lead slot, and would remain there until 2003, with Larry Campbell taking over the slide and pedal steel duties. Billy Burnette had a brief stint in 2003,

HANK, AUDREY AND THE DRIFTING COWBOYS
DURING A RECENT BROADCAST

As a touring musician, Dylan's main later-life influence seems to be Hank Williams, seen here with the Drifting Cowboys. *Left to right*: Cedric Rainwater, Sammy Pruett, Audrey Sheppard, Hank Williams, Jerry Rivers, Don Helms.

MGM Records publicity photo/ Wikimedia Commons/ Public domain

replacing Sexton, before stepping aside for Frenchman Freddy Koella. The following year, Stu Kimball replaced Koella. In 2005, Larry Campbell left the band to join former Dylan compatriot Levon Helm. In his stead, another Austinite, Denny Freeman, who'd played with Stevie Ray Vaughan, was added on lead, with Donnie Herron of country-rockers BR549 on various other stringed instruments. Elana Fremerman joined the band for a couple of dozen gigs on violin. After 441 gigs, Charlie Sexton returned, replacing Freeman, and was available for 536 more gigs, except for a 27-show break for which Duke Robillard filled in.

Dylan is much less fussy about drummers. Plucked like G. E. Smith from the *SNL* band, Christopher Parker was the first Never Ending Tour (NET) drummer in 1988, until Ian Wallace (ex–King Crimson) took his place from 1991 to 1993. In 1992, he used two drummers in the show, when Charlie Quintana of the Plugz sat in with Wallace (who was later replaced by former Arizona electrician Winston Watson) from April to December. Watson held the sticks until 1996, while his successor David Kemper, late of the Jerry Garcia Band, lasted from '96 to 2002. New Orleans's George Receli (Aaron Neville, Dr. John) has handled the drum chores since 2002, except for a few months off, due to illness, early in '02, when Jim Keltner subbed for him. Little Feat's Richie Hayward sat in for a while in 2004.

His Early Bands

Before the Never Ending Tour, Dylan assembled bands pretty much according to what album he had out, going back to his first ever appearance with a live band (other than his high school friends from Hibbing) on July 25, 1965, with Michael Bloomfield on guitar, Al Kooper on organ, Sam Lay on drums, and Jerome Arnold on bass for the pistol shot heard round the world, "Maggie's Farm."

During his most hectic and dangerous period of touring throughout the rest of 1965 and into 1966, he hired Ronnie Hawkins's backup band, the Hawks (Robbie Robertson on guitar, Rick Danko on bass, Richard Manuel on piano, Garth Hudson on organ, and Levon Helm on drums, replaced for 1966 by Mickey Jones). With Helm back in the fold, the Hawks became the Band, joining Dylan for his long recovery period in Woodstock and then on the road again in 1974.

The Rolling Thunder Revue of 1975 and '76 featured Mick Ronson, T Bone Burnett, and David Mansfield on guitars, plus Rob Stoner on bass, Howie Wyeth on drums, and Scarlet Rivera on violin, among many others.

With his life in a shambles and his career now in the hands of Neil Diamond's manager, Dylan's Las Vegas phase of 1978 included Stoner on bass, before he gave way to Jerry Scheff, who'd played with Elvis. Billy Cross, who'd been in the pit for the rock opera *Hair!*, played lead guitar; Steve Soles and David Mansfield also played guitar, with Mansfield handling the pedal steel, mandolin, dobro, and violin. Alan Pasqua, formerly of the Tony Williams Lifetime, played keyboards, and Steve Douglas, formerly of the Phil Spector stable, was on sax. Motown session percussionist Bobbye Hall was another part of the troupe, along with former King Crimson drummer Ian Wallace. The backup singers, whom Dylan sometimes introduced as "my ex-girlfriend, my current girlfriend, and my fiancée," were Jo-Ann Harris, Helena Springs, Debi Dye-Gibson—and Dylan's future wife, Carolyn Dennis.

Many of these backup singers joined Dylan on his gospel tours of 1979–1981, including Regina McCrary, Helena Springs, and Mona Lisa Young in '79; Springs and Young were joined in 1980 by Regina Peeples and Carolyn Dennis; Regina McCrary and Mona Lisa Young were back in 1981, along with Gwen Evans, Mary Elizabeth Bridges, and Clydie King. Fred Tackett, formerly of Little Feat, handled the guitar, Tim Drummond was on bass, Jim Keltner on drums, Terry Young on piano, and Memphis legend Spooner Oldham on organ.

Dylan's European tour of 1984, which was the basis of his *Real Live* album (recorded mostly at Wembley Stadium in London) featured former Rolling Stone Mick Taylor on guitar, Gregg Sutton on bass, Colin Allen on drums, and Ian McLagan on keyboards.

The tours of 1986 and 1987 with Tom Petty and the Heartbreakers were dubbed True Confessions and Temples in Flames. Petty's band consisted of Mike Campbell on guitar, Howie Epstein on bass, Benmont Tench on keyboards, and Stan Lynch on drums, who were joined by the Queens of Rhythm: Queen Esther Marrow, Carolyn Dennis, and Carolyn's mother, Madelyn Quebec.

Ten Instrumental Highlights

Like Dylan's own performances, the work of his instrumentalists has varied widely and wildly through the years. That being said, here are some of the standout moments achieved by these great players—ten guitarists and one violinist—when the boss deigned to let them have the spotlight all to themselves.

1. "Maggie's Farm," Newport, July 25, 1965—Mike Bloomfield
2. "Like a Rolling Stone," Manchester, England, May 17, 1966—Robbie Robertson
3. "Where Are You Tonight (Journey Through Dark Heat)," Camberley, England, July 15, 1978—Billy Cross
4. "Pressing On," Toronto, Ontario, Canada, April 20, 1981—Fred Tackett
5. "When the Night Comes Falling from the Sky," Sydney, Australia, February 24, 1986—Mike Campbell
6. "Gates of Eden," Park City, Utah, June 13, 1988—G. E. Smith
7. "Idiot Wind," San Francisco, California, May 5, 1992—Jerry Garcia
8. "The Times They Are a-Changin'," Konstanz, Germany, July 3, 1996—Boyd Tinsley (violin)
9. "Tangled Up in Blue," San Jose, California, May 19, 1998—Bucky Baxter and Larry Campbell
10. "Just Like Tom Thumb's Blues," London, England, November 23, 2003—Freddy Koella

Opening for Dylan

Being within shouting distance of Bob Dylan's aura can be a humbling experience, and not only for audience members and sidemen. Having toured with Dylan for several dates in 2013, fronting the band Dawes, Taylor Goldsmith managed to put into words what seeing Dylan from that vantage point meant to him in an article for *Esquire* magazine's website. "This tour epitomized what it means to make the music the focus," he wrote. "He was very much about the craft. His commitment to being honest to the experience, it's representative of who he is. You don't need to have snazzy transitions in between songs. And you also don't need to have the voice you did forty years ago. If you have great songs, the right people are going to show up."

Tom Petty's lead guitarist, Mike Campbell, gave a pretty good picture of what a musician had to go through when backing Dylan. "He can be vague as to what or how he wants you to play, but being around him you instinctively soak up a lot of feel, and that's inspiring," he said in an interview I did with him for the November 1990 issue of *Guitar for the Practicing Musician*. "One of the best things we learned from Bob was just to loosen up, because a lot of the times you don't know what he's going to do. You don't know what key the song's going to be in. It might have eighteen chords and you learned it in E and he'll turn around at the mic and say, 'Okay, we're going to do it in B, ready go.' You just get into the frame of mind that you're going to make it work. You go with the flow he's on and that's real exciting."

One of the most obscure artists to be tapped on the head by Dylan was Brenda Kahn, a labelmate at Columbia, who opened for him in Paris, at the Zenith Theater, on February 23, 1993. "I was touring in France and my manager was trying to get me on the Dylan tour for months," she said, when I interviewed her for my book *Working Musicians*. When the okay finally arrived, it came with a bit of bad news: Dylan didn't want a solo acoustic act opening for him. So Brenda had to form a backup band on the fly. "When I opened up for Dylan in Luxembourg, two nights before Paris, they wouldn't let me out of the dressing room. In Paris, I played one song solo acoustic, where the band dropped out, and after I got off stage Dylan's manager says Dylan wants to say hello to me. So I'm freaking out, excited, and shaking his hand. And he said, 'Hey, I really liked that one song you sang solo,' and I had been scared to do it because they said no solo acts, so I said, 'Well, it's not recorded, but as soon as it is, I'll send you a copy.' I didn't know what else to say. We spoke for a few more minutes and then I left."

Forty Artists Who've Appeared with Dylan

Like Scarlet Rivera on the streets of Greenwich Village in the mid-'70s, few artists are apt to turn down the opportunity to play live with Bob Dylan, for a leg of a tour, a couple of shows, or even for a song or two.

- Joan Armatrading
- Asleep at the Wheel
- Beck
- Dickey Betts
- Elvis Costello
- Sheryl Crow
- Dave Matthews Band
- Dion
- John Doe
- Steve Earle
- Garbage
- Grateful Dead
- Merle Haggard
- Ben Harper
- Chrissie Hynde
- Jewel
- Norah Jones
- Rickie Lee Jones
- B. B. King
- Mark Knopfler
- Amos Lee
- Joni Mitchell
- John Cougar Mellencamp
- Van Morrison
- Willie Nelson
- Stevie Nicks
- Tom Petty
- Johnny Rivers
- Leon Russell
- Doug Sahm

- Carlos Santana
- Bob Seger
- Brian Setzer
- Paul Simon
- Bruce Springsteen
- The String Cheese Incident
- Richard Thompson
- Jack White
- Wilco
- Neil Young

39

A Generation's Stepping Stone

Under the Influence of Dylan

The Next Bob Dylans

Ever since the ascent of Bob Dylan in 1963, anyone who wrote words at odds with the prevailing Brill Building standards and sang them in an unpolished style several shades darker than what had ever been heard on *American Bandstand* has been categorized as "the next Bob Dylan," even while the current Bob Dylan was doing his best to avoid any sort of categorization whatsoever. Until folk-rock struck in 1965, in the wake of Dylan and the Beatles' famous meeting of the minds at the Delmonico Hotel in New York City, this was a fairly insignificant number. From 1965 on, however, when a new wave of well-read and predominantly college-educated rockers doffed their caps and gowns in favor of guitars and recording contracts, the ranks of "new Dylans" swelled considerably. In recent years, the somewhat nasal sound of a lone guitarist tilting against the limits of his or her rhyming dictionary and backup band has diminished, yet Dylan's impact remains whenever a poet rises to challenge the slumbering sensibilities of the masses in song.

Paul Simon

In many ways, Paul Simon is Bob Dylan's mirror image. Like Dylan, he was originally a rocker, having gone so far as to appear on *American Bandstand* in 1958 with his pal Art Garfunkel as Tom and Jerry, singing an Everly Brothers–influenced ditty called "Hey Schoolgirl." Also like Dylan, he fell in love with the folk repertoire in college. Unlike Dylan, Simon gained his college degree, but he also shared with Dylan a formative period in England, under the sway of "Scarborough Fair." They also shared a record label, Columbia, and a record producer, Tom Wilson, whose brilliant idea to overdub a rhythm section onto the year-old "The Sound of Silence" had Simon scurrying home from England to find himself a folk-rock star in 1966, capitalizing on the wave Dylan started by charting the Chuck Berry–inspired "Subterranean Homesick Blues" on April 3, 1965.

Simon's early work in Simon and Garfunkel—"The Dangling Conversation," "I Am a Rock," "A Simple Desultory Philippic"—has been compared, even by Simon, to sensitive college-student essays; Dylan wrote the type of essays that would have gotten him thrown out of the same college. As a solo artist, like Dylan, Simon has continued to evolve lyrically and musically, producing a body of work that has been not only commercial but also thought-provoking and rhythmically challenging.

Phil Ochs

Struck by the topical-song bug right about the same time as Dylan in the early '60s, Phil Ochs remained committed to it for his entire songwriting life, which tragically ended in 1977. He immediately left college in Ohio and headed to New York City, where his competition with Dylan spurred him on to creative heights but left him far behind when Dylan sailed off into the realms of the supernatural. In the end, Ochs was brought down by his inability to move beyond protest music.

This was something he was already acutely aware of. "Everything I wrote was on instinct," he said to me in 1974, three years before he committed suicide. "For me, songwriting was easy from 1961 to 1966 and then it got more and more difficult. It could be alcohol; it could be the deterioration of the politics I was involved in. It could be a general deterioration of the country. Basically, me and the country were deteriorating simultaneously and that's probably why it stopped coming. Part of the problem was that there was never any pattern to my writing. The point of discipline is to create your own pattern so you can write, and I haven't done that. I always make plans to do that. I'm now thirty-three and I may or may not succeed. But ever since the late '60s that's constantly on my mind—discipline, training, get it together, clean up your act. I haven't been able to do it yet, but the impulse is as strong as ever. To my dying day I'll always think about the next possible song."

Jim (Roger) McGuinn / the Byrds

Jim (Roger) McGuinn was educated at the Old Town School of Folk Music in Chicago. When he came to New York City in the early '60s to back the folk group the Chad Mitchell Trio, he hung around the same clubs as Dylan. The Chad Mitchell Trio was one of the first groups to cover "Blowin' in the Wind," even before Peter, Paul and Mary turned it into a hit. "He was playing Woody Guthrie songs, and all I knew was that the little girls liked him a lot," McGuinn told me. "I thought of him as just another guy. I was really shocked when he took off."

In no small part, Dylan's ascent was made possible by McGuinn's new folk-rock group, the Byrds, which he formed in Los Angeles soon after the Beatles made rock 'n' roll relevant to the sophisticated music fan. "Dylan was real and the Beatles were plastic," said McGuinn, summarizing the prevailing feeling before 1965. "Then the Beatles got more authentic and Dylan got more Top 40." Solidifying that concept was the Byrds' Dylan-esque recording of "Mr. Tambourine Man," which peaked on the record charts at No. 1 on June 26, 1965. Thereafter, the Byrds would remain one of Dylan's biggest clients, and McGuinn one of his closest friends, recording fourteen of his songs over the years, from obscurities like "Spanish Harlem Incident" and "Lay Down Your Weary Tune" to "My Back Pages" and "You Ain't Goin' Nowhere."

Donovan

If the Byrds were initially thought of as the "American Beatles," Donovan was immediately tabbed the "English Dylan." Although the impish folk singer had been given the snarky Tommy Sands treatment by Dylan during his '65 tour of England, as captured by filmmaker D. A. Pennebaker in *Dont Look Back*, this particular dressing-down wouldn't be widely released until 1967. Having earlier charmed America with the Dylan-esque "Catch the Wind" and "Colours," by then he'd moved on to psychedelic odes like "Mellow Yellow" and "Wear Your Love Like Heaven," before eventually morphing into a latter-day Lord Byron–esque flower-child.

Bob Lind

With Bob Dylan all over the charts in 1965, both with his own work ("Subterranean Homesick Blues, " "Like a Rolling Stone," "Positively 4th Street") and hit covers by the Byrds ("Mr. Tambourine Man"), Cher ("All I Really Want to Do"), and the Turtles ("It Ain't Me Babe"), Denver's Bob Lind found himself at the right place at the right time when he arrived at the offices of World Pacific Records, armed with a tape of five songs he'd recorded at a club in Denver called the Analyst. "The guy said, 'This sounds interesting. Let me talk to the people at Liberty,'" he recalled, in an interview for www.songfacts.com, "and Liberty Records said, 'Well, he kind of sounds like Dylan.' To me, I didn't sound like Dylan. But I guess I was a niche that satisfied their cravings, so they signed me."

"Elusive Butterfly" is thought of as one of the best or one of the worst songs of the entire decade, depending on which list you subscribe to. It was definitely not Lind's personal favorite. "I wrote it in Denver. Originally it was five verses long. I must have sung it on stage about one hundred times and nobody reacted to it any more than they reacted to any other song of mine."

Even though the song reached No. 5, and his debut album was produced by Jack Nitzsche, Lind failed to capitalize on its success, never achieving another Top 40 hit.

David Blue

Starting out among the minions of nasal Dylan acolytes who could generally be found within sniffing distance of the master's aura, if not the master himself, David Blue was easily the most nasal, but not as political as Ochs, as topical as Tom Paxton, or as suavely romantic as Eric Andersen. "These 23 Days in September" was his most fully realized effort, a tone poem in the same league as "Just Like a Woman" and "Visions of Johanna," but dwelling deep in the cellar of that league. Blue eventually found much more of a niche as Dylan's bosom buddy, like Bob Neuwirth, attaching himself to Dylan's right arm whenever he could, and appearing extensively in the movie *Renaldo and Clara*.

Jake Jacobs, then of the Village folk-rock legends the Magicians, and later of Jake and the Family Jewels, vividly recalls Blue in Robbie Woliver's oral history of Greenwich Village, *Hoot*. "Someone said that David Blue was a Bob Dylan clone. If Dylan changed his hairstyle, David would change his hairstyle. If Dylan would wear a white shirt buttoned up to the top, then David would, too. He was ornery and arrogant and abusive."

Leonard Cohen

As an untrained singer with a limited range, an acoustic guitarist of limited ability, and a wordsmith beyond compare, Leonard Cohen shared many traits with the early Bob Dylan. As a published poet and novelist in Canada before signing with Columbia Records, his literary credentials were already impeccable. What he owes to Dylan, then, is the fact that Dylan opened up the marketplace for poets of limited musical prowess to gain an audience. Some of his success he surely owes to Judy Collins, as well, who recorded his "Dress Rehearsal Rag" and "Suzanne" on her album *In My Life*. Judy also persuaded Cohen to become a performer—something he was initially reluctant to do.

Over the years, Cohen has not only gone on to write some of the most complex and beautiful songs in the rock canon, among them "Famous Blue Raincoat" and "Hallelujah," but also to overcome his fear of performing enough to have still been touring at the age of eighty. Seven years older than Dylan, he also seemed to have a handle on pop success right from the beginning. "My training as a writer was not calculated to inflame the appetites," he said, in an interview I did with him for the magazine *After Dark*. "In Montreal in the fifties, when I began to write, people didn't have the notion of superstars. The same prizes weren't in the air as there are today, so one had a kind of modest view of what a writing career was."

Janis Ian

In 1963, when Janis Ian started to write songs under her real name, Janis Fink, female singer/songwriters were virtually nonexistent. In Greenwich Village and Cambridge, Massachusetts, you had Buffy Sainte-Marie getting started around then; Joan Baez, Judy Collins, Odetta, Carolyn Hester, and Mary Travers of Peter, Paul and Mary didn't write their own material. When Ian had her first song, "Hair of Spun Gold," published in *Broadside* magazine at the tender age of twelve, she joined a mostly male bastion including Bob Dylan, Phil Ochs, and Tom Paxton. She was undoubtedly the youngest female ever to play Dylan's favorite Greenwich Village clubs, Folk City and the Gaslight (she took part in a big folk festival at the Village Gate). She wrote the controversial "Society's Child (Baby I've Been Thinking)" in 1965, at the age of thirteen, which was produced by Shadow Morton, known for discovering the Shangri-Las and co-writing "Leader of the Pack."

If "Leader of the Pack" was considered provocative in 1964, "Society's Child" was off the charts, detailing a forbidden interracial romance in an era when Freedom Riders were being shot in the Deep South. It finally made the Top 20 in 1967, on its third release, after Ian appeared on a TV special about the "rock revolution" hosted by Leonard Bernstein. She has been exploring personal relationships and taboo topics ever since. Her biggest hit was "At Seventeen," which reached No. 3 in 1975.

A generation of women was given the artistic freedom to become songwriters through Bob Dylan. First among them was the teenage Janis Fink, soon to become better known as Janis Ian.

Diana Davies, courtesy Ralph Rinzler Folklife Archives and Collections, Smithsonian Institution

Arlo Guthrie

Early in the "New Dylan" era, rough-edged acoustic guitar–playing topical songwriters were referred to as the "Sons of Woody" (Guthrie). Dylan himself was often pejoratively described as the "Son of Jack" (Elliott), for what was taken as his wholesale co-optation of Elliott's heavily Woody Guthrie–influenced persona and singing style. (Jack didn't write his own material, however.)

As far as Woody Guthrie's actual sons, of the three, only Arlo sustained a career as a singer/songwriter, although Joady did put out an album in 1982, produced by Country Joe MacDonald, entitled *Spys on Wall Street*, which features titles like "Red Diaper" and "Draft Me If You Can." Woody's firstborn son, Bill, died in an auto accident at the age of twenty-three.

Arlo met Bob Dylan back when he was fourteen and followed his career in the papers until he heard "Positively 4th Street" on the radio in 1965, when he was attending college in Montana. "I said, 'My God, that's incredible they're playing this song on the radio,'" he told Robbie Woliver. "It was enough to make me leave college just to go to the Village to see what was going on."

Eventually, it would be left to Arlo to carry his father's chalice, leaning more to the folk side of folk-rock, although his eighteen-minute anti-authority opus "Alice's Restaurant" did become an underground hit, with a rock version appearing on the charts in December 1969, following the arrival of *Alice's Restaurant*, the movie.

Loudon Wainwright III

By the dusk of Aquarius at the top of the '70s, with Dylan in hiding, bedridden, brain-dead, or, worse, becoming a country singer, the new decade produced several more singer/songwriters whose sensitive couplets addressing a variety of personal and social issues tried to fill the void for the real thing.

Down in Greenwich Village, with most of the original folk-rock audience having drifted to the Lower East Side, the loping, preppy-looking Loudon Wainwright III arrived from the suburbs with his guitar and a mordant sense of humor. "I played on bills with Dave Van Ronk, but it wasn't Van Ronk's heyday," he told me. "I had friends who wrote great songs, but it wasn't a real scene. It wasn't MacDougal Street, 1961. The Village was in a state of decline. Most of the people in the audience were Japanese tourists. Still, it was exciting to me, because I was really idealistic and hot to trot and have people applaud me. But it wasn't the Newport Generation. It's never going to be Newport '61 again, just like there's no new Bob Dylan."

Nevertheless, Wainwright became a featured attraction on the folk circuit for his comic persona and often-poignant songs about complex family relationships, releasing more than twenty albums on a variety of major and independent labels. In an irony Wainwright would probably appreciate, if not relish, he's most known today as the author of the Top 20 hit "Dead Skunk (in the Middle of the Road)" and as the father of the popular singer/songwriter Rufus Wainwright (who is never referred to as the Next Loudon Wainwright). For his feelings on the matter, it's best to consult "Talking New Bob Dylan," from his 1992 album *History*.

John Prine

A former postman and serviceman whose formative performing years were spent in Chicago, Prine combined the high lonesome sound of the early

Dylan with mid-Dylan poetics about the joys and pains of the average man. "I first heard about Dylan when my older brother told me that the guy who wrote 'Blowin' in the Wind' sounded a lot like Jack Elliott. And I liked Jack Elliott a whole lot," Prine told me. He made an immediate impact with his self-titled 1971 release, produced by early fan Kris Kristofferson, which contains "Sam Stone," the story of a returning Viet vet, the melancholy "Hello in There," which was covered by Bette Midler, and the Grant Woods-ian "Angel from Montgomery," which was covered by Bonnie Raitt.

Like Dylan's before him, Prine's career was launched with a great write-up in the press, in his case from Roger Ebert of the *Chicago Sun-Times*. Dylan himself has been a longtime Prine fan. "Prine's stuff is pure Proustian existentialism," he told the *Huffington Post*. "Midwestern mindtrips to the nth degree." One of his best-known songs is one he refused to take credit for, the hilarious country-music send-up "You Never Even Call Me By My Name," which he wrote with his buddy Steve Goodman, and which David Allen Coe turned into a country hit.

Steve Goodman

Steve Goodman's first album for Buddah Records features a cover of "Donald and Lydia," a song by his friend and fellow Chicago folk-scene veteran John Prine, and a guest appearance by Bob Dylan on the track "Election Year Rag," which was not released in the US. Like Prine, he numbered among his supporters Kris Kristofferson. He also had something profound in common with Bobby Darin (not Dylan): a death sentence hanging over his head that drove his ambitions. Darin had rheumatic fever as a child and packed as much performing and recording into his life as he could until he died after a heart operation at the age of thirty-seven. Goodman was diagnosed with leukemia while he was in college but produced over a dozen albums and many important songs until his death at thirty-six. The best known of these was "The City of New Orleans," which made the Top 20 in a cover version by Arlo Guthrie in 1972, and won Goodman a posthumous Grammy when it was covered by Willie Nelson in 1984.

Though he spent some formative years living across the street from one of Dylan's early Greenwich Village hangouts, the Cafe Wha?, Goodman's heart and soul belonged to the second city, especially its baseball team, the Chicago Cubs. His "Go Cubs Go" is still played after every Cubs win at Wrigley Field, and was presumably heard over the loud speakers by the throngs who congregated in front of that legendary ball park on the night of November 2, 2016, to celebrate the Cubs' first World Series win since 1908.

Don McLean

Befriended by several of the Weavers, including Pete Seeger, McLean was added to the New Dylan ranks in 1972 by virtue of his Dylan-esque take on the decline and fall of pop culture, the massively successful "American Pie," which, he told me when I interviewed him for *Rock* magazine in 1972, "entirely disrupted my value system." For further spleen-venting guilt, see his "The Pride Parade," from 1973's *Don McLean*, an album he called "a study in depression."

McLean is the author of several other enduring gems, including "Vincent," "And I Love You So," and "Castles in the Air," but he didn't find immediate success. His first album, *Tapestry*, recorded in 1969 (three years before Carole King's *Tapestry*), was rejected seventy-two times before finding a taker. In the meantime, he hooked up with Pete Seeger, becoming the house folkie on Seeger's boat, the Clearwater, and documenting its mission to raise awareness about pollution on the Hudson River by coediting *Songs and Sketches of the First Clearwater Crew*. On land he sometimes appeared around the village, but he preferred places out of town, like the Caffe Lena in Saratoga Springs, New York. "Either out of hatred for New York City or out of timidity or out of a lack of self-confidence, I never headed toward anyplace where there was a lot of competition," he said. "I wasn't really anxious to get into a classroom full of the new school of musicians."

Neil Young

Graduating from the Buffalo Springfield in 1970, Neil Young was the first New Dylan to really perk up the ears of the Old Dylan. Young's first two solo albums contain a lot of Dylan-influenced singing and imagery, especially in the nine-minute "Last Trip to Tulsa" from the first and the similarly lengthy "Down by the River" and "Cowgirl in the Sand" from the second. But Young's jangly guitar arrangements were a lot more ambitiously hard-rocking than Dylan's, with "Cinnamon Girl" becoming a standard for future jam bands and punk rockers to emulate. It was apparently Young's fourth album, *Harvest*, that affected the old Bob Dylan the most, with the single "Heart of Gold" attaining the No. 1 status that always eluded Dylan. "The only time it bothered me that someone sounded like me was when I was living in Phoenix, Arizona, in about '72, and the big song at the time was 'Heart of Gold,'" he told Scott Cohen in *Spin* magazine. "I said, 'If it sounds like me, it should be me.'"

Though Young's career since then has ranged far and wide, encompassing almost as expansive a musical spectrum as Dylan's, he apparently served as an inspiration for Dylan to pen one of his most famous songs, "Forever Young." Whether this is true or not, it's a pretty Dylan-esque joke either way.

Bruce Springsteen

Although Bob Dylan never wrote a song called "Forever Bruce," he did write "Tweeter and the Monkey Man" while in the Traveling Wilburys, which contains many references to songs both released and unreleased by 1973's entry in the New Dylan sweepstakes, Bruce Springsteen. Produced by Dylan's first producer, John Hammond, for Columbia Records, *Greetings from Asbury Park* contains a suitcase full of free-associative lyrics attached to joyously energetic R&B grooves.

As a solo artist, Springsteen had been visiting the Village since the mid-sixties, playing matinees at the Cafe Wha? when Frank Zappa's Mothers of Invention were holding down the fort every night at the Garrick Theater and the Fugs were playing at the Player's Theater. Sam Hood at the Gaslight used to throw him the occasional gig. That debut album, although a long time in coming, attracted far better reviews than Dylan's dismal debut. "I think the *Times* compared me to Allen Ginsberg, Rod Stewart, and *El Topo* in the same article," Springsteen told me when I interviewed him for *Rock* magazine.

Like Dylan, Springsteen came naturally to his own kind of instinctual, street-honed poetry. "I went through a year and a half of college and all I remember was getting hassled to no end. People ask me what poets I read. I never read any."

Elliott Murphy

Paul Nelson, Bob Dylan's earliest champion and most consistent critic, chose to pair Elliott Murphy with Bruce Springsteen in his *Rolling Stone* review of their debut albums under the headline, "The Best New Dylans since 1968." The Long Island expatriate, who subsequently moved to Paris, brought his own references to the lost generation (and F. Scott Fitzgerald) on his first four albums: *Aquashow* (1973), containing "Like a Great Gatsby";

Lost Generation (1975), featuring the title song; *Night Lights* (1976), which name-checks the legendary bohemian dancer Isadora Duncan; and *Just a Story from America* (1977), his first album for Columbia Records, home of the old Dylan and the original Springsteen, name-checking Gatsby's narrator, Nick Caraway. Beloved overseas and all-but-unknown in America, Murphy has since put out upward of three dozen albums, published a novel and several short story collections, and won a couple of literary prizes in France.

Patti Smith

More like the female Leonard Cohen than the female Dylan—if Cohen had been raised listening to the Rolling Stones, the Doors, and the Shangri-Las, and reading Rimbaud and Ginsberg—Patti Smith hailed from Springsteen's New Jersey and began her career as a poet turned rock critic turned rock poet on the Lou Reed–haunted streets of Manhattan's Lower East Side. She lived with the controversial photographer Robert Mapplethorpe a little further uptown at the Chelsea hotel on West 23rd Street from 1967 to 1974. Right around this time she helped put the Bowery bar CBGB on the map along with Richard Hell, Television, Talking Heads, Blondie, and the Ramones. Produced by John Cale of the Velvet Underground, her 1975 debut, *Horses*, launched her legendary career, with a version of Van Morrison's "Gloria" as its centerpiece.

In some ways Smith was more an influence on Dylan than the other way around. When Dylan was attempting to recapture his youth on the streets of Greenwich Village in the early '70s, it was Patti Smith's performance with her band, including the esteemed rock critic Lenny Kaye on guitar, that prompted Dylan to create the Rolling Thunder tent show and caravan, reigniting his love/hate relationship with the joys and terrors of the road.

Tom Petty

With the old Dylan's return to form and performing in 1974–1976, and the various New Dylans on the boards and the charts, the baby-boomer generation experienced a cultural relevance it hadn't had since Woodstock—a brief heyday that included the end of the war in Vietnam, the impeachment of archrival Richard Nixon, and the 1975 reunion of Simon and Garfunkel, on the second episode of a subversive late-night comedy show called *Saturday Night Live*. Tom Petty's mixture of Dylan's nasal twang and the Byrds' soaring melodic sense was brought on by his early exposure to Elvis Presley and the Beatles. Featuring guitarist Mike Campbell and keyboard player Benmont Tench, the late-'76 debut album by Tom Petty and the Heartbreakers produced two perennial showstoppers, "Breakdown" and "American Girl," that would establish his sound for years to come, while later songs like "Here Comes My Girl," "Refugee," "The Waiting," "Learning to Fly," and "Into the Great Wide Open" would solidify his Hall of Fame career.

His folk-rock chops would be sorely tested in 1986 and '87, when Bob Dylan invited Petty and his bandmates to back him, first on his True Confessions Tour and a year later on his Temples in Flames Tour. In 1988, Petty's sense of humor would be sorely tested when he formed a supergroup with Dylan, George Harrison, Jeff Lynne, and Roy Orbison called the Traveling Wilburys (who would never travel). Their two-album career produced two platinum sellers and a number of tracks that were better than anything Dylan was putting out under his own name at the time, including "Tweeter and the Monkey Man," "End of the Line," and "7 Deadly Sins."

Steve Forbert

The last New Dylan of the '70s, the dewy-eyed and innocent-looking, Mississippi-born Steve Forbert came to New York City in 1977 to make his mark, much like Bob Dylan in 1961 before him, the main difference being that Forbert never made it to Greenwich Village, setting up shop in Grand Central Station instead. But his highly Dylan-esque *Alive on Arrival*, coproduced by John Simon (who produced the Band's *Music from Big Pink*) was a kind of album-length version of "Bob Dylan's Dream," especially on nostalgic tunes like "Goin' Down to Laurel," "Steve Forbert's Midsummer Night Toast," and "Grand Central Station, March 18, 1977."

His second album, *Jackrabbit Slim*, closed out the decade with an unlikely hit single, "Romeo's Tune." With over a dozen albums to his name since then, many people still connect him to the early Dylan. Forbert is not among them. "It's nothing I take seriously," he told Scott Simon of NPR in 2009. "I don't have to know all the answers like Bob Dylan." Others may remember him most fondly for his brief cameo appearance, in a tuxedo, near the end of Cyndi Lauper's iconic music video for "Girls Just Want to Have Fun," which premiered on MTV at the end of 1983, inaugurating the heyday of that franchise, and in the process bringing to a conclusion the aforementioned cultural relevance of the baby boomers, as far as rock music was concerned.

Cindy Lee Berryhill, Brenda Kahn

With the old, curmudgeonly Bob Dylan turning off audiences to the left with his religious pronouncements, and to the right with his string of lackluster albums, he fell so far out of fashion through the rest of the 1980s that no one in the music business was even looking for a new and improved version anymore. The "New Dylan" label became as pejorative a description as "aging hippie," or, worse, "cranky old folkie." With the Americana surge of the mid-'80s, featuring R.E.M., X, and the Blasters, leading to the alt-country onslaught of the '90s, featuring Uncle Tupelo, Son Volt, and Wilco, the need for a New Dylan was subsumed into a whole lot of "New Byrds" configurations. Even his albums with the Traveling Wilburys were initially dismissed as a feeble last gasp against his inevitable and fast-encroaching total irrelevance.

Thus the way was paved for a couple of female New Dylans to emerge, in a genre of their own called "anti-folk"—a label Dylan himself would have appreciated, had he not been more concerned at that moment with finding his lost muse. If anyone had shown him the debut albums of either of these feisty and word-drunk women, he might have immediately offered them the job. As it was, Cindy Lee Berryhill wound up marrying perhaps the world's foremost rock critic and Dylan expert and confidante, Paul Williams, who passed away in 2013. From *Who's Gonna Save the World*, released in 1987, "Ballad of a Garage Band" is a heady shot of "Gates of Eden," while "She Had Everything" evokes Lou Reed's "Walk on the Wild Side."

Brenda Kahn was riding the crest of her 1990 major label debut, *Epiphany in Brooklyn*, produced by David Kahne (the Bangles, Lana Del Rey), when she landed a spot opening for Dylan in Paris, a gig she termed the high point of her career. But by then, frenetic and powerful songs like "I Don't Sleep, I Drink Coffee Instead," "Mint Juleps and Needles," and "She's in Love" had already established her songwriting credentials.

Ghosts of Dylan Past

For three weeks at the top of 1994, starting on January 22, the ghost of Bob Dylan past returned to the Top 100, bringing back the feel of 1965–1967, a time when the artists involved were hardly out of diapers, and in the case of one of them (Beck) not yet even born. The debut album by the Berkeley-based Counting Crows, produced by Dylan compatriot T Bone Burnett, drew comparisons to Dylan, Springsteen, Van Morrison, and the Band.

They opened for Dylan in Los Angeles in 1992; in 1993, Robbie Robertson heard them at a Rock and Roll Hall of Fame concert and praised them to the skies. Although written for front man Adam Duritz's childhood friend, "Mr. Jones" just happened to name-check one of Dylan's most incisive and legendary characters. In one of the verses of this moody and whimsical No. 1 hit (which was never released as a single), Duritz claims, "I want to be Bob Dylan." In other versions of the song he changed the name of his idol to the more generationally appropriate Alex Chilton, the late Big Star front man who was also favored by the Replacements.

A week later, the oddball lament "Loser" by L.A.'s Beck Hansen, at twenty-three already a veteran of New York's anti-folk movement, arrived on the chart, channeling the basement-era Dylan rediscovering his roots in Woodstock with no thought that what he was doing would ever be heard. In this case, with a slacker's insouciance, a keen ear for sampling, a nod to the Beastie Boys, a thrown-together-after-a night-on-hash feel, and a title evoking John Lennon, the roots of the song lie in Dylan and the Beatles. (Ironically, Dylan had returned to his own roots again in 1992 and '93, with *World Gone Wrong* having been released the previous November. It would win a Grammy for Best Folk Recording in March 1994.) "Loser" hit the Top 10 a few days after the death of Kurt Cobain, a grim defining moment on a par with the deaths of Jimi Hendrix, Janis Joplin, and Jim Morrison for a previous generation, or Buddy Holly for a generation before that.

Most Dylan-inspired of all, on the week of February 5, a song called "Laid" appeared on the charts by a Manchester band called James (thought of at the time to be the new Smiths), led by a straight-out-of-the-Free-Trade-Center vocal by lead singer and cowriter Tim Booth, who was born in 1960. Nobody in the audience could be heard to scream "Judas" as "Laid" climbed all the way to the No. 61 on the pop chart and No. 3 on the modern Rock chart. A few months later, the band played the song on the opening day of Woodstock '94, a concert where Bob Dylan appeared a couple of days later.

Dan Bern

A mere three years later, as Dylan was finishing up his massive comeback album, *Time Out of Mind*, for Columbia Records, the label released the first album by prolific Mount Vernon, Iowa, native Dan Bern, born two days after Dylan launched the rock era with his performance of "Like a Rolling Stone" at Newport. Though his debut album is gifted with lyrically elegant and cynically hilarious songs like the twisted morality tale "Jerusalem" and a joyously convoluted ode to "Marilyn Monroe," Bern adamantly refused to be typecast as the Next Bob Dylan, lampooning those who thought so—as well as himself—in "Talking Woody, Bob, Bruce, and Dan Blues," from his 1998 album *Smartie Mine*, produced by Ani DiFranco.

Bern's subsequent career arc of a dozen worthy but obscure albums and a devoted coffeehouse-sized following has proven how unlikely any New Dylan is to even touch the hem of the garment worn by the Old Bob Dylan in the days when enough elegant and cynically hilarious songs could hoist you up on a pedestal beyond human endurance.

Peter Himmelman, Jakob Dylan

Of Dylan's actual sons, Jesse, Samuel, and Jakob, only Jakob has sustained a career as a musician. However, Dylan's son-in-law, Minnesota native Peter Himmelman, who is married to Bob's adopted daughter, Maria Lownds, has put out more than twenty albums since 1986, as well as several albums of songs for kids. But he may be best known as the composer of the music for the TV dramas *Judging Amy* and *Bones*.

Jakob Dylan attained huge success with the Wallflowers' second album, *Bringing down the Horse*, which was produced by T Bone Burnett and features guest appearances by Mike Campbell of the Heartbreakers and Fred Tackett, formerly of Little Feat, who had previously played with Bob Dylan on the road. The single "One Headlight" won two Grammy Awards in 1998.

In November of the same year, more family history was made when the son's band opened for the father at a private party at the San Jose Arena put on by Silicon Valley's Applied Materials as a gift for its employees on the occasion of its thirtieth anniversary. According to *Rolling Stone*, when word of the show leaked out, "Dylan-related web pages, newsgroups, and mailing lists were flooded with requests for tickets. As it turned out, some fans who showed up at the San Jose Arena were either sold or given extra tickets by Applied Materials employees."

Conor Oberst

In the new millennium, the Dylan torch has been passed to another lonely prodigy from the part of the country Bob Dylan calls the Midwest: Conor Oberst, born in Omaha, Nebraska, in 1980. With influences ranging from the melancholy to the mordant, and from Robert Smith of the Cure to Elliott Smith (who committed suicide in 2003), Oberst released his first independent album at the age of thirteen. He formed and disbanded several groups after that, until settling on the name Bright Eyes at the age of fifteen. He dropped out of the University of Nebraska after three semesters to concentrate on his rock career, and continued releasing powerful and poetic albums with precocious proficiency and a quavery voice that barely contained his youthful dreams and disappointments. National attention arrived in 2005, when *Time* magazine put *I'm Wide Awake, It's Morning* on its list of the ten best albums of the year. Since then, he's been involved in a variety of successful solo and band projects that showcase his downbeat lyrics and happy/sad melodies. In a career move unavailable to Dylan when he started out, one of Oberst's songs from that breakthrough album, the depressive "Lua," entered the wider culture in 2013 through its use in an interactive video game called *Life Is Strange*.

Indeed.

Selected Discography

Although "selected," this discography includes all of Bob Dylan's studio albums through 2016. It includes all of his live albums except for *Live 1961–2000—Thirty-Nine Years of Great Concert Performances*, which includes little to excite any but the unregenerate completist (except for a 1961 performance of "Wade in the Water," recorded in Minneapolis; a 1962 performance of "Handsome Molly" from the Gaslight; "Grand Coulee Dam," from the "Tribute to Woody Guthrie" concert in 1968; and "Dignity" from his *MTV Unplugged* fiasco of 1994). Far more compelling is the thirty-six–CD boxed set of his complete 1966 live performances, released at the end of 2016. This amazing trove of concerts follows the 2015 release of *The Cutting Edge, 1965–1966*, otherwise known as *The Bootleg Series, Volume 12*. Both collections were issued to prevent the bootleggers from having a field day due to the copyright laws in England, which would have put these tracks in the public domain. In the same spirit, expect the release of the Dylan/Cash *Nashville Skyline*–era duets within the next few years.

While I've included all twelve volumes of *The Bootleg Series*, I've omitted a lot of extraneous *Greatest Hits*–type collections, including *Masterpieces*, *Best of Bob Dylan* (*Vols. 1* and *2*), *The Essential Bob Dylan*, *The Bob Dylan Collection*, *The Original Mono Recordings*, *The 50th Anniversary Collection*, and *The Complete Album Collection*. I've included the special 2006 release of *Blues* through Barnes and Noble because it seemed to offer a more unique listening experience than the aforementioned redundant money-grabs proffered above, although the track list is fairly disappointing in its interpretation of the blues, except for the presence of "High Water (for Charley Patton)" and "Blind Willie McTell."

Although Bob Dylan discographies abound in print and on the Internet, I've tried to make this one unique by placing his albums in the chronological order of when he recorded them, rather than when they were released, to thereby facilitate a coherent listening experience for the neophyte as well as the expert, who would like to hear Dylan's body of work as it unfolded in real time, rather than at the whims of the archivists controlling the vaults.

Bob Dylan (March 19, 1962)

You're No Good / Talkin' New York / In My Time of Dyin' / Man of Constant Sorrow / Fixin' to Die / Pretty Peggy-o / Highway 51 / Freight Train Blues / Gospel Plow / Baby Let Me Follow You Down / House of the Risin' Sun / Song to Woody / See That My Grave Is Kept Clean

Live at the Gaslight, 1962 (August 30, 2005)

A Hard Rain's a-Gonna Fall / Rocks and Gravel / Don't Think Twice, It's All Right / The Cuckoo / Moonshiner / Handsome Molly / Cocaine / John Brown / Barbara Allen / West Texas

The Freewheelin' Bob Dylan (May 1963)

Blowin' in the Wind / Girl from the North Country / Masters of War / Down the Highway / Bob Dylan's Blues / A Hard Rain's a-Gonna Fall / Don't Think Twice, It's All Right / Bob Dylan's Dream / Oxford Town / Talkin' World War III Blues / Corrina, Corrina / Honey, Just Allow Me One More Chance / I Shall Be Free

The Bootleg Series Vol. 9: The Witmark Demos: 1962–1964 (October 19, 2010)

Disc 1: Man on the Street / Hard Times in New York Town / Poor Boy Blues / Ballad for a Friend / Rambling, Gambling Willie / Talking Bear Mountain Picnic Massacre Blues / Standing on the Highway / Man on the Street / Blowin' in the Wind / Long Ago, Far Away / A Hard Rain's a-Gonna Fall / Tomorrow Is a Long Time / The Death of Emmett Till / Let Me Die in My Footsteps / Ballad of Hollis Brown / Quit Your Low Down Ways / Baby, I'm in the Mood for You / Bound to Lose, Bound to Win / All Over You / I'd Hate to Be You on That Dreadful Day / Long Time Gone / Talkin' John Birch Paranoid Blues / Masters of War / Oxford Town / Farewell

Disc 2: Don't Think Twice, It's All Right / Walkin' Down the Line / I Shall Be Free / Bob Dylan's Blues / Bob Dylan's Dream / Boots of Spanish Leather / Girl from the North Country / Seven Curses / Hero Blues / Whatcha Gonna Do? / Gypsy Lou / Ain't Gonna Grieve / John Brown / Only a Hobo / When the Ship Comes In / The Times They Are a-Changin' / Paths of Victory /

Guess I'm Doing Fine / Baby, Let Me Follow You Down / Mama, You Been on My Mind / Mr. Tambourine Man / I'll Keep It with Mine

Bob Dylan Live at Carnegie Hall, September 1963 EP (November 15, 2005)

The Times They Are a-Changin' / Ballad of Hollis Brown / Boots of Spanish Leather / Lay Down Your Weary Tune / North Country Blues / With God on Our Side

Bob Dylan in Concert: Brandeis University, 1963 (April 11, 2011)

Honey Just Allow Me One More Chance (partial) / Talking John Birch Paranoid Blues / Ballad of Hollis Brown / Masters of War / Talkin' World War III Blues / Bob Dylan's Dream / Talking Bear Mountain Picnic Massacre Blues

The Times They Are a-Changin' (January 1964)

The Times They Are a-Changin' / With God on Our Side / One Too Many Mornings / North Country Blues / Only a Pawn in Their Game / Boots of Spanish Leather / When the Ship Comes In / The Lonesome Death of Hattie Carroll / Restless Farewell

Another Side of Bob Dylan (August 8, 1964)

All I Really Want to Do / Black Crow Blues / Spanish Harlem Incident / Chimes of Freedom / I Shall Be Free No. 10 / To Ramona / Motorpsycho Nitemare / My Back Pages / I Don't Believe You (She Acts Like We Never Have Met) / Ballad in Plain D / It Ain't Me Babe

The Bootleg Series Vol. 6: Bob Dylan Live 1964: Concert at Philharmonic Hall (March 30, 2004)

The Times They Are a-Changin' / Spanish Harlem Incident / Taking John Birch Paranoid Blues / To Ramona / Who Killed Davey Moore / Gates of Eden / If You Gotta Go, Go Now / It's All Right Ma (I'm Only Bleeding) / I Don't Believe You / Mr. Tambourine Man / A Hard Rain's a-Gonna Fall /

Talkin' World War III Blues / Don't Think Twice, It's All Right / The Lonesome Death of Hattie Carroll / Mama You've Been on My Mind / Silver Dagger / With God on Our Side / It Ain't Me Babe / All I Really Want to Do

Bringing It All Back Home (March 22, 1965)

Subterranean Homesick Blues / She Belongs to Me / Maggie's Farm / Love Minus Zero / No Limit / Outlaw Blues / On the Road Again / Bob Dylan's 115th Dream / Mr. Tambourine Man / Gates of Eden / It's All Right Ma, I'm Only Bleeding / It's All Over Now, Baby Blue

Highway 61 Revisited (August 30, 1965)

Like a Rolling Stone / Tombstone Blues / It Takes a Lot to Laugh, It Takes a Train to Cry / From a Buick 6 / Ballad of a Thin Man / Queen Jane Approximately / Highway 61 Revisited / Just Like Tom Thumb's Blues / Desolation Row

Blonde on Blonde (July 2, 1966)

Rainy Day Women #12 & 35 / Pledging My Time / Visions of Johanna / One of Us Must Know (Sooner or Later) / I Want You / Stuck Inside of Mobile with the Memphis Blues Again / Leopard-Skin Pillbox Hat / Just Like a Woman / Most Likely You Go Your Way (and I'll Go Mine) / Temporary Like Achilles / Absolutely Sweet Marie / 4th Time Around / Obviously 5 Believers / Sad-Eyed Lady of the Lowlands

The Bootleg Series Vol. 4: Bob Dylan Live 1966: The "Royal Albert Hall" Concert (October 13, 1998)

She Belongs to Me / 4th Time Around / Visions of Johanna / It's All Over Now, Baby Blue / Desolation Row / Just Like a Woman / Mr. Tambourine Man / Tell Me Momma / I Don't Believe You (She Acts Like We Never Have Met) / Baby Let Me Follow You Down / Just Like Tom Thumb's Blues / Leopard-Skin Pillbox Hat / One Too Many Mornings / Ballad of a Thin Man / Like a Rolling Stone

Bob Dylan's Greatest Hits (March 27, 1967)

Rainy Day Women #12 & 35 / Blowin' in the Wind / The Times They Are a-Changin' / It Ain't Me Babe / Like a Rolling Stone / Mr. Tambourine Man / Subterranean Homesick Blues / I Want You / Positively 4th Street / Just Like a Woman

John Wesley Harding (January 2, 1968)

John Wesley Harding / As I Went out This Morning / I Dreamed I Saw St. Augustine / All Along the Watchtower / The Ballad of Frankie Lee and Judas Priest / Drifter's Escape / Dear Landlord / The Lonesome Hobo / I Pity the Poor Immigrant / The Wicked Messenger / Down Along the Cove / I'll Be Your Baby Tonight

The Basement Tapes (June 26, 1975)

Disc 1: Odds and Ends / Orange Juice Blues (Blues for Breakfast) / Million Dollar Bash / Yazoo Street Scandal / Goin' to Acapulco / Katie's Been Gone

Disc 2: Lo and Behold! / Bessie Smith / Clothes Line Saga / Apple Sucking Tree / Please Mrs. Henry / Tears of Rage / Too Much of Nothing / Yea! Heavy and a Bottle of Bread / Ain't No More Cane / Crash on the Levee (Down in the Flood) / Ruben Remus / Tiny Montgomery / You Ain't Goin' Nowhere / Don't Ya Tell Henry / Nothing Was Delivered / Open the Door, Homer / Long Distance Operator / This Wheel's on Fire

The Bootleg Series Vol. 11: The Basement Tapes Complete (November 3, 2014)

Disc 1: Edge of the Ocean / My Bucket's Got a Hole in It / Roll on Train / Mr. Blue / Belshazzar / I Forgot to Remember to Forget / You Win Again / Still in Town / Waltzing with Sin / Big River / Folsom Prison Blues / Bells of Rhymney / Spanish Is the Loving Tongue / Under Control / Ol' Roison the Beau / I'm Guilty of Loving You / Cool Water / The Auld Triangle / Po' Lazarus / I'm a Fool for You

Disc 2: Johnny Todd / Tupelo / Kickin' My Dog Around / See You Later Allen Ginsberg / Tiny Montgomery / Big Dog / I'm Your Teenage Prayer / Four Strong Winds / The French Girl / Joshua Gone Barbados / I'm in the Mood / Baby Ain't That Fine / Rock, Salt and Nails / A Fool Such as I / Song for Canada / People Get Ready / I Don't Hurt Anymore / Be Careful of the Stones That You Throw / One Man's Loss / Lock Your Door / Baby Won't You Be My Baby / Try Me Little Girl / I Can't Make It Alone / Don't You Try Me Now

Disc 3: Young but Daily Growing / Bonnie Ship the Diamond / The Hills of Mexico / Down on Me / One for the Road / I'm Alright / Million Dollar Bash / Yea! Heavy and a Bottle of Bread / I'm Not There / Please Mrs. Henry / Crash on the Levee (Down in the Flood) / Lo and Behold / You Ain't Goin' Nowhere / I Shall Be Released / This Wheel's on Fire / Too Much of Nothing

Disc 4: Tears of Rage / Quinn the Eskimo / Open the Door Homer / Nothing Was Delivered / All American Boy / Sign on the Cross / Odds and Ends / Get Your Rocks Off / Clothesline Saga (Answer to Ode) / Apple Sucking Tree / Don't You Tell Henry / Bourbon Street

Disc 5: Blowin' in the Wind / One Too Many Mornings / A Satisfied Mind / It Ain't Me Babe / Ain't No More Cane / My Woman She's a-Leavin' / Santa Fe / Mary Lou, I Love You Too / Dress It Up, Better Have It / Minstrel Boy / Silent Weekend / What's It Gonna Be When It Comes Up / 900 Miles from My Home / Wildwood Flower / One Kind Favor / She'll Be Comin' Round the Mountain / It's the Flight of the Bumblebee / Wild Wolf / Goin' to Acapulco / Gonna Get You Now / If I Were a Carpenter / Confidential / All You Have to Do Is Dream

Disc 6: 2 Dollars and 99 Cents / Jelly Bean / Any Time / Down by the Station / Hallelujah I've Just Been Moved / That's the Breaks / Pretty Mary / Will the Circle Be Unbroken / King of France / She's on My Mind Again / Going down the Road Feeling Bad / On a Rainy Afternoon / I Can't Come in with a Broken Heart / Next Time on the Highway / Northern Claim / Love Is Only Mine / Silhouettes / Bring It on Home / Come All Ye Fair and Tender Ladies / The Spanish Song / 900 Miles from My Home / Confidential

Nashville Skyline (April 9, 1969)

Girl from the North Country (with Johnny Cash) / Nashville Skyline Rag / To Be Alone with You / I Threw It All Away / Peggy Day / Lay Lady Lady / One More Night / Tell Me That It Isn't True / Country Pie / Tonight I'll Be Staying Here with You

Self Portrait (June 8, 1970)

All the Tired Horses / Alberta #1 / I Forgot More Than You'll Ever Know / Days of 49 / Early Mornin' Rain / In Search of Little Sadie / Let It Be Me / Little Sadie / Woogie Boogie / Belle Isle / Living the Blues / Like a Rolling Stone (Live) / Copper Kettle / Gotta Travel On / Blue Moon / The Boxer / The Mighty Quinn (Quinn the Eskimo) / Take Me as I Am (Or Let Me Go) / Take a Message to Mary / It Hurts Me Too / Minstrel Boy / She Belongs to Me (Live) / Wigwam / Alberta #2

The Bootleg Series Vol. 10: Another Self Portrait (1969–1971) (August 27, 2013)

Disc 1: Went to See the Gypsy / Little Sadie / Pretty Saro / Alberta #3 / Spanish Is the Loving Tongue / Annie's Going to Sing Her Song / Time Passes Slowly / Only a Hobo / Minstrel Boy / I Threw It All Away / Railroad Bill / Thirsty Boots / This Evening So Soon / These Hands / In Search of Little Sadie / House Carpenter / All the Tired Horses

Disc 2: If Not for You / Wallflower / Wigwam / Days of 49 / Working on a Guru / Country Pie / I'll Be Your Baby Tonight (Live) / Highway 61 Revisisted (Live) / Copper Kettle / Bring Me a Little Water / Sign on the Window / Tattle O' Day / If Dogs Run Free / New Morning / Went to See the Gypsy / Belle Isle / Time Passes Slowly / When I Paint My Masterpiece

Deluxe Edition, Disc 3: Live at the Isle of Wight Festival 8/31/1969

Deluxe Edition, Disc 4: *Self Portrait* Remastered

New Morning (October 19, 1970)

If Not for You / Day of the Locusts / Time Passes Slowly / Went to See the Gypsy / Winterlude / If Dogs Run Free / New Morning / Sign on the Window / One More Weekend / The Man in Me / Three Angels / Father of Night

Greatest Hits, Vol. 2 (November 17, 1971)

Watching the River Flow / Don't Think Twice, It's All Right / Lay Lady Lay / Stuck Inside of Mobile with the Memphis Blues Again / I'll Be Your Baby Tonight / All I Really Want to Do / My Back Pages / Maggie's Farm / Tonight I'll Be Staying Here with You / She Belongs to Me / All Along the Watchtower / The Mighty Quinn (Quinn the Eskimo) / Just Like Tom Thumb's Blues / A Hard Rain's a-Gonna Fall / If Not for You / It's All Over Now, Baby Blue / Tomorrow Is a Long Time (Live, 1963) / When I Paint My Masterpiece / I Shall Be Released / You Ain't Goin' Nowhere / Crash on the Levee (Down in the Flood)

The Concert for Bangladesh (Apple, December 20, 1971)

Side Five: A Hard Rain's a-Gonna Fall / It Takes a Lot to Laugh, It Takes a Train to Cry / Blowin' in the Wind / Mr. Tambourine Man / Just Like a Woman / Love Minus Zero / No Limit*

* 2005 remaster, disc 2, bonus track

Pat Garrett and Billy the Kid (soundtrack album) (July 13, 1973)

Main Title Theme (Billy) / Cantina Theme (Workin' for the Law) / Billy 1 / Bunkhouse Theme / River Theme / Turkey Chase / Knockin' on Heaven's Door / Final Theme / Billy 4 / Billy 7

Dylan (November 19, 1973)

Lily of the West / Can't Help Falling in Love / Sarah Jane / The Ballad of Ira Hayes / Mr. Bojangles / Mary Ann / Big Yellow Taxi / A Fool Such as I / Spanish Is the Loving Tongue

Planet Waves (Asylum, January 17, 1974)

On a Night Like This / Going, Going, Gone / Tough Mama / Hazel / Something There Is About You / Forever Young / Dirge / You Angel You / Never Say Goodbye / Wedding Song

Before the Flood (Live) (Asylum, June 20, 1974)

Dylan: Most Likely You Go Your Way (and I'll Go Mine) / Lay Lady Lay / Rainy Day Women #12 & 35 / Knocking on Heaven's Door / It Ain't Me Babe / Ballad of a Thin Man / *The Band*: Up on Cripple Creek / I Shall Be Released / Endless Highway / The Night They Drove Old Dixie Down / Stage Fright / *Dylan*: Don't Think Twice, It's All Right / Just Like a Woman / It's Alright Ma (I'm Only Bleeding) / The Shape I'm In / *The Band*: When You Awake / The Weight / *Dylan*: All Along the Watchtower / Highway 61 Revisited / Like a Rolling Stone / Blowin' in the Wind

Blood on the Tracks (January 20, 1975)

Tangled Up in Blue / Simple Twist of Fate / You're a Big Girl Now / Idiot Wind / You're Gonna Make Me Lonesome When You Go / Meet Me in the Morning / Lily, Rosemary and the Jack of Hearts / If You See Her, Say Hello / Shelter from the Storm / Buckets of Rain

Desire (January 5, 1976)

Hurricane / Isis / Mozambique / One More Cup of Coffee (Valley Below) / Oh Sister / Joey / Romance in Durango / Black Diamond Bay / Sara

The Bootleg Series Vol. 5: Bob Dylan Live 1975: The Rolling Thunder Revue (November 26, 2002)

Tonight I'll Be Staying Here with You / It Ain't Me Babe / A Hard Rain's a-Gonna Fall / The Lonesome Death of Hattie Carroll / Romance in Durango / Isis / Mr. Tambourine Man / Simple Twist of Fate / Blowin' in the Wind / Mama, You Been on My Mind / I Shall Be Released / It's All Over Now, Baby Blue / Love Minus Zero / No Limit / Tangled Up in Blue / The Water Is Wide / It Takes a Lot to Laugh, It Takes a Train to Cry / Oh Sister /

Hurricane / One More Cup of Coffee (Valley Below) / Sara / Just Like a Woman / Knockin' on Heaven's Door

Hard Rain (Live) (September 13, 1976)

Maggie's Farm / One Too Many Mornings / Stuck Inside of Mobile with the Memphis Blues Again / Oh Sister / Lay Lady Lay / Shelter from the Storm / You're a Big Girl Now / I Threw It All Away / Idiot Wind / Hurricane

Street-Legal (June 15, 1978)

Changing of the Guards / New Pony / No Time to Think / Baby Stop Crying / Is Your Love in Vain / Señor (Tales of Yankee Power) / True Love Tends to Forget / We Better Talk This Over / Where Are You Tonight (Journey Through Dark Heat)

Bob Dylan at Budokan (April 23, 1979)

Mr. Tambourine Man / Shelter from the Storm / Love Minus Zero / No Limit / Ballad of a Thin Man / Don't Think Twice, It's All Right / Maggie's Farm / One More Cup of Coffee (Valley Below) / Like a Rolling Stone / I Shall Be Released / Is Your Love in Vain / Going, Going, Gone / Blowin' in the Wind / Just Like a Woman / Oh Sister / Simple Twist of Fate / All Along the Watchtower / I Want You / All I Really Want to Do / Knockin' on Heaven's Door / It's Alright Ma (I'm Only Bleeding) / Forever Young / The Times They Are a-Changin'

Slow Train Coming (August 20, 1979)

Gotta Serve Somebody / Precious Angel / I Believe in You / Slow Train / Gonna Chance My Way of Thinking / Do Right to Me Baby (Do unto Others) / When You Gonna Wake Up / Man Gave Name to All the Animals / When He Returns

Saved (June 23, 1980)

A Satisfied Mind / Saved / Covenant Woman / What Can I Do for You / Solid Rock / Pressing On / In the Garden / Saving Grace / Are You Ready

Shot of Love (August 10, 1981)

Shot of Love / Heart of Mine / Property of Jesus / Lenny Bruce / Watered-Down Love / The Groom's Still Waiting at the Altar / Dead Man, Dead Man / In the Summertime / Trouble / Every Grain of Sand

Infidels (November 1, 1983)

Jokerman / Sweetheart Like You / Neighborhood Bully / License to Kill / Man of Peace / Union Sundown / I and I / Don't Fall Apart on Me Tonight

Real Live (November 29, 1984)

Highway 61 Revisited / Maggie's Farm / I and I / License to Kill / It Ain't Me Babe / Tangled Up in Blue / Masters of War / Ballad of a Thin Man / Girl from the North Country / Tombstone Blues

Empire Burlesque (November 1, 1985)

Tight Connection to My Heart (Has Anybody Seen My Love) / Seeing the Real You at Last / I'll Remember You / Clean Cut Kid / Never Gonna Be the Same Again / Trust Yourself / Emotionally Yours / When the Night Comes Falling from the Sky / Something's Burning, Baby / Dark Eyes

Biograph (November 7, 1985)

Disc 1: Lay, Lady Lay / Baby, Let Me Follow You Down / If Not for You / I'll Be Your Baby Tonight / I'll Keep It with Mine / The Times They Are a-Changin' / Blowin' in the Wind / Masters of War / The Lonesome Death of Hattie Carroll / Percy's Song / Mixed-Up Confusion / Tombstone Blues / The Groom's Still Waiting at the Altar / Most Likely You Go Your Way I'll Go Mine / Like a Rolling Stone / Lay Down Your Weary Tune / Subterranean Homesick Blues / I Don't Believe You (She Acts Like We Never Have Met)

Disc 2: Visions of Johanna / Every Grain of Sand / Quinn the Eskimo (The Mighty Quinn) / Mr. Tambourine Man / Dear Landlord / It Ain't Me Babe / You Angel You / Million Dollar Bash / To Ramona / You're a Big Girl Now / Abandoned Love / Tangled Up in Blue / It's All Over Now, Baby Blue / Can You Please Crawl out Your Window / Positively 4th Street / Isis / Jet Pilot

Disc 3: Caribbean Wind / Up to Me / Baby I'm in the Mood for You / I Wanna Be Your Lover / I Want You / Heart of Mine / On a Night Like This / Just Like a Woman / Romance in Durango / Señor (Tales of Yankee Power) / Gotta Serve Somebody / I Believe in You / Time Passes Slowly / I Shall Be Released / Knockin' on Heaven's Door / All Along the Watchtower / Solid Rock / Forever Young

Knocked Out Loaded (August 8, 1986)

You Wanna Ramble / They Killed Him / Driftin' Too Far from Shore / Precious Memories / Maybe Someday / Brownsville Girl / Got My Mind Made Up / Under Your Spell

Down in the Groove (May 30, 1988)

Let's Stick Together / When Did You Leave Heaven? / Sally Sue Brown / Death Is Not the End / Had a Dream About You, Baby / Ugliest Girl in the World / Silvio / Ninety Miles an Hour (Down a Dead End Street) / Shenandoah / Rank Strangers to Me

Dylan & the Dead (February 6, 1989)

Slow Train / I Want You / Gotta Serve Somebody / Queen Jane Approximately / Joey / All Along the Watchtower / Knockin' on Heaven's Door

Oh Mercy (September 18, 1989)

Political World / Where Teardrops Fall / Everything Is Broken / Ring Them Bells / Man in the Long Black Coat / Most of the Time / What Good Am I? / Disease of Conceit / What Was It You Wanted / Shooting Star

Under the Red Sky (September 10, 1990)

Wiggle Wiggle / Under the Red Sky / Unbelievable / Born in Time / T.V. Talkin' Song / 10,000 Men / 2x2 / God Knows / Handy Dandy / Cat's in the Well

The Bootleg Series Volumes 1–3 (Rare and Unreleased) 1961–1991 (March 26, 1991)

Disc 1: Hard Times in New York Town / He Was a Friend of Mine / Man on the Street / No More Auction Block / House Carpenter / Talkin' Bear Mountain Picnic Massacre Blues / Let Me Die in My Footsteps / Rambling, Gambling Willie / Talkin' Hava Negeilah Blues / Quit Your Lowdown Ways / Worried Blues / Kingsport Town / Walkin' Down the Line / Walls of Red Wing / Paths of Victory / Talkin' John Birch Paranoid Blues / Who Killed Davey Moore / Only a Hobo / Moonshiner / When the Ship Comes In / The Times They Are a-Changin' / Last Thoughts on Woody Guthrie

Disc 2: Seven Curses / Eternal Circle / Suze (the Cough Song) / Mama, You've Been on My Mind / Farewell, Angelina / Subterranean Homesick Blues / If You Gotta Go, Go Now / Sitting on a Barbed Wire Fence / Like a Rolling Stone / It Takes a Lot to Laugh, It Takes a Train to Cry / I'll Keep It with Mine / She's Your Lover Now / I Shall Be Released / Santa Fe / If Not for You / Wallflower / Nobody 'Cept You / Tangled Up in Blue / Call Letter Blues / Idiot Wind

Disc 3: If You See Her, Say Hello / Golden Loom / Catfish / Seven Days / Ye Shall Be Changed / Every Grain of Sand / You Changed My Life / Need a Woman / Angelina / Someone's Got a Hold of My Heart / Tell Me / Lord Protect My Child / Foot of Pride / Blind Willie McTell / When the Night Comes Falling from the Sky / Series of Dreams

Good as I Been to You (November 3, 1992)

Frankie and Albert / Jim Jones / Blackjack Davey / Canadee-i-o / Sittin' on Top of the World / Little Maggie / Hard Times / Step It Up and Go / Tomorrow Night / Arthur McBride / You're Gonna Quit Me / Diamond Joe / Froggie Went a-Courtin'

World Gone Wrong (October 26, 1993)

World Gone Wrong / Love Henry / Ragged and Dirty / Blood in My Eyes / Broke Down Engine / Delia / Stack a Lee / Two Soldiers / Jack-a-Roe / Lone Pilgrim

Bob Dylan's Greatest Hits, Vol. 3 (1994)

Tangled Up in Blue / Changing of the Guards / The Groom's Still Waiting at the Altar / Hurricane / Forever Young / Jokerman / Dignity / Silvio / Ring Them Bells / Under the Red Sky / Knockin' on Heaven's Door

MTV Unplugged (1995)

Tombstone Blues / Shooting Star / All Along the Watchtower / The Times They Are a-Changin' / John Brown / Rainy Day Women #12 & 35 / Desolation Row / Dignity / Knockin' on Heaven's Door / Like a Rolling Stone / With God on Our Side

Time Out of Mind (September 30, 1997

Love Sick / Dirt Road Blues / Standing in the Doorway / Million Miles / Tryin' to Get to Heaven / 'Til I Fell in Love with You / Not Dark Yet / Cold Irons Bound / Make You Feel My Love / Can't Wait / Highlands

Love and Theft (September 11, 2001)

Tweedle Dee and Tweedle Dum / Mississippi / Summer Days / Bye and Bye / Lonesome Day Blues / Floater (Too Much to Ask) / High Water (for Charlie Patton) / Moonlight / Honest with Me / Po' Boy / Cry a While / Sugar Baby

The Bootleg Series Vol. 7: No Direction Home: The Soundtrack (August 30, 2005)

Disc 1: When I Got Troubles / Rambler, Gambler / This Land Is Your Land / Song to Woody / Dink's Song / I Was Young When I Left Home / Sally Gal / Don't Think Twice, It's All Right / Man of Constant Sorrow / Blowin' in the Wind / Masters of War / A Hard Rain's a-Gonna Fall / When the Ship Comes In / Mr. Tambourine Man / Chimes of Freedom / It's All Over Now, Baby Blue

Disc 2: She Belongs to Me / Maggie's Farm / It Takes a Lot to Laugh, It Takes a Train to Cry / Tombstone Blues / Just Like Tom Thumb's Blues / Desolation Row / Highway 61 Revisited / Leopard Skin Pill-Box Hat / Stuck

Inside of Mobile with the Memphis Blues Again / Visions of Johanna / Ballad of a Thin Man / Like a Rolling Stone

The Bootleg Series Vol. 8: Tell Tale Signs: Rare and Unreleased 1989–2006 (October 6, 2008)

Disc 1: Mississippi / Most of the Time / Dignity / Someday Baby / Red River Shore / Tell Ol' Bill / Born in Time / Can't Wait / Everything Is Broken / Dreamin' of You / Huck's Tune / Marchin' to the City / High Water (for Charlie Patton)

Disc 2: Mississippi / 32-20 Blues / Series of Dreams / God Knows / Can't Escape from You / Dignity / Ring Them Bells / Cocaine Blues / Ain't Talkin' / The Girl on the Greenbriar Shore / Lonesome Day Blues / Miss the Mississippi / The Lonesome River / 'Cross the Green Mountains

Disc 3: Duncan and Brady / Cold Irons Bound / Mississippi / Most of the Time / Ring Them Bells / Things Have Changed / Red River Shore / Born in Time / Trying to Get to Heaven / Marchin' to the City / Can't Wait / Mary and the Soldier

Modern Times (August 29, 2008)

Thunder on the Mountain / Spirit on the Water / Rollin' and Tumblin' / When the Deal Goes Down / Someday Baby / Workingman's Blues #2 / Beyond the Horizon / Nettie Moore / The Levee's Gonna Break / Ain't Talkin'

Together Through Life (April 28, 2009)

Beyond Here Lies Nothing / Life Is Hard / My Wife's Home Town / If You Ever Go to Houston / Forgetful Heart / Jolene / This Dream of You / Shake Shake Mama / I Feel a Change Comin' On / It's All Good

Tempest (September 10, 2012)

Duquesne Whistle / Soon After Midnight / Narrow Way / Long and Wasted Years / Pay in Blood / Scarlet Town / Early Roman Kings / Tin Angel / Tempest / Roll on John

Christmas in My Heart (October 13, 2009)

Here Comes Santa Claus / Do You Hear What I Hear / Winter Wonderland / Hark the Herald Angels Sing / I'll Be Home for Christmas / The Little Drummer Boy / The Christmas Blues / O' Come All Ye Faithful / Have Yourself a Merry Little Christmas / Must Be Santa / Silver Bells / The First Noel / Christmas Island

Shadows in the Night (February 3, 2015)

I'm a Fool to Want You / The Night We Called It a Day / Stay with Me / Autumn Leaves / Why Try to Change Me Now / Some Enchanted Evening / Full Moon and Empty Arms / Where Are You / What'll I Do / That Lucky Old Sun

Fallen Angels (May 21, 2016)

Young at Heart / Maybe You'll Be There / Polka Dots and Moonbeams / All the Way / Skylark / Nevertheless / All or Nothing at All / On a Little Street in Singapore / It Had to Be You / Melancholy Mood / That Old Black Magic / Come Rain or Come Shine

Triplicate (March 31, 2017)

CD 1—'Til the Sun Goes Down

I Guess I'll Have to Change My Plans / September of My Years / I Could Have Told You / Once Upon a Time / Stormy Weather / This Nearly Was Mine / That Old Feeling / It Gets Lonely Early / My One and Only Love / Trade Winds

CD 2—Devil Dolls

Braggin' / As Time Goes By / Imagination / How Deep Is the Ocean / P.S. I Love You / The Best Is Yet to Come / But Beautiful / Here's That Rainy Day / Where Is the One / There's a Flaw in My Flue

CD 3—Comin' Home Late

Day In, Day Out / I Couldn't Sleep a Wink Last Night / Sentimental Journey / Somewhere Along the Way / When the World Was Young / These Foolish Things / You Go to My Head / Stardust / It's Funny to Everyone but Me / Why Was I Born

Singles and B-Sides

Here is a complete list of Bob Dylan's singles and B-sides.

1962 Mixed Up Confusion / Corrina, Corrina
1963 Blowin' in the Wind / Don't Think Twice, It's All Right
1964 With God on Our Side, Pt. 1 / With God on Our Side, Pt. 2
1965 The Times They Are a-Changin' / Honey Just Allow Me One More Chance (#9 UK)
1965 Maggie's Farm / On the Road Again (#22 UK)
1965 Subterranean Homesick Blues / She Belongs to Me (#39 US, #9 UK)
1965 Like a Rolling Stone / Gates of Eden (#2 US, #4 UK)
1965 Positively 4th Street / From a Buick 6 (#7 US, #4 UK)
1965 Can You Please Crawl out Your Window / Highway 61 Revisited (#58 US, #17 UK)
1966 One of Us Must Know (Sooner or Later) / Queen Jane Approximately (#33 UK)
1966 Rainy Day Women #12 & 35 / Pledging My Time (#2 US, #7 UK)
1966 I Want You / Just Like Tom Thumb's Blues (#20 US, #16 UK)
1966 Just Like a Woman / Obviously Five Believers (#33 US)
1967 Leopard-Skin Pill-Box Hat / Most Likely You Go Your Way (and I'll Go Mine) (#81 US)
1968 All Along the Watchtower / I'll Be Your Baby Tonight
1969 I Threw It All Away / Drifter's Escape (#85 US, #30 UK)
1969 Lay Lady Lay / Peggy Day (#7 US, #5 UK)
1969 Tonight I'll Be Staying Here with You / Country Pie (#50 US)
1970 Wigwam / Copper Kettle (#41 US)
1972 If Not for You / New Morning
1972 Watching the River Flow / Spanish Is the Loving Tongue (#41 US, #24 UK)
1972 George Jackson / George Jackson (#33 US)
1973 Knockin' on Heaven's Door / Turkey Chase (#12 US, #14 UK)
1973 A Fool Such as I / Lily of the West (#55 US)
1974 On a Night Like This / You Angel You (#44 US)
1974 Something There Is About You / Tough Mama

1974 Most Likely You Go Your Way (and I'll Go Mine) / Stage Fright (The Band) (#66 US)

1974 It Ain't Me Babe / All Along the Watchtower

1975 Tangled Up in Blue / If You See Her, Say Hello (#31 US)

1975 Hurricane, Pt. 1 / Hurricane Pt. 2 (#33 US, #43 UK)

1976 Mozambique / Oh Sister (#54 US)

1977 Rita May / Stuck Inside of Mobile with the Memphis Blues Again

1978 Is Your Love in Vain / We Better Talk This Over (#56 UK)

1978 Baby Stop Crying / New Pony (#13 UK)

1978 Changing of the Guards / Señor (Tales of Yankee Power)

1979 Love Minus Zero / No Limit (Live) / Is Your Love in Vain

1979 Gotta Serve Somebody / Trouble in Mind (#24 US)

1980 Man Gave Names to All the Animals / When He Returns

1980 Slow Train / Do Right to Me Baby (Do unto Others)

1980 Solid Rock / Covenant Woman

1980 Saved / Are You Ready

1981 Shot of Love / Heart of Mine

1981 Lenny Bruce / Dead Man, Dead Man

1981 Heart of Mine / The Groom's Still Waiting at the Altar

1983 Union Sundown / Sweetheart Like You (#90 UK, #55 US)

1984 Jokerman / License to Kill

1985 Tight Connection to My Heart (Has Anybody Seen My Love) / We Better Talk This Over

1985 When the Night Comes Falling from the Sky / Emotionally Yours

1986 Band of the Hand / Theme from Joe's Death (#66 UK)

1986 Got My Mind Made Up / The Usual

1988 Silvio / Driftin' Too Far from the Shore (#5 USAT)

1989 Everything Is Broken / Death Is Not the End (#8 USAT, #98 UK)

1989 Slow Train (#8 USAT)

1990 Unbelievable / 10,000 Men (#21 USAT)

1993 My Back Pages (live) / Knockin' on Heaven's Door / My Back Pages (original version) (#26 USAT)

1995 Dignity (live) / John Brown / It Ain't Me Babe (#33 UK)

1996 Not Dark Yet / Tombstone Blues (live)

1996 Love Sick / 'Til I Fell in Love with You (#64 UK)

2000 Things Have Changed / Blind Willie McTell (live) (#58 UK)

2006 Someday Baby (radio edit) / Someday Baby (album version)

2007 Most Likely You Go Your Way (and I'll Go Mine) (remix) / Most Likely You Go Your Way (and I'll Go Mine) (original version) (#51 UK)

2008 Dreamin' of You / Down Along the Cove
2009 Blowin' in the Wind (#93 UK)
2009 Beyond Here Lies Nothin' (download only) / Down Along the Cove
2009 I Feel a Change Comin' On / I Feel a Change Comin' On (album version)
2009 Must Be Santa / 'Twas the Night Before Christmas (#41 UK)
2010 Make You Feel My Love
2012 Duquesne Whistle / Meet Me in the Morning
2014 Full Moon and Empty Arms
2015 The Night We Called It a Day / Stay with Me
2016 Melancholy Mood / All the Way

Selected Bibliography

O f the stacks of books written about Bob Dylan, here are some of the ones I consulted in my research or otherwise came across in my sampling of friends' libraries. From critical studies to interpretive biographies to exhaustive studio logs, there is enough here to satisfy the hungry beginner and the nearly sated devotee alike.

Barker, Derek. *The Songs He Didn't Write: Bob Dylan Under the Influence.* London: Chrome Dreams, 2008.

Bauldie, John (ed.). *Wanted Man: In Search of Bob Dylan.* London: Penguin Books, 1992.

Bell, Ian. *Once Upon a Time: The Lives of Bob Dylan.* London: Mainstream Publishing, 2012.

Corcoran, Neil (ed.). *Do You, Mr Jones? Bob Dylan with the Poets and Professors.* London: Chatto & Windus, 2002.

Cott, Jonathan. *Dylan.* New York City: Rolling Stone Press, 1984.

Cott, Jonathan (ed.). *Dylan on Dylan: The Essential Interviews.* London: Hodder & Stoughton, 2006.

Dalton, David. *Who Is That Man? In Search of the Real Bob Dylan.* New York City: Hyperion, 2012.

Dettmar, Kevin J. (ed.). *The Cambridge Companion to Bob Dylan.* Cambridge: Cambridge University Press, 2008.

Engel, Dave. *Just Like Bob Zimmerman's Blues: Dylan in Minnesota.* Minneapolis: River City Memoirs, 1997.

Epstein, Daniel Mark. *The Ballad of Bob Dylan: A Portrait.* New York City: HarperCollins, 2011.

Gans, Terry Alexander. *What's Real and What Is Not. Bob Dylan Through 1964: The Myth of Protest.* Munich: Hobo Press, 1982.

Gill, Andy. *Classic Bob Dylan: My Back Pages.* London: Carlton, 1998.

Gray, Michael. *Song and Dance Man III.* London: Continuum, 2000.

Gray, Michael. *The Bob Dylan Encyclopedia.* London: Continuum International, 2006.

Griffin, Sid. *Million Dollar Bash: Bob Dylan, the Band, and the Basement Tapes.* London: Jawbone, 2007; revised and updated, 2014.

Hedin, Benjamin. *Studio A: The Bob Dylan Reader.* New York City: W. W. Norton & Company, 2004.

Heylin, Clinton. *Bob Dylan: A Life in Stolen Moments: Day by Day 1941–1995.* New York City: Schirmer Books, 1996.

Heylin, Clinton. *Bob Dylan: The Recording Sessions, 1960–1994.* New York City: St. Martin's Griffin, 1995.

Heylin, Clinton. *Bob Dylan: Behind the Shades: Take Two.* New York City: Viking, 2000.

Heylin, Clinton. *Revolution in the Air: The Songs of Bob Dylan, Volume One: 1957–73.* London: Constable, 2009.

Heylin, Clinton. *Still on the Road: The Songs of Bob Dylan, Volume Two: 1974–2008.* London: Constable, 2010.

Heylin, Clinton. *Bob Dylan: Behind the Shades: 20th Anniversary Edition.* London: Faber and Faber, 2011.

Humphries, Patrick. *Oh No! Not Another Bob Dylan Book.* Garden City: Square One Books, 1991.

Kramer, Daniel. *Bob Dylan: A Portrait of the Artist's Early Years.* New York City: Citadel Underground, 1991.

Lee, C. P. *Like The Night: Bob Dylan and the Road to the Manchester Free Trade Hall.* London: Helter Skelter, 1998.

Lee, C. P. *Like a Bullet of Light: The Films of Bob Dylan.* London: Helter Skelter, 2000.

Marcus, Greil. *Invisible Republic: Bob Dylan's Basement Tapes.* New York City: Picador, 1997.

Marcus, Greil. *Like a Rolling Stone: Bob Dylan at the Crossroads.* New York City: PublicAffairs, 2005.

Marcus, Greil. *Bob Dylan by Greil Marcus: Writings 1968–2010.* New York City: PublicAffairs, 2013.

Marqusee, Mike. *Wicked Messenger: Bob Dylan and the 1960s.* New York City: Seven Stories Press, 2005.

Marshall, Lee. *Bob Dylan: The Never Ending Star.* London: Polity, 2007.

Marshall, Scott. *Restless Pilgrim: The Spiritual Journey of Bob Dylan.* Winter Park: Relevant Books, 2002.

McDougal, Dennis. *Dylan: The Biography.* New York City: John Wiley & Sons, 2014.

McGregor, Craig. *Bob Dylan: A Retrospective.* New York City: William Morrow & Co., 1972.

Mellers, Wilfrid. *A Darker Shade of Pale: A Backdrop to Bob Dylan.* London: Faber and Faber, 1984.

Muir, Andrew. *Razor's Edge: Bob Dylan and the Never Ending Tour*. London: Helter Skelter, 2001.

Muir, Andrew. *Troubadour: Early and Late Songs of Bob Dylan*. New York City: Woodstock Publications, 2003.

Muir, Andrew. *One More Night: Bob Dylan's Never Ending Tour*. Andrew Muir, 2013.

Pichaske, David. *Song of the North Country: A Midwest Framework to the Songs of Bob Dylan*. New York City: Continuum, 2010.

Polizzotti, Mark. *Highway 61 Revisited*. New York City: Continuum, 2006.

Ricks, Christopher. *Dylan's Visions of Sin*. New York City: Penguin/Viking, 2003.

Scaduto, Anthony. *Bob Dylan*. New York City: Grosset and Dunlap, 1972.

Schatzberg, Jerry. *Thin Wild Mercury—Touching Dylan's Edge: The Photography*. London: Genesis Publications, 2006.

Shepard, Sam. *Rolling Thunder Logbook*. New York City: Penguin Books, 1978.

Shelton, Robert. *No Direction Home: The Life and Music of Bob Dylan*. London: Omnibus Press, revised and updated edition, 2011.

Sloman, Larry. *On the Road with Bob Dylan: Rolling with the Thunder*. New York City: Bantam Books, 1978.

Sounes, Howard. *Down the Highway: The Life of Bob Dylan*. New York City: Grove Press, 2001.

Spiotta, Dana. *Eat the Document*. New York City: Scribner, 2006.

Spitz, Bob. *Dylan: A Biography*. New York City: McGraw-Hill, 1988.

Thomson, Elizabeth (ed.). *The Dylan Companion*. New York City: Macmillan Publishers, 1990.

Thompson, Toby. *Positively Main Street: An Unorthodox View of Bob Dylan*. London: New English Library, 1972.

Trager, Oliver. *Keys to the Rain*. New York City: Billboard Books, 2004.

Various. *Younger Than That Now: The Collected Interviews with Bob Dylan*. New York City: Thunder's Mouth Press, 2004.

Wald, Elijah. *Dylan Goes Electric: Newport, Seeger, Dylan, and the Night That Split the Sixties*. New York City: Dey Street Books, 2015.

Weberman, A. J. *Dylan to English Dictionary*. New York City: Yippie Museum Press, 2005.

Wilentz, Sean. *Bob Dylan in America*. New York City: The Bodley Head, 2009.

Williams, Paul. *Bob Dylan, Performing Artist: The Early Years 1960–1973*. San Francisco: Underwood-Miller, 1991.

Williams, Paul. *Bob Dylan, Performing Artist: The Middle Years (1974–1986)*. London: Omnibus Press, 2004.

Williams, Paul. *Bob Dylan, Performing Artist: Mind out of Time (1986–1990 and Beyond)*. London: Omnibus Press, 2005.

Williams, Richard. *Dylan: A Man Called Alias*. New York City: Holt, 1992.

Williamson, Nigel. *The Rough Guide to Bob Dylan*. London: Rough Guides, 2004.

Index

THE FAQ SERIES

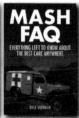

AC/DC FAQ
by Susan Masino
Backbeat Books
9781480394506.................. $24.99

Armageddon Films FAQ
by Dale Sherman
Applause Books
9781617131196...................... $24.99

The Band FAQ
by Peter Aaron
Backbeat Books
9781617136139 ....$19.99

Baseball FAQ
by Tom DeMichael
Backbeat Books
9781617136061...................... $24.99

The Beach Boys FAQ
by Jon Stebbins
Backbeat Books
9780879309879 ....$22.99

The Beat Generation FAQ
by Rich Weidman
Backbeat Books
9781617136016 ....$19.99

Beer FAQ
by Jeff Cioletti
Backbeat Books
9781617136115 .... $24.99

Black Sabbath FAQ
by Martin Popoff
Backbeat Books
9780879309572...................$19.99

Bob Dylan FAQ
by Bruce Pollock
Backbeat Books
9781617136078 ....$19.99

Britcoms FAQ
by Dave Thompson
Applause Books
9781495018992 ....$19.99

Bruce Springsteen FAQ
by John D. Luerssen
Backbeat Books
9781617130939...................$22.99

A Chorus Line FAQ
by Tom Rowan
Applause Books
9781480367548 ....$19.99

The Clash FAQ
by Gary J. Jucha
Backbeat Books
9781480364509 ....$19.99

Doctor Who FAQ
by Dave Thompson
Applause Books
9781557838544....................$22.99

The Doors FAQ
by Rich Weidman
Backbeat Books
9781617130175 .... $24.99

Dracula FAQ
by Bruce Scivally
Backbeat Books
9781617136009 ....$19.99

The Eagles FAQ
by Andrew Vaughan
Backbeat Books
9781480385412.................... $24.99

Elvis Films FAQ
by Paul Simpson
Applause Books
9781557838582...................... $24.99

Elvis Music FAQ
by Mike Eder
Backbeat Books
9781617130496...................... $24.99

Eric Clapton FAQ
by David Bowling
Backbeat Books
9781617134548 .... $22.99

Fab Four FAQ
*by Stuart Shea and
Robert Rodriguez*
Hal Leonard Books
9781423421382........................$19.99

Fab Four FAQ 2.0
by Robert Rodriguez
Backbeat Books
9780879309688..................$19.99

Film Noir FAQ
by David J. Hogan
Applause Books
9781557838551.....................$22.99

Football FAQ
by Dave Thompson
Backbeat Books
9781495007484 .... $24.99

Frank Zappa FAQ
by John Corcelli
Backbeat Books
9781617136030.......................$19.99

Godzilla FAQ
by Brian Solomon
Applause Books
9781495045684 ....$19.99

The Grateful Dead FAQ
by Tony Sclafani
Backbeat Books
9781617130861....................... $24.99

Guns N' Roses FAQ
by Rich Weidman
Backbeat Books
9781495025884 ....$19.99

Haunted America FAQ
by Dave Thompson
Backbeat Books
9781480392625....................$19.99

Horror Films FAQ
by John Kenneth Muir
Applause Books
9781557839503 ....$22.99

James Bond FAQ
by Tom DeMichael
Applause Books
9781557838568...................$22.99

Jimi Hendrix FAQ
by Gary J. Jucha
Backbeat Books
9781617130953.......................$22.99

Prices, contents, and availability
subject to change without notice.